Rabbi Tarfon

BROWN UNIVERSITY
BROWN JUDAIC STUDIES

Edited by

Jacob Neusner
Wendell S. Dietrich, Ernest S. Frerichs, Horst R. Moehring
Richard S. Sarason

Number 7

Rabbi Tarfon: The Tradition, the Man, and Early Rabbinic Judaism
by Joel Gereboff

Rabbi Tarfon: The Tradition, the Man, and Early Rabbinic Judaism

by
Joel Gereboff

Scholars Press

Distributed by
SCHOLARS PRESS
PO Box 5207
Missoula, Montana 59806

Rabbi Tarfon: The Tradition, the Man, and Early Rabbinic Judaism

by
Joel Gereboff

Library of Congress Cataloging in Publication Data

Gereboff, Joel D
  Rabbi Tarfon, the tradition, the man, and early Rabbinic
Judaism.

  (Brown Judaic studies ; v. 7 ; ISSN 0147-927X)
  Bibliography: p.
  1. Tarfon.   2. Talmud—Criticism,   interpretation,   etc.
I. Title. II. Series.
BM502.3.T37G47   296.1'206   78-15220
ISBN 0-89130-257-3
ISBN 0-89130-299-9 pbk.

Printed in the United States of America

1   2   3   4   5

Edwards Brothers, Inc.
Ann Arbor, MI 48106

TABLE OF CONTENTS

PREFACE

This work concludes the analysis of the units of tradition comprising the corpora of Yavnean masters. Like the studies of Jacob Neusner and his students,[1] our investigation of the materials assigned to Tarfon yields two histories: (1) a history of the formation of these items, (2) a biography of Tarfon. We make two advances beyond these previous works. First, having in hand the other studies, we are able to interpret in a more meaningful manner the results of our analysis, for our comparisons of the various findings provide data about the formal and substantive traits of items attributed to other Yavneans. We know, for example, the formulary patterns employed in most corpora and the range of issues usually discussed in these materials. As a result, we see where Tarfon conforms to and where he diverges from these tendencies. Second, because of Neusner's work on the mishnaic Order of Purities,[2] we know a good deal about the literary and substantive characteristics of Mishnah and, therefore, are able to ask a series of questions, not mentioned in previous studies, regarding the legal materials assigned to an individual master. Specifically, we delineate Tarfon's contribution to the unfolding of mishnaic law, and whether or not his items were formulated by the redactors of Mishnah and Tosefta.

My teacher, Professor Jacob Neusner, has read and re-read every page of this manuscript many times. Without his untiring patience and insight, this work would never have been written. I can think of no better way to express my gratitude than to say that Jacob Neusner exemplifies and tries to instill in his students Tarfon's view (M. Avot 2:16), "It is not incumbent upon you to finish the work, but you are not free to desist from it."

The two other readers of my dissertation, Dean Ernest Frerichs of Brown University and Professor Jonathan Z. Smith of the University of Chicago, have offered valuable suggestions. I thank them for their help and advice. My other teachers at Brown University, Professors Horst R. Moehring, Wendell Dietrich, John Giles Milhaven, B. Barry Levy, John P. Reeder, Jr., Sumner B. Twiss, and David R. Blumenthal, have all contributed to my education and have made my years of study both informative and enjoyable. I appreciate the opportunity to have studied with each of them. My two former teachers at the Jewish Theological Seminary of America, both presently at the Hebrew University, Professors Lee Levine and Emmanuel

Etkes, also must be thanked, for they encouraged me to continue my work on the history of Judaism.

The entire work was read over a period of six years in graduate seminars conducted at Brown University by Professor Neusner. I wish to express my gratitude to my fellow students who offered many important comments before, during, and after my presentations: Professors David Goodblatt, Gary Porton, William S. Green, Baruch Bokser, Charles Primus, Tzvee Zahavy, Richard S. Sarason, Jack Lightstone, Rabbi Shammai Kanter, and Mr. Irving Mandelbaum. I am particularly thankful to Jack Lightstone for the continuing dialogue we maintained during our common year of study in Israel. Mrs. Marion Craven typed the manuscript, and I am very grateful for her help and patience.

During my years of study I have been fortunate to receive financial help from a number of sources. Brown University has supported me during all the years of my graduate career. Generous grants from The Lady Davis Fellowship Trust of Jerusalem and the Bureau of Jewish Education of the Jewish Federation of Rhode Island enabled me to study at the Hebrew University during 1974-75. A fellowship from the Memorial Foundation for Jewish Culture aided me during my final year at Brown University. My wife, Barbara Ann Ehrenhaus Gereboff, has given so much of herself during my years of study at Brown. Her encouragement and support have been without end. Even while attending to our newborn son, Avner Gavriel, she found time to type and edit my work.

The publication of this book has been made possible through generous contributions from a number of sources. The Department of Religious Studies of Brown University has made available funds from The Tisch Foundation Grant for the Study of Judaism in Modern Times as well as monies from the Jewish Federation of Rhode Island. That my former mentors should continue to provide financial support after my graduation from Brown is more than I could have ever expected. I thank my teachers for showing their ongoing commitment to me. The Max Richter Foundation and its director, Dr. Jacob Neusner, similarly have continued to show concern for me by granting funds for the publication of this work. For this I am most grateful.

NOTES

PREFACE

[1]Full bibliographical references for the following works are found in the Bibliography: Jacob Neusner, *Development of a Legend*; *The Rabbinic Traditions about the Pharisees*; *Eliezer ben Hyrcanus*; Gary Porton, *Ishmael*; William S. Green, *Joshua*; Shammai Kanter, *Gamaliel of Yavneh*; Tzvee Zahavy, *Eleazar ben Azariah*; Charles Primus, *Aqiva*; Jack Lightstone, *Yose the Galilean*; *Sadoq* (in W. S. Green [ed.], *Persons and Institutions in Early Rabbinic Judaism* [Missoula, 1977]); Diane Levine, *Eleazar Ḥisma* (in W. S. Green [ed.], *Persons and Institutions*).

[2]Jacob Neusner, *A History of the Mishnaic Laws of Purities* I-XXII.

Ah.	'Ahilot
Albeck	H. Albeck (ed.), *Shishah Sidrê Mishnah* I-VI (Jerusalem/Tel Aviv, 1954-1959).
Alfasi	Isaac Alfasi, 1013-1103, *Hilkhot HaRif*, from reprint of Babylonian Talmud, ed. Romm.
Arak.	'Arakhin
ARN	Avot deRabbi Natan
Arndt-Gingrich	William Arndt and F. Wilbur Gingrich, *A Greek-English Lexicon of N.T. and Other Early Christian Literature* (Chicago, 1957).
Arukh	Alexander Kohut (ed.), *'Aruch Completum* I-VIII (Vienna, 1926^2).
Asher	Asher ben Yehiel, d. 1327, Commentary to Mishnah, from Babylonian Talmud, ed. Romm.
Avi-Yonah	Michael Avi-Yonah, *Carta Atlas to the Period of the Second Temple, the Mishnah, and the Talmud* (Heb.) (Jerusalem, 1966).
A.Z.	'Avodah Zarah
b.	Bavli, Babylonian Talmud
b.	ben, as in Aqiva ben Joseph
Bailey	Liberty Hyde Bailey, *The Standard Cyclopedia of Horticulture* I-VI (New York, 1914-1917).
B.B.	Bava' Batra'
Bekh.	Bekhorot
Ber.	Berakhot
Bert.	Obadiah b. Abraham of Bertinoro, d.c. 1500, Commentary to Mishnah, from reprint of Mishnah, ed. Romm.
Beṣ.	Beṣah
Bik.	Bikkurim
B.M.	Bava' Meṣi'a'
B.Q.	Bava' Qamma'

b.V	*Babylonian Talmud, Mss.* in *The Collection of the Vatican Library, Series A, Vat. Ebr. 108, 109, 110, 130, 134* (photocopy, Jerusalem, 1972), *Series B, Vat. Ebr. 111, 112, 114, 118, 119* (photocopy, Jerusalem, 1974).
b. Ven.	*Babylonian Talmud, editio princeps* (Venice, 1520-1523; photocopy, Jerusalem, 1967-1972).
Cant	Canticles
Charles	R. H. Charles, *The Apocrypha and Pseudepigrapha of the Old Testament* (Oxford, 1913).
C.R.	Canticles Rabbah
1 Chr	1 Chronicles
2 Chr	2 Chronicles
Cooke	G. A. Cooke, *Textbook of Northwest Semitic Inscriptions* (Oxford, 1903).
Dan	Daniel
Danby	Herbert Danby, *The Mishnah* (London, 1933).
Deut	Deuteronomy
D.S.	Raphaelo Rabbinovicz, *Sepher Diqduqê Sopherim* I-XII (reprinted, New York, 1960); Moshe Hershler, *Diqduqê Soferim: Tractate Ketubot* I (Jerusalem, 1972); Mayer S. Feldblum, *Diqduqê Soferim: Tractate Giṭṭin* (New York, 1966).
E	Tosefta, Ms. Erfurt
Ed.	'Eduyyot
Epstein, *Mavo*	Y. N. Epstein, *Mavo leNusaḥ HaMishnah* (Jerusalem/Tel Aviv, 1964^2).
Epstein, *Mevo'ot*	Y. N. Epstein, *Mevo'ot leŚifrut HaTanna'im* (Jerusalem/Tel Aviv, 1957).
Epstein, *Prolegomena*	Y. N. Epstein, *Prolegomena ad Litteras Amoraiticas* (Heb.) (Jerusalem/Tel Aviv, 1962).
Eruv.	'Eruvin
Exod	Exodus
Ezek	Ezekiel

F

*Babylonian Talmud, Ms., Florence,
Florence National Library 11 1 7-9,*
intro. David Rosenthal (photocopy,
Jerusalem, 1972).

Feldman

Uriah Feldman, *Simkhê HaMishnah* (Tel
Aviv, n.d.).

Feliks, *Mixed Sowing*

Judah Feliks, *Mixed Sowing, Breading, and
Grafting* (Tel Aviv, 1967).

Feliks, *Ṣemeḥiat*

Judah Feliks, *Maroth HaMishnah* I
(*Semeḥiat HaMishnah*) (New York, 1966).

G

Mishnah, Mss. from Genizah, printed in
Nissan Sacks, *The Mishnah with Variant
Readings, Order Zera'im* I-II (Jerusalem,
1972-1975), and in Abraham I. Katsh,
*Ginze Mishna: One Hundred and Fifty-nine
Fragments from the Cairo Geniza in the
Saltykov-Schedrin Library in Leningrad*
(Jerusalem, 1970); Tosefta, Mss. from
Genizah in Lieberman.

Gärtner

Bertil Gärtner, *The Temple and the Community in Qumran and the New Testament*
(Cambridge, 1965).

Gaston

Lloyd Gaston, *No Stone on Another,
Studies in the Significance of the Fall
of Jerusalem in the Synoptic Gospels*
(Leiden, 1970).

Gen

Genesis

Giṭ.

Giṭṭin

Goldberg

Arnold Goldberg, "Form und Funktion des
Ma'ase in der Mischna," *Frankfurter
Judaistische Beiträge* 2 (1974), pp. 1-38.

Goldin

Judah Goldin, *The Fathers According to
Rabbi Nathan* (New Haven, 1955).

Goldschmidt

E. D. Goldschmidt, *The Passover Haggadah,
Its Sources and History* (Heb.) (Jerusalem,
1969).

GRA

Elijah ben Solomon Zalman ("Elijah Gaon"
or "Vilna Gaon"), 1720-1797, Commentary
to Mishnah, from reprint of Mishnah, ed.
Romm; Commentary to Tosefta, from Tosefta
in Babylonian Talmud; Commentary to Sifra,
from Sifra Hillel.

Green, *Joshua*

William S. Green, *The Traditions of
Joshua ben Ḥananiah. A Form-Critical
Study*, unpublished Ph.D. dissertation,
Brown University (Providence, 1974).

Green, "Name"　　　　　William S. Green, "What's in a Name?
　　　　　　　　　　　The Problematic of Rabbinic 'Biography,'"
　　　　　　　　　　　in W. S. Green (ed.), *Approaches to*
　　　　　　　　　　　Ancient Judaism: Theory and Practice
　　　　　　　　　　　(Missoula, 1978).

Hag　　　　　　　　　　Haggai

Ḥag.　　　　　　　　　　Ḥagigah

Ḥal.　　　　　　　　　　Ḥallah

Halivni　　　　　　　　David Weiss Halivni, *Meqorot uMesorot:*
　　　　　　　　　　　Nashim (Tel Aviv, 1968).

Ḥananel　　　　　　　　Ḥananel ben Ḥushiel, 990-1050, Commentary
　　　　　　　　　　　to Babylonian Talmud, from reprint of
　　　　　　　　　　　Babylonian Talmud, ed. Romm.

Ḥazon Yeḥezqel　　　　Yeḥezqel Abramski, *Ḥazon Yeḥezqel, Bava'*
　　　　　　　　　　　Qamma' (Jerusalem, 1948).

Heinemann, *Aggadah*　Joseph Heinemann, *Aggadah and Its*
　　　　　　　　　　　Development (Heb.) (Jerusalem, 1974).

Heinemann, *Prayer*　Joseph Heinemann, *Prayer in the Period of*
　　　　　　　　　　　the Tannaim and the Amoraim (Heb.)
　　　　　　　　　　　(Jerusalem, 1966²).

Hillel　　　　　　　　Hillel b. R. Eliaqim, c. 12th century,
　　　　　　　　　　　Commentary to Sifra, ed. Shakhna
　　　　　　　　　　　Koleditzky (Jerusalem, 1961).

Hor.　　　　　　　　　Horayot

Ḥul.　　　　　　　　　Ḥullin

Hyman　　　　　　　　　Aaron Hyman, *Toledot Tanna'im Ve'Amora'im*
　　　　　　　　　　　I-III (reprint, Jerusalem, 1964).

Isa　　　　　　　　　　Isaiah

Jastrow　　　　　　　　Marcus Jastrow, *A Dictionary of the*
　　　　　　　　　　　Targumim, the Talmud Babli and Yeru-
　　　　　　　　　　　shalmi, and the Midrashic Literature
　　　　　　　　　　　(reprint, New York, 1967).

Jer　　　　　　　　　　Jeremiah

Josephus　　　　　　　*Josephus in Nine Volumes,* trans. H.
　　　　　　　　　　　St. J. Thackeray, Ralph Marcus, and
　　　　　　　　　　　Louis Feldman (London, 1926-1965).

Abbreviations and Bibliography

K	Mishnah, Ms. Kaufmann A 50; photocopy, Georg Beer, *Faksimile-Ausgabe des Mischnakodex Kaufmann A 50* (The Hague, 1929; reprint, Jerusalem, 1969).
1 Kgs	1 Kings
2 Kgs	2 Kings
Kal. Rab.	Kallah Rabbati
Kanter	Shammai Kanter, *Gamaliel of Yavneh*, unpublished Ph.D. dissertation, Brown University (Providence, 1974).
Kasher, *Haggadah*	Menachem M. Kasher, *Israel Passover Haggadah* (New York, 1975[6]).
Kasher, *Torah*	Menachem M. Kasher, *Torah Shelemah* XI (New York, 1944).
Kel.	Kelim
Ker.	Keritot
Ket.	Ketubot
Kil.	Kil'ayim
Kraus	Samuel Krauss, ed., *Qadmoniyot HaTalmud* I/i (Berlin, n.d.), I/ii (Berlin, 1923), II/i (Tel Aviv, 1929), II/ii (Tel Aviv, 1945).
L	Mishnah, Ms. Cambridge 470, in W. H. Lowe (ed.), *The Mishnah on which the Palestinian Talmud Rests* (Cambridge, 1883; reprint, Jerusalem, 1967).
Lam	Lamentations
Lam. R.	Lamentations Rabbah
Leid.	*Palestinian Talmud- Ms. Leiden Codex Scali 3* (photocopy, Jerusalem, 1971).
Lev	Leviticus
Levi	J. Levi, *Wörterbuch über die Talmudim und Midraschim* I-IV (Leipzig, 1876-1889).
Lieberman, *Hellenism*	Saul Lieberman, *Hellenism in Jewish Palestine* (New York, 1950).
Lieberman, *Moed*	Saul Lieberman, *The Tosefta, The Order of of Mo'ed* (New York, 1962).
Lieberman, *Nashim*	Saul Lieberman, *The Tosefta, The Order of Nashim, Yebamoth, Kethubuth, Nedarim, Nazir* (New York, 1967); *Sotah, Gittin, Kiddushin* (New York, 1973).

Lieberman, *T.K.*   Saul Lieberman, *Tosefta Kifshutah, A Comprehensive Commentary on the Tosefta* I-VIII (New York, 1955-).

Lieberman, *T.R.*   Saul Lieberman, *Tosefeth Rishonim: A Commentary. Based on Manuscripts of the Tosefta and Works of the Rishonim and Midrashim and Rare Editions*: II, *Yevamot-Keritot*; III, *Kelim-Niddah*; IV, *Mikwaoth-Uktzin* (Jerusalem, 1939).

Lieberman, *Zeraim*   Saul Lieberman, *The Tosefta, The Order of Zera'im* (New York, 1955).

Lightstone   Jack Lightstone, *Yose the Galilean: Traditions in Mishnah-Tosefta*, unpublished Ph.D. dissertation, Brown University (Providence, 1977).

lit.   literally

Löw   Immanuel Löw, *Die Flora der Juden* I-IV (Vienna, 1924-1934).

Lon.   London

M   Babylonian Talmud, Codex Munich 95; photocopy, Hermann L. Strack, *Talmud Babylonicum Codicis Hebraica Manacensis 95* (Leiden, 1912; reprint, Jerusalem, 1971).

M.   Mishnah

MA   Ephraim Isaac of Premysla, *Mishnah Aharonah*, published 1882, from reprint of Mishnah, ed. Romm.

Ma.   Ma'aserot

Magen Avraham   Abraham Abele ben Hayyim HaLevi Gombiner, 1637-1683, *Magen 'Avraham*, from reprint of Tos. in Babylonian Talmud, ed. Romm.

Maim.   Moshe ben Maimon, 1135-1204, *Mishnah 'im Perush Rabbenu Moshe ben Maimon* I-VI, trans. Joseph David Qappah (Jerusalem, 1964-1968).

Mak.   Makkot

Maks.   Makhshirin

Malbim   Meir Leibush Malbim, 1809-1879, *Sefer HaTorah VeHamisvah* III, ed. Solomon Drillich (Jerusalem, 1967).

MB   Samuel Avigdor b. Abraham Karlin, *Minhat Bikkurim*, from reprint of Tos. in Babylonian Talmud, ed. Romm.

Me.   Me'ilah

Meg.   Megillah

Meiri   Menaḥem b. Shelomo, 1249-1306, *Bet Habeḥirah, Shabbaṭ*, ed. Isaak S. Lange (Jerusalem, 1971[3]); *Sukkah*, ed. Avraham Leis (Jerusalem, 1971[2]).

Mekh. Ish.   Mekhilta deRabbi Ishmael

Mekh. Sim.   Mekhilta deRabbi Simeon bar Yoḥai

Men.   Menaḥot

Mid.   Middot

Mid.   Midrash

Mid. Ps.   Midrash on Psalms

Mid. Sam.   Midrash Samuel

Mid. Tan.   Midrash Tanna'im

Miq.   Miqva'ot

M.Q.   Mo'ed Qaṭan

MR   Ephraim Isaac of Premysla, *Mishnah Rishonah*, published 1882, from reprint of Mishnah, ed. Romm.

MS   Shelomo bar Joshua Adeni, 1567-1625, *Mel'ekhet Shelomo*, from reprint of Mishnah, ed. Romm.

M.S.   Ma'aser Sheni

Matt   Matthew

N   *Mishnah, editio princeps, Naples, 1492* (photocopy, Jerusalem, 1970).

Naz.   Nazir

Ned.   Nedarim

Neg.   Nega'im

Neh   Nehemiah

Nesiv   Naphtali Ṣevi Yehudah Berlin, 1817-1893, *Sifre with Commentary 'Emeq HaNesiv* I-II (Jerusalem, 1959-1960).

Neusner, *Development*   Jacob Neusner, *Development of a Legend: Studies on the Traditions Concerning Yoḥanan ben Zakkai* (Leiden, 1970).

Neusner, *Eliezer*   Jacob Neusner, *Eliezer Ben Hyrcanus: The Tradition and the Man* I-II (Leiden, 1973).

Neusner, *First*   Jacob Neusner, *First Century Judaism in Crisis* (Nashville, 1975)

Neusner, *HMLP*   Jacob Neusner, *A History of the Mishnaic Law of Purities* I-XXII (Leiden, 1974-1977).

Neusner, "Judaism"   Jacob Neusner, "Judaism in a Time of Crisis, Four Responses to the Destruction of the Second Temple," *Judaism* 21/3 (1972) pp. 313-27.

Neusner, *Phar.*   Jacob Neusner, *The Rabbinic Traditions about the Pharisees before 70* I-III (Leiden, 1971).

Nez.   Nezirot

Nid.   Niddah

Num   Numbers

O   Oxford

Oh.   'Ohalot

Oppenheim   A. Leo Oppenheim, "*kabaru*," in *Assyrian Dictionary* VIII, ed. Ignace Gelb (Chicago, 1964).

Orl.   'Orlah

P   *Mishnah, Ms. Parma De Rossi 138* (photocopy, Jerusalem, 1970).

Par.   Parah

Pb   *Mishnah, Ms. Parma "B" De Rossi 497*, Seder Taharot, intro. M. Bar-Asher (photocopy, Jerusalem, 1971).

Pc   *Mishnah, Ms. Parma "C" De Rossi 984* (photocopy, Jerusalem, 1971).

Pes.   Pesaḥim

Pes. Rab.   Pesikta' Rabbati

Philo   *Philo in Ten Volumes*, trans. F. H. Colson and G. H. Whitaker (London, 1929-1962).

Pliny, *N.H.*   Pliny, *Natural History*, trans. H. Rackman and W. H. S. Jones (Cambridge, 1963).

PM   Moshe Margoliot, d. 1781, *Penê Moshe*, from reprint of Palestinian Talmud, ed. Romm (Vilna, 1922).

Porton	Gary G. Porton, *The Traditions of Rabbi Ishmael* I-II (Leiden, 1976-1977).
Porton diss.	Gary Porton, *The Legal Traditions of Rabbi Ishmael: A Form-Critical and Literary Critical Approach*, unpublished Ph.D. dissertation, Brown University (Providence, 1973).
Pr	*Mishnah, Ms. Paris 328-29* (photocopy, Jerusalem, 1970).
PRE	Pirqé deRabbi Eliezer
Primus	Charles Primus, *Aqiva's Contribution to the Law of Zera'im* (Leiden, 1977).
Prov	Proverbs
Ps	Psalms
QA	Aaron Ibn Hayyim, d. 1632, *Qorban Aharon, Perush LeSefer Sifra* (Dessau, 1749; photocopy, n.p., 1970).
QH	David Frankel of Berlin, 1707-1762, *Qorban Ha'Edah*, from reprint of Palestinian Talmud, ed. Romm (Vilna. 1922).
Qid.	Qiddushin
Qoh.	Qohelet
R.	Rabbi
R.	Rabbah
Rab.	Rabbati
Rabad	Abraham ben David, c. 1120-1198, Commentary to Sifra, from Sifra, ed. Weiss.
Rashba	Shelomo b. Adret, 1235-1310, Novellae to Babylonian Talmud, from reprint of Babylonian Talmud, ed. Makhon Hatam Sofer (Jerusalem, 1968).
Rashbam	Samuel b. Meir, d. 1174, Commentary to Mishnah, from reprint of Babylonian Talmud, ed. Romm.
Rashi	Shelomo b. Isaac, 1040-1105, Commentary to Mishnah and Babylonian Talmud, from reprint of Babylonian Talmud, ed. Romm.
Ratner	B. Ratner, *Ahawath Zion weJeruscholaim* I-XII (reprint, Jerusalem, 1964).
R.H.	Rosh Hashanah

Rich	Anthony Rich, *The Illustrated Companion to the Latin Dictionary and the Greek Lexicon* (London, 1849).
Rom	Romans
Romm	Romm reprint of Mishnah (Vilna, 1887); Romm reprint of Babylonian Talmud (Vilna, 1895).
Rosh	see Asher
Saldarini	Anthony J. Saldarini, *The Fathers According to Rabbi Nathan, A Translation and Commentary* (Leiden, 1975).
1 Sam	1 Samuel
2 Sam	2 Samuel
Sanh.	Sanhedrin
Sem.	Semaḥot
Sens	Samson ben Abraham of Sens, ca. 1150-1230, Commentary to Mishnah, from reprint of Mishnah in Babylonian Talmud, ed. Romm.
Serilio	Solomon ben Joseph Serilio, d.c. 1558, Commentary on Palestinian Talmud (Jerusalem, 1934-1967).
Shab.	Shabbat
Shav.	Shavu'ot
Sheq.	Sheqalim
Shev.	Shevi'it
Smith	R. Payne Smith, *Syriac-English Dictionary* (Oxford, 1903).
Soṭ.	Soṭah
Suk.	Sukkah
Ta.	Ta'anit
Tem.	Temurah
Ter.	Terumot
T.J.	Targum Jonathan
Ṭoh.	Ṭoharot
Tos.	Tosefta

Tosafot Anshé Shem

Tosafot Anshé Shem, Commentary to
Mishnah, from reprint of Mishnah, ed.
Romm.

T.Y.

Tevul Yom

TYT

Yom Tov Lipmann Heller, 1579-1654,
Tosafot Yom Tov, from reprint of Mishnah,
ed. Romm.

TYY

Israel ben Gedaliah Lipschutz, 1782-1870,
Tif'eret Yisra'el Yakhin, from reprint of
Mishnah, ed. Romm.

Uphof

Johannes Cornelis Theodorus Uphof,
Dictionary of Economic Plants (New York,
1959).

Uqs.

'Uqsin

V

Vatican

var.

variant

Ven.

Venice

Vienna

Tosefta, Ms. Vienna Heb. 20

y.

Yerushalmi, Palestinian Talmud

Yad.

Yadayim

Yev.

Yevamot

y. Leid.

see Leid

Y.T.

Yom Tov

y.V

Palestinian Talmud, Ms. Vatican Ebr. 133,
intro. Saul Lieberman (photocopy,
Jerusalem, 1970).

y. Ven.

*Palestinian Talmud, editio princeps,
Venice*, 1523-1524 (photocopy, n.p., n.d.).

Zab.

Zabim

Zahavy

Tzvee Zahavy, *The Traditions of Eleazar
Ben Azariah* (Missoula, 1977).

Zech

Zechariah

Zev.

Zevaḥim

TRANSLITERATIONS

'	=	א
B	=	ב
G	=	ג
D	=	ד
H	=	ה
W	=	ו
Z	=	ז
Ḥ	=	ח
Ṭ	=	ט
Y	=	י
K	=	ך, כ
L	=	ל
M	=	ם, מ
N	=	ן, נ
Ś	=	ס
'	=	ע
P	=	ף, פ
Ṣ	=	ץ, צ
Q	=	ק
R	=	ר
Š	=	שׁ
S	=	שׂ
T	=	ת

INTRODUCTION

The ways in which a community speaks and writes about its
authoritative figures reveal much about the values and the imagination of the members of that group. By examining the literary
and substantive traits of sayings and stories attributed to its
leadership, we discern, for example, the conception of authority
held by a group. When we can trace the history of such items that
have taken shape over several centuries, we may uncover developments and changes in the views of the community. In this study,
we analyze all of the materials attributed by the members of the
rabbinic movement of the first to the eighth centuries to one of
its early masters, R. Tarfon, an authority of the late first and
early second centuries A.D. Reconstruction of the history of the
formation and the preservation of this corpus of items for the
purpose of delineating the factors governing these processes constitutes the primary task of the analysis. By detailing the history of the units of tradition assigned to Tarfon, we gain insight
into the values and the imagination of the members of early rabbinism.

The results of our history of the traditions form the basis
for a second, but limited, history yielded by these various materials, viz., an account of the historical Tarfon. Because of the
nature and the content of these units of tradition, we can say
almost nothing about the actual life of this master. Only a hand-
ful of items claim to provide the type of information normally
included in a biography. But these materials apparently take
shape many centuries after the death of Tarfon, and therefore, are
unlikely to relate reliable data about him. The majority of the
corpus consists of items containing legal rulings assigned to
Tarfon and ideally should give rise to a description of his
thoughts. Once we take into account the history and the traits of
these units of tradition, we may gather from them only some meager
data about our master, for they cannot be shown to have originated
in Tarfon's lifetime, and are cast in highly formalized patterns
obliterating his actual words. The few claims we safely make regarding Tarfon, however, provide information about Judaism in the
late first and early second centuries.

The traits of the literature upon which we draw determine the
methods employed in our study. All of the units of tradition assigned to Tarfon appear in various rabbinic documents composed

1

neither by him nor his immediate disciples. These documents are
highly complex compilations, often containing penultimate units
linked together by redactors. The penultimate materials, including those assigned to Tarfon, themselves are frequently aggregates
of further discrete traditions. Through the use of literary
analysis, by looking, for instance, for accretions, repetitions,
and glosses, we are able to isolate these discrete traditions.
Comparisons of the various versions of a given item also contribute
to this endeavor. In addition, since most of the Tarfon-materials
are highly formalized, form analysis enables us to dissect the
various complex structures. We thereby isolate the most primitive
version of the Tarfon-items and have in hand the data necessary
for tracing the literary history of the Tarfon-corpus. Our literary and formal results also provide the basis for our exegesis of
the materials, for a proper understanding of a given item presupposes a correct literary analysis. Form and literary analyses
thus are indispensable to our exegetical task, and as a result, to
historical knowledge.

This work goes beyond previous studies of Tarfon in that it
raises the issue, ignored in all other studies, of the history of
the Tarfon-materials, and constructs its very limited biography of
this master from a critical analysis of all of these items. The
other attempts to sketch the life of Tarfon suffer from four major
faults.[1] First, they build their descriptions upon incomplete
evidence. In particular, most do not deal with the legal units
of tradition at all. Second, they are completely uncritical, for
they accept the reliability of all attributions and assume that the
items contain verbatim reports of Tarfon's words and deeds. Third,
they try to account for Tarfon's views in terms of character traits
and social and economic considerations mentioned rarely, if at all,
in the items. Fourth, the hermeneutic used in interpreting the
legal materials is very simplistic as it is limited to the questions of whether Tarfon is lenient or strict, and whether he is a
Hillelite or a Shammaite.[2] While none of the historical studies of
Tarfon contribute to our project, the analyses of Jacob Neusner and
of his students of the traditions assigned to other Yavnean masters,
and the former's work on the mishnaic laws of purities provide the
models we follow in this work. As noted, we ask the same range of
questions and employ the identical methods used in these other
studies. In addition to these historical works, the explanations
of both the classical and some modern commentators of Tarfon's
rulings are indispensable. Maimonides, GRA, and Mishnah Rishonah

(Mishnah Aḥaronah) especially have contributed to my exegeses.
Among modern scholars Saul Lieberman occupies a special position.
Without his commentary upon Tos., that document would remain a
closed book. The literary and textual observations of Y. N. Epstein and David Weiss Halivni also have added greatly to my
comments.

    In Chapters I through VII (Part One) we provide a translation
and analysis of all the legal (Chapters I through VI) and the non-
legal (Chapter VII) units of tradition. The translation attempts
to reproduce the syntax, cadence, and formulaic style of the
original Hebrew or Aramaic as far as that is possible within the
limits of intelligible English. The diction of Middle Hebrew and
of the Aramaic of the Talmuds is highly formalized and elliptical.
In order for the translation to remain intelligible, we fill in
these ellipses, placing in brackets all words not appearing in the
original language. When we translate a word whose meaning is uncertain, or where we have given a somewhat free translation, we put
in parentheses a transliteration of the Hebrew or Aramaic. In
making the translation, we have checked the major Mss. for the
various documents. We have listed only those variants from the
standard printed texts[3] that affect the meaning of the text. These
variants also appear in brackets. In order to differentiate Hebrew
from Aramaic texts, the latter are italicized. Citations from the
Bible are placed within single or double quotes. Translations of
biblical verses are based on the RSV except when a particular exegesis requires that we understand the verse otherwise.[4]

    The comments systematically attend to several issues. We
examine the literary traits of each pericope, noting the use of
formulary patterns, for the purpose of isolating the earliest elements of the item. Our analyses of the literary and formal traits
are significant for two reasons. First, on the basis of these results we comment, in Part Two, upon the history of the formation
and redaction of the Tarfon-materials. Second, as noted, our exegeses build upon the findings of our literary analyses. Thus in
our exegetical comments we attempt to discover the primary and
original meaning of the text. We draw upon the classical commentators (and this is quite often) only when they aid in uncovering
this earliest level of meaning. Our comments conclude with remarks
about any historical or biographical information contained in the
pericope, and any evidence of an attestation to the item.[5] We cite
all parallel versions of an item when there are significant differences between them. When Tos. or a document with a later date of

redaction cites M., the quotation from M. appears in italics. The
parallel versions of an item generally are compared in a synoptic
chart for the purpose of tracing the history of the unit of tradition. In these charts, dashes signify that the parallel lacks the
words found in the other version, and quotation marks indicate
that the parallel contains the words in the version cited in the
preceding column.

In Chapters VIII through XIII (Part Two), we synthesize and
refine the data of Part One so that the general characteristics of
the whole corpus emerge. We begin in Chapter VIII with a catalogue
of all the units of tradition indicating in which of the five
strata of the corpus they and their parallels appear. The five
strata in chronological order are: M.-Tos., halakhic midrashim,
beraitot, amoraic materials contained in the Talmuds, later compilations, such as Gen. R. and Pes. Rab. Since by using attestations we are unable to isolate a significant number of items that
can be dated prior to the date of redaction of M.-Tos., the units
of tradition contained in these documents constitute the earliest
stratum of the corpus. Our catalogue indicates that legal materials predominate in the corpus as a whole and tend to appear first
in its earliest levels. By contrast, most of the non-legal units
of tradition first surface in the latest levels of the corpus.[6]
The above results suggest that since the legal materials can be
dated closer to the time of Tarfon, they are more apt than the
non-legal items to contain reliable information about him. Our
reason for this presumption is that materials apparently first
arising long after the death of a person have a greater tendency
to lack close ties to the facts about the actual person. As a
result, we hypothesize that, compared to the legal items, the non-
legal units of tradition may not constitute a coherent complex of
materials. That is to say, these items probably share few formal and substantive traits and therefore have not been formulated
either as a unit or at least in line with each other. The suc-
ceeding chapters of Part Two substantiate this hypothesis.

In Chapter IX we examine the literary traits of the materials.
The legal units of tradition are a coherent set of items, for most
of them have been cast in one of two formulary patterns, the dispute and the *ma'aseh*. The first consists of two or more opposing
sayings, formulated together, each of which is not intelligible on
its own. In the best disputes the opposing dicta contain a
balanced number of syllables or are fixed opposites, such as,
liable/exempt. The *ma'aseh* is the most disciplined of all

narrative patterns. It consists of the formula M'SH B or Š,
followed by a brief statement of a setting, a subject, and a description of his action. The construction of the *ma'aseh* indicates
that its formulators are solely interested in Tarfon, for they
either do not mention other authorities or use them as literary
devices to accentuate Tarfon. The legal materials of the earliest
stratum of the corpus, M.-Tos., have taken shape within the mainstream of the mishnaic redactional process. They have been formulated by the redactors of those documents. Circles primarily interested in Aqiva are responsible for the construction of nearly
half of these items.[7]

By contrast to the legal units of tradition, the non-legal
items appear in a wide variety of loosely structured literary
types. The formulation of many of these items indicates that they
do not center upon Tarfon. For example, his actions often serve
as the basis for lessons assigned in the pericope to other authorities. Tarfon merely supplies a name in many of the non-legal
units of tradition.

The results, given in Chapter X, of our analysis of the substance of the legal materials coincide with our findings in the
preceding chapter. The legal items of the earliest stratum are a
coherent complex of materials, for they focus upon a clearly delineated agendum of issues. The agendum is that of a Pharisee, by
which I mean, that it primarily deals with two topics, purity and
agricultural laws. Sabbath and festival law, family law, and
Temple law are discussed somewhat less than agricultural and
purity laws. Liturgical and civil matters are rarely mentioned.
A second factor pointing to the coherence of the legal materials
is that a number of specific issues is discussed with regard to
different areas of law. Coherence of this sort is fairly uncommon
in materials attributed to named masters. More than one-quarter
of all Tarfon-units of tradition, covering all the broad thematic
concerns of the corpus, relate to the question of whether objective facts, such as the form of an object, or the agent's subjective presumptions, such as his intention to use the object in a
certain way, are the determinative criteria in reaching legal decisions. Similarly, nearly one-third of the items, again dealing
with the major thematic areas of the agendum, pertain to priestly
concerns. The units of tradition first found in the later levels
of the corpus have the same traits as those in M.-Tos.; therefore,
the legal items as a whole are coherent.

In Chapter X we also comment upon the relationship between
Tarfon's legal rulings and those of other Yavneans. The results
again coincide with those of Chapter IX: Tarfon's legal materials
lie within the mainstream of the mishnaic tradition. Thus nearly
all of them either pertain to matters discussed by other Yavneans,
or presuppose views assigned to earlier authorities. While Tarfon's rulings deal with issues referred to by other earlier and
Yavnean masters, they do not generate major developments in mishnaic law. His rulings do not form the conceptual foundation for a
significant portion, e.g., chapter or tractate of M. That is to
say, Tarfon does not articulate fundamental opinions required for
the further unfolding of the law. His rulings for the most part
relate to the fine points of the law. For example, he specifies
dimensions of objects or applies principles to particular cases.

Chapter XI, Formal Exegeses, focuses upon those units of tradition containing a comment by Tarfon upon a citation from Scripture. There is no pattern to these items. They do not center
upon a specific portion of Scripture, discuss a limited set of
issues, or consistently employ the same hermeneutical techniques.
These findings indicate that there is no concern to attribute to a
master a coherent set of exegeses.

Chapter XII forms the counterpart to Chapter X. Here we discuss nearly all of the non-legal items, those attending to homiletical or theological issues. These materials do not constitute
a coherent set of items, for they pertain to a wide range of issues and exhibit little continuity. Topics mentioned in items of
the earliest stratum are ignored in the later levels of the corpus,
and vice versa. Tarfon merely supplies a name either used in
standard stories or appended to sayings also assigned to other
authorities. One theme, the rabbi and the Torah, is discussed in
nearly half of the items. But these discrete units of tradition
share no details, and hence, do not comprise a coherent corpus.

In Chapter XIII we trace the two histories yielded by the 128
units of tradition attributed to Tarfon. In the first of these
accounts, the history of the formation of the corpus, we bring together our findings demonstrating the coherence of its legal
items and the incoherence of its non-legal materials. This difference between the two types of items indicates that the members of
early rabbinism used the name of a master in divergent ways. We
account for this difference in terms of the functions of law and
non-legal ideas in rabbinic Judaism and note what it teaches us
about the values and the imagination of rabbinic Jews of the second

through the eighth centuries.   The second history constructed from
our sources is a very limited account of the historical Tarfon.
We safely say only that he is a Pharisee and a priest who lived at
Lydda after the destruction of the second Temple, and responded to
that crisis by stressing the continuing centrality of the priesthood.   The distinctiveness of this view emerges when compared with
those of other Jews of the first century.

INTRODUCTION

[1]I have consulted the following works: Zvi Kaplan, "Tarfon," *Encyclopaedia Judaica* 15, cols. 810-11 = *Encyclopaedia Hebraica* 19, cols. 73-74; Schulim Ochser, "Tarfon," *Jewish Encyclopedia* 12, pp. 56-57; A. Orenstein, "Lidmut Diyuqno shel Rebbi Tarfon," *Sinai* 39 (1956), pp. 182-88; Jacob Brüll, *Mavo HaMishnah* I (reprinted; Jerusalem, 1970), pp. 100-03; Zecharias Frankel, *Darkhê HaMishnah* (reprinted; Tel Aviv, n.d.), pp. 107-12; Louis Finkelstein, *Akiba* (New York, 1970); Mordechai Margolioth, *Encyclopedia of Talmudic and Geonic Literature* I (Tel Aviv, 1944-45), cols. 381-86; B. Z. Bacher, *Aggadot HaTannaim* I (Berlin, 1922[2]), pp. 80-87; Gershom Bader, *The Jewish Spiritual Heroes* I (New York, 1940), pp. 270-75; A. Hyman, *Toledot* II, pp. 524-29; J. Derenbourg, *Essai sur l'histoire et la geographie de la Palestine* (Paris, 1867), pp. 376-83; Jacob Neusner, "A Life of Rabbi Tarfon, ca. 50-130 C.E.," *Judaica* 17 (1961), pp. 141-67.

[2]See the works of Ochser and Orenstein.

[3]Throughout study we base translations upon the following editions:
Mishnah: H. Albeck, ed., *Shishah Sidrê Mishnah* (Jerusalem, 1954-59).
Tosefta: S. Lieberman, ed., *The Tosefta* (New York, 1955-73) and M. S. Zuckermandel, ed., *The Tosefta: Based on the Erfurt and Vienna Codices* (reprinted; Jerusalem, 1963).
Halakhic Midrashim: Y. N. Epstein and E. Z. Melamed, eds., *Mekhilta D'Rabbi Sim'on b. Jochai* (Jerusalem, 1955); L. Finkelstein, ed., *Sifre on Deuteronomy* (New York, 1969); H. S. Horovitz, ed., *Sifre D'Be Rab: Sifre on Numbers and Sifre Zuṭṭa* (reprinted; Jerusalem, 1966); H. S. Horovitz and I. A. Rabin, eds., *Mechilta D'Rabbi Ismael* (reprinted; Jerusalem, 1970); I. H. Weiss, ed., *Sifra deBe Rab or Sefer Torat Kohanim* (reprinted; New York, 1963).
Palestinian Talmud: Venice edition of *Talmud Yerushalmi* (reprinted; n.p. and n.d.), with attention to B. Ratner, *Sefer Ahavat Zion weJeruscholaim.*
Babylonian Talmud: Vilna edition of *Talmud Babli* (reprinted; New York, n.d.), with attention to R. Rabbinovicz, *Diqduqê Soferim.*
Editions used for less frequently cited documents are recorded after the relevant texts.

[4]There are a number of peculiarities in translation, transliteration, and capitalization. The diacritical marks on those proper names frequently cited in the text, i.e., Tarfon, Aqiva, Eliezer, Eleazar, Ishmael, and Yose are left out. Hebrew terms fairly well accepted in English have not been italicized. Halakhah, midrash, amora, tanna, and baraita appear in normal type. Many words often capitalized are given in this study in lower case, e.g., mishnaic, rabbinic, tannaitic, and amoraic. I can think of no reason for not capitalizing "biblical" while capitalizing the above terms.

[5]An attestation is data indicating knowledge of the unit of tradition prior to the date of redaction of the document in which it appears.

[6]The Tarfon-corpus in this respect parallels those of other Yavneans.

[7]In this respect the Tarfon-materials again are comparable to those of other Yavneans.

PART ONE

SOURCES

CHAPTER I

ZERA'IM

A. The House of Shammai say, "In the evening everyone
should recline (YṬW) and recite the *Shema*',[1] and in the
morning they should stand up [and recite it].

B. "For it is written, 'And when you lie down and when
you rise up'" [Deut 6:7].

C. The House of Hillel say, "Everyone recites the
Shema' in his own way.

D. "For it is written, 'And when you walk by the way'"
[Deut 6:7].

E. If so, why does it say, "And when you lie down and
when you rise up?"

F. [The meaning of the verse is not what you say]
[K,L,P: but] [that one should recite the *Shema*'] at the time
that people lie down and at the time that people rise up.

G. Said R. Tarfon, "I was on the way, and I moved to
the (HYṬTY) [alternatively, reclined] to recite the *Shema*',

H. "in accordance with the words of the House of Shammai,

I. "and I put myself in jeopardy by reason of robbers."

J. They said to him, "You were worthy to be liable for
your own punishment (KDYY HYYT LḤWB B'ṢMK), because you
transgressed the words of the House of Hillel."

M. Ber. 1:3

Comment: A and C are independent sayings which have not been
redacted into a neatly balanced dispute form. B glosses A, and D
glosses C by supplying proof texts. E-F explain by means of a
question and answer how the opinion of the House of Hillel relates
to the proof text of B. G is a first person report by Tarfon.
This is a formulary pattern which frequently appears in the traditions of Tarfon. H+I gloss G, while J responds to H and I.

The Houses' opinions relate to the manner in which one may say
the *Shema*' (Deut 6:4-9). Tarfon's saying in G, depending on how
one translates the verb HYṬTY, may be interpreted in two ways.
The redactor treats HYṬTY as identical to the verb YṬW in A. Tarfon's saying is taken to show, as H asserts, that Tarfon acted
according to the opinion of the House of Shammai. I-J utilize this
claim to develop an anti-Shammaite polemic. One problem with interpreting Tarfon's saying in this manner is that G does not indicate, as we would expect in a statement relating to the Shammaite

13

ruling, whether it was at night or in the morning that the incident occurred.

We can explain G differently if we translate HYṬṬY as "turn"
or "to turn off the road."[2] Accordingly, G relates that, while on
a journey, Tarfon turned off the road to recite the *Shema'*. This
statement addresses the issue of whether or not one may say the
Shema' while moving, while literally on the way. The biblical
verse gives rise to this question, for Deut 6:7 states, "You should
teach these words, [which in M.-Tos. means, "you should recite the
Shema'"], when you lie down, when you rise up, and when you walk
by the way." If we interpret HYṬṬY in this manner, then we see
that the redactor has taken advantage of the double meaning of the
root NṬH and has turned Tarfon's saying into a pro-Shammaite assertion. This statement then serves as the basis for the anti-
Shammaite polemic. We should assume that this transformation of
G took place during the time of the conflict between the Houses;
therefore, it should predate the formation of M. Yev. 1:4. M. Yev.
depicts the conflict as having ceased, or at least diminished.

This is the only tradition of Tarfon in M.-Tos. which connects his view with those of the House of Shammai. There is a
tradition in y. Shev. 4:2 which ties a saying of Tarfon to an
opinion of the House of Shammai, but as we shall see, the association of the two in that pericope is the work of third century
rabbis. There is, therefore, no sustained effort to depict Tarfon
as a Shammaite.

A.   [P,L, Maim. Ms. Enelow 270, Maim. Ms. 0 393: And]
[As to] one who drinks water to quench his thirst, he says--
B.   That all exists by his word.
C.   R. Tarfon says, "The creator of many living things
[G,L,P,K,Leid.,M,N: and their wants]."

M. Ber. 6:8 (b. Eruv. 14b,
Deut. R. 3:8)

Comment: A-C are a variation of a dispute form: anonymous law
+ x says = gloss. A-B thus are a declarative sentence which C, an
alternate opinion, depends upon for its superscription.

The context of this pericope is a series of laws concerning
the blessings recited after eating. The two preceding laws in M.
Ber. 6:8 and all of M. Ber. 7 deal with the grace after meals. A
of our pericope does not specify whether it concerns the blessing
said before or the one said after drinking the water. All of the

commentators ignore the context and claim that A deals with the
prayer said before drinking the water. This interpretation is
generated by B. According to rabbinic law, the blessing, "That
all things exist...," is said only before eating. M. Ber. 6:3
specifies that for all things which do not grow from the earth one
says this blessing. Thus the commentators treat our pericope as
an example of M. Ber. 6:3. The blessing Tarfon suggests appears
nowhere else in M.-Tos. It does appear in b. Ber. 37a-38b as a
blessing one recites after eating certain foods.

Tos. Ber. 4:4 utilizes Tarfon's opinion as the basis for an
aggadic discussion. We treat Tos. below (p. 221).

> A. R. Eliezer says, "Land that can be sown with a
> quarter (BYT RWB') [of a *qav* of produce] is liable for *pe'ah*."
>
> B. R. Joshua says, "That which produces two *se'ah* [is
> liable]."
>
> C. R. Tarfon says, "[Land that is] six *tefaḥim* by six
> *tefaḥim* [is liable]."
>
> D. R. Judah [O,L,Leid.,Serilio,K,P: R. Joshua] says,
> "Sufficient to harvest and repeat [i.e., enough grain so that
> one may move the sickle back and forth]."
>
> E. And the law is according to his opinion.
>
> F. R. Aqiva says, "Any land is liable to *pe'ah*, first
> fruits,
>
> G. and [it is permitted] to have a *prozbul* written on
> it, and to acquire with it movable objects by means of
> money, writ, or usucaption.

M. Peah 3:6

Comment: A-D are a dispute in which the superscription appears in the first opinion, A. The sayings are not balanced. E
glosses the above. F-G are an autonomous saying.

Lev 19:2, 23:22, and Deut 24:19-21 specify that a person must
leave the corner of his "field" unharvested so that the poor may
gather from it. The opinions in this pericope use different criteria to establish the amount of land liable for *pe'ah*. A is in
terms of the amount of grain that can be sown. M. Kil. 2:9 treats
this as a fixed amount of land, a square ten and one-half *amot* by
ten and one-half *amot*. B and D use the criterion of the amount of
grain the land produces. C gives a linear measurement. Maim.,
Bert., and TYY explain that the opinions are in descending order.

The rulings of Judah b. Bathyra and Aqiva do not relate to a
real field. The "field" of the Torah means for them any piece of
land. But as the *gemara* in y. Peah 3:6 points out, the opinions
of the first three masters deal with amounts of land which are
treated in mishnaic law as fields. According to M. Kil. 2:9 a
piece of land which can be sown with a quarter of a *qav* of produce
is considered a field, such that one may plant, without incurring
liability, diverse kinds of grain in adjacent pieces of land of
this size. The *gemara*'s explanation of Joshua's ruling is based
upon M. Peah 6:6 which states that two *seah*s of produce left behind by the harvesters are not considered forgotten sheaf. The
gemara explains that two *seah*s of produce constitute a field. Now
since Deut 24:19 stipulates that one must leave the sheaf which he
forgets *in his field*, he need not leave two *seah*s of produce. The
amount of land prescribed by Tarfon constitutes the minimum size
of adjacent plots of land in which one may sow diverse kinds of
vegetables (M. Kil. 2:10). A square of land six *tefaḥim* by six
tefaḥim, therefore, is considered a field.

> A. Said R. Simeon Shezuri, "M'SH Š [b.: One time]:
> My fruits that needed tithing became mixed [b. adds: with
> already tithed common-produce],
>
>   B. "and I came and asked R. Tarfon [what to do],
>   C. "and he said to me, 'Go and purchase for yourself
> [some] produce from the market place (MN HŠWQ) and tithe
> with them [for the untithed crops that have become mixed
> with the already tithed crops].'"

Tos. Demai 5:22, ed. Lieberman,
p. 92, lns. 93-94 (b. Men. 31a)

Comment: The M'SH consists of two elements, a setting, A-B,
and Tarfon's legal advice, C.

In our analysis we first explain Tarfon's opinion. We then
compare it with the anonymous law of Tos. Demai 5:12. Finally, we
contrast the reading in this version of the tradition with that of
y. Demai 5:9 and attempt to determine the earlier of the two
readings.

Simeon's problem in A is as follows: Since his crops requiring tithing have become mixed with already tithed crops, he can no
longer merely extract the required amount of tithe from the mixture. Tithe may be given only from untithed crops. If Simeon
simply takes out the required amount of tithe from the mixture,

he may include in the tithe some of the already tithed crops.
Tarfon advises Simeon to purchase some (untithed) produce from the
market place and separate the tithe from this purchased produce
for his other untithed produce. According to Tarfon's advice, if,
for example, Simeon has mixed 100 bushels of crops requiring
tithing with 100 bushels of already tithed crops, he should now
purchase 12 bushels of crops from the market and tithe from the
newly purchased crops in behalf of the untithed crops now in
the mixture. After combining all his crops which still require
tithing, Simeon would now give 11.2 bushels of crops as tithe,
10 for the 100 in the mixture, and 1.2 for the newly purchased
crops.

        Lieberman notes that Tarfon's opinion does not conform to the
anonymous law of Tos. Demai 5:12 which reads:

>   A. [Concerning] untithed produce which became mixed
> with common produce [i.e., already tithed crops], lo, this
> [the untithed produce] completely forbids [the use of the
> already tithed crops (HRY ZH 'WŚR KL ŠHW')].
>   B. And if he has some other income (PRNŚH MMQWM 'HR)
> [i.e., some other crops], he removes [from them tithe]
> according to the [required] amount.
>   C. And if not [if he does not have other produce], he
> takes all the common produce corresponding to [as much as is
> required for] heave-offering and heave-offering of tithe
> for the untithed crops.

>   Tos. Demai 5:12, ed. Lieberman,
>   p. 89, lns. 54-56

According to A, the mixture of crops is completely forbidden to
the individual. B and C stipulate what the person can do if he
wants to reclaim some of the mixture. But as Lieberman notes
(*Zeraim*, p. 89 n. to lns. 52-53), B and C do not respond to the
claim that "they are completely forbidden," rather, to the problem
of what the person can do to reclaim his crops. Which solution
the person chooses (B or C) is determined by whether or not he has
other crops. If he has other crops, then he merely tithes from
them in behalf of the now mixed crops (so Lieberman, n. to ln. 53).
If he does not have other crops, then according to Lieberman,
(*T.K.* I, p. 256), following Serilio, he should take from the mixture
the amount of crops corresponding to the complete amount of common
produce plus ten percent of the amount of the untithed crops. This
explanation of C agrees with the anonymous law of M. Demai 7:7:

> If one hundred [bushels] of tithed common produce [become
> mixed with] one hundred [bushels] of untithed produce, he
> should take one hundred and ten [bushels and give them
> as tithe].

M. Demai 7:7

If we now compare the rulings of Tos. Demai 5:12 and M. Demai 7:7
to Tarfon's advice (Tos. Demai 5:22), we see that Tarfon's suggestion agrees with B of Tos. but with one very important difference.
According to B, only if the person already has the other crops, may
he tithe from them in behalf of the now mixed crops. If he does
not already have other crops, then he must forfeit (C) all his
already tithed crops to be certain that he gives tithe from untithed crops. Tarfon's advice thus keeps Simeon from incurring
the substantial economic loss of all of his already tithed crops.

This is the only Tarfon-tradition transmitted by Simeon
Shezuri. It is also the only M'SH among the traditions of Simeon.

> A. DTNY: Said R. Simeon Shezuri, "M'SH Š: Fruits that
> needed tithing became mixed with my [already tithed] crops,
> B. "and I came and asked R. Tarfon [what to do],
> C. "and he said to me, 'Go and purchase them [other
> crops] from a gentile (GWY) and tithe upon it.'"

y. Demai 5:9 24d

Comment: Our pericope now appears with one major change: "From
a gentile" instead of "from the market." The reading in y. may be
simply an alternative version of Tarfon's advice, or it may be the
result of an intentional change. I cannot determine which alternative is correct.

There is evidence to support both interpretations. A statement in b. Men. 31a suggests that y. preserves an alternative reading. After b. cites Tos.'s version of the pericope, an anonymous
statement follows which reads, "There are some who say, He said,
'Go and purchase them from a gentile.'" If we assume that this
statement was made without knowledge of the tradition preserved in
y. Demai, then it is evidence that y. may preserve a different
version of Tos.

Alternatively, the role the pericope plays in y. suggests that
the reading "from a gentile" is the result of an intentional change.
y. Demai 5:9 is an amoraic discussion about whether or not a heathen

has property rights in the land of Israel. The *gemara* opens by
citing a dispute between Meir and Judah:

> A. R. Meir said, "The heathen does not have the right
> to acquire [land] in the land of Israel which would absolve
> him [his crops] from tithes."
> B. R. Judah and R. Simeon say, "A heathen does have
> the right to acquire [land] in the land of Israel which
> exempts him [his crops] from tithes."

y. Demai 5:9

The reasoning of all parties is that if a heathen has the right
to acquire land, then his crops are his own; therefore, they do
not require tithing. But if the heathen lacks this right, then
his crops are not considered his own; therefore, a Jew who buys
these crops must tithe them. Judah b. Pazzi and R. 'Osha'iah
cite Tarfon's instructions to Simeon as a precedent for Meir's
claim. Tarfon's directions to Simeon to purchase the gentile's
crops, which require tithing, imply, although they do not explicitly state, that a heathen does not have property rights
in the land of Israel. Tarfon's saying can serve as a precedent
only if it reads "from a heathen." Furthermore, the phrase "from
the market" is vague, which again suggests that y. may be an
interpretation of Tos.

> WHTNY: R. Simeon in the name of R. Tarfon says, "The
> crops of this Israelite [who has deposited crops with a
> gentile] have rendered ('SW L) the crops of this [Serilio,
> Responsa of R. Bezalel Ashkenazi, ed. Ven. #1: gentile]
> [y. Ven.,Leid.,V: Cuthean[4]] *demai*."

y. Demai 3:4 23c

Comment: This tradition, except for a different attributive
formula, is identical to Tos. Demai 4:25. In order to facilitate
our discussion, I present in parallel columns the Tos. and the M.
upon which it comments.

M. Demai 3:4	Tos. Demai 4:22, 24, 25
1. [As to] one who brings wheat to a Cuthean miller, or to a miller [who is an] 'am-ha'areṣ, they maintain their previous status with regard to tithes and the Sabbatical year.	1. - - - -

M. Demai 3:4	Tos. Demai 4:22, 24, 25
2. To a gentile miller, [they are] *demai*.	2. - - - -
3. [As to] one who deposits his crops with a Cuthean or with an *'am-ha'areṣ*, they maintain their previous status with regard to tithes and the Sabbatical year.	3. [As to] one who deposits his crops with an *'am-ha'areṣ*, " " " " " " " " " " " " [Tos. Demai 4:22. Tos. comments upon this law.]
4. [See above #3.]	4. [As to] one who deposits crops with a Cuthean, they maintain their previous status with regard to tithes and the Sabbatical year. [Tos. Demai 4:24. Tos. comments upon this law.]
5. [If he deposited them] with a gentile, [they are] like his crops [i.e., they must be tithed].	5. [As to] one who deposits crops with a gentile, lo, he scruples [about them] regarding tithes and regarding the Sabbatical year.
6. R. Simeon says, [They are] *demai*.	6. R. Simeon b. Gamaliel and R. Simeon say, The crops of the Israelite have rendered the crops of this gentile *demai*. [Tos. Demai 4:25]

M. 3:4 and the two following it, M. 3:5,6 (not presented here),
deal with the problem of doubt about whether or not crops deposited
with or milled by someone else are deemed having been mixed with
the crops of other people. There are three possible alternatives.
The crops certainly have not been mixed; they certainly have been
mixed; they may have been mixed. In light of these three possibilities, the crops may fall into one of three categories. If
they have not been mixed, they maintain their previous status. If
they certainly have been mixed, then they acquire the status of
the other person's crops. If they may have been mixed, they are
demai. According to 1 and 3 of M. = 3 and 4 of Tos., millers and
storehouse owners, who are Cutheans or *'amme-ha'areṣ*, are trustworthy. Crops deposited with them maintain their status. Gentiles,
however, are never trustworthy. But there is a difference between
a gentile miller (2 of M.) and a gentile storehouse owner (5 and 6
of M.). According to the anonymous law of 2 of M., wheat given to

the miller is treated as *demai*. We are uncertain that he has
switched the wheat. Fruits deposited with a gentile, according to
the anonymous law of 5 of M., are like the gentile's crops, i.e.,
they must be tithed. We assume that the gentile has mixed the
crops.[5] Simeon regards these crops as *demai*; we are not sure that
they have been mixed with those of the gentile.[6] In Tos. this
opinion is given in the names of Simeon and Simeon b. Gamaliel,
and in y., in the names of Simeon and Tarfon. There is clearly
uncertainty concerning the attribution. But the principle underlying this ruling is in line with one found throughout Tarfon's
traditions (see M. Yev. 15:6-7, Tos. Miq. 1:16-19); namely, in
cases of doubt one may act leniently even if this involves the
possibility of a transgression. Thus by following Simeon's opinions, according to which the crops are considered *demai*, one may
eat produce from which heave-offering has not been separated.
One gives only tithes for *demai*-produce. Adherence to sages'
opinion eliminates this possible transgression, for since the
crops in their view have the same status as those of the gentile,
one must separate heave-offering and tithes for them.

     A. Hemp (HQNBŚ)--

     B. R. Tarfon says, "[It is] not diverse kinds
[K: in a vineyard]."

     C. But sages say, "[it is] diverse kinds."

M. Kil. 5:8

Comment: The pericope appears in the standard dispute form.
The sayings are balanced. Only Ms. K contains the words "in a
vineyard." Lacking these words, we do not know what type of
diverse kinds are discussed. The two surrounding pericopae contain internal evidence which indicates that the question at hand
is diverse kinds in a vineyard. It is, however, only on the basis
of external evidence, the context, that we assume that our pericope discusses diverse kinds in a vineyard.

    Deut 22:9 states, "Thou shall not sow thy vineyard with di-
verse kinds lest the fullness of the seed which you have sown be
forfeited together with the increase of the vineyard." Yehudah
Feliks (*Mixed Sowing*, p. vii) states, "A problem [regarding the
laws of diverse kinds] is that of the criterion for defining, for
the purpose of *kila'yim*, species of 'the same kind' and of
'diverse kinds.'" Furthermore, Feliks notes that the botanical
categories we use cannot be strictly applied to rabbinic law.

The best approach for determining the reason for the classification of certain crops as diverse kinds, therefore, is to
describe the plants.

   Hemp, *cannabis sativa*, is an annual herb. Hemp yields fibers
used for clothing, edible oil, and marijuana. Hemp does *not* look
at all like grapevines. M. Kil. 5:5 states that herbs (YRQWT) are
diverse kinds in a vineyard. The ruling of sages in our pericope
thus agrees with the law of M. Kil. 5:5. If this is the basis for
the sages' decision, then Tarfon either does not consider herbs
diverse kinds in a vineyard, or he does not classify hemp as an
herb. The botanical evidence concerning hemp supports the latter
explanation.[7]

   A. Cuscuta (KSWT)--
   B. R. Tarfon says, "[It is] not diverse kinds [b.: in
a vineyard]."
   C. But sages say, "[It is] diverse kinds [b.: in a
vineyard]."
   D. Said R. Tarfon [E: to them], "If it [constitutes]
diverse kinds in a vineyard, let it [constitute] diverse
kinds in seeds. But if it [does] not [constitute] diverse
kinds in seeds, let it not [constitute] diverse kinds in a
vineyard."

                            Tos. Kil. 3:16, ed. Lieberman,
                            p. 217, lns. 58-60 (A-C =
                            b. Shab. 139a)

Comment: The pericope is incomplete, for a debate containing
only an opinion attributed to Tarfon, D, follows the well-balanced
dispute, A-C. Furthermore, Lieberman (*T.K.* II, p. 6) points out
the second part of Tarfon's saying in D, "If it is not...," seems
to indicate that sages contend that cuscuta is not diverse kinds
in seeds. Lieberman states, "One responds to another person
according to the saying of the other person." Thus Tarfon's saying presupposes an opinion of sages concerning cuscuta planted with
seeds. But such a saying is not preserved.

   There is a disagreement concerning the identification of
cuscuta. Feldman points out (p. 252) that in Talmudic literature,
KSWT designates two different crops, cuscuta and *humulus lupulus*
or hops.[8] Cuscuta, the identification given by Löw (IV, p. 71),
Feliks (*Mixed Sowing*, p. 146), and Lieberman (*T.K.* II, p. 636)
for KSWT mentioned in our pericope, is an annual, parasitical,
leafless, twining vine bearing clusters of flowers. Once the

crop attaches itself to a plant, its roots die and it lives
entirely off the other plant. Pliny notes (13:46) that cuscuta
is used as an herb to flavor wine. Tos. Kil. 1:11 states KSWT
is a YRQ. Lieberman claims that sages in our pericope classify
cuscuta as a YRQ, and since they consider herbs diverse kinds
in a vineyard, they forbid its use in a vineyard. In explaining
Tarfon's statement in our pericope, Lieberman argues that according to him, cuscuta is a tree. The basis for his conjecture
probably is the context in which the pericope appears. The
already cited definition of YRQWT and trees (p. 36 n. 7) appears
immediately preceding this pericope. Since cuscuta does not send
forth its leaves from its roots, according to Lieberman, Tarfon
does consider cuscuta a YRQ. He, therefore, does not classify it
as diverse kinds in a vineyard. Cuscuta thus is an intermediate
case--it may be considered either an herb or a tree. Since it
looks like a tree, Tarfon allows its use in a vineyard. This is
the same reason we have given for his not forbidding hemp in a
vineyard. Thus for Tarfon the appearance, and not the botanical
classification, is the key factor for determining diverse kinds.

A. *From what time at the conclusion of the Sabbatical
year is one permitted to take arum* (LWP) from any place [even
from a place in which the laws of the Sabbatical year may not
have been observed]--

B. *R. Judah says, "At once."*

C. 1. Said R. Judah, "M'SH W: We were in Ein Kushi[9]

2. "and we did eat [y.: ate] arum at the conclusion
of the festival [of Sukkot] [y. adds: of the conclusion] of
the Sabbatical year,

3. "on the instruction of ('L PY) R. Tarfon" [y.
inserts C3 after "arum" in C2].

D. 1. Said to him R. Yose, "Is that [incident] proof
[for your opinion] [y. omits D1]?

2. "I was with you, and it was [y.: none other than]
the conclusion of Passover."[10]

Tos. Shev. 4:4, ed. Lieberman,
p. 180, lns. 7-10

Comment: Tos. Shev. 4:4 supplements M. Shev. 5:5 which reads:

A. From what time at the conclusion of the Sabbatical
year is one permitted to take arum--
B. R. Judah says, "At once."

> C. But sages say, "[He may take the arum] once the
> new [part of the crop] has come up."

M. Shev. 5:5

A-B of M. are identical to A-B of Tos. except that A of Tos.
contains the words "from any place." C adds a precedent in support of Judah's view; Yose in D challenges this report. Judah's
first person report, C, consists of three elements: (1) a setting,
(2) a description of his actions, and (3) a justification for these
actions. But without the third element, C3, C1+2 are a perfectly
intelligible report. Furthermore, Yose in D does not mention
Tarfon's advice, but simply challenges Judah's recollection of the
facts. Tarfon's authority thus stands outside of the exchange
between Judah and Yose. C1+2 and D, therefore, are a unit. When
the redactor joined this tradition to A-B, he had to insert a
clause like C3, otherwise C1+2 are no more than a report that
Judah followed his own view. We can account for the choice of
Tarfon's name in C3 in light of (1) those traditions in which Judah
Judah asserts that he did something with Tarfon's approval, and
(2) as we shall now see, the substance of the law discussed here.

Rabbinic law mandates that one may not eat crops purposely
grown during the Sabbatical year. M. Shev. 6:4 states that after
the conclusion of the Sabbatical year one may not eat herbs (YRQWT)
until a new part of the herb has begun to grow. Arum is an herb.
Judah thus disagrees with the ruling in M. Shev. 6:4. His disagreement may be based on the botanical nature of arum. Arum is
left in the ground for three years in order to grow (Feliks, *Mixed
Sowing*, p. 218; Löw I, p. 214; Lieberman, *T.K.* I, p. 444; *T.K.* II,
p. 497; M. Kil. 2:5). Furthermore, Tos. Shev. 2:11 states that
one may leave arum in the ground during the Sabbatical year.
Judah, therefore, may reason that the arum one finds at the conclusion of the Sabbatical year very likely has been planted prior
to the Sabbatical year, and was not cultivated during that year.[11]
The doubt concerning the status of the arum, i.e., that it may
have been planted and cultivated during the Sabbatical year, does
not override the normal presumption that arum is several years old.
In cases of doubt we act as usual unless there is probative contrary evidence. As we shall see, this principle is articulated in
several of Tarfon's traditions (M. Yev. 15:6-7, Tos. Miq. 1:16-19,
y. Demai 3:4). Accordingly, the author of this pericope may have
added Tarfon's name in C3.

> Testified R. [first ed., E lack: R.] Judah b. Isaiah,
> the spice maker, before R. Aqiva in the name of R. Tarfon
> that balsam (QTP) is [subject to (ŠYŠ)] the [laws of the]
> Sabbatical year.

> Tos. Shev. 5:12, ed. Lieberman,
> p. 188, lns. 28-29

Comment: The pericope uses the following testimony form:

> Testified + authority + before x + in the name of y +
> that (Š) + ruling.

This pericope and Tos. Ḥul. 3:7 (b. Ḥul. 55b), the tradent of which
also is Judah b. Isaiah, are the only two traditions attributed to
Tarfon which use the testimony form. Judah b. Isaiah appears in
M.-Tos. only in these two items.

This pericope centers upon the issue of whether or not an
inedible crop, QTP, which may be either a resin-producing tree or
the resin itself,[12] falls within the category of those plants
which one may neither cultivate nor harvest during the Sabbatical
year. Tarfon rules that QTP is subject to these prohibitions.
He thus agrees with the anonymous law of M. Shev. 7:6 which states
that QTP, as well as rose, henna, and cistus are subject to the
laws of the Sabbatical year. These other substances, like QTP,
are used for making perfume.[13] M. Shev. 7:6 also contains the
following statement attributed to Simeon which disagrees with
Tarfon's opinion:

> R. Simeon says, "Balsam (QTP) is not [subject to
> the laws of] the Sabbatical year, because it is not a
> fruit (PRY)."

Thus for Simeon the laws of the Sabbatical year apply only to
fruits, edible substances. According to Tarfon, however, a greater number of items, substances which grow and which humans use,[14]
are subject to these laws.

> A. [As to] one who gives more [than the required amount]
> of heave-offering--
> B. R. Eliezer says, "[He may give up to] one tenth [of
> his total produce],
> C. "as is the case with heave-offering of tithe.
> D. "[If he wants to give] more than this, let him make
> it [the surplus] heave-offering of tithe [for produce] else-
> where."
> E. R. Ishmael says, "[He may designate] half [as]
> common produce and half [as] heave-offering.

F. R. Tarfon and R. Aqiva say, "[He may give as much
as he desires] so long as he leaves [some] common produce."

M. Ter. 4:5

Comment: A is a superscription to which B, E, and F respond.
The opinions are in ascending order in terms of the amount of
produce which may be given as heave-offering. C-D gloss B. F is
one of three statements (Tos. Yev. 14:10, M. Mak. 1:10) among the
traditions of Tarfon which is attributed to him and to Aqiva.

Biblical law, which mandates that one must set aside part of
his crops as a heave-offering for the priest, does not specify the
amount of this offering. The Houses in M. Ter. 4:3 (Tos. Ter.
5:3) disagree about the minimum one must give. The Yavnean authorities in our pericope discuss the maximum one may set aside as
heave-offering.[15] The logical sequence of ideas, therefore, coincides with the chronological order of the masters. The opinion
attributed to Tarfon and to Aqiva is given anonymously in M. Hal.
1:9.

A. And it [a field mistakenly sown with heave-
offering] is subject to [the laws of] gleanings, forgotten
sheaf, and *pe'ah* [L,N: and poorman's tithes].

B. And the poor Israelites and the poor priests glean
[from it].

C. And the poor Israelites sell their portion to the
priests at the price of heave-offering, but the money is
theirs [the poor Israelites'].

D. [K,P,M,Pr,N,b.Ven.,b.F,O,M,L: Said] R. Tarfon
[Serilio,y.Ven.,Leid.,: says], "No one shall glean except
the poor priests,

E. "lest they [the poor Israelites] forget and place it
[the crops] in their mouths."

F. Said to him R. Aqiva, "If that be the case,

G. "no one shall glean except clean [M,Pr 362:
priests[16]]."

M. Ter. 9:2

H. And it is subject to tithes and to poorman's tithe.

I. And the poor Israelites and the poor priests take
[thereof].

J. And the poor Israelites sell their portion to the
priests at the price of heave-offering, but the money is
theirs.

M. Ter. 9:3

Comment: A-C and H-J are a unit. A parallels H; I repeats B, except for the appropriate change of "glean" to "take"; J is identical to C. Tarfon in D disagrees with B. His opinion in the majority of the Mss. has the attributive formula, "Said R. x." The dispute between Tarfon and B can be reduced to the following:

poor Israelites and poor priests vs. only poor priests.

E glosses Tarfon's opinion. Let us now discuss A-E and then turn to F-G.

A presents an intermediate case. A field mistakenly sown with heave-offering is treated like a normal unconsecrated field and is subject to all agricultural obligations. But its produce has the status of consecrated crops. Who may glean from such a field? Should the governing factor be the laws of heave-offering or those of gleaning? B treats the field like a normal one; all poor people may glean from it. Tarfon's view, however, takes account of the special nature of the field. It is a field sown with heave-offering; therefore, only priests may glean from it. Israelites may accidentally eat some of the food.[17] Tarfon's opinion is consistent with his priestly office.

In F-G Aqiva responds to Tarfon in the form of a *reductio ad absurdum*. He challenges Tarfon by pointing out that the latter has not fully applied the logic of his reasoning. Tarfon should restrict the gleaning of the field to only clean priests, for an unclean priest, like an Israelite, may forget his status and eat the crops. But Tarfon can admit the validity of this argument and still maintain the reasoning attributed to him in E. Thus as is common throughout the entire Tarfon-corpus, Aqivan redactors have attempted to portray Aqiva as the wiser of the two masters. But in the present pericope, they have not given Aqiva a good argument.

      A.   [As to] a vine that is planted in a yard--

      B.   "One takes the whole [K lacks: the whole] cluster,

      C.   "and similarly with regard to pomegranate,

      D.   "and similarly with regard to watermelon,"

      E.   the words of R. Tarfon.

      F.   R. Aqiva says, "He picks [the grapes] one at a time (MGRGR) from the cluster,

      G.   "and he splits (WPWRṬ) the pomegranate,

      H.   "and he slices (WŚWPT) the watermelon.

M. Ma. 3:9

Comment: A mentions only vines. Thus only B and F respond
to A. Primus (pp. 72-73) suggests that G and H may have been
added to F, because the three items and the technical language
mentioned in F-H occur together in M. Ma. 2:6. C and D were then
added in order to balance G-H. The dispute between Tarfon and
Aqiva therefore is as follows:

> As to a vine that is planted in a yard--
> One takes the (whole) cluster, the words of R. Tarfon.
> R. Aqiva says, He picks [the grapes] from the cluster.
>
> NWṬL ʾT (KL) HʾŠKWL
> MGRGR BʾŠKWL.

If we follow the reading of Ms. K, which lacks the word "whole,"
then the opinions are perfectly balanced.

An explanation of the laws found in this pericope reveals
that A deals with an intermediate case. Different laws of tithing
apply to each of the following four stages of the growth and of
the harvesting of crops: 1) from the time the crop begins to grow
until it becomes ripe; 2) from the time it becomes ripe until
gemar melakhah, the act which indicates that one deems the crop
fit for consumption (this is generally indicated by piling up the
crops); 3) the period between *gemar melakhah* and the bringing of
the crops into one's house or courtyard; 4) the period after one
has brought the crops into these places. The law differs as to
how much of the crop one may eat during the different periods.
During the first period, one may eat all he wants; he may eat a
regular meal and does not have to give any tithes (Maim., "Laws of
Tithes" [Maim. IV] 2:3). Once the crops have become ripe and thus
liable for tithes, but before *gemar melakhah*, one may eat a random
meal from the crops (M. Ma. 1:5; Maim., "Laws of Tithes" 3:1). A
random meal consists of eating the food one piece at a time.
During the third period, one may still eat a random meal from the
crops (Maim., "Laws of Tithes" 3:2; Tos. Ma. 1:1). During the
fourth period, however, one may not eat any of the crops until
they have been tithed.

Since the crops in A grow in a courtyard, they are treated as
if the owner has already brought them into the yard. But the person has not indicated that the crops are at the point of *gemar
melakhah*. The issue, therefore, is how one must pick (and eat) the
crops while in the courtyard and not indicate that the crops have
reached *gemar melakhah*.

MR and Maim. ("Law of Tithes" 4:17, 5:3) point out that our
pericope deals specifically with the question of how one may pick

the crop. This is in distinction to the surrounding pericopae,
M. 3:8 and 3:10, which treat the issue of how one may eat crops
that grow in a courtyard. The ruling in those other pericopae is
that one may eat the food, dates, only one at a time. If one
wants to eat together two dates, he has in effect made a pile from
the dates, thereby indicating that they have reached *gemar melakhah*. But may one pick a fruit which consists of several pieces,
fruits such as a cluster of grapes, a watermelon, or a pomegranate?
Does the fact that one will hold in his hand what he will eat in
more than one act determine whether or not he may pick such a
fruit (so Serilio)? Aqiva rules it does; therefore, one must pick
the fruits one piece at a time. What will occur in the future
determines the present status of an object. Tarfon rules that one
may take the whole fruit from the vine or the tree. Thus, for
Tarfon, the future considerations are irrelevant. While on the
vine, the fruit appears as a single item; therefore, one may pick
the entire fruit.

> A. Vetches of second-tithe may be eaten when in green
> condition [but not when fully grown].
> B. And they come into [are brought into] (WNKNŚYN)
> Jerusalem and go out [are taken out from Jerusalem] (WYṢ'YN).
> C. [If] they have become unclean--
> D. R. Tarfon says, "They may be distributed among lumps
> of dough (YTḤLQW L'YŚWT)."
> E. But sages say, "They may be redeemed."

M. M.S. 2:4

Comment: A and B are anonymous declarative sentences. C-E are
a well formulated dispute form. A supplies the subject for "they"
in C. The key words in the opinions of Tarfon and sages are YTḤLQW
vs. YPDW.

Rabbinic law, based on Deut 14:22,27, prescribes that in the
first, second, fourth, and fifth years of the Sabbatical cycle, one
must give a second-tithe in addition to heave-offering and first-
tithe. The individual must take some crops to Jerusalem and consume them there. Once these second-tithe crops have been brought
into Jerusalem, they may not be taken out (M. Ma. 3:5). Alternatively, the person redeems his crops by setting aside 125% of the
crops' value. He then takes the money to Jerusalem and spends it
there.

Our pericope focuses upon an intermediate case, vetches.
Vetches can be eaten by humans only when they are green. Accordingly, as A states, they may be used as second-tithe only in that
condition. Only food which can be consumed by humans may be used
as second tithe. At all other times only animals eat vetches.

B notes that one may take vetches of second-tithe out of
Jerusalem even after they have already been brought into the city.
Thus one does not treat vetches as normal food subject to the law
of second-tithe. As noted, one may not normally take second-tithe
out of Jerusalem.

C considers the issue of what one does if his second-tithe
vetches become unclean. Sages claim the person redeems the unclean vetches. Thus sages treat the vetches of second-tithe as
any other unclean second-tithe; it is normal food. The vetches,
once they are redeemed, are unclean common produce. Tarfon, however, does not prescribe the application of the laws of redemption;
rather, he rules that one distributes the vetches among lumps of
dough. Because they are not food, one need not treat vetches as
he treats other unclean second-tithe. Thus Tarfon's opinion concurs with the view of B. Maim., Bert., TYY, and GRA explain
Tarfon's ruling as follows: Since the vetches are second-tithe,
one may not simply do whatever he wishes with them. Thus one may
not redeem the vetches and then feed them to animals. The person
instead distributes small enough amounts, a *beṣa*, of the unclean
vetches among larger lumps of clean dough and thereby avoids rendering the clean dough unclean. The person, by following this
course of action, avoids paying the fine for redeeming the crops,
25% of their value. Similarly, we have seen above (Tos. Demai
5:22) that one may interpret Tarfon's ruling regarding untithed
produce which has become mixed with tithed produce as a means for
avoiding financial loss.

This pericope is found among a series of Houses' disputes,
M. M.S. 2:3,4. What is its relationship to them? We present these
pericopae in parallel columns in order to facilitate our analysis.

M. M.S. 2:3	M. M.S. 2:4
1. Second-tithe of fenugreek [TLTN] may be eaten when in green condition.	1. Second-tithe vetches may be eaten when in green condition,
2. - - - -	2. and they come into Jerusalem and go out.
3. - - - -	3. [If] they have become unclean,

M. M.S. 2:3	M. M.S. 2:4
4. - - - -	4. R. Tarfon says, They may be distributed among lumps of dough.
5. - - - -	5. But sages say, They may be redeemed.
6. As for heave-offering [fenugreek]--	6. As for heave-offering [vetches]--
7. The House of Shammai say, Whatsoever concerns it [is done] in cleanness, save combing [the head therewith].	7. The House of Shammai say, They soak and rub in cleanness, but they give as food [to cattle] in uncleanness.
8. And the House of Hillel say, Whatsoever concerns it [is done] in uncleanness, save the soaking of it.	8. And the House of Hillel say, They soak in cleanness, but they rub and give as food in uncleanness.

Omitting 2, 3-5, the form, but not the language, of the two pericopae is identical. 1 states when these crops fit into the category of second-tithe. Both of these crops may be eaten by humans only when green. Thus both crops fit into the category of second-tithe only when green. 6-8 contain a Houses' dispute, concerning the required cleanness for these crops when used as heave-offering. The respective opinions of the Houses are the same with regard to both of these crops. The House of Shammai contend that, since these crops *may* be eaten by humans, one must maintain their cleanness until he is sure that a human will not eat them. Thus the House of Shammai treat these crops always as food until certain that they will not be used as food. But the House of Hillel treat these crops as food only when the person is certain that a human will eat them. The House of Hillel, therefore, rule that one must maintain the cleanness of these crops only when he is sure that a human will eat them. The anonymous law in 2 and the opinion of Tarfon, 4, are far less extreme than either of the Houses' opinions.

According to the law of 2 and Tarfon's opinion, vetches are sufficiently like food so that one may not merely discard them if they have become unclean second-tithe. But the vetches are sufficiently not-food, so that the person does not treat the vetches as other unclean second-tithe.

> A. [As to] one who changes a [silver] *sela* of second-tithe money in Jerusalem--
> B. The House of Shammai say, "[He exchanges] the whole *sela* [for] copper coins (M'WT)."

C. And the House of Hillel say, "[He exchanges it for]
one *sheqel*['s worth in] silver and one *sheqel*['s worth in]
copper coins."

D. They that made argument before the sages say, "[He
exchanges it for] three *denar*s of silver and one *denar* of
copper coins."

E.   R. Aqiva says, "[He exchanges it for] three *denar*s
of silver, and one quarter [of the remaining *denar* must be
in] copper."

F. R. Tarfon says, "[He exchanges it for three *denar*s
of silver, and the remaining *denar* for] four *asper*s of silver
[and one *asper* of copper]."

G. Shammai says, "Let him deposit it in a shop and
[gradually] consume its value."

                            M. M.S. 2:9 (M. Ed. 1:10)

Comment: The pericope is a composite. A-C are a Houses' dispute. The opinions of the Houses appear verbatim in M. M.S. 2:8.
D-E respond to A but stand outside the framework of B-C. They
introduce *denar*s of which B-C make no mention. Both D and E use a
b-. The opinions of Tarfon and Shammai bear no formal relationship to the foregoing. Tarfon's opinion is not given in full and
is dependent upon the first part of D and E. B-F are in ascending
order in terms of the amount of silver one takes.

We have explained in our discussion of the previous pericope
that one may exchange for money his crops of second-tithe, and then
bring the money to Jerusalem. M. M.S. 2:8 discusses the rules
governing the exchange of money once in Jerusalem. The concern it
addresses is how does one exchange his second-tithe money so that
its purchasing power does not decrease. (If the purchasing power
of the coins decreases, then the pilgrim will not have redeemed
all of his second-tithe produce; he will not be able to buy in
Jerusalem crops equal to the second-tithe produce he has sold and
redeemed before coming to Jerusalem.) The opinions in this pericope attempt to keep Gresham's law from coming into effect.
Gresham observed that when currencies of different metallic contact but of the same face value are in circulation at the same
time, the tendency is to hoard the more valuable currency, the
good money, thereby flooding the market with the bad money. Con-
commitantly, if only the poorer coins are in circulation, there
will be a general rise in prices, for people will not have confi-
dence in the bad currency. Furthermore, because of the pilgrims'

demand for produce, its price at this time normally is inflated.
The House of Hillel, and the opinions in D-F, try to avoid a loss
in the purchasing power of the pilgrim's money by having him exchange his silver coins for both silver and copper. The market
will not be flooded with copper coins, bad money, and as a result,
there will not be an inflation in prices. But if the pilgrim ex-
changed his silver for only copper coins, their purchasing power
would decrease. I cannot account for the ruling of the House of
Shammai in light of these economic principles. Their opinion,
however, may attempt to compensate for the effects of Gresham's
law by the principle of liquidity. Thus if a person exchanges his
silver coins for copper coins, he will quickly spend them, thereby not allowing their purchasing value to decrease.

A. R. Jonah taught [in the name] of R. Simeon b. Yoḥai,
R. Joshua b. Levi taught [in the name] of R. Simeon b. Yoḥai,[18]
B. DTNY: R. Simeon b. Yoḥai [says], R. Tarfon says, "It
says 'dough-offering' (ḤLH) here [in Num 15:20, 'Of the first
of your meal you shall set aside dough as an offering'], and
it says 'dough' there [in Lev 8:26, 'dough-cake (ḤLT) of bread
made with oil']. Just as the dough that is mentioned there
[refers to dough that] is made with oil, so too the dough that
is mentioned here [refers to dough that] is made with oil."

y. Ḥal. 2:3 58c

Comment: Tarfon's exegesis is based upon a *gezerah shavah*, a
deduction which follows from the mention of the same word in two
biblical verses. Since Lev 8:26 speaks of dough which is mixed
with oil, we may deduce that one must separate dough-offering (Num
15:20) from dough mixed with oil. The meaning of Tarfon's exegesis is unclear. We do not know whether it means that only dough
mixed with oil is liable to dough-offering, or that dough mixed
with oil, as well as dough made with other liquids, is liable to
dough-offering. The saying appears in an amoraic discussion about
whether or not only the seven liquids mentioned in M. Maks. 6:4,
one of which is oil, render flour mixed with them subject to dough-
offering. The amoraim use Tarfon's saying to prove that only these
seven liquids have this effect. They thus oppose the anonymous law
of M. Ḥal. 2:3 which rules that a lump of dough mixed with fruit
juice, which is not one of the seven liquids, is liable to dough-
offering.

NOTES

CHAPTER I

[1]The term LQR' is used by itself throughout M.-Tos. Ber.
chapters 1-3 to mean, "to recite the *Shema'*."

[2]HYṬṬY frequently has the meaning in M.-Tos. of "to deviate,"
i.e., to turn off the path. M. Sanh. 14:4 contains the expression
"to turn off the way" (LHṬWT MN HDRK). Tos. Zev. 1:8 preserves a
first person saying of Tarfon which uses HYṬṬY with the meaning
"to turn."

[3]M.-Tos. do not preserve any opinions which address this
question. A baraita in b. Ber. 112, however, reads as follows:

> TNW RBN: The House of Hillel say, "They stand and
> recite the *Shema'*, they sit and recite the *Shema'*, they
> recline and recite the *Shema'*, they walk along the way
> and recite the *Shema'*, they engage in their work and recite
> the *Shema'*." (b. Ber. 11a)

This baraita is probably a development of M. Ber. 1:3C. It does,
however, indicate that a question could arise about reciting the
Shema' while walking on the way.

[4]Lieberman prefers the reading of Serilio because it is the
same as in Tos., and because the amoraic context in y. demands it.

[5]Three explanations may be given for the difference between
the rulings of 2 and 5 of M. The amoraim in y., GRA, Sens, Rashi,
and MS note that 1 of M. deals with piles of wheat, while 3 of M.,
with loose pieces of fruit. The latter certainly will be switched
with the crops of the gentile; therefore, they are treated like
his crops. Piles of wheat are not easily switched. Accordingly,
we regard them as *demai*. A second interpretation, offered by Maim.,
Bert., and TYY, distinguishes between the crops which the miller
grinds and those deposited in a gentile's storehouse. The miller
grinds crops of 'amme-ha'areṣ; the gentile storehouse owner keeps
his own crops there. In the case of the miller we assume that he
mixes the crops with those of an 'am-ha'areṣ; therefore, they are
demai. The storehouse owner switches his own crops with those deposited with him. Accordingly, the latter are treated as those of
the gentile. Rosh and MR build upon this second explanation and
add an economic consideration. The miller has little to gain by
mixing the crops of two other people. We therefore are not certain
that he has mixed the crops. As a result, they are treated as
demai. But the owner of a storehouse may substitute some of his
own poorer crops for the better crops of the Israelite. Accordingly, the fruits of the Israelite are treated like those of the
gentile.

[6]Simeon's ruling agrees in principle with the view of Judah
in Tos. 1:14. According to Judah, any amount of Israelite crops
mixed with those of a gentile render all the crops *demai*. Meir
disagrees with the ruling that the majority of the crops determines
the status of the whole. I have not interpreted the anonymous laws
of M. 3:4 in light of this dispute, because to do so involves reading a great deal into the pericope, and also leaves one without an
explanation for the difference between 2 and 5 of M.

35

[7]Hemp, as the following discussion of the term "herb" indicates, is an intermediate case, for it has characteristics both of a tree and of an herb. According to its botanical definition, an herb is a plant whose stem either dies to the ground each year or at least does not become woody (Bailey III, p. 1461). But Bailey further points out that no clear distinction can be made between herbs, woody plants, or trees, for there are tender herbs which in a warmer climate will become shrubs or even trees. Feliks (*Mixed Sowing*, p. 144), in discussing M. Kil. 1:7, which states that one may not graft one kind of tree to another, or one kind of an herb to another, etc., cites all the Talmudic sources containing this terminology. He contends that the one characteristic which may be applied to all herbs, appearing in the cited sources, is that herbs do not become woody. Lieberman (*Hellenism*, pp. 180-82), in discussing the Talmudic definition of herbs, cites Tos. Kil. 3:15, "This is the general rule, any plant that sheds forth its leaves from its roots is a species of herb, and any plant that does not shed forth its leaves from its roots is a species of tree." The problem with regard to hemp is that according to the definition of Tos. Kil. 3:15 it is not an herb. The leaves of hemp grow from its stem and not from its roots. But according to the botanical definition of herbs, hemp is an herb. Thus hemp is an intermediate case. We can now explain Tarfon's opinion as follows: He classifies hemp, on the basis of its form, its appearance, as a tree and not as an herb. Accordingly, it is not diverse kinds in a vineyard.

Lieberman notes that the rabbis are aware that their classification of herbs and trees is not applicable to all plants. There are certain plants such as cabbage which, according to Tos. Kil. 3:15, are trees, but these plants are always regarded as herbs. Lieberman further notes that Theophrastus uses the same criteria as Tos. for distinguishing between herbs and trees. Theophrastus also states that an exact classification of plants is impossible, and in some cases one must employ other criteria in making classifications. As Lieberman notes, practical life, e.g., determining the laws of diverse kinds, gave birth to the rabbis' subdivision of the category of herbs into cereal, pulse, and greens (YRQ). We can now see that YRQ has at least two meanings in rabbinic literature. YRQ stands for the general category of herbs whose definition has been given above. As noted, hemp does not satisfy the criteria for belonging to this category. YRQ also serves as the designation for a subdivision within the category of herbs. The definition formulated by Maim. and Naḥmonides on the basis of the usage of this term in Talmudic literature is a seed which cannot be eaten, but whose fruit, i.e., the fruit produced from that seed, can be eaten. Hemp fits this category of YRQWT, since it yields an edible oil.

[8]Feldman (p. 253), Rashi, and R. Gershon suggest that KSWT in our pericope refers to hops. Hops are a perennial, twining vine, reaching a height of 25-30 feet, bearing cones which look very much like grape clusters and are used to make beer. If this is the correct identification of KSWT, then we may conjecture that sages restrict its use in a vineyard because of its resemblance to grape vines. Tarfon disagrees with the sages' opinion because he does not restrict the use of crops resembling grapes.

[9]Ein Kushi is mentioned in one other rabbinic source, b. A.Z. 31a (y. A.Z. 5:4). According to that tradition, Ein Kushi is in the vicinity of other places in Samaria (see Avi-Yonah, map 95).

[10]There is no statement in M.-Tos. which defines the end of
the Sabbatical year. M. R.H. 1:1, however, states that it begins
on the first of Tishré. Furthermore, M. Soṭ. 7:8 describes *haqhel*
as occurring at the conclusion of the festival day of Sukkot.
This ceremony was performed at the end of the Sabbatical year.

[11]Tos. Shev. 2:2 indicates that arum continues to grow even
when it is untended.

[12]Feldman (p. 314) claims that QṬP designates merely the
balsam-resin that flows from certain trees. Lieberman (*T.K.* I,
p. 557, following Maim.), Krauss (II/i, p. 125), and Feliks
(*Ṣemeḥiat*, p. 125) identify QṬP with the balsam tree, *commiphora
opobalsamum* ('PRŚMWN). Löw (III, p. 390) claims that QṬP is the
name for the tree *styrax officinalis*. Both trees, the balsam
and the styrax, have similar characteristics. Pliny (12:115-20)
notes that both trees are common to Palestine, and that when the
bark of these trees is split, it yields a balsam-resin used for
making perfume. Talmudic sources (y. Yoma 4:5 and b. Ker. 6a)
indicate that the amoraim also identified QṬP with trees from
which one extracts balsam-resin (ṢRY).

[13]According to Bailey (V, p. 2982), rose yields a fragrant
oil, attar, used for making perfume. Certain species of roses
yield fruits which are made into preserves. Whether or not the
species growing in Palestine can serve this purpose is unclear.
Feldman (p. 302) mentions only that roses were used to yield an
oil which was used for medicinal purposes, for anointing, and for
a spice. Henna, not a plant, is the dye produced from the
lawsonia inermis (Bailey IV, pp. 1830-31). Uphof (p. 210) notes
that the dye is a powder made from the dried leaves of the plant.
In addition to the dye, the rose colored flowers of the *lawsonia*
yield a fragrant oil. Similarly, cistus, or rock rose, which
also has flowers resembling those of a rose, yields a resin called
ladanum (Feldman, p. 244; Löw I, p. 362). This resin is used
both for perfume (Bailey II, pp. 776-77) and for medicine (Uphof,
p. 94).

[14]There is a further tradition, attributed to a fourth
generation amora, which discusses the classification of balsam.
It reads:

> Said R. Pedat, "*Who teaches that balsam is a fruit?*
> R. Eliezer." (b. Nid. 8a)

Pedat's comment explains why balsam is subject to the laws of the
Sabbatical year; it is a fruit. Thus it seems that for Eliezer,
if indeed b. Nid. 8a is Eliezer's opinion, and for Simeon, a crop
is subject to the laws of the Sabbatical year if it is a fruit.
There is no reason to presume that this line of reasoning lies
behind Tarfon's opinion.

[15]Maim. links the opinions to various biblical verses.
Eliezer contends, since the heave-offering of tithe mentioned in
Num 18:26 is one-tenth of the tithe and is referred to as heave-
offering, normal heave-offering may be one-tenth. Ishmael bases
his opinion on Deut 18:4 which reads, "The first of your grain,
your wine...you shall give to him [the priest]." This indicates
that the first part, fifty percent, of your crop may be given as
heave-offering. Tarfon's view relies upon Num 15:21 which states,
"From the first of your dough, you shall give heave-offering to
God." This teaches that the person must keep some crops in order
to indicate the source of his offering.

[16]Epstein (*Mavo*, pp. 448-49) argues that our text of M.,
which lacks the word "priests," was emended on the basis of the
comments in y. Ter. 9:2.

[17]In a further development of this tradition, the amoraim in
y. Ter. 9:2 apply Tarfon's ruling in M. Ter. 9:2 to Tos. Toh. 8:4.

    1.   TNY: The wife of an '*am-ha'areṣ* mills [grain] with
the wife of a *ḥaver* when she [the '*am-ha'areṣ*] is unclean.
    2.   But when she [the '*am-ha'areṣ*] is clean, she [the
'*am-ha'areṣ*] may not mill [grain with the wife of a *ḥaver*],
    3.   because she ['*am-ha'areṣ*] holds herself [to be] more
pure than her [the *ḥaver*'s wife]. (Tos. Toh. 8:4)

    A.   And according to the words of (WKDBRY) R. Tarfon:
    B.   Even when she is unclean, she [the '*am-ha'areṣ*] may
not mill [grain with the wife of the *ḥaver*],
    C.   lest she may forget and place [some food] in her
mouth. (y. Ter. 9:2 46c [A-C = Tos. Toh. 8:4])

[18]Epstein (*Prolegomena*, p. 376 n. 23) and Ratner (III,
p. 123), basing themselves on the readings in responsa of Rosh and
Rashba, and on that of Serilio, argue that the correct attributive
formula is, "R. Jonah taught [in the name] of R. Simeon b. Yoḥai,
R. Tarfon says."

A. They do not light [the lamp], on the holiday, with [heave-offering] oil [that has become unclean and] must be burnt.

B. R. Ishmael says, "They do not light with resin, out of respect for the Sabbath."

C. But sages permit [kindling the lamp] with all [kinds of] oil:

D. with sesame oil, with nut oil, with fish oil, with colocynth oil, with resin, and with naphtha.

E. R. Tarfon says, "They light [the lamp] exclusively ('L' BLBD) with olive oil."

M. Shab. 2:2

Comment: A, B, and E are autonomous sayings phrased in simple declarative sentences. C disputes with B, while D glosses C.

A concerns lighting the lamp on the holiday. B deals with lighting on the Sabbath. Tarfon, in E, does not specify whether his ruling concerns the Sabbath or holidays. The pericope thus contains a number of thematically related sayings. As we shall see, the parallel in Tos. preserves several more sayings concerning the lighting of the lamp. For a detailed discussion listing possible explanations of the development of this pericope, see Porton I, pp. 54-57.

Tarfon allows the use of only pleasant smelling, but expensive, olive oil. The parallel tradition in Tos. points out the difficulties this restrictive view causes.

A. R. Simeon b. Leazar says, "They do not light with balsam."

B. R. Ishmael says, "[As to] everything that exudes from a tree, they do not light with it."

C. R. Ishmael b. R. Yoḥanan b. Beruqah says, "They light only with that which exudes from a fruit."

D. *R. Tarfon says, "They light exclusively with olive oil."*

E. 1. R. Yoḥanan b. Nuri stood up upon his feet and said,

2. "What will the people in Babylonia do who have
only sesame oil? What will the people of Media do who have
only nut oil? What will the people of Alexandria do who
have only fish oil? What will the people of Cappadoccia do
who have neither this nor that [b.,y.Leid. add: and have
only naphtha]?

3. "You have only that which they [b.: sages] said
('YN LK 'L' MH Š'MRW) [you may use only that which the sages
permitted] [y.: You have only that which the first ones
(R'ŠWNYN) have permitted]."

> Tos. Shab. 2:3, ed. Lieberman,
> pp. 6-7, lns. 7-13 (y. Shab.
> 2:2 4a, b. Shab. 26a)

Comment: A-D are autonomous sayings. A-B are phrased nega-
tively, listing items which one may not use. C-D detail the items
which one may use. E is phrased as a protest to D.

The pericope contains opinions of both Ushans, A and C, and
Yavneans, B and D. Yoḥanan b. Nuri, E, is a late Yavnean. None
of the sayings, as well as the context, specify whether the issue
is lighting on the Sabbath, or whether it is lighting on the holiday. The redactor, however, has organized the opinions in a logical manner. A prohibits the use of balsam, a derivative from a
tree. In B Ishmael forbids the use of all derivatives from trees.
Thus Ishmael's opinion is more extreme than A. C-D concern the
use of fruits, and again the more extreme opinion, that of Tarfon,
comes second. Thus in both cases, A-B and C-D, the opinions of
the Ushans are less restrictive than those of the Yavneans.

Yoḥanan b. Nuri objects to an opinion which severely limits
the types of oil one may use. This could be either that of Tarfon
or that of Ishmael b. R. Yoḥanan.

A. TNY': Said R. Judah, "One time we spent the Sabbath
in the upper chamber of the House of Nithzeh in Lydda, and
they brought us an eggshell, and we filled it with oil, and
perforated it, and placed it over the mouth of the lamp.

B. "And R. Tarfon and the elders [and his associates]
were there, and they said nothing to us."

> b. Shab. 29b

Comment: b. Shab. 29b parallels Tos. Shab. 2:5, which in turn
supplements M. Shab. 2:4. We, therefore, present these pericopae
in a chart.

M. Shab. 2:4	Tos. Shab. 2:5	b. Shab. 29b
1. One may not pierce an eggshell, fill it with oil, and place it over the mouth of the lamp, so that the oil will drip from it [into the lamp].	1. See below #5.	1. See below #5.
2. But R. Judah permits.	2. - - -	2. - - -
3. - - -	3. Said R. Judah,	3. " " "
4. - - -	4. When we used to stay in the upper chamber of the House of Nithzeh in Lydda,	4. One time we spent the Sabbath in
5. See above #1.	5. they used to perforate an eggshell, and fill it with oil, and place it over the mouth of the lamp,	5. They brought before us an egg-shell, and we filled it with oil, and we perforated it, and we placed it over the mouth of the lmap.
6. - - -	6. on the eve of the Sabbath at nightfall,	6. - - -
7. - - -	7. so that it would be lit and shining on the Sabbath eves.	7. - - -
8. - - -	8. And the elders were there, and not one of them said anything.	8. And R. Tarfon and the elders " " "
9. But if the potter joined [the eggshell with the lamp] from the first, it is permitted in that it is a single vessel.	9. - - -	9. - - -

b. adds Tarfon's name in 8. This addition may be based upon the
appeal by Judah in other *ma'asim* to the authority of Tarfon, and,
as we shall now see, upon the substance of Judah's ruling. Lieberman explains, on the basis of M.9, that the dispute between Judah
and the anonymous law in M.1 centers upon the fact that the eggshell and the lamp are not one vessel. He cites the comments of
the amoraim in b. and y. who point out that since the eggshell and
the lamp are not joined as one vessel, the person may forget and
remove the eggshell or the oil in it, and thereby extinguish the
fire, an act forbidden on the Sabbath. Accordingly, the anonymous
law in M.1 prohibits this arrangement. Judah, however, does not
take into account future possibilities; therefore, he rules that
one may place the eggshell over the lamp. Thus for Judah, it is
the present status of the lamp and eggshell which determines the
law. The principle that the objective facts, and not future possibilities, are the key in deciding matters of law is found
throughout the rulings of Tarfon. His name, therefore, may have
been added to 8.

> A. 1. Said R. Judah, "M'SH B: R. Tarfon
>   2. "went out (YṢ')
>   3. "on Sabbath eves
>   4. "[first ed., E: to] [Lon.: from] the *Bet Midrash*,
>   5. "and they gave him
>   6. "a linen covering (ŚDYN),
>   7. "and he held it with both hands,
>   8. "and went out with it
>   9. "because of the rain."
>
> B. They go out (1) with a thick woven cloth (ŚGYŚ),
> (2) with a tent cloth (YRY'H), (3) and with a thick woven
> garment made from camel hairs (HML'), (4) with a shirt made
> of leather (ŚQWRṬY'), (5) with a leather covering (QTBWLY')
> because of the rain.
>
> C. But [they do not go out] (1) in a chest, or (2) in a
> basket (QWPH), or (3) in a mat made of heavy reeds because of
> the rain.
>
>   Tos. Shab. 5:13-14, ed. Lieberman,
>   p. 22, lns. 30-34

Comment: A is independent of B-C. I have included the latter
because of the evidence it supplies concerning the context of A.
The only essential items in A are 1, 2, 3, 6 (if introduced by a
b), and 9. A M'SH containing only these items reads:

M'SH B: R. Tarfon went out on Sabbath eve with
[wearing] a linen covering because of the rain.

Rabbinic law mandates that one may not carry objects on the
Sabbath from one domain to another. Clothing, however, does
fall under this prohibition. But what constitutes clothing? Is
it something which functions as an article of clothing, or must it
also have the appearance of clothing? The anonymous laws of B and
C show that one may wear on the Sabbath only objects which look
like a garment. An object which merely functions as a garment,
one which protects a person from the rain, does not constitute a
garment which one may wear on the Sabbath. Similarly, Tarfon wore
a piece of linen, because in addition to functioning as a garment,
it looks like one. Thus this M'SH is a further instance in which
Tarfon's opinion is based on the formal nature of the item under
discussion.

A. [As to] the scrolls and the books of sectarians
(HMYNYM)--

B. they do not save [them on the Sabbath] from a fire;

C. rather, they are [left to] burn in their place, they
and the divine names [contained] in them [b. lacks C].

D. R. Yose the Galilean says, "On the weekdays one cuts
out their divine names, and hides them (GWNZN), and [then]
burns the remainder."

E. Said R. Tarfon, "May I bury my son, for if they [the
books of the sectarians] should come into my hands, I will
burn them and the divine names which are in them.

F. "For   .

G. 1. "even if a pursuer [were] chasing me, I [would]
enter a temple of idolatry, but I [would] not enter their
houses [of worship; y.: of the sectarians].

2. "For idolaters do not know Him and deny Him;
but these [y.: sectarians] know Him and deny Him.

H. "And with regard to them Scripture said, 'And behind
the door and the doorpost you have set up your memorial' [Isa
57:8] [y.: 'Do not I hate, O Lord, those that hate You' (Ps
139:21)]."

I. Said R. Ishmael, "If in order to make peace between
a man and his wife Heaven said, 'Let a book [containing the
divine name] which is written in holiness be blotted out in
water,' [then] the books of sectarians, which cause enmity

between the children of Israel and their Father in heaven,
how much the more so [should] they and their divine names be
blotted out [in water].

J. "And of them Scripture said, 'Do not I hate, O Lord,
those that hate You,' etc. ['And do not I strive with those
that rise up against You,] I hate them with utmost hatred,'
etc. ['I count them among my enemies' (Ps 139:21-22)]."

> Tos. Shab. 13:5, ed. Lieberman,
> pp. 58-59, lns. 18-28 (b. Shab.
> 116a, y. Shab. 16:1 15c)

Comment: The context of this pericope is a discussion concerning holy objects which, on the Sabbath, one saves from a fire.
But only A-B address this question. C glosses A by claiming that
even the divine names contained in these books need not be saved
from a fire. The remainder of the pericope turns to a different
question, what one does if sectarian writings come into his hands.

Tarfon and Yose, in D-E, disagree about whether on a weekday[1]
one burns the entire sectarian book, or whether he first removes
the divine names and then burns the book. But their sayings, unlike those in disputes involving Tarfon and Aqiva, have not been
placed in a neatly balanced dispute form. Such a dispute would
read:

> [As to] the scrolls and the books of sectarians--
> R. Yose the Galilean says, "One cuts out the divine
> names contained in them and then burns the remainder."
> R. Tarfon says, "One burns them and the divine names
> contained in them."

We will discuss below the substance of this dispute.

F joins G to E. G, however, does not support E, for it
merely is a statement about the infidelity of sectarians. H is a
Scriptural proof text which corroborates G by indicating that the
sectarians have taken "the memorial of God," his Torah, and have
placed it "behind their door"; they have disregarded it.

Ishmael's autonomous saying, I, provides a third opinion
concerning what one does with sectarian documents. Like Tarfon,
Ishmael rules that one does not spare the divine names. Ishmael,
however, prescribes that one blots out in water the divine names.
Neither Tarfon nor Yose mention this method.

The opinions in D, E, and I ultimately concern whether or not
the name of God, when written, has intrinsic sanctity. Yose seems
to claim it does. The context in which the name appears is irrelevant. Tarfon and Ishmael, however, appear to feel that the location of the name of God affects its status.

A. "[As to] one who settled down [on the eve of the
Sabbath] on the road, and rose up [after nightfall] and saw,
and lo, he was near (ŚMWK) [K,M: QRWB] to a town,

B. "because it had not been his intention [prior to
the beginning of the Sabbath] to do so (HW'YL WL' HYTH KWNTW
LKK),

C. "he may not enter [the town]," the words of R. Meir.

D. R. Judah says, "He may enter."

E. 1. Said R. Judah, "M'SH HYH W: R. Tarfon entered
[a town under the above conditions],

2. "without having [previously] intended (BL' MTKWN)
[to do so]."

M. Eruv. 4:4

Comment: A+C and D are a balanced dispute. B is an internal
gloss. It is clear from A that when the person settled down he
did not know that he was close to the city. It, therefore, obviously was not his intention to enter the town. The M'SH in E is
extremely elliptical. It consists of two elements, a description
of what Tarfon did and a statement of the operative conditions.
But it lacks a clause detailing the setting. The context supplies
this information.

The commentators' interpretations of this pericope focus upon
two words, "near" and "enter." They explain the pericope in terms
of the following rules governing travel on the Sabbath. One may
walk on the Sabbath from his place of residence two thousand cubits
in all directions. This area in which the person is permitted to
walk is known as his THWM ŠBT, his Sabbath-limit. If a person
lives in a city, he may traverse the entire city and a further
distance from it of two thousand cubits. Conversely, if someone
lives within the two thousand cubit area surrounding the town, he
is considered a member of the town and may walk throughout its
entirety. In light of these rules, Maim., Bert., and TYY interpret "near" to mean within the Sabbath-limit of the town. They
reason that if "near the town" means outside the Sabbath-limit of
the town, the person obviously may not enter the town. The person
who sat down on the road may travel only two thousand cubits from
"his place of residence," and this would not bring him to the city
proper. It follows from this explanation of "near" that "to enter"
does not literally mean "to enter the city." If the person is within
two thousand cubits of the city and he may travel a distance of two
thousand cubits, then the area in which he is permitted to walk

includes the boundaries of the city proper. "To enter," therefore,
must mean "to enter the town and establish one's Sabbath-residence
in the town," to enter the town and be able to travel throughout
the entire town (so TYY; Bert.; MS; Meiri; Maim., "Laws of Sabbath"
[Maim. I] 27:10). A-B, therefore, discuss whether or not a person who settles down before the Sabbath within the Sabbath-limit
of a town is automatically considered a resident of that town.

Judah rules that as long as a person before the Sabbath is
within the Sabbath-limit of a town, he is considered a resident of
the town. Tarfon's actions seem to conform to this rule. B accen-
tuates that the person's lack of intention is of no consequence.
Meir, however, rules that the person may not enter the town. A person must intend a certain place to be his residence for the Sabbath.

The legal principle underlying Tarfon's actions is the con-
verse of a principle articulated in many of his rulings. Several
of Tarfon's opinions indicate that, for him, a person's future
intentions are inconsequential for matters of law. It is the
present condition of the person which is determinative. E of our
pericope demonstrates that a person's lack of intention is of no
consequence in establishing his legal rights. It is the condition
in which he finds himself that is determinative.

A. 1. TNY': Said R. Judah, "M'SH B: R. Tarfon was
walking on the way and dusk fell, and he spent the night
outside (ḤWŞ) a town.

2. "In the morning [some] herdsmen discovered him.
They said to him, 'Rabbi, lo, the town is before you, enter.'

3. "He entered [the town],

4. "and sat down in the *Bet HaMidrash,* and delivered
discourses all the day."

B. 1. They [M, b.V 109, Solonika: R. Jacob; She'iltot:
R. Aqiva] said to him [to Judah], "Is that incident any proof?

2. "Perhaps [when the Sabbath set in] it [the town]
was in his mind,

3. "or [perhaps] the *Bet HaMidrash* was encompassed
within his Sabbath-limit."

b. Eruv. 45a

Comment: The following chart demonstrates that b. expands
M. Eruv. 4:4.

M. Eruv. 4:4	b. Eruv. 45a
1. M'SH HYH B: R. Tarfon	1. M'SH B: R. Tarfon
2. - - -	2. was walking on the way and dusk fell, and he spent the night outside a town.
3. - - -	3. In the morning herdsmen discovered him. They said to him, Rabbi, lo, the town is before you, enter.
4. entered [a town]	4. He entered,
5. - - -	5. and sat down in the *Bet Midrash* and delivered discourses all the day.
6. without having [previously] intended [to do so].	6. - - -

2-3 of b. detail the setting of Tarfon's action, 4, and also indicate that, prior to the beginning of the Sabbath, Tarfon did not intend to enter the town (= M.6). 5 is a standard addition.

B raises two objections to the use of the M'SH as a precedent for allowing a person to enter a town on the Sabbath under the conditions stipulated in A. B2 asks whether or not the reason Tarfon entered the town was that he intended prior to the beginning of the Sabbath to do so. This objection completely ignores the description in A1-2, which indicates that Tarfon did not know that he was near the town. B3 suggests that the incident does not demonstrate that Tarfon entered the town and acquired the rights of a resident of the town with regard to travelling on the Sabbath, but that Tarfon entered that part of the town which was already within his Sabbath-limit. This objection indicates that the person responsible for it knows that "to enter" may mean to enter and acquire the rights of travel of a resident of the town.

A. 1. They said, "And was not the *Bet Midrash* of R. Tarfon within [the limit of] two thousand cubits,

2. "or perhaps already from the time that the Sabbath set in he intended to establish his residence in the town"?

B. *I find*, TNY': In the morning, the sun shone. They said to him [to Tarfon], "Master, lo, the city is before you, enter." [This proves that he did not at the beginning of the Sabbath have the town in mind.]

y. Eruv. 4:4 21c

Comment: The pericope is circular; A is formulated to introduce B. A raises both questions found in B of b. Eruv. 45a. But
B of this pericope responds to only one of the objections in A,
that of prior intention, and clearly indicates that prior to the
beginning of the Sabbath, Tarfon did not intend to enter the town.
It is only part of some other tradition, for it presupposes the
referent of "him" and also the conditions under which the incident
occurred. Furthermore, it does not tell us who "they" are. A possible source for B, as the following synoptic table shows, is A of
b. Eruv. 45a.

b. Eruv. 45a	y. Eruv. 4:4
1. TNY: Said R. Judah, M'SH....	1. TNY - - -
2. In the morning [some] herdsmen found him.	2. In the morning the sun shone
3. They said to him, Master, lo, the city is before you, go in.	3. " " " " " "

A. How far does one recite [the *Hallel* (Psalms 113-18)]?

B. The House of Shammai say, "To 'A joyful mother of
children'" [Ps 113:9].

C. And the House of Hillel say, "To 'A flintstone into
a springwell'" [Ps 114:8].

D. And he concludes with a prayer for redemption (WḤWTM
BG'WLH).

E. R. Tarfon says, "He that redeemed us and redeemed
our fathers from Egypt, and brought us to this night [L,N,Pr,
and other texts, see D.S. III, p. 363: to eat therein unleavened bread and bitter herbs]. But he does not recite a
concluding blessing [P,K,L,Pr,y.Ven.,y.Leid.: W'YNW ḤWTM]
[N,M: But he does not recite a concluding blessing]."

F. R. Aqiva says, "Therefore, O Lord our God and God of
our fathers, bring us in peace to [L,M,b.V.: set feasts and]
[M,b.V.: other] festivals, may they reach us in peace, to re-
joice in the building of Thy city and to be joyful in Thy
worship, and we shall eat [K,P: to eat] there from the sacrifices of the Passover-offering and from the peace-offerings
whose blood has reached with acceptance the wall of Thy altar,
and we shall praise Thee [L,M,P,Pr: with a new song] for our
redemption. Blessed art thou, O Lord [K,P:] the one who redeems Israel [N,L,Pr,b.Ven.,y.Leid,y.Ven.: The one who redeemed
Israel]."

                            M. Pes. 10:6

Comment: A-C are a well-balanced dispute. D glosses C and
introduces the comments of Tarfon and Aqiva, E-F.

At the *Seder* one recites part of the *Hallel* before the meal
and part of it after the meal. The Houses dispute about which
paragraphs of the *Hallel* one says before eating. The issue between the Houses is whether or not one should speak of redemption
before eating, for the Israelites were not redeemed from Egypt
until after they ate the Passover-offering (see Tos. Pisḥa 10:9).
The House of Shammai contend that one recites the *Hallel* before
the meal only until Psalm 113. Thus one does not read Psalm 114
which speaks of redemption. The House of Hillel, however, rule
that one does recite Psalm 114. D builds upon the reasoning of
the House of Hillel, for like the House of Hillel, it asserts that
one speaks of redemption before the meal. E-F respond to D by
providing alternative prayers of redemption. These differ with
regard to both their content and their conclusion. Aqiva's prayer
ends with a concluding blessing; Tarfon's prayer does not.[2]

The content of the respective blessings of the two rabbis is
noteworthy. Tarfon's blessing emphasizes the present by stating
"who has brought us to this night." In addition, his formulation,
as recorded in some manuscripts, mentions only two of the major
symbols of the *Seder*, the unleavened bread and the bitter herbs,
but not the third, the Passover-offering. Thus according to the
saying attributed to Tarfon, we thank God for His having saved us
in the past, and His now allowing us to eat unleavened bread and
bitter herbs. But there is no mention or request in Tarfon's
blessing of either the future rebuilding of the Temple or of the
sacrifices to be offered in it. Aqiva's blessing stresses those
factors not mentioned by Tarfon. Aqiva prays that in the future
Israel will be able to celebrate more festivals, to rebuild the
Temple and Jerusalem, and once again to partake of the Passover
sacrifice. It is only in the closing benediction that Aqiva
offers thanks for God's past redemption of Israel.

1. [They mixed for him] the fourth [cup of wine],

2. he concludes [N: over it] the *Hallel* and recited
over it "The Blessing of the Song" (BRKT HŠYR).

M. Pes. 10:7

A. What is "The Blessing of the Song"?

B. Rav Judah said, "May all praise thee, O Lord,
our God."

C. R. Yoḥanan said, "The soul of all life shall
bless you."

D. 1. TNW RBNN: "[They mixed for him] the fourth
cup of wine],

2. "he concludes over it the *Hallel* and recites
'The Great *Hallel*,'" the words of R. Tarfon.

E. Others say, "The Lord is my shepherd I shall not
want" [Psalm 23].

F. From where [does] "The Great *Hallel*" [begin]?

G. Rav Judah says, "From 'O Give thanks unto the Lord'
[Psalm 136] until 'By the Rivers of Babylon'" [Psalm 137].

H. R. Yoḥanan says, "From 'A Song of Ascent' [Psalm 134]
until 'By the Rivers of Babylon'" [Psalm 137].

b. Pes. 118a

Comment: M. Pes. 10:7 and D and E of b. are three different
opinions concerning the prayers one says over the fourth cup of
wine at the *Seder*. Tarfon and the anonymous law of M. agree that
one concludes the *Hallel* over this cup. But they disagree about
the additional prayers one recites. M. Pes. 10:7 claims one recites "The Blessing of the Song," which is defined in B-D of b.
Tarfon asserts that one says "The Great *Hallel*." G-H define this
prayer. M. Pes. 10:7 and D could yield the following dispute:

1. They mixed for him the fourth cup of wine, he
concludes over it the *Hallel*,
2. and [recites over it] "The Blessing of the Song."
3. R. Tarfon says, [He recites over it] "The Great
Hallel."

One reason we do not have this dispute is that the Tarfon-tradition
may not have originally dealt with the fourth cup of wine. Goldschmidt (p. 66, n. 24) and Kasher (*Haggadah*, pp. 332-35) note that
Alfasi, R. Ḥannanel, Rosh, and certain geonim, the Solonika Ms. of
the Talmud and Aggadot HaTalmud (see D.S. III, p. 371) preserve a
different version of Tarfon's saying:

[They mixed for him] the fifth [cup of wine], and he
says [over it] "The Great *Hallel*."

This tradition differs in two respects from that preserved in the
majority of the Mss. It concerns the fifth cup of wine.[3] Accordingly, no mention is made of concluding the *Hallel*, since M. Pes.
10:7 specifies that one concludes the *Hallel* over the fourth cup
of wine. Thus the sayings of Tarfon and M. Pes. 10:7 may not have
been redacted together because they originally did not concern the
same issue.

1.   How do they roast (ṢWLYN) the Passover-offering?

2.   "They bring a skewer of pomegranate wood, [and]
thrust it from its [the lamb's] mouth through to its anus,
and they place its legs and its entrails (BNY M'YW) into it
(LTWKW) [the lamb's cavity]," the words of R. Yose the
Galilean.

3.   R. Aqiva says, "This is like a type of boiling
(BŠWL).

4.   "Rather, he hangs them [the legs and the entrails]
outside of it."

M. Pes. 7:1

A.   "TWK BR [inside, outside]," the words of R. Tarfon.

B.   R. Ishmael says, "MQWLŚ."

C.   *R. Tarfon follows* [the opinion of] *R. Aqiva, and
R. Ishmael follows* [the opinion of] *R. Yose the Galilean.*

D.   DTNY: R. Yose the Galilean says, "What is a GDY
[lamb] MQWLŚ?   [One which is] completely roasted (KWLW ṢLY),
'its head with ('L) its legs, and with its insides (QRBW)'"
[Exod 12:9].

y. Pes. 7:1 34a

Comment: Exod 12:9 prescribes the following concerning the
Passover-offering: "Do not eat any of it raw, or boiled with
water, but roasted (KY 'M ṢLY 'Š), its head with ('L) its legs,
and with its insides."   Aqiva and Yose in M. disagree concerning
where one places the legs and the entrails.   They make no mention
of the head.   Yose claims that one places these parts inside the
cavity of the lamb, while Aqiva asserts that one hangs them outside the lamb.   If they are placed inside the lamb, they will be
boiled.

A-B are a problematic tradition.   First, they lack a superscription.   They probably answer M.1.   Second, the parallel versions
of the pericope indicate that there is some confusion concerning
the attributions and also concerning the proper reading for A.
Finally, the terms given in A-B are subject to a number of interpretations,[4] one of which is presented by the amoraim in C-D.
They treat A-B as contradictory sayings and interpret them in
terms of the dispute between Yose and Aqiva in M.   Tarfon's statement TWK BR, inside outside, means that one places the insides of
the lamb, the entrails, outside of it and then roasts it.   Tarfon
thus agrees with Aqiva.   MQWLŚ according to C-D, when read with
Yose's saying in M., means that the exterior portions of the lamb

should be placed inside it, and then one roasts the lamb.   Ishmael
thus agrees with Yose.

      A.   "But roast with fire," etc. [Exod 12:9]--

      B.   "He would place its head, and its legs, and its
entrails into it," the words of R. Yose the Galilean.

      C.   1.   Said to him R. Aqiva, "But they shall be
parched and boiled inside it!

          2.   "Rather, he hangs them outside it."

      D.   R. Ishmael calls it a GDY MQWLŚ.

      E.   1.   R. Tarfon calls it TWKBR,

          2.   for its insides are like its outsides (ŠTWKW
KBRW).

Mekh. R. Simeon b. Yohai Bo'
12:9, ed. Epstein, p. 14, lns.
24-30

Comment: The numbers refer to the chart on pp. 54-55. Mekh. R.
Simeon treats M. and the tradition involving Tarfon and Ishmael as
a unit.   It is the best formulated version of these items.   The
attributive formula for Aqiva's response to Yose appropriately is,
"Said R. Aqiva." 5 of Mekh. is much more forceful than 5 of y.
The attributive formulae for the sayings of Ishmael and Tarfon are
identical.   "Calls it" is an appropriate formula, since these two
authorities assign names to the Passover-offering.   Tarfon's saying in Mekh. Simeon is the single word TWKBR.   8 glosses this saying by indicating that it means that the insides of the lambs
should be like their outsides.   This implies that the entrails
should be hung outside the lamb, which agrees with the interpretation of Tarfon's saying given by the amoraim in y.   Mekh. 3 also
adds the word "head" in 3, thereby clarifying where the head is
placed.

      A.   TNY': R. Ishmael calls it TWK TWK [inside, inside]
[D.S. III, p. 221 lists the following variants: TKBR,
TWK WBR].

      B.   R. Tarfon calls it GDY MQWLŚ.

      C.   TNW RBNN: What is a GDY MQWLŚ, which [we are]
forbidden, at this time, to eat on the night of Passover?

      D.   One which is roasted as one [piece (KL ŠṢL'W K'ḤD)].

b. Pes. 74a

Comment: In b. the attributions are reversed. Furthermore, there are several variant readings for A. The one preserved in the printed editions, TWK TWK, inside, inside, probably means that the inside portions of the lamb, the entrails, should be cooked inside it. This is the opposite of the way in which TWKBR is understood in y. and in Mekh. R. Simeon. D gives another definition of GDY MQWLŚ, a lamb roasted as one piece. This probably means, as Aqiva claims, that the inside portions should be hung on the outside. Thus the meaning of GDY MQWLŚ here is the opposite of that in y.

     A. "Its head with its legs, and with its insides" [Exod 12:9]--

     B. "TWK WBR," the words of R. Aqiva [Yalqut Saloniki 1526-27: R. Eliezer].

     C. R. [Yalqut: R. Aqiva; O, M, Midrash Ḥakhamim, Midrash Sekhel Tov: R. Eliezer] says, "MQWLŚ."

Mekh. de R. Ishmael Pisḥa 6,
ed. Horowitz, p. 21, lns. 8-9

Comment: Mekh. Ishmael knows nothing of Tarfon and Ishmael. There is confusion regarding the attributions. But in most of the Mss., Tarfon's saying is assigned to Aqiva.

Let us now compare the four versions of this tradition.

M. Pes. 7:1 / y. Pes. 7:1	Mekh. R. Simeon	b. Pes. 74a	Mekh. R. Ishmael
1. How do they roast the Passover-offering?	1. "But roast with fire" [Exod 12:9].	1. - - -	1. "Its head, with its legs, and with its insides" [Exod 12:9].
2. They bring a skewer of pomegranate wood, thrust it from its mouth through to its anus,	2. - - -	2. - - -	2. - - -
3. and they place its legs and its entrails into it, the words of R. Yose the Galilean.	3. He would place its head " "	3. - - -	3. - - -
4. R. Aqiva says,	4. Said to him R. Aqiva,	4. - - -	4. - - -
5. This is like a type of boiling.	5. But they shall be parched and boiled inside it!	5. - - -	5. - - -
6. Rather, he hangs them outside of it.	6. " " " "	6. - - -	6. - - -
7. TWK BR, the words of R. Tarfon.	7. R. Tarfon calls it TWKBR,	7. TNY': R. Ishmael calls it TWK TWK [var.: TKBR, TWK WBR].	7. TWK WBR, the words of R. Aqiva [var.: Eliezer].
8. - - -	8. for its insides are like its outsides.	8. - - -	8. - - -
9. R. Ishmael says, MQWLS.	9. R. Ishmael calls it GDY MQWLS.	9. R. Tarfon calls " "	9. R. [var.: Aqiva; Eliezer] says, MQWLS.

(y. Pes. 7:1 begins at item 7 in the first column.)

y. Pes. 7:1	Mekh. R. Simeon	b. Pes. 74a	Mekh. R. Ishmael
10. R. Tarfon follows R. Aqiva, and R. Ishmael follows R. Yose the Galilean.	10. - - -	10. - - -	10. - - -
11. DTNY: R. Yose the Galilean says, What is a GDY MQWLŚ?	11. - - -	11. TNW RBNN: What is a GDY MQWLŚ,	11. - - -
12. - - -	12. - - -	12. which [we are] forbidden at this time to eat on the night of Passover?	12. - - -
13. [One which is] completely roasted, "Its head, with its legs, and with its insides" [Exod 12:9].	13. - - -	13. One which is roasted as one [piece].	13. - - -

The chart above all indicates the poor state of this tradition.
The attributions are not firm. The spelling of the term used in 7
differs in the four versions of the tradition. This suggests that
its meaning is unclear. We have offered in our discussion of y.
Pes. several alternative interpretations for it. MQWLŚ is interpreted differently in y. Pes. = Mekh. R. Simeon and b. Pes. We
have listed below (pp. 69-70 n. 4) other definitions for this
term. On the other hand, as we have noted, Mekh. R. Simeon has
formulated its material well.

> 1.   It is a commandment for a man to make his wife and
> his children joyful on the festival [on Passover].
> 2.   With what does he make them joyful?
> 3.   With wine.
> 4.   As it is written, "And wine gladdens the heart of
> man" [Ps 104:15].
> 5.   R. Judah says, "Women [are made joyful] by means
> of what is appropriate for them, and children by means of
> what is appropriate for them."

Tos. Pisha 10:4, ed. Lieberman,
p. 196, lns. 8-10

> A.   *Women by means of what is appropriate for them*, for
> example, shoes and bright colored garments. *Children by
> means of what is appropriate for them*, nuts and almonds.
> B.   *They say R. Tarfon used to do this.*

y. Pes. 10:1 37b

Comment: B asserts that Tarfon acted in accordance with
Judah's view. Thus, this is another tradition which builds upon
the association of the two masters.

> A.   R. Ishmael says, "Three myrtle branches, and two
> willow branches, [M: and] one palm branch, and one citron
> [comprise the four kinds, Lev 23:40]."
> B.   1.   [M,y.Ven.,y.Leid.: And] even
>   2.   [if there are] two which have broken off [parts]
> (QṬWMYM) and one which does not have a broken off [part,
> they are fit].
> C.   R. Tarfon says, "Even [if] all three have broken off
> [parts, they are still fit]."

D.   R. Aqiva says, "Just as [there is] one palm branch
and one citron, so too [there is] one myrtle branch and one
willow branch."

M. Suk. 3:4 (B-D = b. Suk. 34b)

Comment: The pericope consists of two disputes. B2-C have
been interpolated by means of "even," B1, into A and D (see Porton
II, p. 27). B-C are well balanced; however, they lack a superscription. Myrtles is the only object, mentioned in A, of which
one must take three branches; therefore, the amoraim in both b.
and y., as well as Bert., Rashi, Rosh, TYT, and Meiri, identify
it as the subject of the dispute. The redactor, accordingly, has
inserted B-C in between A and D, since these opinions concur with
Ishmael's view that there must be three myrtles.

M. Suk. 3:2 lists the defects which render a myrtle unfit.
The commentators explain that certain defects have this effect
because they detract from the beautification of the *miṣvah (hiddur
miṣvah)* of taking the four kinds. One of the defects which renders a myrtle unfit is a broken-off tip. B-C of our pericope do
not specify the part of the myrtle under discussion. But if we
assume that B-C deal with the tips of the myrtles, then both sayings oppose the anonymous law in M. Suk. 3:2. According to these
rulings, a myrtle with a broken-off tip is still considered a
myrtle; therefore, one may use it to fulfill the commandment.
TYY and TYT suggest that the myrtles are fit, because the thick-
ness of their leaves covers up the broken-off tips.

A.   R. Ishmael expounded [Sifra: says], "'The fruit of
a goodly tree' is one; 'palm branches' is one; and 'boughs
of thick trees' are three; and 'willows of the brook' are two."

B.   [y. Ven., y. Leid, Sifra V 66: *And] two* vine
branches trained to an espalier, [Sifra adds: and] *one which
does not have broken off* [*parts*].

C.   *R. Tarfon says*, "[*They are fit*] even [*if*] *all three
have broken off* [*parts*]."

D.   Aqiva says, "'Fruit of a goodly tree' is one; and
'palm branches' is one; and 'boughs of thick trees' is one;
and 'willows of the brook' is one.

E.   "Lo, *just as* [*there is*] *one palm and one citron, so
too*, [*there is*] *one myrtle and one willow branch*."

Sifra 'Emor Pereq 16:7, ed.
Weiss, 102d (A-C = y. Suk. 3:4
53c)

Comment: This version has DLYWT and not QṬWMYM in B. DLYWT
means vines trained to an espalier. Ratner (VII, p. 100) cites
the exegetical tradition which interprets DLYWT as a synonym
for QṬWM. But I agree with Rabad (commentary to Sifra), and cannot offer a reason for the use of DLYWT.

      A. The measure of the myrtle and the willow [is]
      three handbreadths, and [for] the palm, [the measure is]
      four [first ed., Lon.: handbreadths].

      B. R. Tarfon says, "A cubit of [E: B'MH BT; first ed.,
      Lon.: B'MH ŠL] five handbreadths."

Tos. Suk. 2:8, ed. Lieberman,
p. 264, lns. 52-53 (b. Suk. 32b)

Comment: A is an independent anonymous law. B glosses A.
Our problem is to determine whether B supplements A, or whether
A-B are a dispute consisting of a statement plus a gloss.

Lieberman (*T.K.* IV, p. 862) explains, in agreement with the
interpretation of the amoraim in b. and y., that Tarfon supplements
A. Tarfon gives the length of the handbreadths mentioned in A; it
is a handbreadth that is one-fifth of a cubit. This explanation
assumes that the length of the cubit is fixed, and that one com-
putes the length of the handbreadth in terms of it.

The problem with the above explanation is that the content
of Tarfon's saying "with a cubit of five handbreadths" occurs in
Tos. Kel. B.M. 6:13 in a statement attributed to Meir, and there
its meaning is the opposite of the interpretation given by Lieberman. Meir's saying reads:

      R. Meir says, "All the measurements which sages said
in Kerem BeYavneh, for example...all of them are in terms
of a cubit of five handbreadths (B'MH ŠL) [see Lieberman,
T.R. III, pp. 54-55 for variant BT], except for...which
are in terms of a cubit of six handbreadths."
      [The pericope continues by citing, in support of Meir,
Ezek 43:13 which reads:] "And these are the measurements of
the altar in terms of cubits."
      "In terms of cubits" [teaches us that there are two
cubits. One which is] a cubit, [and one which is] a cubit
and a handbreadth, which is one more handbreadth than its
fellow cubit.

Tos. Kel. B.M. 6:13

From this tradition it is clear that in the expression, "with a
cubit of five handbreadths," the handbreadth is the fixed measure,
and the cubit is computed in terms of it. If this interpretation
of the expression is correct, then Tarfon does not gloss A by defining the length of the cubit. Tarfon, rather, disputes with A's

measure for the palm. Tarfon, using the formula SYWR B, claims
that the length of the palm is not four handbreadths but a cubit
of five handbreadths.[5] Thus we have another tradition of Tarfon
in which he comments upon the dimensions of certain objects.

> A. TNY: [The required length for] the myrtle and
> the willow is three [handbreadths] and [for] the palm, it
> is four [handbreadths].
> B. TNY: "With a cubit (B'MT) of five [handbreadths],"
> the words of R. Tarfon.
> C. But sages say, "With a cubit of six [handbreadths]."
>
> y. Suk. 3:1 53c

Comment: We now have a dispute between Tarfon and sages. The
opinions are neatly balanced. The attributive formula for Tarfon's
saying is not "R. Tarfon says," as in Tos., but "the words of R.
Tarfon." The interpretation given in the *gemara* for these sayings
is that Tarfon's handbreadth is six-fifths of that of sages. Thus
the amoraim treat these sayings as supplementary to A.

> 1. [If] its [a *lulav*'s] leaves become separated
> completely [from the stem (NPRṢW)], it is unfit.
> 2. [If] its leaves become separated (NPRDW) [such
> that they are attached to the stem but are not close
> together], it is fit.
> 3. R. Judah says, "He should tie it together (Y'GDNW)
> at the top."
>
> M. Suk. 3:1

> A. "Palm branches" (KPWT TMRYM) [Lev 23:40]--
> B. R. Tarfon says, "[This means they must be] KPWT
> TMRYM [i.e., 'bunches of palms']."
> C. R. Aqiva says, "'Palm branches' [means that they
> must be] as their name implies (KŠMN)."
> D. R. Judah says, "If it is separated, he should tie
> it together."
>
> y. Suk. 3:1 53c

Comment: A-C are a peculiar dispute. The superscription, A,
is a citation of a biblical verse. B repeats the words of A. C
also repeats A and adds KŠMN. By themselves, A-C are unintelligible.
But when read with D, they are a good dispute. The issue discussed
in this dispute is the condition required for a fit palm, *lulav*.

According to Tarfon, the palm must be in bunches, KPWT. Aqiva,
however, rules that the palm simply must be branches. This is all
"palm branches" in Scripture indicates. Judah's ruling, which
appears in M. Suk. 3:1 and disagrees with its anonymous law, extends Tarfon's view. According to Judah, not only must the palm
initially be in bunches, but even if the leaves become separated,
they must be tied back together.

A.   *"Palm branches"*--

B.   1.   *R. Tarfon says,* "[*This means they must be
kept in*] *bunches.*

2.   "If they become separated, he should put them
in a bunch (YKPTNW)."

> Sifra 'Emor Pereq 16:4, ed.
> Weiss, 102d (Pesikta deRav
> Kahana 27:8, ed. Mandelbaum,
> p. 413, ln. 12)

Comment: Sifra understands Tarfon's saying to mean that the
palm branches must be in bunches. It has glossed Tarfon's saying,
B1, with a statement, B2, very similar to that of Judah. The only
difference between the two is the verb, "he should put them in a
bunch," vs. "he should tie it together." Aqiva does not appear in
Sifra.

A.   *And does not R. Judah demand that the palm branches
shall be goodly?*

B.   WHTNN: R. Judah says, "He should tie them together
at the top."

C.   *What is his reason* [for this injunction]? *Is it
not that he wants* [*them to be*] *goodly?*

D.   No, the reason is as it has been taught (KDTNY):

E.   1.   R. Judah says in the name of R. Tarfon, "'Palm
branches' [means that they must be in] bunches.

2.   "And if it is separated, he should put it in a
bunch."

> b. Suk. 31a, 32a

Comment: E has conflated the sayings of Tarfon and Judah.
Aqiva's opinion again does not appear.

A.   [As to] a beast that died [on the Festival day],
one may not move it from its place.

B.   1.   M'SH [N,Pr,K,L,P,y.Ven.,y.Leid.:] Š [M,b.V 134:
W]: They asked R. Tarfon about this [matter ('LYH)] and
about the dough-offering that had become unclean,

2.   and he went into the *Bet Midrash* and inquired
(WŠ'L),

3.   [L,M,b.V 134: and] they said to him, "One may
not move them from their place."

M. Beṣ. 3:5

Comment: B serves as an illustration of A.   The M'SH is odd
in that Tarfon is not credited with an opinion but simply inquires
in the *Bet Midrash*, where the anonymous "they" answer his question.
The pericope relates to the following law of *muqṣeh*.   In order to
use an object on a Festival day, one must have that intention
prior to the beginning of the day.   If he lacks this prior intention, the object is considered *muqṣeh* on the Festival day and may
not be moved.   Since the owner of the animal that died on the
Festival and of the dough-offering that became unclean on that day
did not intend to feed, on the Festival, these items to animals,
the purpose for which they may be used, they are *muqṣeh*.   One,
therefore, may not move them.

A.   TNY': [As to the members of a] Sanhedrin who observed one [person] who killed [another] person--

B.   "some were made witnesses and some were made
judges," the words of R. Tarfon.

C.   R. Aqiva says [R.H.:], "All of them are made
witnesses [B.Q., M, and all Mss. R.H.: All of them are
witnesses].

D.   "And a witness is not made a judge."

b. R.H. 25b-26a (b. B.Q. 90b)

Comment: A-C are a well-balanced dispute.   The key words are
some, MQṢTN, vs. all, KWLN.   D glosses C.

The wording of this baraita is very similar to a statement
attributed to Aqiva in b. Mak. 12a.   This statement in turn parallels Tos. Mak. 3:7.   We present these pericopae in a chart:

Tos. Mak. 3:7	b. Mak. 12a	b. R.H. 25b-26a
1. R. Aqiva says,	1. " " "	1. - - -
2. [If] a court observed that he killed [someone], lo, this one is not [immediately] exiled [to a city of refuge].	2. - - -	2. - - -
3. - - -	3. Whence do we know that	3. - - -
4. [If] a high court (BYT DYN GDWL) observed that he killed [someone], lo, this one is not [immediately] exiled.	4. a Sanhedrin which observed one who killed [another] person	4. DTNY' " " "
5. - - -	5. - - -	5. some were made witnesses and some were made judges, the words of R. Tarfon.
6. And they do not immediately put him to death.	6. that they do not put him to death	6. - - -
7. Rather, they seat other judges, and they [the members of the court who observed the murder] testify before them.	7. until he stands [trial] before a different court?	7. R. Aqiva says, All of them are witnesses.
8. For it is written, "[The man-slayer] may not die [until he stands before the congregation for judgment]" (Num 35:12).	8. It is written, " " " " " " " "	8. - - -
9. - - -	9. [This teaches that he is not put to death] until he stands [trial] before another court.	

The chart indicates that a ruling of Aqiva has been formulated
differently in the three versions of this tradition. In one of
these versions, b. R.H., it has been placed in a dispute with an
opposing opinion of Tarfon.

This tradition appears in an amoraic discussion of M. R.H.
3:1, which states that if only the members of a court saw the new
moon, some of its members act as witnesses and some as judges. M.
agrees in principle with Tarfon's view in the baraita, for he
rules that the members of a court who observe a crime may judge
the case. He assumes that their observation of the crime does not
prejudice their judgment. Aqiva contends that these witnesses may
not act as judges. They are not unprejudiced.

> A.   1.   [If] they were fasting and rain fell before the
> sunrise, they should not complete [the fast].
>
> 2.   [But if the rain fell] after the sunrise, they
> should [complete the fast].
>
> B.   1.   R. Eliezer says, "[If the rain fell] before
> midday, they should not complete [the fast].
>
> 2.   "[But if the rain fell] after midday, they
> should complete [the fast]."
>
> C.   1.   M'SH Š: They decreed a fast in Lydda, and the
> rain fell before midday.
>
> 2.   Said to them R. Tarfon, "Go and eat, and drink,
> and keep this as a Festival day."
>
> 3.   And they went and ate, and drank, and kept it
> as a Festival day, and in the afternoon they came and recited
> "The Great *Hallel*" [Psalm 136].

M. Ta. 3:9

Comment: A-B are a well-balanced dispute. C is an autonomous
tradition. The redactor uses it as an illustration of B since it
shows that in Lydda, Eliezer's supposed place of residence, they
observed the law in accordance with his view. C consists of three
elements: (1) the setting, (2) Tarfon's ruling, (3) a statement
detailing the people's adherence to Tarfon's view. C1+2 suffice
to convey Tarfon's opinion.

> A.   Said R. Judah, "I was a minor and I read it [the
> *Megillah*, the book of Esther] before R. Tarfon [b.: and the
> elsers] in Lydda, [b.,y. omit: and he accepted me] [my
> reading of it (WQBLNY)]."

B.   Said Rabbi, "I was a minor and I read it before
R. Judah at Usha, and there were elders there, and not one
of them said a thing."

C.   They said to him, "One does not bring proof from
[a case involving the] one who permits."

D.   From that time onward minors were directed (HWNHGW)
to read it [the *Megillah*] to the public (LRBYM).

> Tos. Meg. 2:8, ed. Lieberman,
> p. 350, lns. 24-27 (b. Meg. 20a,
> y. Meg. 2:4 73b)

Comment: Judah's testimony serves as a precedent for his
ruling in M. Meg. 2:4, which permits a minor to read the *Megillah*.
Sages, in M., disagree with him. A and B have been formulated
together. A is another tradition which depicts Judah as relying
upon the actions of Tarfon.

DTNY: R. Simeon b. Yoḥai [says], R. Tarfon says,
"'*Karet*' [death by the hand of heaven] is stated [in Scripture as the punishment for violations of] the Sabbath, and
'*karet*' is stated [as the punishment for violations of] Yom
Kippur. Just as no stripes are inflicted [for those viola-
tions] of the Sabbath [for which the person is liable to]
karet, so too no stripes are inflicted [for those violations
of] Yom Kippur [for which the person is liable to] *karet*."

> y. Meg. 1:8 71a (y. Ket. 3:1 27c)

Comment: Tarfon's exegesis is based upon a *gezerah shavah*.
"*Karet*" is prescribed by the Bible as the punishment for violations both of the Sabbath and of Yom Kippur. Since no stripes are
inflicted when a person is liable to *karet* for violations of the
Sabbath, we may deduce that a person who is liable to *karet* for
violations of Yom Kippur is not scourged. PM and QH explain Tarfon's ruling as follows: A court may not inflict stripes for violations of a negative commandment for which they may punish a
person, if they have previously warned him. Now a person is subject to punishment by a court if he transgresses the Sabbath =
violating a negative commandment, after having been warned. The
court executes him. Accordingly, he is not flogged. This is the
rule whether he is to suffer death by the court or by heaven. As
noted, if he has previously been warned, the court executes him.
He is punished by heaven if he has not been warned. Since one
liable to *karet* for violations of the Sabbath is not flogged, then

one liable to *karet* for violations of Yom Kippur also should not
be scourged. Tarfon's opinion disagrees with the anonymous law of
M. Mak. 3:2, which states that one who works on Yom Kippur = violating a negative commandment for which one is subject to *karet*,
is flogged.[6]

     A.   [Vienna: W] M'SH Š: Alexsa died in Lydda, and the
people of the city [Lon.: of his city; E, first ed.: of the
villages; b.: all of Israel] came to eulogize him.
     B.   1.   Said to them R. Tarfon,
           2.   "Go away,
           3.   "one does not eulogize on the Festival day
(BYWM ṬWB)." [b. reads: And R. Tarfon did not allow them
(to eulogize him), because it was the holiday of Pentecost.]

                        Tos. Ḥag. 2:13, ed. Lieberman,
                        p. 386, lns. 92-93 (b. Ḥag. 18a)

Comment: A implies, by mentioning that all the people came,
that it was an accepted practice to eulogize on Festival days.
Tarfon's prohibition, B3, against eulogizing agrees with the laws
implicit in M. Ḥag. 2:4 and in M. M.Q. 3:8. This is the only tradition in rabbinic literature about Alexsa (see Hyman I, p. 157).

     A.   1.   M'SH B: R. Tarfon was walking by the way.
           2.   An old man met him.
           3.   He [the man] said to him, "Why do the people
jeer you, are not all your teachings true and correct but
that
           4.   you receive heave-offering on the rest of the
days of the year from anyone"?
     B.   1.   Said R. Tarfon, "May I bury my son, if I do not
have in my hand a *halakhah* from Rabban Yoḥanan b. Zakkai who
said to me, [E,G lack: to me].
           2.   [E: "'One] You are permitted to receive heave-
offering on the rest of the days of the year from anyone.'
     C.   1.   "Now [that] all the people jeer me,
           2.   "I take a vow upon myself that
           3.   "I shall not receive heave-offering on the rest
of the days of the year from anyone,
           4.   "unless he tells me, 'I have [placed] in it a
quarter [of a *log*] of sanctified [food].'"

                        Tos. Ḥag. 3:33, ed. Lieberman,
                        p. 393, lns. 71-77

Comment: The pericope is not unitary, for despite Tarfon's
appeal in B1 to the authority of Yoḥanan b. Zakkai, Tarfon in C
reverses his opinion. A-B, however, are a perfectly intelligible
M'SH. Furthermore, as we shall see, the context in which the
pericope appears suggests that C has been added to A-B in order to
have Tarfon agree with the anonymous law of Tos. Ḥag. 3:32. In
the analysis which follows we shall first discuss Tarfon's opinion, B2, and then turn to the law attributed to him in C4.

This pericope relates to the following laws in Tos. Ḥag. 3:30,
32 (M. Ḥag. 3:4):

> A. In Judaea they [the *'amme-ha'areṣ*] are deemed trust-
> worthy all the days of the year regarding the cleanness of
> wine and of oil [to be used for sacrifices]. But [they are]
> not deemed trustworthy] regarding heave-offering.
> B. At [the time] of the vats and the winepresses [they
> are deemed trustworthy] even with regard to [the cleanness]
> of heave-offering.
>> Tos. Ḥag. 3:30, ed. Lieberman,
>> p. 392, lns. 63-64

> A. [When] the vats and the winepresses passed, they
> [the heave-offering of wine and of olives] return to their
> former prohibition [i.e., they are deemed unclean].
> B. If they [the *'amme-ha'areṣ*, after the season of
> the vats,] brought him a barrel of wine of heave-offering,
> he may not receive it from them, unless he said to him,
> "I have [placed] in it a quarter [of a *log*] of a Holy
> [thing]."
>> Tos. Ḥag. 3:32, ed. Lieberman,
>> p. 393, lns. 69-70

Maim. explains that the principle underlying these rules is that
when an *'am-ha'areṣ* intends to fulfill a biblical injunction, he is
careful to maintain the cleanness of his produce. Thus Tos. 3:30A
states that an *'am-ha'areṣ* is deemed trustworthy at all times regarding any wine or oil which he dedicates to the Temple. Similarly, in B, since at the time of the preparation of his wines and
his olives the *'am-ha'areṣ* has in mind the commandment of giving
heave-offering, one may at this time accept his heave-offering.
But as Tos. 32A states, once the season for the preparation of
wines and of olives passes, one may no longer accept the heave-
offering of the *'am-ha'areṣ*. At these times we do not presume
that the *'am-ha'areṣ* had the heave-offering in mind; therefore, he
probably did not maintain the cleanness of his wine. Tarfon's
opinion in B2 implicitly disagrees with this law.[7] Tarfon rules
that one may accept heave-offering, from anyone, at any time, i.e.,
not only at the time of the vats but even on the rest of the days
of the year. Lieberman explains that Tarfon considers an

'am-ha'areṣ always trustworthy regarding the cleanness of heave-
offering. One, therefore, may always accept his offering.

In C Tarfon revises his opinion. But the view attributed to
him in C4 is identical to that of Tos. 3:32B. Maim. explains this
law as follows: Tos. 3:30A states that the 'amme-ha'areṣ, in
Judaea, are deemed trustworthy the entire year with regard to the
cleanness of Holy produce. Now since we trust the 'am-ha'areṣ
with regard to the quarter of the log of sanctified oil which he
places in the barrel, we assume that he places it only into a
barrel containing clean liquid. The person, therefore, may accept, under the above conditions, the heave-offering of the
'am-ha'areṣ = Tos. Ḥag. 3:32b.

This is the only tradition in which Tarfon claims that he has
received a law from another authority. It is striking that whoever added C to A-B allows the criticism of Tarfon's contempor-
aries to override the authority of Yoḥanan b. Zakkai.

[1]I concur with Lightstone (pp. 29-33) who argues that no authority would permit purposely burning books on the Sabbath. The
opinions in D-E, therefore, relate to weekdays. Lightstone also
contends that "on weekdays" is not integral to Yose's saying and
have been added to join D to A-C.

[2]Rashi, Bert., TYT, MS, TYY offer the following explanation
for this difference: Since Aqiva's prayer is one of request, it
concludes with a blessing. Tarfon's prayer, however, is only a
prayer of thanks; therefore, it does not require a concluding
blessing. Tarfon considers the blessing over the *maṣṣah* as the
blessing which concludes the story-section of the *Haggadah*.
Heinemann (*Prayer*, pp. ix, 108-112) concludes that the rules
concerning the use of blessings were not formalized until amoraic
and geonic times.

[3]Kasher notes that certain Haggadot do mention the drinking
of a fifth cup of wine and the recitation of "The Great *Hallel*"
over it. Goldschmidt argues that Rashi and his students, Rashbam
and Tosafot, in light of the practice of drinking only four cups,
emend the text in the *gemara* to read, "They mixed for him the
fourth cup...." Thus, according to Goldschmidt, the reading preserved by Rashi is not a variant he knew, but simply a correction
he made because of the legal observance of this rule.

[4]The first problem with regard to A is that there is some
uncertainty with regard to its reading. As we shall see, the
parallel versions of this tradition have different readings for
Tarfon's saying, such as, TWKBR, TWK WBR, and TWK TWK. Krauss
(II, pp. 257-58), Jastrow (p. 1667), Levi (p. 641), and Kasher
(*Torah* XI, p. 108) all suggest that TKBR(') is the correct reading
for A. This word appears in T.J. to 1 Sam 25:18 in the translation of "five prepared lambs" (ḤMŠH ṢWN 'SWYWT), WḤMYŠ 'N TKBR'.
This clearly indicates that TKBR(') is a term used in connection
with sacrifices or the cooking of animals. The above scholars
derive TKBR(') from the root KBR, and claim that it means "stuffed
like a basket." *Kabāru* appears in Akkadian and means "to become
fat and thick." It is used with reference to animals and parts of
the body. Thus one can see some connection to the idea of stuffed
(see Oppenheim VIII, pp. 4-5). According to this interpretation
of A, Tarfon claims that the parts of the lamb should be cooked
inside it. This is the opposite of C's interpretation of A.
    The definition of MQWLŚ is somewhat more difficult. There is
no way to determine what the term means in B. D of our pericope
defines MQWLŚ by citing the biblical verse. But without M.2 we
would not know how Yose interprets the verse. A definition of
MQWLŚ also appears in Tos. Beṣ. 2:15. It reads:

        A.   What is a GDY MQWLŚ?
        B.   [One that is] completely roasted, its head,
[first ed. and Lon. add: and] its legs, and its insides.
        C.   [If] they boil any part of it, or [if] they
seeth (SLQ) any part of it, it is not a GDY MQWLŚ.

Lieberman (*T.K.* V, p. 957) interprets this to mean that one places
the entrails, the legs, and the head outside the lamb, roasting
the entire lamb. This does not agree with Yose's definition, 2 of
M. Pes. 7:1 and y. Pes. D. Lieberman also notes that Ms. E has a

different reading for Tos. B, "Its head, and its legs inside of
it (LTWKW)." According to this reading, MQWLŚ is interpreted in
a manner similar to Yose's explanation. A number of other definitions of the term can be offered. Krauss (II, pp. 257-58)
claims it comes from the Greek χαυλος and means "helmeted" (*Helm
galem*). This explanation is also given by Levi, Jastrow, the
Arukh (VII, p. 106), and Rashi. According to this explanation,
a GDY MQWLŚ would have its entrails and its legs wrapped around
the head so as to form a helmet. This is the opposite of the
gemara's definition of MQWLŚ in G, but agrees with the reading in
the first ed. and the Lon. Ms. of Tos. Kohut (supplement to the
Arukh, p. 363), however, rejects this explanation. Another possible derivation of the term is from the Greek for "beautiful,"
καλος. If this explanation is correct, then a GDY MQWLŚ would
simply be a beautiful lamb. Alternatively, Syriac preserves the
word QLŚ', deriving from the Greek καλως which refers to an animal
led on a string. The Arukh also gives κωλος, meaning "intestines,"
as a definition for QLŚ. Finally, the word κολος in Greek means
"a hornless animal." MQWLŚ would then simply be a hornless sheep.
If this explanation is correct, then Ishmael's comment has nothing
to do with the discussion in this pericope.

[5]b. Suk. 32b preserves a comment by Rava on our pericope
which understands Tarfon's saying as an alternative opinion to A.
This statement reads:

> Said Rava [b. V 134: R. Huna], "May the master forgive
> R. Tarfon. Now we cannot find myrtles of [even] three
> [handbreadths]; is one of five [now] required"? [b. V:
> "Who can find one (of) five (handbreadths)"?]

Rava interprets Tarfon's statement as an opinion in dispute with A.
My explanation agrees with Rava's interpretation of the function
of Tarfon's comment but disagrees with regard to the object to
which it refers.

[6]The anonymous law is in agreement with the sayings attributed
to Aqiva and to Ishmael in the following baraita (b. Mak. 13a-b):

> A. DTNY': "Those liable to *karet* are the same as
> those liable for death by [human] court, they all are
> within the rule of forty stripes," the words of R. Ishmael.
> B. R. Aqiva says, "Those liable to *karet* are within
> the rule of forty stripes....Those liable to death by a
> [human] court are not within the rule of forty stripes...."

Both Aqiva and Ishmael, in opposition to Tarfon, agree that one
liable to *karet* should be flogged.

[7]B2 makes no mention of Judaea and also does not specify the
product for which the '*am-ha'areṣ* gives the heave-offering. But
since it implies that one may receive any heave-offering from anyone on the rest of the days of the year, it implicitly includes
the '*amme-ha'areṣ* in Judaea.

CHAPTER III

NASHIM

> Said R. Tarfon, "I am desirous that (T'YB) the
> co-wife of my daughter[1] would fall to me, and I would
> cause her to marry (W'ŚY'NH) into the priesthood."

> Tos. Yev. 1:10, ed. Lieberman,
> p. 3, ln. 3 (y. Yev. 1:6)

Comment: According to Deut 25:5-10 a man is required to take
as his wife his brother's widow if his brother dies childless.
This is known as Levirate marriage. If, however, the brother refuses to marry the widow, he must submit to the ceremony of
ḥaliṣah. But if the widow is among those forbidden to the surviving brother (Lev 18:6-18), he does not perform the Levirate
marriage, nor must he submit to *ḥaliṣah* (M. Yev. 1:1). The Houses
(M. Yev. 1:4), however, dispute about what must be done with regard to the co-wives of the woman forbidden to the surviving
brother. Does the co-wife forbidden to the brother exempt the
other co-wives from entering into Levirate marriage, and if the
surviving brother refuses to marry them, does she also exempt them
from performing *ḥaliṣah*? The House of Shammai contend that the
co-wife forbidden to the brother does not have this effect; therefore, the other co-wives must enter into Levirate marriage with
the surviving brother. If the brother refuses to marry them,
they must perform *ḥaliṣah*. If they perform this ceremony, then in
accordance with the anonymous law in M. Yev. 2:4 they may not
afterwards marry a priest. The House of Hillel rule that the co-
wife forbidden to the brother exempts the other co-wives from
entering into Levirate marriage and also from performing *ḥaliṣah*.
According to the House of Hillel, even if the other co-wives perform *ḥaliṣah*, they do not acquire the status of a *ḥaluṣot*, for they
were not required to perform the ceremony. Thus in any case,
according to the House of Hillel, the other co-wives may subsequently marry a priest.

Tarfon's remark appears after those of several other Yavneans
relating to the Houses' opinions. Yoḥanan b. Nuri attempts to
compromise the Houses' opinions; Joshua clearly agrees with the
ruling of the House of Hillel. Similarly, Tarfon's saying tries
to explain how the law is to be observed. Tarfon's saying lends
itself to two interpretations, one of which supports the opinion
of the House of Shammai, the other that of the House of Hillel.

Thus Tarfon's saying may mean that he would arrange for a co-wife
of his daughter to marry a priest, or that he would marry his
daughter's co-wife.[2] According to the first interpretation, Tarfon
agrees with the House of Hillel, for he does not consider the wife
a ḥaluṣah. If the co-wife of Tarfon's daughter observed the law
in accordance with the ruling of the House of Shammai, she would
have this status. The second interpretation of Tarfon's saying
has him agree with the opinion of the House of Shammai, for Tarfon
would marry the co-wife of his daughter. Thus if Tarfon's daughter
were married to his brother,[3] and the latter died, Tarfon could of
course not perform Levirate marriage with his daughter, but, according to the view of the House of Shammai, he must perform it
with her co-wife.

> A. *Come and Hear*: For said R. Tarfon, "I am desirous
> [for] the time [that] the co-wife of my daughter would
> fall to me, and I would marry her (W'S'NH)."
> B. *One should say* ('YM'), "And I would cause her
> to marry (W'SY'NH)."
> C. But he said, "I am desirous (T'YBNY)." [I am
> desirous implies he disagrees with some previous state-
> ment, or that he is teaching some new law.]
> D. *It* [I am desirous] *implies an objection to the
> statement of R. Yoḥanan b. Nuri* [who says one needs to
> perform ḥaliṣah].

b. Yev. 15a

Comment: This version of Tarfon's saying contains the verb
"I would marry" and not the verb "I would cause to marry." Although the latter construction of the verb may also mean that
Tarfon would marry the girl, the construction of the verb in this
pericope eliminates all doubt as to who would marry the girl; it
is Tarfon. Accordingly, Tarfon's saying supports the view of the
House of Shammai and not that of the House of Hillel.

B's purpose is to indicate that Tarfon would not be the one
marrying the girl and thereby eliminates the implication that
Tarfon adheres to the Shammaite position.

[The *gemara* discusses the period of time a widow or a widower
must wait before remarrying. These matters are dealt with in M.
Yev. 4:11. A widow may not remarry for thirty days. But a widower
normally must wait three festivals before remarrying. But if he
does not have children, or if he does not have someone to wait on

him, or if he has young children, he may remarry immediately.
The *gemara* cites the following M'SH to support these rules.]

    A. For example:

    B. M'SH Š: The wife of R. Tarfon died.

    C. While he was still in the cemetery, he said to her
[his wife's] sister, "Marry [me], and bring up the children
of your sister."

    D. Nevertheless [Alfasi: Even though], [Sens omits:]
he married her,

    E. but [Alfasi omits but] he did not have relations
with her until thirty days had passed since her [his wife's
death].

y. Yev. 4:11 6b (Sem. 7:15)

Comment: B-E give a biographical story about Tarfon. B-C can
stand alone. The redactor appropriately ties the M'SH to the preceding *gemara*. The M'SH illustrates that a widower with small
children may remarry immediately. The order of the first two
words in D should be reversed. D-E respond to the problem discussed in the *gemara* of whether or not a widower must observe a
period of mourning. Tarfon's actions are a compromise. He remarried immediately, but he did not have relations for thirty days.

    b. M.Q. 23b preserves a story identical to B-E. But it con-
cerns Joseph the Priest. Since the two stories are identical, I
present them in a chart.

y. Yev. 4:11	b. M.Q. 23b
1. M'SH Š The wife of R. Tarfon died.	1. M'SH Š The wife of Joseph the Priest died.
2. While he was still in the cemetery, he said to her [his wife's] sister,	2. And he said to her [his wife's] sister in the cemetery,
3. Marry [me] and bring up the children of your sister.	3. Go and provide for the children of your sister.
4. Nevertheless, he married her, but did not have relations with her until thirty days passed since her [death].	4. Nevertheless, he did not have relations with her (L' B' 'LYH) until after a considerable time.
5. - - -	5. What is a considerable time?
6. - - -	6. Said R. Papa, Until after thirty days.

Whose name is primary? There are only five traditions ascribed to
Joseph the Priest preserved in M.-Tos. (M. Ḥal. 4:11, M. Miq.
10:1, Tos. Shab. 13:12, Tos. Pisha 8:10, Tos. A.Z. 1:8). Each is
set in a narrative. b. Zev. 100a preserves an additional story
about Joseph the Priest:

> M'SH B: Joseph the Priest [whose] wife died on the
> eve of Passover, and he did not want to make himself
> unclean....

Thus we have two traditions about the death of the wife of Joseph
the Priest. We have no such other tradition for Tarfon. The
simplest explanation for the existence of y. Yev. and b. M.Q. is
that y. Yev., the story involving Tarfon, and b. Zev., the story
about the death of Joseph the Priest's wife on the eve of Passover, are two independent traditions. Someone knowing these two
traditions could easily switch Tarfon's name with that of Joseph
the Priest and thereby create b. M.Q.

        A. 1. [As to] a woman and her husband who went to
the province beyond the sea (LMDYNT HYM), and she came
[back] and said, "My husband died,"
            2. she may remarry and collect [the money pre-
scribed in] her *ketubah*,
            3. but her co-wife is forbidden [to remarry].
        B. [If] she [the co-wife] was the daughter of an
Israelite [and was married] to a priest--
        C. "She may [continue] to eat heave-offering," the
words of R. Tarfon.
        D. 1. R. Aqiva says, "This is not a way to remove
her from transgression;
            2. "until she is [both] forbidden to remarry,
and forbidden to eat heave-offering."
        E. 1. [If] she said "My husband died and after
that my father-in-law [died],"
            2. she may remarry and collect her *ketubah*,
            3. but her mother-in-law is forbidden [to remarry].
        F. [If] she [the mother-in-law] was the daughter of
an Israelite [married] to a priest--
        G. "She may [continue] to eat heave-offering," the
words of R. Tarfon.
        H. 1. R. Aqiva says, "This is not a way to remove
her from transgression;

2. "until she is [both] forbidden to remarry, and
forbidden to eat heave-offering."

I. [If] a man betrothed (QDŠ) one of five women,
and it is not known which of them he betrothed, [and] each
one [of them] says, "He has betrothed me,"

J. "he gives a *get* to everyone of them and leaves
[the amount of one] *ketubah* among them, and departs," the
words of R. Tarfon.

K. 1. R. Aqiva says, "This is not a way to remove
him from transgression;

2. "[he may not leave] until he gives a *get* and
[the amount] of a *ketubah* to each one of them."

L. [If] a man stole from one of five [people], and
it is not known from which of them he stole, [and] each
one says, "He stole from me,"

M. "he leaves the stolen article among them and
departs," the words of R. Tarfon.

N. 1. R. Aqiva says, "This is not a way to remove
him from transgression;

2. "[he may not leave] until he pays each one
of them the [full] amount of the stolen article."

M. Yev. 15:6-7 (L-N = b. B.Q.
103b, b. B.M. 37a)

Comment: A dispute in principles between Tarfon and Aqiva has
generated two types of cases, A-H and I-N; each of these types is
spelled out in two examples A-B, E-F; I and L. Aqiva's sayings,
which respond to those of Tarfon, are not phrased as balanced
opposites to those of the latter. Thus for example, a balanced
response to C is, "She may not eat heave-offering"; while for L it
is, "He pays each of them." Aqiva's opinions, rather, are formulated in each case in line with the expression common to all of
them, "This is not a way to remove her (or him) from transgression," D1, H1, K1, and N1.

The dispute between Tarfon and Aqiva comes down to the following: In cases involving doubt do we continue to act in the normal
manner, until there is probative evidence, even if this involves
the possibility of transgression, or does the concern that some
transgression may be committed override the lack of probative evidence? Tarfon agrees with the former principle; Aqiva adheres to
the latter. Thus Tarfon rules in A and E that, because the testimony of the wife is not probative so as to allow the co-wives or

the mother-in-law to remarry, it is not strong enough to cause the
forfeiture of the right to eat heave-offering. (A woman from non-
priestly stock may eat heave-offering only while she is married to
a priest.) Similarly, for I and K, Tarfon's opinion is that the
mere assertions of the plaintiff do not necessitate the defendant
giving the value of five *ketubot* or of five stolen articles.
(When a man divorces his wife, he must pay her the amount specified in the *ketubah*.) The plaintiffs must produce stronger evidence than their own claims. Aqiva in all cases is concerned
that some transgression, some wrong in a broad sense of the word,
may be committed. Thus in A and E, if the husband is dead, then
an Israelite woman would eat heave-offering while not married to a
priest. Similarly, in I and L, unless the defendant gives each
person the worth of the *ketubah* or of the stolen articles, the one
party who has a valid claim may not receive the complete sum owed
him. Aqiva, therefore, rules that the person must follow the more
extreme course of action.

> A. 1.   [If] a man betrothed one of five women, and it
> is not known which of them he betrothed, and each one of
> them says, "He betrothed me,"
>
>   2.   [or if] a man purchased something (LQḤ MQḤ)
> from [one of] five [people], and it is not known from which
> one he purchased it, and each one of them says, "He pur-
> chased it from me."
>
> B. 1.   Said R. Simeon b. Leazar, "R. Tarfon and R.
> Aqiva did not disagree about [the one] who betrothed one of
> five women, and it is not known which of them he betrothed,
> for [they both agree that] he places the amount of money
> of the *ketubah* among them and departs.
>
>   2.   "About what did they disagree? [They dis-
> agreed about the one] who cohabited (ŠB'L) [with one of
> the women, and he did not known which one it was].
>
>   3.   "And they did not disagree about [the one]
> who purchased something from [one of] five people, and it
> is not known from which one he purchased it, for [they both
> agree] that he places the amount of the purchase among
> them and departs.
>
>   4.   "About what did they disagree? [They disagreed
> about the one] who stole [from one of five people, and he
> did not know which one it was]."

C. R. Tarfon admits [that the law is correct with
regard to]

D. 1. one who says to two people, "I stole from one
of you a *maneh*," and it is not known which one, or [if he
says], "the father of one of you deposited a *maneh* with
me," and he does not know which one [it is], he gives each
one of them a *maneh*,

2. since he has admitted it [his liability]
himself.

> Tos. Yev. 14:2, ed. Lieberman,
> pp. 50-51, lns. 10-18 (B = b.
> Yev. 118b; C-D = b. B.M. 37a,b,
> y. Yev. 15:9 15b; B-D = b. B.Q.
> 103b)

Comment: A has the form of a superscription, but no opinions
follow. Lieberman (*T.K.* VI, p. 169) argues that A presupposes the
opinions of Tarfon and Aqiva and is an explanation of M. Yev. 15:
6-7I and N. M.I and N assert that Tarfon and Aqiva disagree (1)
about a man who betrothed one of five women, an act not involving
the commission of a crime, and (2) about a man who stole from one
of five people, a criminal act. Tos. A refines M by claiming that
the two authorities dispute about two cases which involve no
illegal action, that of betrothal and that of purchasing an
article from one of five people. As Lieberman explains, according to A there can be no disagreement about cases in which the
person has committed a crime, i.e., theft from one of five people.
Tarfon agrees with Aqiva that in this case the thief must give
each person the monetary equivalent of the stolen item. Thus A
brings Tarfon over to Aqiva's view.

Simeon in B disagrees with A, and thus attests the opinions
of Tarfon and Aqiva. Simeon asserts (B1 and B3) that the two
authorities did not disagree about the cases of betrothal and of
purchasing an item. Both parties agree that in cases involving
no active transgression, the person must pay the value of only one
of the *ketubot*, or that of the stolen object. Thus Simeon, as
opposed to A, brings Aqiva over to Tarfon's view. The dispute
between Tarfon and Aqiva, according to Simeon, focuses upon two
illegal acts, that of theft and that of illegal cohabitation.

C-D are spun out of M. Yev. 15:6-7I-L and out of M. B.M. 3:3.
The latter pericope reads:

> [If a man] said to two [others], "I stole from one
> of you a *maneh*, and I do not know [from] which one of you
> [I stole it]"; or [if he says], "One of your fathers left

as collateral with me a *maneh* and I do not know which
one," he gives this one a *maneh* and that one a *maneh*,
because he admitted it himself.

The redactor of Tos. Yev. 14:2 has joined this anonymous tradition
to A-B by adding C. D2 gives the reason for Tarfon's agreement
with this law. Since the defendant makes a partial admission, he
must pay the full amount. This is in contrast to the cases given
in B and in M. Yev. 15:6-7 in which the plaintiffs accuse the
defendant, but the latter makes no admission. Thus the redactor
who added D to A-B has built upon the details given in M.I and L
and has drawn a logical conclusion from them.

    A. *Objected Rava* M'SH B: A pious man purchased an
article from two persons, but he did not know from which
one of them he purchased it,

    B. 1. and he came before R. Tarfon.

    2. He [Tarfon] said to him, "Leave the amount
of your purchase between them and depart."

    C. 1. He came before R. Aqiva.

    2. He [Aqiva] said to him, "There is no remedy
(TQNH) for you, unless you pay each of them."

              b. B.Q. 103b

Comment: According to the M'SH presented by Rava, Tarfon and
Aqiva do disagree concerning the law which pertains to the pur-
chasing of an object. The story cited by Rava thus agrees with
Tos. A and disagrees with Simeon b. Leazar's statement, Tos. B.

This M'SH has been generated from M.-Tos. It contains two
refinements of the latter. First, M.-Tos. mention five women and
five plaintiffs. But the case is the same whether there are two
or five plaintiffs. Thus b. has refined M.-Tos. by changing five
to two. Second, b. adds "a pious man" as the subject in A.

    A. It is an obligation (MṢWH) for the judges [to
recite this verse, Deut 25:10, "The man that has had his
shoe loosened, the man that has had his shoe loosened,"
but] it is not an obligation for the students [to recite
the verse].

    B. R. Judah says, "It is an obligation for all those
standing there to say, 'The man that has had his shoe
loosened, the man that has had his shoe loosened.'"

C. Said R. Judah, "[Vienna:] M'SH W [first ed.
lacks W; E: One time]: We were seated before R. Tarfon and
he said to us, 'All of you answer, "The man that has had
his shoe loosened, the man that has had his shoe
loosened."'"

> Tos. Yev. 12:15, ed. Lieberman,
> p. 45, lns. 69-71 (B-C = Sifre
> Deut. 291; C = b. Yev. 101b,
> 106b, b. Qid. 14a)

Comment: C can stand by itself. Here it serves as a precedent for Judah's opinion in the dispute A-B. It is another example of a tradition in which Judah claims to have acted in accordance with Tarfon's decision.

The pericope deals with the procedure for the ceremony of
ḥaliṣah (Deut 25:7-10). The opinions in A and B (= C) regarding
who must recite the verse are based on different interpretations
of the words in Deut 25:10, "And his name shall be called in
Israel." The verse does not specify who shall call the name.
Does "in Israel" indicate that all Israelites present at the ceremony must recite the verse, or is the important point that "his
name shall be called," i.e., that those responsible for the ceremony shall recite the verse? The anonymous law, A, adheres to
the latter interpretation; Tarfon and Judah to the former.

A. They do not rigorously cross-examine (BWDQYN
BDRYŠH WBHQYRH)[4] witnesses [who testify in behalf] of a
woman [that her husband has died].

B. R. Tarfon and R. Aqiva say, "They do rigorously
cross-examine witnesses [who testify in behalf] of a
woman."

C. 1. M'SH B: An individual came before R. Tarfon
to testify in behalf of a woman [so that] she could remarry.

2. He [Tarfon] said to him, "My son, how do you
happen to have testimony in behalf of this woman?"

3. He said to him, "Rabbi, he [the deceased] was
with us on a journey (BŠYYRH) and pirates (GYYŠ) fell upon
us, and he [the deceased] grasped the branch of a fig-tree
and pulled it down, and he chased away the pirates. I said
to him, 'I thank you, Lion ('RY).'

4. "He said to me, 'You have spoken well, you
have guessed my name (KYWNTH LŠMY). Thus I am called in
my town, Yoḥanan b. Jonathan, the Lion of Kefar Shaḥira.'"

5. He [Tarfon] said to him, "You have spoken
well, my son, [about] Jonathan b. Yoḥanan, the Lion of
Kefar Shaḥira."

6. He said to him, "No, Rabbi, rather Yoḥanan
b. Jonathan, the Lion of Kefar Shaḥira."

7. He said to him, "And did you not say thus,
Jonathan b. Yoḥanan, of Kefar Shaḥira, the Lion?"

8. He said to him, "Rather, Yoḥanan b. Jonathan,
[E: the Lion] of Kefar Shaḥira."

9. [y.: After a few days he (Yoḥanan b.
Jonathan) became ill and died.]

10. R. Tarfon examined his testimony three
times, and his [statements] were found to agree, and he
married [performed the marriage of] the woman on the
basis of his testimony.

D. From that time onward (MYKN WHLK) they used to
carefully cross-examine witnesses [who testify in behalf
of] women.

> Tos. Yev. 14:10, ed. Lieberman,
> p. 54, lns. 63-72 (C = y. Yev.
> 16:5 15d)

Comment : A-B are a neatly balanced dispute. B is attributed
to both Tarfon and Aqiva. But the story which follows relates
only to Tarfon. On the basis of C, someone may have added Tarfon's
name to B.

C is a very long M'SH, which, as we shall now see, contains
several smaller units. The preceding pericope, Tos. Yev. 14:9,
preserves a tradition that is almost identical to C3, 4, and 9[5] of
our pericope; therefore, it indicates that C3, 4, and 9 are an
independent story which has been joined to the other elements in C.
In order to facilitate our discussion, we present in parallel
columns Tos. Yev. 14:9 and Tos. Yev. 14:10C3, 4, and 9.

Tos. Yev. 14:10C3, 4, 9	Tos. Yev. 14:9
1. He was with us on a journey, and pirates fell upon us.	1. M'SH B Two men were pursuing pirates.
2. And he grasped the branch of a fig tree, and pulled it down, and he chased away the pirates.	2. And one [of them] pulled himself up by the branch of an olive tree, and he pulled it down, and he ran after the raiding gang, and [then] returned,

Tos. Yev. 14:10C3, 4, 9	Tos. Yev. 14:9
3. I said to him, I thank you, Lion.	3. and his friend said to him, May your strength return, Lion.
4. He said to me, You have spoken well; you have guessed my name.	4. He said to him, How do you know me, for I am [my name is], Lion.
5. Thus I am called in my town, Yoḥanan b. Jonathan, the Lion of Kefar Shaḥira.	5. " " "
6. After a few days, he [Yoḥanan b. Jonathan] became ill and died.	6. After three days, " " "
7. - - -	7. And [on the basis of the other person's testimony] they performed the marriage of his the deceased's wife.

There are only some minor differences[6] between Tos. 14:9 and Tos.
14:10; therefore, we conclude that the two are fundamentally the
same independent story. If we remove 3, 4, and 9 from C of Tos.
14:10, we are left with two different groups of elements: 1+10, a
brief M'SH involving Tarfon; 2, 5-8 which have been generated when
1+10 were joined to 3, 4, and 9. A M'SH consisting of 1+10 reads:

> M'SH B: An individual came before R. Tarfon to
> testify in behalf of a woman [so that] she could remarry.
> R. Tarfon examined his testimony three times, and his
> statements were found to agree, and he [Tarfon] married
> [performed the marriage of] the woman on the basis of
> his testimony.

This M'SH, like others involving Tarfon, consists of a statement
of the operative conditions, the setting, and Tarfon's actions.
Let us now turn to the substance of this M'SH.

According to rabbinic law, a woman whose husband has gone away
and has not returned may not remarry until someone brings evidence
that the husband has died. Tos. Yev. 14:8 states that a witness
who testifies in behalf of a woman must know the deceased's name,
his father's name, and his place of residence. Our pericope discusses the procedure the judges should follow in examining these
witnesses. Sages rule that one need not carefully cross-examine
these witnesses; Tarfon contends that cross-examination is required. D has the anonymous law agree with Tarfon.

A. 1. TNW RBNN: An individual came to testify before
R. Tarfon in behalf of a woman.

   2. He said to him, "How do you [come to] have
testimony concerning this woman?"

   3. He said, "He [the deceased] and I were going
on the way, and pirates pursued us, and he pulled himself
up on the branch of an olive tree, and pulled it down, and
chased away the pirates. I said to him, 'Lion, May your
strength return.'

   4. "He said to me, 'How do you know that Lion is
my name? Thus they call me in my town, Yoḥanan b. Jonathan,
Lion of Kefar Sheḥiya.'"

   5. After a few days he became sick and died, and
R. Tarfon performed the marriage of his wife.

B. Does not R. Tarfon, [however] hold that rigorous
[cross-examination is necessary]?

C. 1. WHTNY: M'SH B: An individual came before R.
Tarfon to testify in behalf of a woman [so that] she could
remarry.

   2. He [Tarfon] said to him, "My son, how do you
happen to have testimony in behalf of this woman?"

   3. He said to him, "Rabbi, he [the deceased] and
I were going on the way, and pirates were pursuing us, and
he pulled himself up on the branch of a fig tree, and he
pulled it down, and he chased away the pirates. I said to
him, 'May your strength return, Lion.'

   4. "He said to me, 'Good, you have guessed my
name, for thus they call me in my town, Yoḥanan b. Jonathan,
Lion of Kefar Sheḥiya.'"

   5. After a few days he became sick and died.

   6. He [Tarfon] said to him, "Did you not say to
me, Yoḥanan b. Jonathan of Kefar Sheḥiya, Lion?"

   7. He said to him, "No, rather I said thus to you,
Yoḥanan b. Jonathan, Lion of Kefar Sheḥiya."

   8. And he examined him carefully (DQDQ) two or
three times, and his statements agreed, and R. Tarfon performed the marriage of his [the deceased's] wife.

b. Yev. 122b

Comment: b. both refines and confuses certain elements of
Tos. It treats Tos. 14:9 and 14:10 as two separate stories and
has attributed both to Tarfon. But as a result, Tarfon now seems

to hold contradictory opinions, one does (C8) and one does not
(A5) cross-examine witnesses. Lieberman (*T.K.* VI, pp. 182-83)
accounts for this confusion by noting that there is some evidence
that an alternative version of Tos. Yev. 14:10A-B reads:

> A.   "They do not carefully cross-examine witnesses
> [who testify in behalf] of a woman," the words of R.
> Tarfon.
> B.   R. Aqiva says, "They do carefully cross-examine
> witnesses [who testify in behalf] of a woman."

This version of Tos. generated b.A. b.C refines Tos. by shorten-
ing the exchange between Tarfon and the witness, 6-7 (= Tos.
14:10C5-8).

> A.   1.   They give
>
>   2.   a virgin,
>
>   3.   after her [future] husband has asked her [to
> marry him (MŠTB'H)],
>
>   4.   twelve months to provide for herself.
>
> B.   And just as they give [this period of time] to a
> woman, similarly, they give [this amount of time] to a
> man to provide for himself.
>
> C.   And to a widow [they give] thirty days.
>
> D.   1.   [If] the time [for marriage] arrived and they
> were not married [K,P,Pc,L add: or their husbands died],
>
>   2.   they eat from his [property], and [if he is a
> priest], they eat from heave-offering.
>
> E.   R. Tarfon says, "They give her the whole [as]
> heave-offering."
>
> F.   R. Aqiva says, "[They give her] one half common
> produce and one half heave-offering."

M. Ket. 5:2

Comment: A is a simple declarative sentence which B glosses.
C relies upon A1+3. The anonymous law D relates to both A and C.
The dispute between Tarfon and Aqiva glosses D1. Aqiva's opinion
is phrased so as to depend on that of Tarfon to supply the words,
"They give." The key words in these sayings are HKL vs. MḤṢH
WMḤṢH.

Maim., Bert., and others explain that A concerns a woman who
is betrothed ('RWŚ) to a man and who subsequently is asked by him
(TB'H) to perform the ceremony of *nissu'in*, to marry him. D in-
forms us that if the couple has not married within the allotted

period of twelve months, the woman then acquires the right to be
provided for by the husband.[7] It is phrased in terms of what the
woman now consumes. The fact that the husband must provide for
his future wife is a penalty imposed upon him, for he must now,
to a certain extent, treat the woman as if she were already his
wife. Tarfon and Aqiva agree about this principle, but disagree
about the extent of the husband's obligation. Their opinions are
phrased in terms of what the future husband gives the woman. For
a priest, it is of course cheaper to give her heave-offering than
to give her common produce. A priest either receives heave-
offering gratuitously or buys it at a low price.[8] Tarfon, as
Halivni states, "allows the future husband to fulfill (PWṬR) his
obligation to feed his wife by giving her her entire provisions in
the form of heave-offering."[9] Aqiva, however, imposes a more
severe penalty upon the husband, for he claims that he must give
her half common produce and half heave-offering. As we shall see,
Tos. asserts that these are the amounts which a married woman receives. Thus Aqiva has the husband treat the woman as if she were
already married. For Tarfon, what will occur in the future does
not dictate the husband's present obligation.

A. A woman of age (HBGR) is like one who has been
asked to perform *nissu'in* (KYBY'H); *they give her twelve
months* [to prepare].

B. If she was a minor, either she or her father can
postpone [the marriage].

C. *R. Tarfon says, "They give the whole [as] heave-
offering."*

D. Under what circumstances was this said? When she
is betrothed.

E. But when she is married, R. Tarfon admits that
they give her half common produce and half heave-offering.

F. Under what circumstances was this said? With
[regard to] the daughter of a priest [who is betrothed]
to a priest.

G. But with [regard to] the daughter of an Israelite
[betrothed] to a priest, all agree that they give her
(M'LYN) [during the period of her betrothal] all her food
from common produce.

H. Judah b. Bathyra says, "[He gives her] two handfuls
of heave-offering and one of common produce [twice as much
heave-offering as common produce]."

I.   R. Judah says, "She sells the heave-offering and
purchases, with the money [she receives], common produce."

J.   R. Simeon b. Gamaliel says, "Whenever they mentioned heave-offering, he gives double common produce
(NWTN KPWL ḤWLYN)."

K.   This [the opinion that an Israelite betrothed to
a priest may eat heave-offering prior to her *nissu'in*, is
the] first *mishnah*.

L.   Our rabbis said, "The daughter of an Israelite
does not eat heave-offering until she enters into marriage
('D ŠTKNŠ LḤWPH)."

M.   Said R. Menaḥem b. Nappaḥ in the name of R. Liezer
the Qappar, "M'SH B: R. Tarfon [y.: the father of all
Israel] betrothed three hundred women [in order] to enable
them to consume [E: and fed them] heave-offering, for
they were years of want."

N.   1.   WKBR: Yohanan b. Bagbag sent to R. Judah b.
Bathyra at Nisbis.

2.   He said to him, "I heard that you say a
daughter of an Israelite who is betrothed to a priest
eats heave-offering."

O.   1.   He [Judah] sent [a reply] to him, saying,
"I assumed you were an expert in the fine points of the
Torah; do you know how to reason [by means of] a *qal
vaḥomer*?

2.   "If a Canaanite bondswoman who is not entitled
to eat heave-offering, [when betrothed by means of] cohabitation, is entitled to eat heave-offering, [when
betrothed by means of] money, then the daughter of an
Israelite who is entitled to eat heave-offering, [when
betrothed by means of] cohabitation, surely is entitled
to eat heave-offering, [when betrothed by means of] money.

P.   "But what can I do, for lo, sages said, The
daughter of an Israelite betrothed [to a priest] does not
eat heave-offering until she enters into marriage."

Tos. Ket. 5:1, ed. Lieberman,
pp. 71-72, lns. 1-18 (H = y.
Yev. 4:12 6b)

Comment: Tos. serves as commentary to M.   A supplements A of
M. by stating that a woman of age is like a virgin who has been
asked by her future husband to perform *nissu'in*.   M. mentions only
the virgin.   B adds information not contained in M.   C, as Lieberman (*T.K.* VI, p. 258) notes, is a citation from M.   D-G qualify

this statement and thereby reduce the conflict between Tarfon and
Aqiva to the case of a daughter of a priest during her period of
betrothal. We have discussed E above. G's modification of the
dispute has both Tarfon and Aqiva agree with the law attributed
in L to the rabbis. Similarly, someone has modified by means of
P the tradition (N-O) involving Yoḥanan b. Bagbag and Judah b.
Bathyra. The view of L is that until *nissu'in* have been performed, until there has been a complete acquisition (*qinyan*) of
the wife, an Israelite woman does not acquire the prerogative to
eat heave-offering. This modification of the opinions of Tarfon
and Aqiva does not flow from the logic of their rulings, but from
the external considerations of Tos. L.

H-J are the comments of three Ushans. Judah b. Bathyra's
ruling occupies a middle position between those of Tarfon and
Aqiva, a frequent stance of a later authority. He rules that the
woman receives her provisions in the proportion of two-thirds as
heave-offering and one-third as common produce. Judah's saying,
I, which agrees with the principle of Tos. L, glosses M.D2 by
stating that although the husband may fulfill his obligation by
giving the woman heave-offering, the latter must sell it. Thus
for Judah an Israelite woman prior to *nissu'in* does not acquire
the prerogative to eat heave-offering. The meaning of Simeon b.
Gamaliel's saying is unclear.[10]

We have already discussed the importance of L. M is cited in
the names of a contemporary of Judah the Patriarch, Liezer b.
Qappar, and a tanna who is mentioned nowhere else, Menaḥem b.
Nappaḥ. What is the relationship between M and Tarfon's ruling in
M. Ket. and the modifications of that opinion in Tos. D-G? According to M, Tarfon gave heave-offering to some women whom he had
betrothed. The story, however, specifies neither the status of
these women, nor the time after which Tarfon gave them the heave-
offering, nor the amount of the heave-offering. Now we may assume
that the women were daughters of Israelites, for daughters of
priests, by virtue of their own prerogatives, may eat heave-
offering. Furthermore, the story appears to imply that Tarfon
gave them the heave-offering immediately upon betrothing them.
We have noted in our discussion of M. that Tarfon's ruling there
does not imply that he contends that an Israelite woman betrothed
to a priest may eat heave-offering only after the expiration of
the period of twelve months. Thus Tos. M and M. are not inconsis-
tent but are probably independent of each other. M, however,

disagrees with G's modification of Tarfon's opinion, according to
which he admits that an Israelite woman betrothed to a priest receives only common produce.

> A. Said Abaye, "The dispute [applies only] to the
> daughter of a priest who [was betrothed] to a priest, but
> with [regard to] the daughter of an Israelite [who was
> betrothed] to a priest, the opinion of all is [that she
> receives] one-half common produce and one-half heave-
> offering."
>
> B. And said Abaye, "The dispute [applies] to one who
> was betrothed, but [with regard] to one who was married,
> the opinion of all is [that she receives] one-half common
> produce and one-half heave-offering."
>
> C. TNY' NMY HKY: *R. Tarfon says*, "*They give her*
> *the whole [as] heave-offering*."
>
> D. *R. Aqiva says*, "*[They give her] one-half common*
> *produce and one-half heave-offering*."
>
> E. 1. Under what circumstances was this said?
>
> 2. With [regard to only] the daughter of a
> priest [betrothed] to a priest, but with [regard to] the
> daughter of an Israelite [betrothed] to a priest, the
> opinion of all is that [she receives] one-half common
> produce and one-half heave-offering.
>
> F. 1. Under what circumstances was this said?
>
> 2. With [regard to] one who was betrothed, but
> with [regard to] one who was married, the opinion of all
> is that [she receives] one-half common produce and one-
> half heave-offering.

b. Ket. 58a

Comment: C-D are a citation of the opinions in M. Abaye's
sayings A-B and the anonymous comments E2 and F2 are identical.
b. agrees with Tos. concerning the matters about which Tarfon and
Aqiva disagree. These authorities do not concur with regard to a
daughter of a priest betrothed to a priest (A, E2) and about her
rights during her period of betrothal (B, F2). Thus b., like Tos.,
claims that Tarfon and Aqiva agree about the case of an Israelite
betrothed to a priest, and about her rights after marriage.
b. (A, E2), however, does not concur with Tos. G which asserts
that all agree she receives only common produce. According to b.
she receives half as heave-offering and half as common produce.

The effect of this statement is to have the qualifications of A-B
(= E and G) agree in principle with Aqiva's view, D.

    A. 1. TNY: *R. Tarfon says*, "*They give her the*
whole [as] heave-offering,
        2. "because heave-offering is found everywhere
(MṢWYH BKL MQWM)."
    B. 1. *R. Aqiva says*, "*[They give her] one-half*
common produce and one-half heave-offering,
        2. "because women are prone to make unclean
that which is clean."
                         y. Ket. 5:3 29d

Comment: The opinions of Tarfon and Aqiva have now been
glossed. The meaning of the gloss of Tarfon's statement is unclear. Lieberman (*T.K.* VI, p. 255, n. 1) offers two explanations.
Either the comment means that heave-offering is found everywhere
among all priests, that is, there is plenty of heave-offering;
therefore, it is no problem to give the woman heave-offering.
Alternatively, it means that heave-offering is easy to sell in
all places. Thus, giving the woman heave-offering does not cause
her great difficulty.

    A. These are [the women who] go forth [from marriage,
are divorced] without [receiving the amount of their]
ketubah:
    B. 1. One that transgresses the Law of Moses,
        2. and Jewish [practice (WYHWDYT)].
    C. And what is [considered transgressing] the Law
of Moses?
    D. (1) She [who] feeds him [her husband] that which
is not tithed, or (2) has intercourse with him [when she
is] menstrual, or (3) does not set aside dough-offering,
or (4) utters a vow and does not fulfill it.
    E. And what is [considered transgressing] Jewish
[practice]?
    F. (1) She goes out and her head is uncovered, or
(2) strolls about in the market, or (3) talks with any man.
    G. Abba Saul says, "Even the one [the woman] who
curses his parents in his presence."
    H. R. Tarfon [y.: R. Joshua] says, "Even the
scolding [woman (HQWLNYT)]."

I.   What is [considered] a scolding [woman]?   [The
title applies] to one who speaks in her house and her
neighbors hear her voice."

                              M. Ket. 7:6 (I = Tos. Ket. 7:7)

Comment: A Jewish woman, when divorced, is entitled to receive the amount of money prescribed in her *ketubah*. But as we
learn from A-B, certain women, by virtue of their actions, forfeit
this money. A-B state the anonymous law is a simple declarative
sentence. The rest of the pericope is a gloss which gives examples
of the violations mentioned in B. D contains four examples of a
transgression of the Law of Moses, a transgression of a biblical
commandment. But F contains only three examples of violations of
Jewish practice, i.e., immodest behavior. G and H offer alternative, fourth examples. I glosses H by defining "a scolding woman."

A.   [As to] a man who died and left a wife, and a
creditor and heirs,
B.   and had [either goods as] collateral or [as]
a loan in the possession of another--
C.   R. Tarfon says, "They [the property] shall be
given to the weakest among them."
D.   1.   R. Aqiva says,
     2.   "One does not show pity in [matters of] law;
     3.   "rather,
     4.   "they shall be given to the heirs,
     5.   "since all [the others] need [to take] an
oath [in order to acquire the property], but the heirs
do not have [to take] an oath."
E.   [If] he left crops uprooted from the ground,
F.   whoever comes first gains possession of them.
G.   1.   [If] the wife acquired more [than the amount
of] her *ketubah*, or the creditor more than the amount of
the debt,
     2.   [what do we do with] the surplus?
H.   R. Tarfon says, "They shall be given to the
weakest among them."
I.   1.   R. Aqiva says,
     2.   "One does not show pity [in matters of] law;
     3.   "rather,
     4.   "they shall be given to the heirs,

5. "since all the [others] have to swear, and
the heirs do not have to swear."

M. Ket. 9:2-3

Comment: The pericope on the face of it is a good example of
the spelling out of the same legal problem in two parallel cases
(A+B, A+E-G). But both formal and substantive considerations indicate that this is not correct. A+B and A+E-G serve as superscriptions for the opinions of Tarfon and Aqiva, C = H and D = I.
A-B pose no problem. But in E-I the opinions, which contain a
plural passive verb, respond to a protasis whose subject is in the
singular, surplus, G2. Furthermore, E-G are not formally parallel
to their counterpart, B. If, however, we take A+E as the topic
sentence for the opinions in H-I, the formal difficulties are
eliminated. The reconstructed pericope, therefore, has the form:

A'. [As to] a man who dies and left a wife and a creditor
     and heirs,
B'. and had [either goods as] collateral or [as] a loan
     in the possession of another--
C'. R. Tarfon says, "They..."
D'. R. Aqiva says, "One..."
E'. [If] he left crops uprooted from the ground--
F'. R. Tarfon says, "They..."
G'. R. Aqiva says, "One..."

A' serves both B' and E', and together with them forms the superscriptions for the opinions in C'-D' and F'-G'. The opinions of
Tarfon and Aqiva may be reduced to C vs. D1+4. The key words in
the dispute are balanced:

LKWŠL

LYWRŠYN

A discussion of the substance of the pericope supports our argument for reconstructing it.

According to Jewish law, a father's property, particularly
his movable property (MṬLṬLYN), passes at his death to his children. Any other claimant, in order to receive anything, must
substantiate his demand. M. Ket. 9:7, therefore, states that a
wife who wants to receive the value of her *ketubah* from her children must swear that her *ketubah* entitles her to the particular
objects in question. Similarly, a creditor must take an oath regarding any money owed to him by the deceased. Our pericope deals
with a case in which a man dies leaving a wife and creditors. The
items claimed by these parties, however, do not fall exactly into
the category of movable objects; rather, they may be treated as

intermediate cases. B discusses movable objects, collateral. But
these items are not in the possession of the deceased. They,
therefore, are not like other movable objects which are in the
deceased's possession at the time of his death. Money out on a
loan also is not quite like movable objects. Similarly, uprooted
crops, E, are somewhat like crops still in the ground so as to
raise some question concerning their status. We can easily explain Aqiva's ruling regarding A+B. Aqiva treats these items as
movable articles; therefore, he contends that the heirs automatically gain possession of them. (MS points out that the argument in D5, all others must take an oath in order to extract these
properties from the heirs, is secondary.) But, as the amoraim in
b. Ket. 84a-b note, Aqiva's opinion with regard to A+E-G is not
consistent with his view with regard to A+B. Aqiva in I should
rule that the inheritors automatically receive all the uprooted
crops. If, however, we treat only A+E as the superscription for
Aqiva's opinion in I, the discrepancy is eliminated. Thus as our
formal analysis indicated, the superscription for the opinions in
H-I should be A+E.[11]

Tarfon disagrees with Aqiva and argues that the goods fall to
the "weakest" among the parties. The exact meaning of this phrase
is uncertain. The amoraim (b. Ket. 84a-b, y. Ket. 9:2) offer two
interpretations: physically weakest, the woman; legally weakest,
the creditor. Maim., Bert., TYY, TYT explain that Tarfon allows
the weakest to claim the property because, as noted, the items
mentioned in this pericope fall into the gray area between movable
and non-movable objects. They, therefore, do not come under the
normal rules for the inheritance of movable objects. This pericope preserves another fundamental dispute in principles between
Tarfon and Aqiva. Tarfon rules one may act leniently when the
issue at hand is an intermediate case. Aqiva contends that laws
are definite, and there is no latitude for exceptions.

> A. 1. [As to] one who vows [to abstain] from meat,
>
>   2. he is permitted [to eat] broth and meat sedi-
> ment (WBQYPH).
>
> B. But R. Judah [Pc: Joshua; Pr: Yose] forbids.
>
> C. Said R. Judah, "M'SH W: R. Tarfon forbade me [to
> eat] eggs which had been cooked [M: with it] [K,N,L,P,Pc,
> Pr,y.Leid.,y.Ven.: it it]."

D.   They said to him, "Is that so? When [('YMTY)
under what circumstances]?

E.   "[One is forbidden only] when (BZMN) he says,
'Let this particular meat [be forbidden] to me.'"

M. Ned. 6:6 (C-E = b. Ned. 52b)

Comment: The pericope consists of a well-balanced dispute
(A-B), a M'SH (C), which is cited in support of Judah's opinion in
B, and a response in D-E to Judah's opinion. But the wording and
the substance of the M'SH, as well as the wording of E, suggest
that C has been interpolated. C is very elliptical. It requires
the context to supply not only the antecedent of "it," the broth,
but also the setting, Judah took a vow to abstain from meat.
Furthermore, C and A-B do not deal with identical cases. According to A, one who makes a general vow to abstain from something,
in this case meat, is permitted to eat its direct derivatives, the
broth and the meat sediment. C, however, speaks of an item at two
removes from the meat, eggs cooked in meat broth. Thus C does not
relate to Judah's view in B. It, however, could be placed into a
context which discusses cooking eggs with some forbidden substance,
such as with carrion flesh, or with sanctified food, or in a pot
with milk and meat. In all these cases one may not eat the eggs
because they have absorbed the flavor of the forbidden substance.
Furthermore, for none of these other cases must we supplement the
M'SH with the assumption that Judah took a vow to abstain from
some food.

As noted, the wording of E also suggests that C has been
interpolated. The language in E is impersonal, a third person
singular verb, and not a second person singular verb. We would
expect a reply to C to read, "He must have forbidden you, when you
took a vow to abstain from this meat." E, however, is a good
reply to B. In this case it modifies Judah's opinion in B, by
stating that one is forbidden to eat all the derivatives from a
piece of meat, even that which has absorbed its flavor, only when
he takes the specific vow, "Let this meat be forbidden to me."

A.   [If six] persons were on a journey and another
was coming toward them [and] one of them said, "I will be
a Nazirite, that (Š) this is so and so."

And one said, "I will be a Nazirite that this is
not so and so."

[And a third said], "I will be a Nazirite if
one of you is a Nazirite."

[And a fourth said], "If one of you is not a
Nazirite."

[And a fifth said], "If both of you are
Nazirites."

[And a sixth said], "If all of you are Nazirites."--

B.   The House of Shammai say, "They all are Nazirites."

C.   And the House of Hillel say, "None of them is a
Nazirite except he whose words were not confirmed."

D.   And R. Tarfon says, "None of them is a Nazirite."

M. Naz. 5:5

Comment: A serves as a superscription for the opinions in B-D.
The opinions appear in a descending order of stringency.   The rulings of the Houses in this pericope are consistent with those
found in M. Naz. 5:1.   According to the House of Shammai, if someone dedicates something in error, its dedication is binding, while
according to the House of Hillel, it is not binding.   As Neusner
(*Phar*. II, pp. 219-21) observes, the dispute between the Houses
comes down to the question of the force of saying, "I am a Nazir."
For the House of Shammai, the person becomes a Nazirite, whether
or not he intentionally uttered the saying, or whether or not the
relevant facts coincide with his stipulations.   The House of
Hillel, however, rule that in order for a person to become a
Nazirite he must clearly have this intention in mind.   Tarfon goes
beyond the ruling of the House of Hillel and says that not one of
the persons is a Nazirite.   No reason is supplied for Tarfon's
ruling.   But Tos. provides an explanation.

> [Tos. cites M. Naz. 5:5A-C with minor changes and
> glosses.]

A.   R. Judah says in the name of *R. Tarfon*, "*None of
them* [first ed. and G add: *is a Nazirite*],

B.   "since Naziriteship does not apply except [when
there is a] distinct [utterance]."

Tos. Nez. 3:19, ed. Lieberman,
p. 35, lns. 61-67 (b. Eruv. 82a;
Sanh. 25a; Ḥag. 10a; Naz. 34a,
62a; Ned. 19b, 21a; y. Naz.
5:6 54b)

Comment: On the basis of the gloss, B, we may explain Tarfon's
saying in two ways. The persons stating, "I will be a Nazirite,"
had no intention of becoming Nazirites. They used this language
merely to add force to their statements. According to Tarfon, for
a person to become a Nazirite, he must use the formula, "I will be
a Nazirite" with the appropriate intention. But if he utters the
vow merely to accentuate his claim, then he does not become a
Nazirite. Tarfon thus seems to follow the reasoning of the House
of Hillel, that in order to become a Nazirite one must intend to
do so.

Alternatively, Tarfon stipulates that for a vow to be binding,
the conditions contained in the vow must be clear. From the comments of R. Judah and Abaye in b. Naz. 32b-33a, it is evident that
a vow using the form "š," "that it is so and so," may be interpreted in two ways. The person uttering the statement intends to
become a Nazirite, if in fact the person approaching is so and so.
On the other hand, the person uttering the statement may mean, "I
am so certain that the person who is approaching is so and so that,
if he turns out not to be so and so, I will become a Nazirite."
Tarfon's comment is to the effect that if the exact meaning of a
vow is not certain, a person's vow is not binding.

The principle underlying Tarfon's view in this pericope is
consistent with one found throughout his traditions. One may not
make legal decisions, or undertake legal obligations, on the basis
of what *may be the facts at hand*. In the case described here, it
is uncertain who is approaching. One may, therefore, not become
a Nazirite depending on whom this may be.

> A. The cutting of the hair [for a Nazirite who
> contracted] uncleanness, how is it [to be done]? [Danby:
> What was the rite prescribed for the cutting of the hair
> after contracting uncleanness?]
> B. He was sprinkled on the third and the seventh
> [days with water of purification, Num 19:11] and cut his
> hair on the seventh [day], and brought his sacrifices on
> the eighth [day].
> C. 1. "[N,M,Pc: And] if he cut his hair on the
> eighth [day],
>   2. he brings his sacrifice on that same day,"
> the words of R. Aqiva.
> D. Said to him R. Tarfon, "What is the difference
> between this [one's purification rites] and [those of]
> the leper"?

E. 1. He said to him, "[L,K,N,M,P,Pc: That] this
one [the unclean Nazirite], his cleanness depends upon
[waiting the prescribed number of] days, and a leper,
his cleanness depends upon his cutting his hair,

2. "and he does not bring a sacrifice unless he
has waited until sunset."

M. Naz. 6:6 (Sifra Mesora'
Pereq 2:7, ed. Weiss, 71c)

Comment: This pericope is an example of the use of Tarfon's
name by Aqivan-redactors as a literary device. A-B are an anonymous law in the form of a question, A, and an answer, B. C1
raises a secondary question to which Aqiva responds in C2. We
now expect a contrary opinion attributed to Tarfon. This opinion
would read, "a leper who cuts his hair on the eighth day brings
his sacrifice on the ninth day." Instead of this ruling, however,
we have what looks like the beginning of a debate, D. But in the
present formulation of the pericope, D merely sets up Aqiva's explanation, E, of the view attributed to him in C. Thus Aqivan
redactors have either dropped an opinion of Tarfon, if he ever had
one, or more likely simply inserted his name and the question as
a literary device. Since Tarfon's role in the pericope is
strictly literary, I shall not discuss its legal issue.

1. [As to] one who vowed to become a Nazirite and
he was in a cemetery,

2. even if he was there for thirty days,

3. [these days] do not count for him among the
number [of days of his Naziriteship],

4. and he does not bring an offering for uncleanness.

5. [If] he went out and came [back] in,

6. [the days in between his departure and his
return] are counted for him among the days [of his
Naziriteship],

7. but he brings an offering for uncleanness.

8. R. Eliezer says, "[He does not bring an offering
for uncleanness if he went out and returned] on the same
day,

9. "for it is written, 'But the former days [of a
Nazirite who becomes unclean] shall be void' [Num 6:12].

10. "Not until he has former days [is he required to
bring an offering for uncleanness]."

M. Naz. 3:5

A.   [*If*] *he went out and came* [*back*] *in*--

B.   R. Tarfon exempts [him from the sacrifice].

C.   But R. Aqiva declares [him] liable.

D.   Said to him R. Tarfon, "And did he add a defilement (ḤLL) to his defilement? [Since he was not liable
to bring an offering for his first defilement, he should
not be liable to bring an offering because of his departure and return to the cemetery]."

E.   Said R. Aqiva, "When he was there [in the ceme-
tery], he rendered [others] unclean for seven days.
[When] he departed (PYRS), [if he touched others], he
rendered [them] unclean overnight. [If] he went out and
came [back] in, he rendered [others] unclean [Ven.,Leid.:
overnight] [printed text: seven days]."

F.   Said to him R. Tarfon, "Aqiva, Everyone who
separates himself from you is as if he separates from
his life."

y. Naz. 3:5 52d

Comment: A cites M.5. But the opinions in B+C also presuppose
M.1. The pericope, therefore, must circulate along with M. A-C
are a dispute which employs the fixed opposites PṬR vs. ḤYB. The
debate, D-F, is typical for those of Tarfon and Aqiva. Aqiva wins,
and Tarfon, in F, as usual, extols the virtues of Aqiva.

The biblical law to which the dispute between Tarfon and
Aqiva relates is the liability to bring a sacrifice of a Nazirite
who contracts uncleanness. Num 6:1-2 mandate that, if a Nazirite
becomes unclean, he must bring a peace-offering and a purification-
offering as a purification from his uncleanness. But what is the
liability of a person who becomes a Nazirite while in contact with
a source of uncleanness, and then leaves and returns to this
source of uncleanness? Even though he is not a clean Nazirite who
becomes unclean, must he still bring an offering for coming in
contact with uncleanness? According to 7 of M. the person brings
a sacrifice. Aqiva agrees with this anonymous ruling. Eliezer
refines the ruling of 7. The person does not bring an offering if
he returns on the same day. Tarfon apparently goes beyond Eliezer's
ruling, for his opinion that the person is exempt from bringing the
sacrifice is not limited to one who returns on the same day.

We may explain the opinions of Tarfon and Aqiva in terms of
their arguments in the debate D-E. (As we shall see, Tarfon's
argument is a "foil" for Aqiva.) According to Tarfon, the departure

and the return by the person to the cemetery does not change his
status regarding his uncleanness; he has not added a defilement to
his previous defilement. If a Nazirite does not have to bring a
sacrifice when he vows while in a cemetery (M.1-4), then because
his return to the cemetery does not change his status, he still
should not have to bring a sacrifice. Aqiva treats defilement in
a different way, and thus Tarfon's argument sets up that of Aqiva.
For Aqiva, defilement refers not only to the Nazirite's own status
vis à vis uncleanness, but also to his ability to render others
unclean. While in a cemetery the person renders others unclean
for seven days. When outside the cemetery, he renders others unclean overnight. But if he returns to the cemetery, he again renders others unclean for seven days. (The reading in the printed
ed., which QH and PM assert is correct, is appropriate in terms of
both Aqiva's argument and the laws of uncleanness.) Thus the dispute between Tarfon and Aqiva comes down to the definition of uncleanness. For Tarfon, only the Nazirite's own status regarding
uncleanness is legally significant. According to Aqiva, the
Nazirite's ability to render others unclean also is legally
important.

> A. 1. [If] he [a priest] was standing and bringing
> his dead,
>> 2. while he still ('D Š) is standing at the grave,
>> 3. he receives [corpses] from others and buries
> [them].
> B. 1. [If] he left [the grave],
>> 2. lo, this one may not become unclean [again].
> C. [If] he became unclean on that same day--
> D. R. Tarfon says, "He is liable [to bring a
> sacrifice]."
> E. R. Aqiva says, "He is exempt."
> F. 1. [If] he became unclean after that day,
>> 2. all agree that he is liable,
>> 3. because he negates (ŠWTR) one day [of the
> days of his purification].

>> M. Sem. 4:10, ed. Higger,
>> pp. 119-20, lns. 38-41

Comment: The rulings of Tarfon and Aqiva now appear in relation to a case similar to that of y. Naz. 3:5. A priest may only
under special circumstances become unclean (Lev 21:9). What are

the legal requirements of a priest, who already unclean because of
corpse-uncleanness, contracts additional corpse-uncleanness? Must
he bring a sacrifice? The attributions in Sem. are reversed.
Tarfon declares him liable; Aqiva exempts.

> A. R. Tarfon says, "All the memory offerings
> [(ZKRWNWT) any sacrifice which brings forth some remem-
> brance] that are in the Torah, are mentioned [in relation]
> to good [occasions], except for that [concerning which]
> it is written, 'A meal offering of remembrance bringing
> iniquity to remembrance'" [Num 5:15]. [This verse refers
> to the sacrifice offered by the suspected adulteress.]
> B. R. Aqiva says, "Even this [one] is [mentioned]
> for good, for it is written, 'If the woman [the suspected
> adulteress] is not unclean, but is clean, then she shall
> be cleared and shall conceive seed'" [Num 5:28].

> Tos. Soṭ. 1:10, ed. Lieberman,
> p. 154, lns. 42-45

Comment: A-B are in a modified dispute form. Tarfon's opinion contains the superscription. B is phrased so as to respond to
A. The sayings are well balanced. The Scriptural verses are
integral.

The dispute between Tarfon and Aqiva is of no legal significance. They merely offer different classifications for the
memory-offering brought by the woman suspected of adultery. Each
cites a verse to support his classification. According to Tarfon,
since Num 5:15 states that the memory offering brought by the
suspected adulteress recalls iniquity, this indicates that it is
brought in relation to a bad occasion. Aqiva, however, notes that
Num 15:28 says that if the woman is innocent, then she shall be
declared not guilty and shall conceive. This indicates that even
the memory offering brought by the suspected adulteress is brought
with regard to a good occasion.

> A. "A meal offering of remembrance" [Num 5:15]--
> B. 1. *"All the memory offerings that are in the*
> *Torah [are] for good,*
> 2. "and this one is for punishment (LPWR'NWT),"
> 3. the words of R. Tarfon.
> C. *R. Aqiva says, "Even this one is for good, for it*
> *is written,* 'And if the woman is not unclean'" [Num 5:28].

> Sifre Naso' 8, ed. Horowitz,
> p. 14 (Num. R. 9:34)

Comment: Sifre B2 describes the memory offering of the woman as one for punishment and not simply, as in Tos., one which does not bring forth good remembrances.

A. TNY: *R. Tarfon says, "All the memory offerings
that are mentioned in the Torah [are in reference] to good
[occasions] except for* this one [whicn is] for punishment."

B. Said to him R. Aqiva, "If it is said, 'a meal
offering of jealousy' [Num 5:15], and [had] stopped, I
would agree with your words. Lo, it does not say 'a meal
offering of remembrance' [ibid.] except for good."

y. Soṭ. 3:4 8d

Comment: y.'s version sharpens up Aqiva's view by noting
that, since the passage does not end with v. 15, this memory
offering is for good. y.'s version of the tradition presupposes
another version, for it does not give Aqiva's reason for classify-
ing it as a sacrifice which brings forth good.

1. [If] one witness said I saw her that she was made
unclean,

2. she [the suspected adulteress] did not drink.

3. But not only this (WL' 'WD), even a slave, even
a bondswoman, lo, these are trustworthy;

4. even to cause her to lose her *ketubah*.

M. Soṭ. 6:2

A. The *mishnah* [was taught] after R. Aqiva admitted
to R. Tarfon [that his opinion was correct].

B. R. Tarfon says, "One witness is trustworthy to
make her [the suspected adulteress] unclean, but one
witnesses is not trustworthy to cause her to lose her
ketubah."

C. R. Aqiva says, "Just as one witness is trustworthy
to make her unclean, so too one witness is trustworthy to
cause her to lose her *ketubah*."

D. Said to him R. Tarfon, "Where have we found one
witness [trustworthy concerning] monetary [cases]? Nowhere.
[The woman, therefore, should not lose her *ketubah*]."

E. Said to him R. Aqiva, "And where have we found one
witness [trustworthy concerning matters] of a man's wife?
Nowhere.

F.   "Rather, just as [we make an exception in this case and rule that] one witness is trustworthy to make her unclean, so too one witness is trustworthy to cause her to lose her *ketubah*."

G.   R. Aqiva began to teach (ḤZR LHYWT ŠWNH) like R. Tarfon.

y. Soṭ. 6:2 21a

Comment: Our discussion will first deal with B-F and then turn to the relationship between B-F and M. Soṭ. 6:2. B-F are a dispute + debate involving Tarfon and Aqiva. B-C present the opinions of the two masters in the form of balanced, declarative sentences. Aqiva's saying responds to that of Tarfon. The two authorities agree that one witness causes the woman to be de-clared unclean, but they disagree about the ability of one witness to cause her to lose her *ketubah*. The dispute between Tarfon and Aqiva, therefore, could be phrased as follows:

The testimony of one witness with regard to a woman suspected of adultery--
R. Tarfon says, "It does not cause her to lose her *ketubah*."
R. Aqiva says, "It does cause her to lose her *ketubah*."

The opinions include statements about declaring the woman unclean because the debate presupposes the agreement of the two authori-ties on this issue.

The debate contains identically formulated arguments, D-E. F spells out Aqiva's reasoning. Aqiva wins the debate. But G asserts that Aqiva adopted Tarfon's view. We would expect G to read, "R. Tarfon began to teach like R. Aqiva." As we shall now see, the claim of A also is backwards.

A asserts that M. Soṭ. 6:2 agrees with the opinion of R. Tarfon. But as all the commentators note, M. agrees with Aqiva. 1-3 of M. make no mention of the woman's *ketubah*. The use of "even" in 4, however, implies that the rule of 4 also applies to 1. Thus the force of 3-4 is that a slave, like a normal person, can cause the woman not to drink and, like a normal person, he even can cause her to lose her *ketubah*. M., therefore, agrees with Aqiva that the testimony of one witness causes the woman to lose her *ketubah*. But A asserts that M. follows the opinion of Tarfon. Thus the claim of A, like the claim of G, is backwards. The sim-plest solution to this discrepancy is that someone has reversed the names in A and G. Epstein proposes the more complicated

solution that the person responsible for A had before him a different version of M.[12] We now turn to the legal issue of this
pericope.

This pericope is a further illustration of a dispute between
Tarfon and Aqiva about the effect of doubt on the law; namely,
there is insufficient evidence, that of one witness. Tarfon's
opinion is consistent with his rulings in the other pericopae
dealing with this issue. Since there is doubt and not certitude
regarding the woman's status, we continue to act under the normal
presumption. The woman is not definitely an adulteress; therefore, she does not forfeit her *ketubah*. We may explain Aqiva's
opinion as follows: Since the woman may be an adulteress, giving
her the *ketubah* may involve a transgression. The possibility of
this transgression necessitates that we can no longer act as if
there were no uncertainty.

The debate is typical for those between Tarfon and Aqiva.
Tarfon, in D, begins the debate by offering what appears to be a
very convincing argument. But the argument is a foil which Aqiva
turns against Tarfon. Tarfon contends, in D, that there is no
monetary case in which the testimony of one witness is probative.
The testimony of one witness, therefore, should not cause the suspected adulteress to lose her *ketubah*. Aqiva, in E, builds upon
Tarfon's observation by noting that, with the exception of the
woman suspected of adultery, the testimony of one witness is not
probative in cases of marital relationships. Since we make an
exception in the case of this woman with regard to her marital
status, we therefore may make an exception with regard to her
monetary status. The woman should not receive her *ketubah*.

      A. On that day (BW BYWM)

      B. R. Tarfon observed a lame [priest] standing and
blowing [WMRY'] the horns. [Num 10:1-10 tell Moses to
make horns which the priests should use on special
occasions.]

      C. On that basis [Vienna: he observed (R'H) and
said] [E: R. Tarfon observed and said; first ed.: they
said],

      D. "A lame [priest] blows (TWQ') [the horn] in
the Temple."

                        Tos. Soṭ. 7:16, ed. Lieberman,
                        p. 196, lns. 131-35

Comment: A is redactional language. It joins B-D to the preceding pericopae which discuss the festival of assembly, *Haqhel*.[13]
A, therefore, gives the setting of Tarfon's observation. (*Haqhel*
was celebrated on Sukkot in the year following the Sabbatical
year.) B can stand alone. It could belong to a corpus of Tarfon-
traditions which detail his observations of Temple practices.[14]
C is joining language which links D to B. D, which uses terminology slightly different from B,[15] can stand by itself. It is a law
in the form of a simple declarative sentence.

Lev 21:17-24 stipulate that a priest with a physical defect,
such as lameness, may not offer sacrifices or present the showbread
in the Temple. Num 10:1-10, which mandate that Moses should make
horns to be used by the priests, the sons of Aaron, in order to
summon the nation on special occasions, do not mention whether or
not the priests, who perform this function, must be without physical defect. Tarfon's report, B, and the statement in D indicate
that a priest with a physical defect may blow the horns. There
are no other pericopae, except the parallels of this tradition,
which deal with the issue at hand.

A. Said R. Jonah, "And is he [the high priest] not
inside [the Temple] when he performs the ceremony, and is
it [not] outside [that] he asks? Could they make a mistake between [something done] inside and [something done]
outside"?

B. And did not R. Tarfon, the father [y. Hor.: the
master] of all Israel, make a mistake [in failing to dis-
tinguish] between the blowing of the horns at the festival
of *Haqhel* and the blowing [to announce] the sacrifices?

C. DTNY: "The sons of Aaron [who] shall blow the
horns" [Num 10:8]--

D. "[They shall be] whole and not with defects,"
the words of R. Aqiva.

E. 1. Said to him R. Tarfon,

2. "May I bury my sons,

3. "if I did not observe Simeon, my maternal
uncle, [who] was lame in one foot, and he [was] standing
in the Temple-court, his horn in his hand, and blowing it?"

F. Said to him R. Aqiva, "Perhaps you did not observe
him except at the festival of *Haqhel*, and I say [that the
priest who blows the horns] at the time [of the offering
of] the sacrifices [has to be without defects]."

G. Said to him R. Tarfon, "May I bury my sons, for
you did not deviate either to the left or to the right.
I am the one who observed [y. Hor.: heard about] this
incident, and forgot [what happened], and I did not know
how to explain it, and you [now] explain it so that it
accords with the tradition (WMŚKYM LŠMW'H). Behold, anyone who separates himself from you is as if he separates
from his life."

> y. Yoma 1:1 38d (y. Meg. 1:12
> 72b, y. Hor. 3:5 47b)

Comment: The numbers in the following discussion refer to the
chart on pp. 105-107. This version of the pericope is another example of the reworking of a Tarfon-tradition by Aqivan hands. Tarfon serves simply as a foil for Aqiva. The Aqivan redactors have
taken the brief tradition, Tos. 11, expanded it, and then built
the remainder of the pericope (4-10, 12-21) around it. 2-3 are
the amoraic context. 4 is phrased like a superscription, but only
an opinion of Aqiva, 6, follows. 8-13 give us a debate. In 8,
10-11, Tarfon presents evidence which indicates that a lame priest
may blow the horn. As noted, he cites the expanded version of
Tos. 11. Aqiva in 12 suggests that Tarfon has forgotten the facts
relating to the incident, and in 13 he offers an explanation for
the report. 15-21 have Tarfon accept Aqiva's explanation. By
means of 13, the editors have also limited Aqiva's opinion in 6.
Aqiva now claims that only the priests who blow the horns at the
time of sacrifices must be without defect. Furthermore, the redactors of this version of the tradition have neglected the context of Tarfon's tradition in Tos., a discussion about *Haqhel*.
They have Aqiva suggest, in 11, that Tarfon observed his uncle at
this festival.

A. "The priests" [Num 10:8]--
B. "whether whole or whether with defects [may blow
the horns]," the words of R. Tarfon.
C. R. Aqiva says, "[They are to be] whole and not
with defects.
D. "It says, 'a priest' there [Lev 1:5, "And Aaron's
sons, the priests, shall present the blood" etc.] and it
says 'a priest' here. Just as the priests there are whole
and not with defects, so too the priests here are whole
and not with defects."

E. 1. Said to him R. Tarfon, "How long will you put
words together and bring them against us (MGBB WMBY' 'LYNW)?
I cannot endure [this any longer].

2. "May I bury my sons

3. "if I did not observe Simeon, my maternal
uncle, who was lame in one foot, standing and blowing the
horns."

F. He said to him, "Rabbi, [you are] correct, [but]
perhaps you observed this at the festival of *Haqhel*, for
[priests] with defects are fit [to blow the horns] at the
festival of *Haqhel*, and on the Day of Atonement, and at
the Jubilee festival."

G. He said to him, "[I swear] by the Temple service
that you did not invent this. How worthy is Abraham, our
father, [that he] has Aqiva as his descendant. Tarfon
observed [the incident] and forgot; Aqiva explains it by
himself so that [the report] accords with the law. Behold,
anyone who separates himself from you is as if he separates
from his life."

> Sifre Baha'alotkha 75, ed.
> Horowitz, p. 70, lns. 1-8

Comment: Sifre is the most elaborate version of the tradition. Sifre 4-6 has a well-balanced dispute. y. has only an
opinion of Aqiva. Aqiva, in 7, is supplied with a Scriptural
proof text to support his opinion. In 9, Tarfon reacts rather
antagonistically to Aqiva. Finally, in 18, Tarfon is very effu-
sive in his praise of Aqiva.

Tos. Soṭ. 7:16

20. - - -

21. - - -

y. Yoma 1:1

20. and you explain it so that it accords with the tradition.

21. Behold, anyone who separates himself from you is as if he separates himself from his life.

Sifre 75

20. Aqiva explains it by himself so that [the report] accords with the law.

21. " " "

A. [*As to*] *one who divorces his wife and said to
her,* "*Lo, you are permitted* [*to marry*] *anybody except for
so and so*"--

B. *R. Eliezer permits* her to be married by any man
except by that man [forbidden to her by her former husband].

C. R. Eliezer admits that, if she married another
[man] and was widowed or was divorced, she is permitted
to be married by the one who was [previously] forbidden
to her.

D. After the death of R. Eliezer four elders came in
to respond to his words, R. Tarfon, R. Yose the Galilean,
R. Eleazar b. Azariah, and R. Aqiva.

E. 1. Said R. Tarfon, "[If] she went and was married
by his [the one forbidden to her] brother and he died without offspring, how can she enter into Levirate marriage
with him?

2. "Would not he [the first husband] turn out to
be making a stipulation contrary to that written in the
Torah? [first ed., E: And (anyone) who makes a stipulation
contrary to that written in the Torah, his stipulation is
invalid].

3. "Thus we have learned that this is not cutting
off [a valid divorce]."

F. 1. Said R. Yose the Galilean, "Where have we
found in the Torah a forbidden connection ('RWH) who is
permitted to one [person] and forbidden to one [person]?

2. "Rather, one who is permitted [E: to one
person], is permitted to all men. And one who is forbidden [E: to one person], is forbidden to all men.

3. "Thus we have learned that this is not cutting
off."

G. R. Eleazar b. Azariah says, "'Cutting off' [Deut
24:3], it is something that separates him from her [Vienna,
first ed.: Thus we have learned that this is not cutting
off]."

H. Said R. Yose [E: the Galilean], "I [agree with]
the words of R. Eleazar b. Azariah."

I. 1. Answered [N'NH] R. Simeon b. Eleazar saying,
"Lo, [if] she went and married another and he divorced her
and said to her, 'Lo, you are permitted to every man,' how
can this one permit what the first one forbade?

2.   "Thus we have learned that this is not cutting off."

J.   1.   [E: Said] R. Aqiva [Vienna, first ed.: says] "Suppose that the one forbidden to her was a priest and the one divorcing her died;

2.   "would she not be considered a widow [with regard to] him [the priest] and a divorced woman to his fellow priests?

3.   "Thus we have learned that this is not cutting off" [E lacks J3].

K.   1.   "Another matter: And with regard to what [case] was the Torah more stringent, in general [with regard to] a divorce, or in general [with regard to] a widow?

2.   "A divorcee is more stringent[ly dealt with than] a widow.

3.   "[Now in this case] if the widow [who is dealt with] more stringently is forbidden to the one [the priest] permitted to her, is it not the case [that] the divorcee [who is] more stringent[ly dealt with] should be forbidden to the one permitted to her?

4.   "Thus we have learned that this is not cutting off."

L.   1.   "Another matter: [If] she went and married another man and had children with him and [he] died, when she returns to the one forbidden to her, are not the children of the first [husband] considered bastards [since how can she marry the one forbidden to her? Is it not the case that the bill of divorce was invalid? Hence when she remarried for the first time she was not properly divorced as she was still married to her former husband, and therefore, the children born from her first remarriage are bastards].

2.   "Thus we have learned that this is not cutting off."

Tos. Giṭ. 9:1, ed. Lieberman, pp. 272-73, lns. 1-22 (A-B = M. Giṭ. 9:1, y. Giṭ. 9:1 50a, b. Giṭ. 83a, Sifre Deut. 269, ed. Finkelstein, p. 289, lns. 8-20

Comment: Tos. Giṭ. 9:1 supplements M. Giṭ. 9:1 which reads:

A. [As to] one who divorces his wife and said to her,
"Lo, you are permitted to [marry] anybody except for so
and so"--
B. R. Eliezer permits.
C. But sages forbid.

A and B of Tos., with a slight addition, are a citation from M.
C glosses B.[16] D is a literary device which provides a setting
for the opinions which follow, E-L. We may eliminate several elements in E-L. I is assigned to an Ushan. All the other authorities who offer objections are Yavneans. Similarly, H is not integral; it is attributed to an Ushan and also is not an objection.
We are now left with E, F, G, and J-L. All of the objections are
conceptually independent of each other. There are, however, formal similarities between some of these opinions, and this may
enable us to identify the various units of this tradition. E and
F both use the attributive formula, "Said R. x." Furthermore,
both sayings consist of (1) a statement which notes an anomaly
that follows from adherence to Eliezer's ruling, and (2) a lemma
which spells out the implications of this anomaly. G, unlike E
and F, uses the attributive formula, "R. x says." Its content
also differs from that of E and F. G is an exegesis of the words
KRYTWT, "cutting off." It can stand by itself. The redactor who
placed it in this pericope has not changed the attributive formula
so as to make it identical to those of E and F. Aqiva's saying,
J, like those of Yose and Tarfon, points out an anomaly. There is
conflicting evidence regarding its attributive formula. Only in
Ms. E does Aqiva's saying, like those of Yose and Tarfon, have the
attributive formula, "Said R. x." Furthermore, J, unlike E and F,
is followed by a very lengthy statement, K, which spells it out.
This, along with the conflicting evidence regarding the attributive formula, suggests that Aqiva's saying does not belong to the
same unit as E+F. We, therefore, may isolate three formal units,
E+F, G, and J-L. Let us now briefly turn to Tarfon's objection.
    Tarfon notes that under the appropriate circumstances, i.e.,
if the woman was married to the brother of the man forbidden to
her and he then died, she would not be able to enter into Levirate
marriage. The conditions dictated by the husband at the time of
the divorce, therefore, contain a stipulation contrary to a law of
the Torah. Eliezer's ruling, as a result, is wrong. The admission
in C, however, make Tarfon's objection impossible. According to C,
Eliezer admits that if the husband of the first remarriage dies,

the woman may then marry the man forbidden to her by the first
husband. Thus under the appropriate circumstances, she could enter
into Levirate marriage. The fact that C makes Tarfon's objection
impossible indicates that either the version of the pericope, which
the person responsible for Tarfon's objection had, lacked C, or C
was formulated as a response to E.

The opinion of sages in M. Giṭ. 9:1, with which all the authorities mentioned in E-L agree, is to the benefit of the woman;
her former husband may not dictate her future actions. It also is
in accordance with both the anonymous law and Joshua's view in
M. Giṭ. 9:3 which prescribe that the *geṭ* must contain the clause,
"You are permitted to marry any man."

> A. *Abaye found R. Joseph who was sitting and com-*
> *pelling* [men to give] *writs* [of divorce].
>
> B. *He* [Abaye] *said to him*, "*But we are* [only] *laymen*
> (HDYWṬWT)."
>
> C. 1. WTNY': R. Tarfon [Tanḥuma: Simeon; She'iltot:
> Meir] did say, "Any place that you find market places
> ('GWRY'WT) [in which legal transactions occur[17]]
> [M: recording offices] of heathens,
>
> 2. "even though their laws are like the laws of
> Israel,
>
> 3. "You are not permitted to put yourself in a
> position of dependence upon them (LHYZQQ LHN).
>
> D. "For it says,
>
> E. "'And these are the judgments (MŠPṬYM) which you
> shall set before them' [Exod 21:1],
>
> F. "before them but not before heathens."
>
> G. Another explanation: Before them but not before
> laymen. [The *sugya* continues with Joseph explaining why
> they, as laymen, are allowed to compell men to give writs
> of divorce.]

>   b. Giṭ. 88b (She'iltot Genesis
>   2, Tanḥuma Mishpatim 6)

Comment: A-B, and the materials following G, are the amoraic
context in which the baraita, C-G, appears. C is a saying, in
standard attributive form, which is followed by a proof text, E,
and two exegeses, F and G. Only the first, F, is relevant to
Tarfon's statement.[18] The evidence from She'iltot and Tanḥuma indicates that there is some uncertainty regarding the attribution
of C.

Tarfon's statement that one should not become dependent upon
gentile courts apparently means only that one should not use these
facilities; one should not adjudicate cases in them. The exegesis
in E-F indicates that judicial matters should be handled in Jewish
and not in gentile courts. This exegesis is based on the hermeneutical principle of *miyyut*, exclusion, the presence of a word
in a verse for the purpose of limiting its application. The words
"before them" thus indicate that cases should be heard only in
Jewish courts. The other opinions in M.-Tos. which relate to the
use of gentile courts deal with the issue of whether or not decisions issued or validated in them are valid (see M. Giṭ. 1:5, 9:8;
Tos. Giṭ. 1:4; Mekh. R. Ishmael Neziqin 1). Tarfon's saying does
not mention the terms valid or invalid; therefore, the relationship between his saying and those of the pericopae noted above is
unclear. It is, however, evident from these pericopae that the
issue is Yavnean. Tos. Giṭ. 1:4 contains a tradition of Aqiva.
The saying in Mekh. is attributed to Eleazar b. Azariah.

    A.   R. Tarfon says, "*Mamzerim* can be purified [N,Pc:
Mamzerim are able to purify themselves]."
    B.   How so?
    C.   [P,K,M: (If) a *mamzer* married] [N,L,Pc,Pr,y.Leid.:
(As to) a *mamzer* who married] a bondswoman, the offspring
[produced by them] is a slave.
    D.   [If] he [the woman's master] sets him [the slave]
free, he [L,P,K: the son] is a free man.
    E.   R. Eliezer says, "Lo, he is a slave [Pc,N,L: and
and a] *mamzer*."
                              M. Qid. 3:13

Comment: Lying behind the apparent dispute between Eliezer and
Tarfon are an autonomous saying attributed to Tarfon, A, and a dispute between the anonymous law, C, and the contrary view assigned to
Eliezer, E. D glosses C. The redactor has created an artificial
dispute between Tarfon and Eliezer by joining C-E to A by means of B.
    Tarfon's saying can be interpreted in two ways. A means either
that a *mamzer*, one born from a prohibited relationahip, can purify
himself, or that *mamzerim*, although they cannot purify themselves,
may purify their lineage. It is thus possible for *mamzerim*, or at
least their offspring, to reenter the congregation of God. It is
unclear to me how Tarfon interprets Deut 23:3 which states, "A *mamzer* may not enter into the congregation of God; even until the
tenth generation, he may not enter into the congregation of God."

C gives an example of a *mamzer* who purifies his stock. A child born from the union of a *mamzer* and a bondswoman is simply a slave. He acquires the status of his mother. The ruling of C is in agreement with the anonymous law of M. Qid. 3:12 which states, "And every [woman] who does not have valid betrothal with him or with anyone else, the child is like her. And who is this? This is a bondswoman and a gentile woman." According to this law, a child of a bondswoman, no matter who the father is, has its mother's status; it is a slave. Thus even if the father is a *mamzer*, the offspring is merely a slave. Eliezer, however, contends that the offspring of the union described in C is a slave and a *mamzer*. We may explain that according to Eliezer, the explicit statement in Deut 23:3 that a *mamzer* and his offspring may not enter the congregation of God overrides any rules which may be deduced from the law of M. Qid. 3:12.

> A.   TNW RBNN: Because of all of these [maimings of the tips of limbs and the knocking out of an eye or of a tooth], a slave goes free.
>
> B.   "And he needs [from his master] a writ of emancipation," the words of R. Simeon [Giṭ. V 130: R.].
>
> C.   R. Meir says, "He does not need [the writ]."
>
> D.   R. E. (') [Giṭ. V 130, Qid. V 111: Eleazar] says, "He does need [it]."
>
> E.   R. Tarfon says, "He does not need [it]."
>
> F.   R. Aqiva says, "He does need [it]."
>
> G.   1.   Those arguing before the sages (HMKRY'N) say, "The words of R. Tarfon are acceptable (NR'YN) with regard to [the loss of] a tooth or [of] an eye,
>
>   2.   "since the Torah gave him the right [to go free for the loss of either a tooth or an eye].
>
> H.   1.   "But [we agree with] the words of R. Aqiva with regard to the [maiming] of the other limbs,
>
>   2.   "because in this case it is a fine (QNŚ) of the sages [imposed upon the master]."
>
> I.   *Is that a fine?*
>
> J.   *Do they thus deduce it from Scripture?*
>
> K.   Rather, [he needs the writ] because it is [only] a deduction of the sages.
>
>   b. Qid. 24b (b. Giṭ. 42b)

Comment: A requires a context to supply the referent of "these." Once we insert the proper words, A can stand alone. B-F are a catalogue of sayings attributed to Ushans (B-D) and to Yavneans (E-F). They have been joined to A, which serves as their

protasis, by use of "and" in B.   B uses the formulary pattern,
"words of R. x."   C-D and E-F are nearly balanced sayings in dispute form.   They rely upon B to supply the antecedent of "it."
G-H attest the opinions of Tarfon and Aqiva, and not those of Meir
and Eleazar, and interpret them as responses to A.   I-K glosses H.

The issue discussed in this pericope is whether or not a
slave who is freed by his master must receive a writ of emancipation.   Biblical law makes no mention of such a writ.   The anonymous law of M. Qid. 1:3 states that a slave may acquire his freedom by means of a writ.   M. does not explain the need for this
document.   R. Tam and Rashba state that the writ serves as proof
for the slave's freedom and thereby enables him to avoid any possible attempt of reclamation by his former master.   Alternatively,
as I-K of our pericope indicate, rabbinic law, by means of an
exegesis, derives the need for a writ of emancipation.   If we
treat the sayings in our pericope as responses to the general
question of whether or not a slave needs a writ, then we see that
Simeon, Eleazar, and Aqiva require the writ, while Tarfon and Meir
do not.   Those who reject the necessity of this document may contend that Scripture makes no mention of the writ, and the reasons
suggested for it are not valid.   Thus what may happen is not important for Tarfon.   If Tarfon in principle rejects the institution of the writ of emancipation, it follows that he does not require it for the cases described in A.   The redactor, however, has
placed Tarfon's opinion as a response to A.   If we read Tarfon's
opinion in this way and assume that he recognizes the institution
of a writ of emancipation, I cannot determine why he does not require the writ for the cases mentioned in A.

G-H treat B-F as responses to A.   They, however, explain
Tarfon's ruling only with regard to the knocking out of a tooth or
of an eye.   In order to understand G-H we must first review the
biblical and rabbinic law relevant to A.   Exod 21:26-27 stipulate
that a master must free his slave if he knocks out the slave's eye
or tooth.   An anonymous law in Tos. Qid. 1:6 states that a slave
acquires his freedom because of injuries to the tips of his limbs.
G-H adjudicate between the opinions of Tarfon and Aqiva as follows.
Since the Torah stipulates that a slave goes free because of the
loss of an eye or a tooth, the slave does not need the writ.   No
one can have any recourse.   But in cases involving maiming of a
limb, the slave receives a writ; it is a fine imposed upon the
master.   I-J ask why this is a fine.   J-K indicate that the need
for a writ is based on a deduction from Scripture.   b. Qid. 24b
continues by giving such an exegesis.[19]

[1]The expression "co-wife of the daughter" appears nowhere else in M.-Tos. b. Yev. 15a,b, 16a, however, use the expression, and in these traditions it means the co-wife of the daughter of the person who is speaking.

[2]The use of the *hif'il*, 'SY'NH, the causative, suggests that Tarfon is going to arrange the marriage of the girl into the priesthood. But the *hif'il* can also mean that Tarfon would marry the girl. A *qal* is the preferred construction to express this idea.

[3]Biblical law and rabbinic law do not forbid marrying one's niece.

[4]The phrase DRYŠH WHQYRH appears in the Torah (Deut 13:15) in the passage which deals with a report about people who encouraged Israel to worship foreign gods. Deut 13:15 states that, "If you have searched and examined (WDRŠT WHQRT) the matter and the report is true, then the people should be punished."

[5]Tos. lacks 9. But this detail is necessary to the story and may have been omitted accidentally, or it may simply be assumed.

[6]In 14:9 the men pursue the pirates, while in 14:10 the pirates fall upon the men. 2 of 14:9 has an olive branch, while the other formulation of the story has a fig branch. The dialogue between the deceased and the witness is not the same in both stories. In 14:9(3) the witness says, "May your strength return," while in 14:10(3) he says, "I thank you, Lion." The deceased responds in 14:9(4), "How do you know my name is Lion?" But in 14:10(4) he says, "You have spoken well, you have guessed my name."

[7]Halivni (pp. 200-202) notes that D does not relate to the question of when an Israelite woman betrothed to a priest acquires the right to eat heave-offering. It simply deals with the issue of the point in time that the husband acquires the obligation to provide sustenance for his future wife. Halivni demonstrates that the discussion in the *gemara* upon this pericope presupposes that an Israelite woman betrothed to a priest may eat heave-offering from the time of the betrothal. Sifre Num. 117 derives this rule from Num 17:11, while Ulla, in the *gemara* upon our pericope, derives it from Lev 22:11.

[8]Since only priests buy heave-offering, and since it is abundant, its price is low.

[9]Halivni, pp. 200-202.

[10]It may mean, that whenever it says that the woman receives heave-offering, this indicates that she must receive no heave-offering but double her amount of common produce, or that she must receive two times more heave-offering than common produce.

[11]The present formulation of the pericope may be the result of an attempt to harmonize E+H-I with the anonymous law of M. Ket. 8:7, which states that uprooted crops become the property of the first to claim them. The editor of the pericope, therefore, added

F, and then formulated a new superscription, G. G is simply based
on the principle that a woman or a creditor may not claim more
than the amount due to them.

[12]Epstein (*Mevo'ot*, pp. 411-12) argues as follows: The remainder of M. Soṭ. 6:2 reads:

> Her mother-in-law, the daughter of her mother-in-law,
> her co-wife, her husband's brother, the daughter of her
> husband, lo, these are trustworthy but not to cause her to
> lose her *ketubah*; rather, so that she will not drink.

Epstein contends that the M., which the person who inserted A of
y. had, lacked 4. It, therefore, read as follows:

A. [If] one witness said...she did not drink.
B. But not only this even a slave, even...are trustworthy.
C. Her mother-in-law, the daughter....
D. These are trustworthy.
E. But not to cause her to lose her *ketubah*.
F. Rather, so that she will not drink.

According to this version of M., the testimony of one witness, or
of those included in B and C are not sufficient to cause the woman
to lose her *ketubah*. This agrees with Tarfon's opinion. The
claim of A of y., therefore, is correct. This solution, however,
does not account for the discrepancy between the assertion of G of y.
and the structure of the debate.

[13]Tos. Soṭ. 7:13 opens by quoting M. Soṭ. 7:8 which states
that they made in the Temple court a platform of wood for the king.
A saying of R. Eliezer b. Jacob follows which claims that the platform was on the Temple mount. Neh 8:3-6 and 2 Chr 23:13 are then
quoted. Nehemiah states that Ezra read the Torah on a wooden platform in front of the water gate. 2 Chronicles reads, "And she
[Athaliah] looked, and behold the king [Yosah] stood on his platform at the entrance, and the captains and the trumpets by the
king...." The redactor has then joined Tos. Soṭ. 7:15 to the
above by using the words "on that same day ('WTW HYWM)." Tos. Soṭ.
7:15 states, "On that day the priests stood on the entrances and
on the walls of the Temple and had golden horns in their hands,
and if a priest did not have a golden horn, the people would say
that the person was not a priest." The redactor clearly takes
7:15 to refer to the ceremony for the king. Similarly, Tos. Soṭ.
7:16, our pericope, is assumed by the redactor to refer to this
ceremony. Thus "on that day" indicates that Tarfon's observation
was dependent upon the ceremony for the king. Tos. Beṣ. 4:14 uses
"on that day" in just this way. See Lieberman (*T.K.* VIII, p. 683)
for a discussion of the views relating to the historicity of Tarfon's report.

[14]See b. Qid. 71a.

[15]It uses the verb TQ' and not RW'. It also does not mention
"horns," therefore, it could also apply to the blowing of the
shofar.

[16]None of the objections in E-L presupposes this admission.
In fact, as we shall see, it renders Tarfon's objection impossible.

[17]Both Homer and early Christian materials indicate that *agora*
can refer to a market place which is the scene of lawsuits (see
Arndt-Gingrich, p. 12).

[18]Only E+G, however, are relevant to the amoraic context.
The citation of C-G by the redactor and not just E+G indicates
that the entire baraita circulated as a unit.

[19]The *gemara* offers the following exegesis (b. Qid. 24b):

    A. What is the reason of R. Simeon?
    B. He learned [the rule concerning] "sending out"
[from the rule concerning] "sending out." [Deut 24:1
states that when a man divorces his wife, "he shall send
her from his house with a bill of divorce." Similarly,
Exod 21:26, which speaks of the emancipation of the
slave, states that "the master shall send the slave to
freedom."]
    C. Just as a woman [is sent out] with a document,
so too a slave [is sent out] with a document.

Mekh. R. Simeon b. Yoḥai records the same line of reasoning but
with the attributive formula "R. Simeon says." It reads:

    It says "sending forth" here, and it says "sending
forth" there [Deut 24:1]. Just as the sending forth
mentioned there [is with a] writ, so the sending forth
here [is with a] writ.

Mekh. R. Ishmael (Deniziqin 9, ed. Horowitz, p. 279), however,
attributes the identical saying to R. Eliezer. Thus Eliezer
agrees with Aqiva.

NEZIQIN

A. [As to] an ox which causes damage in the domain of the injured party--

B. How?

C. It gored, pushed, bit, lay down, or kicked--

D. [If it occurs] in the public domain, he pays [a restitution equal to] half [of the amount of] damage.

E. In the domain of the injured party--

F. R. Tarfon says, "[The owner of the ox pays a restitution equal to the] full [amount of] damage."

G. But sages say, "[A restitution equal to] half [of the amount of] damage."

H. Said to them R. Tarfon, "Since it dealt leniently, exempting payment in the case of damages [caused by] the tooth and the foot in the public domain, [and] it has dealt stringently, requiring [payment equal to the] full [amount of] damage for these [damages when] incurred in the domain of the injured party; [then surely] in a case in which it has dealt stringently requiring [payment equal to half [of the amount of the] damage for damages caused by the horn in the public domain, is it not logical ('YNW DYN) that we should deal stringently with it [these damages] requiring [payment equal to the] full [amount of the] damage [when incurred] in the domain of the injured party?"

I. 1. They said to him, "What is inferred can be [only as strict as] that from which it is inferred (DYW LB' MN HDYN LHYWT KNDWN).

     2. "If [for damages done] in the public domain [he pays a restitution equal to] half [of the amount of the] damage, then also [for damages done] in the domain of the injured party [he should pay a restitution equal to] half [of the amount of the] damage."

J. 1. He said to them, "I shall not infer [the rule for] the case of a horn from the [rule for] the case of a horn, [rather] I shall infer [the rule for] the case of a horn from [the rule for] the case of a foot.

2. "And since in a case in which it dealt
leniently with damages [caused by] the tooth and the
foot in the public domain, it has dealt stringently with
damages [caused by] the horn, [then] in the case in which
it has dealt stringently with damages [caused by] the
tooth and the foot in the domain of the injured party,
is it not logical that we should deal stringently with
damages [caused by] the horn [in this domain]?"

K. 1. They said to him, "What is inferred can be
[only as strict as] that from which it is inferred.

2. "If [for damages done] in the public domain
[he pays a restitution equal to] half [of the amount of]
the damage, then also [for damages done] in the domain
of the injured party [he should pay a restitution equal
to] half [of the amount of] the damage."

M. B.Q. 2:5

Comment: A, F, G are a balanced dispute. B-E gloss this dispute by specifying the type of damage the ox caused.[1] In the debate H-K, Tarfon is assigned two arguments, H and J, in support of
his view. Sages in I and K refute both. Exod 21:35-36 distinguishes between damages caused by an ox about which the owner has
not been warned, and those inflicted by an ox about which the
owner has been warned. If the former does damage, the owner pays
a restitution equal to half of the amount of the damage. If the
latter causes harm, the owner pays a full restitution. Scripture
makes no mention of the place in which the damage occurs. This is
the question which Tarfon and sages discuss. Tarfon rules that
the person whose ox causes damage in the domain of the person whose
property is injured must pay a full restitution. Thus Tarfon applies the rule governing an ox about which the owner has been
warned to the ox discussed in our pericope. Sages rule that the
owner of such an ox pays only half damages. They, therefore,
classify the ox mentioned in A as one about which the owner has
not been warned. As we shall see, the parallel versions of this
tradition refine sages' opinion by distinguishing between oxes
about which the owners have been warned and those about which the
owners have not been warned.

The debate in H-K is probably artificial.[2] In both I and K
sages give the same argument. Both of Tarfon's arguments contain
the same error. Furthermore, the term "horn," which is used to
cover those damages mentioned in C, appears nowhere else in M.-Tos.

It, however, is repeatedly used in the *gemarot*. In both arguments Tarfon derives the rule for damages of the horn inflicted in the domain of the injured party from the rule governing damages of the horn which occur in the public domain. But as sages point out, since the owner of such an ox, when an accident occurs in the public domain, pays a restitution equal to half of the value of the damaged property, we may derive from this only a rule of equal stringency for accidents which occur in the domain of the injured party. Thus the owner of the ox in such cases must pay restitution of half-damages.

Tos. B.Q. 1:9 records a dispute between Meir and sages which parallels and refines our pericope. It reads:

> 1. *An ox that causes damage in the domain of the injured party*--
>   2. *How?*
>   3. *It gored, pushed, bit, lay down, or kicked*--
>   4. R. Meir says, "[The owner of the ox] pays [a restitution equal to the] full [amount of] damage."
>   5. *But sages say*, "For [damages caused by] the tooth or the foot he pays [a restitution equal to the] full [amount of the] damage. For [damages caused by] goring, or pushing, or laying down, or kicking, [if the ox was] an attested danger, he pays [a restitution equal to the] full [amount of the] damage, [if it was] a harmless [ox], he pays [a restitution equal to] half [the amount of the] damage."

Tos. B.Q. 1:9c, ed. Zuckermandel, p. 347, lns. 17-20

Tos. 1, 2, and 3 are identical to A, B, and C of M. Tos. has refined M. by dropping D-E and by expanding sages' opinion.[3] Tarfon's opinion in M. is assigned to Meir.

> A. R. Eleazar and R. Simeon say, R. Tarfon says, "For all ('L HKL) he pays [a restitution equal to the] full [amount of the] damages."
>
> B. 1. But sages say, "For [damages done by] the tooth or the foot he pays [a restitution equal to the] full [amount of the] damage;
>   2. "for [damages done by] goring, or pushing, or biting, or laying down, or kicking,
>   3. "[if the ox was an] attested danger, he pays [a restitution equal to the] full [amount of the] damage,
>   4. "[if it was a] harmless [ox], he pays [a restitution equal to] half [of the amount of the] damage."

Tos. B.Q. 1:9b, ed. Zuckermandel, p. 347, lns. 15-17

Comment: A cannot stand alone, for it does not specify the
referent of Tarfon's saying. I follow Magen Avraham, Minḥat Bikkurim, Ḥazon Yeḥezqel and Epstein (*Mavo*, p. 639, n. 4) in treating
A as a comment upon M. B.Q. 2:5. A-B are a different way of saying, "Tarfon and sages did not disagree about x but about y." Thus
according to A-B, the only area of dispute between Tarfon and
sages is about a harmless ox which causes damage by goring, pushing, biting, laying down, or kicking in the domain of the party
whose property is injured. We have explained in note 1 to our
discussion of M. B.Q. 2:5 that the gloss, B-E, in M. in effect
reduces the dispute between Tarfon and sages to this question.
The opinion of sages in B of Tos. also is identical to that ascribed to sages in the dispute with Meir, Tos. B.Q. 1:9c.

1. [As to one] who brought his ox into the yard
of a householder without [his] permission--
2. [If] it fell into his pit and spoiled its water,
3. he is liable.
4. [If] his father or son were in it,
5. he pays the *kofer* [redemption money].

M. B.Q. 5:3

A. [If an ox brought into the plaintiff's property
without his permission] *fell into the pit and spoiled its
water* ·[= M. B.Q. 5:3],
B. "he [the owner of the ox] is liable [to pay] a
fine for the redemption of his life (KWPR)," the words
of R. Tarfon.
C. But R. Aqiva exempts [him] from the fine.
D. [If] there was a servant or a bondwoman in it,
E. "he gives thirty *selas*," the words of R. Tarfon.
F. But R. Aqiva exempts [him] from [paying] the
thirty *selas*.

Tos. B.Q. 5:12, ed. Zuckermandel, p. 354, lns. 6-8

Comment: Tos. B.Q. 5:12 comments upon M. B.Q. 5:2,3. A is a
citation of M.2. The opinions of Tarfon and Aqiva, B-C, however,
also presuppose and relate to M.4. Tarfon's view agrees with the
anonymous law of M.5. The rulings of Tarfon and Aqiva use the
fixed opposites PṬR vs. ḤYYB. Tos. D-E add another ruling to M.'s
scenario of 2-5. In E-F, the key words are NWTN vs. PWṬR.

Exod 21:28-32 give a scenario of laws concerning an ox which
is an attested danger, and which then causes damage. If such an
ox kills a man, the owner of the ox should be put to death. The
Bible, however, stipulates that, alternatively, the owner of the
ox pays a fine, a *kofer*, for the redemption of his life. The same
law applies if the ox kills a minor. But if the ox kills a slave
or a bondwoman, the owner of the ox must give thirty *selas* to the
slave's master. Tarfon and Aqiva apply these rules to a slightly
different case from the one described in the Bible. A does not
specify that the ox is an attested danger; rather, it deals with
one which causes damage in another man's property after it has
been brought there without the property owner's permission. The
issue, therefore, becomes, does such an ox constitute an attested
danger? Since Tarfon applies the rules of Exod 21:28-32 in this
case, then, according to Tarfon's opinions, an ox which causes
damage in another man's property is considered an attested danger.
According to Aqiva's rulings, the two types of oxen are not
comparable.

Tarfon's opinion in Tos. B.Q. 5:12 probably has been generated from M. B.Q. 2:5 and M. B.Q. 5:3. These two pericopae discuss almost identical cases, except that, according to 5:3, the
ox was brought into the domain of the person whose property was
injured *without his permission*. If a redactor knew these two
pericopae, he could easily construct Tarfon's opinion for M. 5:3.
Tarfon rules in 2:5, which does not specify that the ox was brought
in without the owner's permission, that we treat the ox like one
which is an attested danger. He therefore surely considers an ox
brought in without the owner's permission an attested danger (Tos.
5:12).

A. "[If he] brought his ox into the yard of the
householder without permission, and it [the ox] gored the
householder, and he died,

B. "the ox is stoned,

C. "and the owner [of the ox],

D. "whether it was a harmless one, or whether it
was an attested danger,

E. "pays the full *kofer*," the words of R. Tarfon.

b. B.Q. 26a

Comment: This version is the latest of all the Tarfon-
traditions on this subject. It contains the refinement that the

ox was brought in without the householder's permission. Furthermore, it explicitly states that it makes no difference whether
prior to the accident the ox was a harmless one or whether it was
an attested danger. The redactor, by including this fact, has
captured the important point in Tarfon's decision. It is not the
status of the ox that determines the owner's liability; rather, it
is the location of the accident. Finally, B adds the law regarding the ox; it is stoned.

> A. 1. [As to objects which have been found]--
> everything that earns its keep, shall earn its keep.
> 2. But that which does not earn its keep shall
> be sold,
> 3. for it is written, "And you shall restore it
> to him" [Deut 22:2].
> 4. [This teaches us] see, how you shall restore
> it to him [so that he does not lose money].
> B. What shall be done [until it is returned] with
> the money [the finder receives after selling the object]?
> C. R. Tarfon says, "He may use it;
> D. "therefore, if it is lost, he is responsible
> for it."
> E. R. Aqiva says, "He may not use it;
> F. "therefore, if it is lost, he is not responsible
> for it."

M. B.M. 2:7

Comment: A gives an anonymous law, which the dispute (B, C,
and E) glosses. The opinions in C and E are perfectly balanced.
D and F gloss these rulings,[4] and again are in perfect balance.

This pericope and the one which follows it discuss the obligations of a person who finds an object. The finder should act in
such a way that the owner of the item does not incur any financial
liability to him. Furthermore, the finder may use the object only
if he does not harm it, and only if he does not derive personal
benefit from it in excess of his costs for maintaining it. A,
accordingly, states that the finder should not sell an animal
which earns its keep. But if the animal does not earn its keep,
he should sell it. If he does not sell it, but instead feeds it,
then the owner of the animal, when he comes to claim it, must pay
the finder for the feed. The opinions of Tarfon and Aqiva do not
deal with a lost object, but with its substitute, the money received

in selling it. We thus have another dispute between Tarfon and
Aqiva concerning an intermediate case. Do we treat the money received in selling it as equivalent to the object itself and, accordingly, not allow the finder of the object to derive benefit
from it, or do we treat the money differently from the object and
allow the finder to derive benefit from it? Aqiva rules the finder may not use the money. Thus Aqiva treats the substitute for
the object as equivalent to the object itself. Tarfon, however,
rules that the finder may use the coins. Thus Tarfon does not
apply the rules governing the use of the object to its substitute.
The two are not synonymous cases.

> A. Rav Judah [said] in the name of Rav, "The law
> is according to R. Tarfon, in the case of something that
> has identifying marks."
> B. R. Abba and Rav Judah [said] in the name of Rav,
> "M'SH HYH W: Rabbi taught according to the words of R.
> Tarfon with regard to something that had identifying marks."

                           y. B.M. 2:9 8c

Comment: According to R. Abba, Rav Judah, and Rabbi Judah
the Patriarch, B, Tarfon's opinion--that one may use the money--
is the law for cases in which the lost object has identifying
marks. PM explains that, since the object has these marks, the
owner will not give up hope but will search for it. If the finder
sells the object, the owner still will be able to retrieve its
value, the coins, because it is identifiable.

> A. Defrauding (H'WN'H) [is constituted by an over-
> charge or an undercharge of] four pieces of silver out of
> the twenty-four pieces of silver [which comprise] a *sela*,
> B. [an overcharge of] one-sixth the [correct] pur-
> chase price.
> C. Until when is [he who is defrauded] permitted to
> return [the article and receive his money back]? Until
> [sufficient time has elapsed so that] he is able to show
> it to a merchant or to his relative.
> D. Taught R. Tarfon at Lydda, "Defrauding [is an
> overcharge or an undercharge of] eight pieces of silver
> out of a *sela*,
> E. "one-third the purchase price."
> F. And the merchants of Lydda were happy.

G. 1. He said to them,

2. "He [the one who is defrauded] may return
[the article] all day."

H. They said [L: to him], "R. Tarfon, leave us, as
we were before."

I. And they returned to the words of sages.

M. R.M. 4:3 (Sifra Behar
Parasha 3:5)

Comment: The pericope gives us a dispute in an odd form, an
anonymous law phrased as a simple declarative sentence and as a
question and answer vs. a narrative. The two units, however, have
been formulated together. Thus A and the saying in D are identical, except for the numbers, 4 vs. 8. B, which glosses A, parallels E.[5] C and G2 are not perfectly balanced. Instead of the
formulary pattern of question and an answer in C, we expect "and
he may return it until he shows it to a merchant or to his rela-
tive."

Lev 25:14 states, "And if you sell something to your neighbor
or buy of your neighbor's hand, you shall not deceive [overcharge]
one another." Maim. ("Laws of Sale" [Maim. V] 12:1-4) summarizes
the rabbinic laws on this subject. If the overcharge or undercharge does not equal or exceed the prescribed amount allowed for
an overcharge, then the sale is final. If the overcharge equals
the prescribed amount, either party can demand the return of the
amount overpaid. If the overcharge exceeds the prescribed amount,
then the sale may be invalidated. The dispute between Tarfon and
the anonymous law concerns both the percentage which is considered
an overcharge and the period allowed for return of the object.
Scripture does not address either of these issues. A-B inform us
that an overcharge of one-sixth the purchase price constitutes defrauding; therefore, the person may return the item. C adds the
further stipulation that before the sale is considered final the
customer must be given at least enough time to show the article to
an expert. Tarfon, in D, allows the merchants a profit margin of
one-third, twice that permitted by A-B. But Tarfon also stipulates
that the person has the entire day to return the article. H-I indicate that it is preferable to make a smaller profit and to be
able to conclude a sale quickly, than to make a larger profit but
to have to wait the entire day to finalize the sale.

If we review Tarfon's three rulings in the area of torts, we
see that two out of the three opinions relate to very basic issues

of law. M. B.M. 2:5 and its numerous parallels state Tarfon's
opinion concerning damage done in the plaintiff's property, while
M. B.M. 4:3 deals with the amount of the permitted overcharge.
In both of these cases, Tarfon's opinions presuppose only biblical
law. M. B.M. 2:7 is only one step removed from biblical law.
Tarfon and Aqiva discuss the secondary issue of what is to be done
with the money one receives after selling an animal he has found.

CHAPTER IV

[1]B-E are a very good gloss. M. B.Q. 1:4 specifies those
damages which are considered attested dangers (MW'DYM) for which
the person pays a restitution equal to the value of the damage,
and those which are considered harmless damages (ṬMYM) for which
the person pays a compensation equal to half of the value of the
damage. The five damages mentioned in C are classified as harmless; hence, when these types of injury occur, the owner of the ox
pays a compensation equal to half the value of the damage. Among
the damages which are considered to be "attested dangers" are
those caused by an ox while walking in its normal manner, and
damage occurring within the domain of the injured party. If we
combine the above rules, we see that the only case in which there
can be a doubt concerning the amount of the restitution is when a
"harmless damage" occurs in the domain of the injured party. The
redactor of our pericope by glossing A, F, and G with B-E, has
focused upon this very case. In this manner he has eliminated the
contradiction between sages' opinion in G and the rule of M. B.Q.
1:4. Thus, according to our pericope, sages do not always rule
that the owner of the ox pays a restitution equal to half of the
amount of the damage. It may be only for the types of damage mentioned in C that he pays this compensation. B-E, in addition to
clarifying the opinion of sages, also supply in C-D the information necessary for the debate in H-K.

[2]An excellent discussion of the debate appears in Abraham
Weiss, *Studies in the Law of the Talmud on Damages* (New York, 1966).

[3]Sages' opinion in Tos. indicates that all parties agree that
the owner of the ox pays a full restitution for damages of the
tooth and the foot, and for damages caused by goring when done by
an ox who is an attested danger (one which has gored three times
and about whom the owner has been warned). Thus sages' statement
agrees with M. B.Q. 1:4. The only area of dispute concerns goring, when inflicted by a harmless ox, which occurs within the domain of the injured party. This agrees with our explanation in
the previous footnote. The expanded version of the sages' opinion,
however, ignores 2-3.

[4]The comments of the amoraim in D and F point out that, for
the following reason, F is problematic: They discuss the opinions
of Tarfon and Aqiva in relation to the four types of watchmen.
Since, according to Tarfon, the person may use the money--that is,
he has use of something and does not pay anything for it--he is
considered a borrower. A borrower is responsible for something
whether or not he uses it. Furthermore, a borrower is responsible
even if the loss was because of an accident. Thus the amoraim read
Tarfon's saying as follows: "Therefore, if it is lost, even if he
did not use it, and even if by accident, he is responsible." Aqiva
rules the person may not use the money; therefore, he is considered
an unpaid watchman, somebody who guards something but receives
nothing in return for his services. An unpaid watchman may not
derive any benefit from what he watches. But at the same time he
is liable only for loss because of negligence. The "therefore"-
clause of Aqiva's statement is as a result taken to mean, "therefore, if he does not use it, he is not responsible." If the watchman, however, uses the money, he is of course responsible for it.

The two "therefore"-clauses, D and F, thus apply to different
cases; Tarfon's to whether or not he uses it, while Aqiva's only
to his not using the money. The amoraim note that in effect
Aqiva's statement tells us nothing we would not know by deduction.
It is suggested in the *gemara* that the "therefore"-clause in
Aqiva's statement appears solely for formal reasons, to balance
the "therefore"-clause in Tarfon's saying.

[5]Rav and Samuel (b. B.M. 40b) explain the necessity for these
glosses. They point out that A, and similarly D, do not make
clear whether the overcharge is computed on the basis of the number of coins paid, or on the basis of the correct value of the
article. Thus, for example, if a person paid twenty-eight pieces
of silver for an article worth twenty-four pieces of silver, the
overcharge equals one-sixth the purchase price (twenty-four pieces).
But if we compute the overcharge in terms of the number of coins
paid, then it is an overcharge of one-seventh the number of coins
paid (4/28). It is obvious that computing the overcharge in terms
of the correct purchase price is to the benefit of the customer.
In our case the merchant can overcharge only up to twenty-eight
pieces of silver. But if the overcharge is computed in terms of
the number of coins paid, he could charge up to twenty-eight and
four-fifths pieces of silver. Thus B and E clarify A and D respectively by stating that the overcharge is computed on the basis
of the purchase price.

QODASHIM

A. 1. R. Tarfon says,

    2. "If he cooked in it [a metal pot] from the beginning of the festival (HRGL),

    3. "he may cook therein

    4. "the entire festival."

B. But sages say, "Until ('D) the time of eating."

C. Scouring and rinsing--

D. 1. Scouring [must be done] like the scouring of the cup.

    2. Rinsing [must be done] like the rinsing of the cup.

M. Zev. 11:7 (Sifra Ṣav
Pereq 7:2, ed. Weiss, 32d)

Comment: This pericope poses both formal and substantive problems. We first must determine the extent of the sages' opinion, whether it consists of B+C or only B, and the part of A to which it responds. We then must try to establish the issue discussed in the dispute between Tarfon and sages.[1]

On formal and literary grounds, I follow the view of TYY, and also that of the printer of the first printed edition of Sifra, and treat only B as sages' opinion.[2] If we take only B as the sages' lemma, then A-B are a common variation of the dispute form, "R. x says + superscription + ruling, R. y says + ruling." In this pericope, A4 and B are in dispute.

As we have noted in our discussion of M. Beṣ. 3:5, on a festival one may use only those objects which he had in mind at the beginning of that day. It is obvious that when someone intends to use something he has in mind a particular purpose. Thus, for example, when a person at the beginning of a festival cooks food in a pot, he intends to eat that food at some point during the day. One may on a festival prepare food only for consumption on that day. Sages and Tarfon disagree in our pericope about the effect of one's prior intention upon his use of the pot on the festival (A3). Does one's prior intention determine how long he may use the pot, or does the fact that the pot is already in use and, therefore, not *muqṣeh*, govern how he may use it? Sages hold the former opinion. They rule that one may cook in the pot only until the time of eating, that is, he may use the pot only until the point at

which it has fulfilled the purpose he had in mind at the beginning
of the festival. Tarfon, however, rules that the person's prior
intention is inconsequential; therefore, he may cook in the pot
the entire day. Since the pot is already permitted for use on the
festival, and hence not *muqseh*, the person may continue to cook in
the pot even after the time of eating. Thus this pericope is
another illustration of a decision of Tarfon based upon the objective facts, the condition of the object, and not upon subjective
intentions.

A. *R. Tarfon says, "[If] he cooked in it at the
beginning of* (BTKYLT) *the festival, he cooks in it the
entire festival"* [= M. Zev. 11:7A].

B. After the festival, it does not require scouring
and rinsing.

C. Said R. Nathan, "R. Tarfon spoke exclusively
about less holy [sacrifices]."

Tos. Zev. 10:13, ed. Zuckermandel, p. 495, lns. 16-18

Comment: Tos. comments on M. by extending, in B, Tarfon's
comment to an issue not mentioned in M., and by modifying it in C.
Nathan attests to Tarfon's comment, and to its application to the
question of *notar*. B is not a good gloss, for it ignores the substance of A.[3] C, however, is a very good modification of Tarfon's
view. As we have explained (p. 179 n. 1), Tarfon's opinion makes
sense only if one assumes that less holy sacrifices, such as
peace-offerings, are cooked in the pot. But if one cooks more
holy sacrifices in the pot, by the second day the residue
becomes "remnant."

A. *What is the reason of R. Tarfon?*

B. 1. *Because Scripture states,* "And you shall turn
in the morning and go unto your tents" [Deut 16:7]. [This
verse refers to Passover. The one following it says, "You
shall eat unleavened bread for six days."]

2. [This indicates that] the Bible treats the
whole [of the festival] as one morning.

C. *Demurred R. Aḥabdoi b. Ammi,* "Is there no *piggul*
during the festival, is there no remnant during the
festival?"

D. 1. *And should you say that indeed is so, but it
was taught* (WHTNY):

2.   R. Nathan says, "R. Tarfon spoke only about
this [only about scouring and rinsing, but he made no
mention about the general rules of remnant and *piggul*]."

E.   1.   Rather, the reason is as R. Naḥman taught.

2.   For said R. Naḥman said Rabbah b. Abbuha,
"Each day affects scalding (GY'WL) for it fellow [i.e.,
previous day]."

Zev. 97a

Comment: B and E are two different responses to A. B provides a Scriptural basis for Tarfon's opinion. Since the Bible
treats the entire festival as a single day, one does not have to
scour and rinse the pot each day of the festival. According to E,
the view articulated by the commentators in their analyses of M.,
the food cooked in the pot each day of the festival in effect removes any remnants of the previous day's sacrifices. C raises the
logical question, if B is correct--that the entire festival is
considered as one day--there should not be any *piggul* or remnant
during this period. D answers this objection by citing a version
of Nathan's comment which is slightly different from that given in
Tos. Nathan's saying indicates that Tarfon's ruling does not imply that in general there is not any remnant on the festival.
Tarfon's ruling applies only to the case of cooking sacrifices in
the pot. If we compare the two versions of Nathan's comment, we
have:

Tos. - Said R. Nathan, L' HYH RBY TRPWN 'WMR 'L' BQDŠYN QLYM BLBD
b.   - R. Nathan says, L' 'MR RBY TRPWN   'L' ZW   BLBD

A.   Expounded R. Aqiva, "From what verse [do we learn
that] the receiving of the blood must be [done] only by a
perfect [unblemished] priest [dressed] in the vestments of
service?

B.   "The text reads, 'And the sons of Aaron shall
bring the blood to him' [Lev 1:5]. [This exegesis presupposes that "bring the blood" means "receive the blood."]

C.   "One might suppose this [verse refers to] sprinkling [the blood]. [One may interpret "to bring" in two
ways. It may mean to bring the blood in a vessel, i.e.,
to receive the blood. Alternatively, "to bring" may
refer to bringing the blood before the altar, i.e., to
sprinkle the blood.]

D. "When it [Scripture] states, 'And they shall
sprinkle' [Lev 1:5], this refers to sprinkling. But here
it [the verse] states, 'And he shall bring,' [which
refers to] only receiving the blood.

E. 1. "[Since the verse speaks of both sprinkling
and receiving], it compares receiving to sprinkling.

2. "Just as sprinkling [is done] by a perfect
priest [dressed] in the vestments of service, so too in
carrying, receiving [is done] by a perfect priest [dressed]
in the vestments of service.

F. 1. "And there it says, ['You shall bring them
(Aaron's) sons also and put coats on them. And anoint
them to serve Him'] [Exod 40:14,15].

2. "Just as the priest referred to there is a
perfect priest [dressed] in the vestments of service, so
too the priest referred to here [in the verse cited in B]
is a perfect priest [dressed] in the vestments of service."

G. 1. Said to him R. Tarfon,

2. "Aqiva, how long will you continue to gather
[words] and bring [them] against me?

3. "May I bury my sons,

4. "if I did not hear a distinction (HPRŠ)
between receiving and sprinkling, and you equate receiving
and sprinkling."

H. He said to him, "Permit me to say before you what
you have taught me."

I. He said to him, "Speak."

J. 1. He said to him, "[For] receiving, intention is
not [tantamount to] action. [But in the case of] sprinkling,
intention is [tantamount to] action.

2. "One [a priest] who receives it [the blood]
outside [the sanctuary], is fit [Lieberman: exempt], but
one who sprinkles it outside [the sanctuary] is unfit
[Lieberman: liable].

3. "[If] unfit ones [priests] received it, they
are not liable on its account. [If] unfit ones sprinkled
it, they are liable on its account."

K. He said to him, "[I swear] by the Temple-service,
that you have not deviated either right or left. I heard
[it] and could not explain [it], and you expound so that

it accords with the law. Behold, anyone who separates
from you is as if he separates [himself] from his life."

> Tos. Zev. 1:8, ed. Zucker-
> mandel, p. 480, lns. 16-27
> (B-E = Sifra Vayiqra'
> Parashata 4:4-5, ed. Weiss, 6a

Comment: Since as our analysis will show, Tarfon serves
merely as a literary device in this pericope, we shall deal only
with its formal and literary aspects. The central portions of
this pericope are two thematically related teachings of Aqiva,
both of which deal with receiving sacrificial blood: (1) A-F, and
(2) J. These units have been joined together by means of G-I and K.

B-F contain two different responses to A: (1) B+F, (2) B-E.
B+F answer A by comparing two Scriptural verses. Exod 40:15 states
that the sons of Aaron shall be consecrated while wearing the vestments of service. Since Lev 1:5, which deals with receiving sacrificial blood, also uses the words, "the sons of Aaron," we may deduce that the priests who receive the blood must be dressed in the
vestments of service. B-E respond to A by drawing an analogy between receiving and sprinkling; both actions are mentioned in the
parallel stichs of Lev 1:5. Since, as E2 presupposes, the priest
who sprinkles the blood must be unblemished and dressed in the
vestments of service, it follows that the priest who receives the
blood must meet the same requirements. C-E are necessary for Tarfon's question in G; accordingly, the redactor has inserted them
into A, B, and F in order to set up the remark in G. G in turn
leads us to Aqiva's second saying, J, which deals with sprinkling
and receiving. The remainder of G-K (G-I and K) serves both as an
anti-Tarfon polemic, and also as a device for uniting the two
thematically related teachings of Aqiva. G2-3 and K are standard
for anti-Tarfon traditions. Tarfon is portrayed in H-I and K as
having forgotten his own teaching. This is similar to a charge
found in y. Yoma 1:1 (Tos. Soṭ. 7:16). In that pericope Aqiva re-
minds Tarfon of the setting of an event which he, Tarfon, but not
Aqiva, observed. Of note, y. Yoma 1:1, like our pericope, discusses whether or not priests who perform certain Temple functions
must be unblemished. The same circle of redactors probably have
constructed both pericopae.

A. 1. Said R. Aqiva, "From what verse [do we learn
that] the receiving of the blood must be [done] only by a
fit priest [GRA adds: (dressed) in the vestments of service]?

2. "It says here 'priestly outfit' (KYHWN).
[This word does not appear in the Bible. Rabad claims
it refers to Lev 1:5.] And it says there 'priestly outfit.' [According to Rabad the second KYHWN refers to
Num 3:3 which is cited in the parallel version of this
tradition, b. Zev. 13a. Num 3:3 states, "These are the
names of the sons of Aaron, the anointed priests, when
he ordained (ML' YDM) to minister in the priest's office."
On the basis of Exod 29:29, Rabad determines that
"ordained," ML' YDM, refers to wearing the vestments of
service. Exod 29:29 reads, "The holy garments of Aaron
shall be for his sons after him, to be anointed in them
and ordained in them (WLML' BM 'T YDM).]

3. "Just as the 'priestly outfit' stated there
[refers to] a fit priest [dressed] in the vestments of
service, so too the 'priestly outfit' stated here [refers
to] a fit priest [dressed] in the vestments of service."

B. 1. Said to him R. Tarfon,

2. "How long will you gather [words] and bring
[them] against us?

3. "May I bury my son,

4. "if I did not hear that there is a distinction
between receiving and sprinkling, and I cannot explain it."

C. He said to him, "Permit me to say before you what
you have taught me."

D. He said to him, "Speak."

E. 1. He said to him, "[For] receiving, intention
is not [tantamount to] action. [But in the case of]
sprinkling, intention is [tantamount to] action.

2. "The one who receives it outside [the sanc-
tuary] is exempt. But the one who sprinkles it outside
[the sanctuary] is liable.

3. "[If] unclean ones [priests] received it, they
are not liable on its account. [If] unclean ones sprinkled
it, they are liable on its account."

F. Said to him R. Tarfon, "May I bury my son, for
you have not deviated either right or left. I am the one
who heard [it], and could not explain [it], but you expound so that it accords with the tradition (LŠMW'H).
Behold, anyone who separates from you is as if he separates
[himself] from his life."

Sifra Vayiqra' Parashata 4:4-5,
ed. Weiss, 6a

Comment: The numbers refer to the chart on pp. 139-40. 9-18
of Sifra, except for minor changes, are identical to 9-18 of Tos.
1-2; 7-8 of Sifra parallel the same sections in Tos. They, however, use an analogy different from that given in Tos. in order to
derive the rule given in 8. Sifra compares two usages of the word
KYHWN. We have noted in our translation that this word does not
appear in the Bible. Accordingly, we have cited Rabad's explanation. Sifra lacks 3-6 of Tos. and, as a result, Tarfon's question
in 11 is unintelligible.

    A. 1. Said R. Aqiva, "From what verse [do we learn
that] the receiving must be [done] only by a fit (KŠR)
priest and [dressed] in vestments of service?

    2. "It says, 'The sons of Aaron' here [Lev 1:5]
[while] there it says, 'These are the names of the sons of
Aaron, the priests that were anointed' [Num 3:3]. [For
an explanation of the use of this verse, see Sifra.]

    3. "Just as there [it refers to] fit priests
[dressed] in the vestments of service, so too here [it
refers to] fit priests [dressed] in the vestments of
service."

    B. 1. Said R. Tarfon,

    2. "May I bury my sons,

    3. "if I did not hear [that one should] make a
distinction between receiving and sprinkling, and I cannot
explain [what it is]."

    C. 1. Said R. Aqiva, "I will explain.

    2. "[In the case of] receiving, intention is
not [tantamount to] action; [whereas in the case of]
sprinkling, intention is [tantamount to] action.

    3. "[If] he received [the blood] outside [the
sanctuary], he is not liable for extirpation; [whereas
if] he sprinkled [it] outside [the sanctuary], he is
punished by extirpation.

    4. "[If] unfit ones received it, they are not
liable on its account. [If] unfit ones sprinkled it, they
are liable on its account."

    D. Said to him R. Tarfon, "[I swear] by the Temple
service, you have not deviated either right or left. I
heard [it], yet could not explain it; you expound so that
it accords with the tradition (LŠMW'H)."

E.   In these words he addressed him: Aqiva, anyone
who separates himself from you is as if he separates from
his life.

b. Zev. 13a

Comment: As the following chart indicates, there are several
differences between b. and Tos.

Tos. Zev. 1:8	Sifra 4:4-5	b. Zev. 13a
1. Expounded R. Aqiva, From what verse [do we learn that] the receiving of the blood must be [done] only by a perfect priest [dressed] in the vestments of service?	1. Said R. Aqiva, " " " a fit priest " "	1. Said R. Aqiva, " " " a fit priest " "
2. The text reads, "And the sons of Aaron shall bring the blood to him" [Lev 1:5].	2. It says "priestly outfit" here.	2. It says, "The sons of Aaron" here.
3. One might suppose this [refers to] the sprinkling of the blood?	3. – – –	3. – – –
4. When it states, "And they shall sprinkle" [Lev 1:5], this refers to sprinkling. But here it states, "And he shall bring" [which refers to] only receiving the blood.	4. – – –	4. – – –
5. It compares receiving to sprinkling.	5. – – –	5. – – –
6. Just as sprinkling [is done] by a perfect priest [dressed] in the vestments of service, so too receiving [is done] by a perfect priest [dressed] in the vestments of service.	6. – – –	6. – – –
7. And there it says, "And you shall anoint them to serve him" [Exod 40:15].	7. and it says "priestly outfit" there.	7. And there it says, "These are the names of the sons of Aaron, the priests that were anointed" [Num 3:3].

Tos. Zev. 1:8	Sifra 4:4-5	b. Zev. 13a
8. Just as the priest referred to there is a perfect priest [dressed] in the vestments of service, so too the priest referred to here is a perfect priest [dressed] in the vestments of service.	8. Just as the "priestly outfit" stated there [refers to] a fit priest " " " so too the "priestly outfit" stated here [refers to] a fit priest " "	8. Just as there it [refers to] " " " " " " so too here it [refers to] " " " " " "
9. Said to him R. Tarfon,	9. " " " "	9. Said R. Tarfon
10. Aqiva, how long will you continue to gather [words] and bring them against me?	10. How long " " " us?	10. - - -
11. May I bury my sons if I did not hear a distinction between receiving and sprinkling, and you equate receiving with sprinkling.	11. " " " " " " " " " " " " and I cannot explain it.	11. " " " " " " " " " and I cannot explain it.
12. He said to him, Permit me to say before you what you have taught me.	12. " " " " " " "	12. Said R. Aqiva, I will explain.
13. He said to him, Speak.	13. " " " "	13. - - -
14. He said to him, For receiving....	14. " " " "	14. " " "
15. He said to him, [I swear] by the Temple service,	15. He said to him, May I bury my sons,	15. Said to him R. Tarfon, [I swear] by the Temple service,
16. for you have not deviated either right or left.	16. " " " " " " "	16. " " " " " "
17. I heard [it] and could not explain [it], and you expound so that it accords with the law.	17. " " " " " " " the tradition.	17. " " " " " " the tradition.
18. Behold, anyone who separates himself from you is as if he separates from his life.	18. " " "	18. In these words he addressed him " " "

Aqiva's exegesis in b. (1-2, 7-8), as in Sifra, consists merely of
two proof texts and a statement which spells out the implications
of these sources. The second verse (Num 3:3), cited to substantiate Aqiva's claim, is different from that in Tos. 9-11, like the
same sections in Sifra, are unintelligible. The remainder of b.
parallels the versions in Tos. and Sifra, except that in b. the
exchange between Tarfon and Aqiva is not as antagonistic. Tarfon's
statement lacks the complaint, 10, that Aqiva gathers words. Furthermore, Aqiva, in 12, does not assert that Tarfon has forgotten
his own teaching; rather, he simply explains the differences between sprinkling and receiving.

> A. "They vow free-will offerings of wine, but they
> do not vow free-will offerings of oil," the words of R.
> Aqiva.
> B. R. Tarfon says, "They [P adds: even] vow free-will
> offerings of oil."
> C. Said R. Tarfon, "Just as we found with regard to
> wine that it is given as an obligation, and it is given as
> a free-will offering, so too oil, [K,L,P,Pr: which is
> given as an obligation, may be given as a free-will offering][4]
> [N,M: comes as an obligation and comes as a free-will
> offering.]"
> D. Said to him R. Aqiva, "No, if you said with regard
> to wine, which is offered up by itself as an obligation,
> [that one may vow it as a free-will offering], will you say
> [the same] with regard to oil, which is not offered up by
> itself as an obligation?"

> M. Men. 12:5

Comment: In the dispute, A-B, Tarfon's opinion comes second
and is phrased as a gloss of Aqiva's saying. This is one of the
two pericopae in which Aqiva appears first. The dispute could be
formulated:

> Oil--
> R. Aqiva says, They do not vow [to give it as a]
> free-will offering.
> R. Tarfon says, They vow [to give it as a]
> free-will offering.

The two masters disagree about whether or not one may vow to
give oil as a free-will offering. (This dispute does not deal with
the question of whether or not one may offer up oil by itself as a
free-will offering.) Aqiva rules that one may not designate oil as

a free-will offering; Tarfon rules that one may. We may explain
these opinions in terms of the debate, C-D. Tarfon argues, in C,
on the basis of an analogy that, just as wine is given as an obligatory offering and as a free-will offering, so too oil, which
is given as an obligatory offering, may be given as a free-will
offering. Aqiva rejects this argument by pointing out that wine
and oil are not completely analogous. Wine is offered up by itself as an obligatory offering. But oil is not offered up by itself as an obligatory offering. Tarfon may, therefore, not derive
by means of an analogy the laws with regard to vowing to give oil
as a free-will offering. D, in addition to refuting Tarfon's
argument (C), also helps us to explain Aqiva's opinion in A. For
Aqiva, the future use of the oil, how it may be sacrificed, determines the laws which apply at a prior stage. Thus if one may not
sacrifice oil by itself, one may not vow to give it as a free-will
offering. For Tarfon, however, the future use of the oil is irrelevant; one may, therefore, vow to give it as a free-will offering. The anonymous law in M. Men. 12:4, which discusses vowing to
give a meal-offering as a free-will offering, is in agreement with
the logic of Aqiva's opinion. Simeon comments upon M. Men. 12:4,
and thus provides an Ushan attestation to the issue.

> A. [As to] one who vows free-will offerings of wine,
> according to the words of [Lieberman emends (*T.R.* II, p.
> 263): R. Aqiva (and R. Tarfon)], they put [the wine] in
> the basins.
> B. Oil, according to the words of R. Tarfon, is
> sacrificed on the [altar's] fires.
>
> > Tos. Men. 12:10a, ed. Zucker-
> > mandel, p. 532, lns. 6-7[5]

> A. *Come and hear:*
> B. Wine, according to the words of R. Aqiva, is for
> the basins.
> C. Oil, according to the words of R. Tarfon, is for
> the fires.
>
> > b. Zev. 91b

Comment: My explanation of Tos. is in accordance with Lieberman's emendation, which is supported by the parallel in b. A-B comment upon M. by explaining the manner in which the wine and the oil,
given as free-will offerings, are offered as sacrifices. Tos. thus
interprets A-B of M. to mean that one vows to give, *and offers up*

by themselves, wine and oil. According to A-B and b., they put
the wine in the basins; they sacrifice the oil on the altar's
fires. A further comment in b. Zev. 91b, not presented here, explains that they put the wine in the basins and not on the fires
in order not to extinguish them. Oil, however, burns well and,
accordingly, it may be put directly on the altar's fires.

    A. From what verse do we learn that an individual
vows a free-will offering of oil?

    B. It is the logical conclusion and it is the answer.

    C. "The text teaches, '[And when a person offers] a
sacrifice [of meal-offering...]' (Lev 2:1)]. [The inclusion
of the word "sacrifice" indicates that one may bring a
free-will offering of any part, including the oil, of a
meal-offering]," the words of R. Tarfon.

    D. *Said R. Tarfon, "Just as we have found with regard
to wine that it comes as an obligation and comes as a free-
will offering, so too oil, which comes as an obligation,
may come as a free-will offering."*

    E. *Said to him R. Aqiva, "No, if you said [the above
with regard to] wine, which is sacrificed by itself as an
obligatory offering, will you say [the same with regard to]
oil which is not sacrificed by itself as an obligatory
offering?"*

                        Sifra Vayiqra' Parashata 8:7,
                        ed. Weiss, 9c (C-D = M. Men.
                        12:5C-D)

Comment: Sifra joins C-D of M. = D-E of Sifra to a Scriptural
proof text. Sifra is clearly dependent upon M., for Aqiva's appearance in E is unexpected. A asks a question. B is formulaic.
C answers A. The exegesis, which we have explained in our translation, is based on a *ribbui*, the inclusion of an extra word in a
verse whose purpose is to teach some additional law. If the text
wanted to teach that one may bring only a meal-offering consisting
of a mixture of the three items, then it should have simply read,
"offers a meal-offering."

    A. 1. Said R Simeon, "If you saw oil which was spread
about the Temple-court, you need not ask, 'What is it?'
Rather, [it is] the excess of the meal-offering-wafers of
an Israelite, or the leper's *log* of oil.

2.   "If you saw oil which was put on the [altar's]
fire, you need not ask, 'What is it?' Rather, [it is] the
excess of the meal-offering wafers of the priests, or the
meal-offering of the anointed [high] priest.

B.   "[It must be one of the items mentioned in A2]
for they do not make free-will offerings of oil."

C.   R. Tarfon says, "They vow free-will offerings
of oil."

M. Zev. 10:8

Comment: Tarfon's saying concerning the use of oil as a free-
will offering now appears with a saying of Simeon. B, which
glosses Simeon's saying, A, is identical to the part of Aqiva's
saying that deals with oil. A-B indicate that the redactor understands Tarfon's saying to mean that oil may be given and sacrificed
by itself as a free-will offering.

A.   TNW RBNN: "'And you shall offer [on Pentecost]
with the bread-offering [seven lambs a year old without
blemish...' (Lev 23:18)].

B.   "[You might think this implies that it is] an
obligation [to sacrifice the seven lambs] with the bread-
offering.

C.   "[The verse continues:] 'Seven lambs without
blemish' [Lev 23:18].

D.   "[This shows that you may offer the lambs] even
though there is no bread-offering.

E.   "If so, what does 'with the bread-offering' teach?

F.   "It teaches that they were not obligated [to bring
these] lambs prior to their having been obligated [to bring]
the bread-offering,"

G.   the words of R. Tarfon.

b. Men. 45b

A.   "'And you shall bring with the bread' [Lev 23:18].

B.   "[This means it is] an obligation [to sacrifice
the seven lambs] with the bread-offering.

C.   "'And you shall bring with the bread seven lambs
without blemish in the first year' [Lev 23:18].

D.   "[This indicates that one may bring] the lambs
even though there is no bread-offering,"

E.   the words of R. Tarfon.

      F. If so, why does it say "bread"?

      G. This teaches that they were not made liable [for
the] lambs until they were made liable for the bread.

Sifra 'Emor Pereq 13:4,
ed. Weiss, 101b

Comment: A-F are a very common form for an exegesis. A cites
part of a verse; B then notes the apparent inference to be drawn
from the verse. C cites the remainder of the verse; D then spells
out the implications of this part of the verse, thereby indicating
that the inference recorded in B is incorrect. The tradition could
end at this point, as it does in Sifra, since Tarfon's opinion
comes in D. E asks what is the purpose of the part of the verse
cited in A; F answers this question.

     This pericope discusses the offerings of Pentecost. Lev 23:
15-21 list these sacrifices, among which are seven lambs without
blemish and two loaves of bread made from new grain. Our pericope
asks whether or not one may bring the lambs without the bread-
offering. As we shall see below, the question may also be phrased
as follows: Does the omission of one of the items invalidate the
sacrifice of the other? Tarfon's opinion is that one may offer
the seven lambs without the bread-offering. QA explains Tarfon's
exegesis as follows: If the Torah wanted to indicate that the
bread-offering *must* accompany the seven lambs, then the verse
should have read, "And you shall offer seven lambs with the bread-
offering." Such a verse shows that the bread-offering is the primary sacrifice. But since the verse is not phrased in this way,
we conclude that the bread-offering need not accompany the sacrifice of the lambs. E-F complete the pericope by indicating what
we learn from the words "with the bread-offering." The Israelites
were not required to bring the offering of the seven lambs prior
to their obligation to bring the bread-offering.

     The issue to which Tarfon's exegesis relates is also discussed
in M. Men. 4:3; the portions of that M. relevant to our pericope
are as follows:

      A. "The bread offering [by its omission], invalidates
(M'KB) the lambs, but the lambs [by their omission], do not
invalidate the bread-offering," the words of R. Aqiva.
      B. 1. Said R. Simeon b. Nannos, "Not so, rather,
          2. "the lambs [by their omission], invalidate
the bread-offering, but the bread-offering [by its omis-
sion], does not invalidate the lambs."

M. Men. 4:3 and Tarfon's exegesis formulate the issue in different
ways. M. phrases the matter in terms of whether or not the omission of one of the items invalidates the sacrifice of the other.
Tarfon says that one may offer one of the items without the other.
But if one is permitted to bring the lambs without the bread-
offering, as Tarfon claims in D of the baraita, then the sacrifice
of the lambs without the bread is not invalid. This is Ben Nannos'
opinion in M. Ben Nannos and Tarfon, therefore, agree with regard
to the offering of the lambs without the bread-offering. Whether
or not they agree concerning the sacrifice of the bread-offering
without the lambs cannot be determined. Since Tarfon agrees with
Ben Nannos, he accordingly disagrees with Aqiva regarding the
offering of the lambs without the bread. A redactor who knew both
Tarfon's opinion and those in M. Men. 4:3 could have created the
following disputes:

I   As to lambs brought on Pentecost--
           R. Aqiva says, "One may not offer them without the
           bread-offering."
           R. Tarfon and Ben Nannos say, "One may offer them
           without the bread-offering."

II   As to the bread-offering which should be offered with
           the lambs--
           R. Aqiva says, "Its omission invalidates the offering
           of the lambs."
           R. Tarfon and Ben Nannos say, "Its omission does not
           invalidate the offering of the lambs."

           1. The [bringing of] the *omer* [on the second day of
Passover] would render permissible [the consumption of the
new grain] in the provinces [throughout the land of Israel].
           2. And [the bringing of the] bread-offering [on
Pentecost would render permissible the new grain] in the
Temple.
           3. They do not bring [from the new grain] meal-
offerings, or first fruits, or meal-offerings [that
accompany] animal [offerings] prior to [the bringing of]
the *omer*.
           4. If he brought [such an offering prior to this
time], it is unfit.
           5. Prior to [the bringing of] the two loaves [which
are the bread-offering], he may not bring [the offerings
mentioned in C, if they are made from new grain].
           6. If he brought [such an offering prior to this
time], it is fit.

                          M. Men. 10:6

A.   "[On the day of first fruits when you offer] a
meal-offering of new grain [to the Lord" (Num 28:26)]--

B.   [This teaches] that it shall be new in relationship
to all the meal-offerings such that another meal-offering
[made from the new grain] shall not precede it.

C.   On the basis of this [verse] they said,

D.   *They do not bring [from the new grain] meal-
offerings, or first fruits, or meal-offerings [that
accompany] an animal [offering] prior to the [bringing
of the]* 'omer.

E.   *"And if he brought [it], it is unfit.*

F.   *"Prior to the [bringing of the] two loaves, he
may not [bring the offerings].*

G.   *"But if he brought [it], it is fit."*

H.   What difference is there between the 'omer and
the two loaves [such that the laws of E and G differ]?

I.   Lo, prior to [the bringing of] the 'omer it is
prohibited to raise it [the new produce up as an offering],
and it is prohibited for a common person [to eat it].

J.   Therefore, if he offered it, they shall not be
accounted [as fulfilling the obligations].

K.   But prior to the [bringing of the] two loaves,
it is forbidden to raise it [up as an offering], but it
is permitted for a common person.

L.   Therefore, if he offered it, they are accounted
[as fulfilling the obligations].

M.   R. Tarfon says, "Since the [offering of the]
'omer permits and the [offering of the] two loaves permits
[the consumption of the new grain];

N.   "if I have learned concerning the meal-offerings,
that are brought before the [offering of the] 'omer, that
they are unfit, then also the meal-offerings, that are
brought before the [offering of the] two loaves, shall
be unfit."

O.   Said to him R. Judah b. Naḥman [V and Lon.:
Neḥemiah],

P.   1.   "No, if you said [the above] with regard to
meal-offerings which are brought before the [offering of
the] 'omer [and] which [are made from the new grain which]
they have not declared fit either to raise up [as an
offering] or for a common person,

2. "will you say with regard to meal-offerings
[made from new grain], which are brought before the
[offering of the] two loaves,

3. "that they are unfit,

4. "even though they were not declared fit to
[be] raised up [as offerings], they were declared fit for
a common person?"

Q. R. Aqiva looked at him, and his [Judah's] face
brightened.

R. He [Aqiva] said to him, "Judah b. Naḥman, your
face has brightened because you have refuted the elder.

S. "I should be amazed at you if you will live long
in this world."

T. 1. Said R. Judah bar Ilai, "It was on Passover
that this incident occurred,

2. "and when I came for Pentecost I said,
'Where is Judah b. Naḥman?'

3. "They said to me, 'He has died.'"

Sifre Pinḥas 148, ed. Horowitz,
p. 195, lns. 1-12 (D-G = 3-6
of M. Men. 10:6)

Comment: A-B are an exegesis which C joins to D-G = 3-6 of M.
Men. 10:6. The question and answer, H-L, glosses D-G. In M-N we
have an argument attributed to Tarfon. M-N could respond to I-L
or directly to D-G.[6] The fact that O-P, which reply to M-N, is
identical in substance to I-L suggests that M-N should follow
directly after D-G. H-P thus are a composite consisting of (1)
M-N, which disagree with D-G, and a response in O-P to this ruling, and (2) an anonymous question and answer, H-L, which, like
O-P, offer a reason for the ruling in D-G. The homily Q-T is
attached to O-P. Its ironic lesson, R-S, is that it is deadly to
feel prideful because of one's refutation of an elder. Thus Judah
b. Naḥman won the argument about Passover but did not survive until Pentecost to enjoy his victory.

Lev 23:14 states that no one may eat any new grain until the
'*omer* has been brought on the second day of Passover. This implies,
as 1 of M. states, that after this time people may eat the new produce. Lev 23:16-17 specify that on Pentecost, seven weeks after
the bringing of the '*omer*, a bread-offering consisting of two
loaves of bread is sacrificed. Lev 23:16 also states that at this
time you shall offer a new meal-offering. This is the law of M.2.

Once the bread-offering has been presented on Pentecost, one may
then make meal-offerings from the new grain. 3 of M. indicates
that, prior to the bringing of the 'omer, meal-offerings were made
from the old grain. 5 claims that old grain was used until the
bread-offering was presented. Thus, prior to the bringing of the
bread-offerings, one should not make meal-offerings from the new
grain. There is a distinction, however, between meal-offerings
made from new grain which one presents prior to the bringing of
the 'omer, and those which one presents prior to the bringing of
the bread-offering. The former are unfit (M.4), while the latter
are fit (M.6). Thus there is a distinction between the laws
governing the offerings made during these two periods.

Tarfon disagrees with M. arguing that the 'omer and the bread-
offering are analogous. Both of these offerings, as 1 and 2 of M.
indicate, permit the consumption of the new grain. Once the 'omer
is brought, the new grain may be eaten outside the Temple. Once
the bread-offering is presented, the new grain may be used in the
Temple. Since the two offerings are analogous, then if meal-
offerings brought before the bringing of the 'omer are unfit,
meal-offerings brought before the bringing of the bread-offering
should be unfit. Judah's response to this argument, like it,
agrees with 1 and 2 of M. But it takes these laws and uses them
to illustrate that the 'omer and the bread-offering are not
analogous. New grain may not be eaten by the common person before
the bringing of the 'omer, but it may be eaten by such people
prior to the bringing of the bread-offering. M-N and O-P thus presuppose the same laws, but derive opposite conclusions from them.

     A. *R. Tarfon was sitting and it* [the following ques-
tion] *bothered him*:

     B. What is the difference between [the period] prior
to [the bringing of] the 'omer and [the period] prior to
the [bringing of the] two loaves?

     C. Said before him Judah bar Nehemiah,

     D. 1. "No, if you said [that] prior to [the bring-
ing of] the 'omer

     2. "[in relation to] which the law did not permit
by implication [the consumption of the new grain] by the
common person, [an offering made of the new grain is unfit],

     3. "will you say [that] prior to [the bringing
of] the two loaves,

4. "[in relation to] which the law did permit
by implication [the consumption of the new grain] by the
common person, [an offering made of new grain is unfit]?"

E. R. Tarfon was silent.

F. The face of R. Judah b. Neḥemiah brightened
[with joy].

G. Said to him [to Judah] R. Aqiva, "Judah, your
face has brightened because you have refuted (ŠHŠBT) the
elder. You will amaze me if you live long."

H. 1. Said R. Judah bar Ilai, "This incident
('WTW HPRK) occurred a fortnight [before] Passover.

2. "When I came up [to Jerusalem] for Pentecost,
I inquired concerning Judah b. Neḥemiah [and asked] where
he was.

3. "And they said to me [that] he was dead and
departed."

b. Men. 68b

Comment: This is a defective version of this tradition. An
argument attributed to Tarfon is missing and, as a result, the
refutation in D does not make sense as a response to the question
B.[7] A is redactional language which has been added in order to
anticipate the mention of Tarfon in E. A comparison of b. and
Sifre indicates that they are two versions of the same tradition.

Sifre Pinḥas 148	M. Men. 10:6 + b. Men. 68b
1. They do not bring meal-offerings, or first fruits, or meal-offerings [that accompany] an animal prior to the [bringing of the] 'omer.	1. " " " " " " " " " " " "
2. If he brought it, it is unfit.	2. " " "
3. Prior to the [bringing] of the two loaves,	3. " " "
4. if he brought it, it is fit.	4. " " "
5. What difference is there between the 'omer and the two loaves?	5. [See below #11]
6. Lo, prior to the 'omer it is prohibited to raise it, and it is prohibited for a common person.	6. - - -
7. Therefore, if he offered it, they shall not be accounted [as fulfilling the obligations].	7. - - -

Sifre Pinḥas 148	M. Men. 10:6 + b. Men. 68b
8. But prior to the two loaves it is forbidden to raise it, but it is permitted for a common person.	8. - - -
9. Therefore, if he offered it, they are accounted [as fulfilling the obligations].	9. - - -
10. R. Tarfon says,	10. *R. Tarfon was sitting and it bothered him.*
11. [See above #5]	11. What is the difference between [the period] prior to the [bringing of the] 'omer and [the period] prior to the [bringing of the] two loaves?
12. Since the 'omer permits, and the two loaves permit,	12. - - -
13. if I have learned concerning meal-offerings, that are brought before the [offering of the] 'omer, that they are unfit, then also the meal-offerings, that are brought before the [offering of the] two loaves, shall be unfit?	13. - - -
14. Said to him R. Judah b. Naḥman,	14. Said before him Judah bar Neḥemiah,
15. No, if you said with regard to meal-offerings which are brought before the [offering of the] 'omer [and which are made from new grain which] they have not declared fit either to raise up [as an offering] or for a common person, [that they are unfit],	15. No, if you said [that] prior to the [bringing of the] 'omer, [in relation to] which the law did not permit by implication [consumption] by the common person, [that an offering made of new grain is unfit],
16. will you say with regard to meal-offerings which are brought before [the offering of] the two loaves,	16. will you say [that] prior to the [bringing of the] two loaves,
17. that they are unfit,	17. - - -
18. even though they were not declared fit to be raised up [as an offering], they were declared fit for a common person?	18. [in relation to] which the law did permit by implication [consumption] by the common person, [that it is unfit]?
19. - - -	19. R. Tarfon was silent.
20. R. Aqiva looked at him,	20. - - -

Sifre Pinḥas 148	M. Men. 10:6 + b. Men. 68b
21. and his face brightened.	21. The face of R. Judah b. Neḥemiah brightened.
22. He [Aqiva] said to him, Judah b. Naḥman, your face has brightened since you have refuted the elder.	22. Said to him R. Aqiva, Judah, your " " "
23. I should be amazed at you if you will live long in this world.	23. You will amaze me if you live long.
24. Said R. Judah bar Ilai,	24. " " "
25. It was on Passover that this incident occurred,	25. This incident occurred a fortnight [before] Passover.
26. and when I came for Pentecost I said, Where is Judah b. Naḥman?	26. When I came up for Pentecost I inquired concerning him,
27. They said to me, He has died.	27. and they said to me, He has died and departed.

The formulaic patterns in the two versions are the same. 5 of
Sifre = 11 of b., and in both versions Judah has an argument using
the language, "No, if you said...will you say." The wording of b.
and Sifre significantly differ, but the substance of the parallel
sections are the same. b. and Sifre, therefore, are two versions
of the same tradition. We cannot, however, prove that one of them
is dependent upon the other. Sifre simply gives us a correct
version.

> A. *An animal stripped of its hide--*
> B. *R. Meir declares fit.*
> C. *But sages declare unfit.*
> D. Said R. Simeon b. Eleazar, "R. Meir and sages did
> not dispute about an animal stripped of its hide that it
> is unfit."
> E. Testified R. Judah b. Isaiah [b.: R. 'Oshaiah the
> son of R. Judah], the spice-maker, before R. Aqiva who
> said in the name of R. Tarfon concerning an animal stripped
> of its hide that it is unfit.

> Tos. Ḥul. 3:7, ed. Zuckermandel,
> p. 504, lns. 16-19 (A-C = b.
> Ḥul. 55b, M. Ḥul. 3:2)

Comment: A-C are a citation from M. Ḥul. 3:2 which D-E supplement. D attests the dispute in A-C, but is incomplete. It lacks
a further clause which states either about what Meir and sages did

disagree, or that either Meir or sages changed their opinions.
E is an autonomous tradition. We have already discussed its form
above (p. 25).

Exod 22:30 prescribes that one may not eat any animal which
has been torn to pieces (*terefah*). Rabbinic law expands the category of *terefah* to include those animals which, because of either
internal or external defects, could not continue to survive (M.
Ḥul. 3:1). An animal which suffers from a defect which would
cause its death thus is considered unfit for consumption. The
present pericope discusses the status of an animal that suffers
from the defect of lacking its hide. Tarfon, as well as sages,
consider such an animal unfit for consumption; Meir rules it is fit.

   A. 1. [As to] a sheep that had not before given
birth, and it gave birth to two males,
     2. and their heads came forth at the same time--
   B. 1. R. Yose the Galilean says, "Both [are given]
to the priest,
     2. "for it is written, 'The males shall be the
Lord's'" [Exod 13:12].
   C. 1. But sages say, "It is impossible [for both
heads to come out at the same time]; rather,
     2. "one [is given] to him [the owner] and the
other to the priest."
   D. R. Tarfon says, "The priest chooses the better
[of the two animals] for himself."
   E. R. Aqiva says, "They compromise between them
(MŠMNYM BYNYHN)."
   F. And the second is left to pasture until it
suffers a blemish.
   G. And it [the second] is subject to [Priest's] dues.
   H. But R. Yose exempts [it from the dues].
   I. If one of them [the sheep] died--
   J. R. Tarfon says, "They divide [the value of the
living one]."
   K. R. Aqiva says, "The burden of proof lies on him
who would exact something from his fellow."
   L. [If the offspring were] a male and a female, the
priest [can claim] nothing.
   M. 1. [As to] two sheep that had not before given
birth, and they gave birth to

2. two males, he [the owner] gives both to the priest.

3. [If they gave birth to] a male and a female, the male [is given] to the priest.

4. [If they gave birth to] two males and a female, one male [is given] to him [the owner] and the other to the priest.

N. R. Tarfon says, "The priest chooses the better for himself."

O. R. Aqiva says, "They compromise between them."

P. And the second is left to pasture until it suffers a blemish.

Q. And it is subject to [Priest's] dues.

R. But R. Yose exempts.

S. [If] one of them died--

T. R. Tarfon says, "They divide [the value of the living one]."

U. R. Aqiva says, "The burden of proof lies on him who would exact something from his fellow."

V. [If the offspring were] two females and a male, or two males and two females, the priest [can claim] nothing.

W. [As to two sheep], one that already has given birth and one that had not before given birth, and they gave birth to two males, one [is given] to him [the owner] and the other to the priest.

X. R. Tarfon says, "The priest chooses the better for himself."

Y. R. Aqiva says, "They compromise between them."

Z. And the second is left to pasture until it suffers a blemish.

AA. And it is subject to [Priest's] dues.

BB. 1. R. Yose exempts,

2. for R. Yose used to say, "[As to] all [animals] whose substitute the priest has, it [the other beast] is exempt from [Priest's] dues."

CC. R. Meir declares it liable.

DD. [If] one of them died--

EE. R. Tarfon says, "They divide [the value of the living one]."

FF.   R. Aqiva says, "The burden of proof lies on
him who would exact something from his fellow."

GG.   [If the offspring were] a male and a female,
the priest [can claim] nothing.

M. Bekh. 2:6-8

Comment: The pericope consists of three sets of parallel
examples;[8] accordingly, we present it in parallel columns. We
omit A2-C1, which are a separate dispute, because all the other
opinions in the pericope agree with sages' view, C2.

M. Bekh. 2:6

1. A sheep that had not before given birth, gave birth

   a. - - -

   b. - - -

   c. to two males, one is given to him and the other to the priest.

2. R. Tarfon says, The priest chooses the better for himself.
   R. Aqiva says, They compromise between them.

3. And the second is left to pasture until it suffers a blemish.

4. a. And it is subject to [Priest's] dues.

   b. R. Yose exempts.

   c. - - -

   d. - - -

5. [If] one died--
   R. Tarfon says, They divide the value of the living one.
   R. Aqiva says, The burden of proof lies on him who would exact something from his fellow.

M. Bekh. 2:7

1. Two sheep that had not before given birth, gave birth

   a. to two males, both are given to the priest;

   b. to a male and a female, the male is given to the priest;

   c. to two males and a female, one is given to him and the other to the priest.

2. " = = =
   " = = =
   " = = =
   " = = =

3. " = = =
   " = = =

4. a. " = = = =

   b. " = = = =

   c. - - -

   d. - - -

5. " = = =
   " = = =
   " = = =
   " = = =

M. Bekh. 2:8

1. Two sheep, one had and one had not before given birth, gave birth

   a. - - -

   b. - - -

   c. to two males, one is given to him and the other to the priest.

2. " = = =
   " = = =
   " = = =
   " = = =

3. " = = =
   " = = =

4. a. " = = = =

   b. " = = = =

   c. For R. Yose used to say, All animals whose substitute the priest has, it [the other animal] is exempt from [Priest's] dues.

   d. R. Meir declares it liable.

5. " = = =
   " = = =
   " = = =
   " = = =

M. Bekh. 2:6

6. [If the offspring of the sheep
in 1 were] a male and a female,
the priest [can claim] nothing.

M. Bekh. 2:7

6. " " "
two females and a male, or
two males and a female, " " "

M. Bekh. 2:8

6. " " "
a male and a female,
" " "

The rules given in 1 and 6 also appear in M. Bekh. 1:3-4 with regard to asses, and in M. Bekh. 8:3-5 with regard to humans. Thus
the redactor of our pericope has inserted the remaining materials,
2-5, into the framework of 1-6. We may break down 1-6 into three
types of cases: (1) 1a-b, the male or males must be firstlings and
therefore are given to the priest; (2) 1c, one of two males must
be a firstling, but we are uncertain which one it is; and (3) 4,
5, and 6, the male or males may, but need not, be firstlings.

       The first dispute between Tarfon and Aqiva (2) relates to a
case involving doubt. As noted, we are uncertain as to which of
two males is the firstling. Tarfon rules that the priest receives
the benefit of the doubt; therefore, he chooses the better of the
two animals. Aqiva's opinion is not phrased as the opposite of
that of Tarfon, i.e., "weaker of them," but as MŠMNYM BYNYHN.
Albeck (pp. 387-88) summarizes the various explanations of this
term. It may mean either that they estimate the value of both
animals and then the person who receives the better of the two
animals must compensate the other person, or that the priest receives the weaker of the two animals.[9] According to the first
interpretation, Aqiva rules that, since this is a case of uncertainty, the two parties compromise. According to the second interpretation, Aqiva, as in the cases given in 5, asserts that the
priest must supply evidence if he wants to claim the better of the
two animals. This second interpretation of Aqiva's saying is
based upon the reading in Tos., which was bothered by the unclar-
ity of Aqiva's ruling. Accordingly, it has for Aqiva's saying,
"the weaker of them." Tarfon's ruling in 5 is consistent with his
view in 2. Tarfon takes into account that the surviving animal
may be the firstling. The priest receives the benefit of the
doubt; therefore, he and the owner divide its value.

       The ruling in 3 agrees with the principle behind Tarfon's
opinion. The second animal may be a firstling; therefore, it must
be treated as a doubtful firstling. It is left to pasture until
it suffers a blemish, and the owner then consumes it. Yose in 4
also agrees with the principle behind Tarfon's opinion. As M. Bekh.
2:8 4c explains, an animal, in this case the now-dead animal which
the priest took, can be regarded as a substitute for another animal,
in this case the surviving animal, only if the latter is regarded
as having belonged to the priest. Since the surviving animal was
once the property of the priest, but the priest subsequently relin-
quished his rights to it, it is not subject to Priest's dues. The

anonymous ruling which opposes Yose, and which in M. Bekh. 2:8 4d
is attributed to Meir, agrees in principle with Aqiva. According
to Meir, we assume that the animal which the priest originally
claims is the firstling. The remaining animal, therefore, is not
sacred. It, as a result, is subject to Priest's dues. Similarly,
Aqiva rules in 5 that the surviving animal is not the firstling;
therefore, to receive it the priest must substantiate his claim.
The anonymous ruling in 6, which states that the priest can claim
nothing, also agrees in principle with Aqiva's view in 5. In
cases of doubt we assume that the animal is not a firstling. As
we shall see, Tos. supplements this anonymous rule with a stipulation which is in line with Tarfon's view.

The opinions of Tarfon and Aqiva in this pericope belong to
the group of their disputes which relates to how one acts in cases
of doubt. Their rulings here are consistent with their views in
M. Yev. 15:6-7.

> A. [As to] a sheep that had not before given birth and
> it gave birth to two males, and their heads came forth at
> the same time--
>
> B. 1. R. Yose the Galilean says, "Both [are given]
> to the priest,
>
> 2. "for it is written, 'The males shall be the
> Lord's'" [Exod 13:12].
>
> C. But sages say, "It is impossible [for both to come
> out at the same time]; rather,
> "one [is given] to him [the owner] and the other to the priest."
>
> D. R. Tarfon says, "The better of them [is given to the
> priest]."
>
> E. R. Aqiva says, "The weaker of them."
>
> F. The second is left to pasture until it suffers a
> blemish.
>
> G. And it is subject to [Priest's] dues.
>
> H. But R. Yose exempts.
>
> I. [If] one of them died--
>
> J. R. Tarfon says, "They divide [the value of the living
> one]."
>
> K. R. Aqiva says, "The burden of proof lies on him who
> would exact something from his fellow."
>
> L. 1. [If the offspring were] a male and a female,
>
> 2. and it is not known [which came first],

3. *the priest [can claim] nothing.*

4. Rather, it [the male] is left to pasture until it suffers a blemish, and it is [then] sold, and it shall be eaten with its blemish by the owner.

M. 1. *[As to] two sheep that had not before given birth and they gave birth to*

2. *two males, he gives both to the priest.*

3. *[If] a male and a female, the male [is given] to the priest.*

4. *[If] two males and a female, one male [is given] to him [the owner] and the other to the priest.*

N. *R. Tarfon says, "The better of them."*

O. *R. Aqiva says, "The weaker of them."*

P. *The* koi *is left to pasture until it suffers a blemish.*

Q. *And it is [then] subject to [Priest's] dues.*

R. *But R. Yose exempts.*

S. *[If] one of them died --*

T. *R. Tarfon says, "They divide [the value of the living one]."*

U. *R. Aqiva says, "The burden of proof lies on him who would exact something from his fellow."*

V. 1. *[If the offspring were] two females and a male, or two males and two females,*

2. and it is not known [which came first],

3. *the priest [can claim] nothing.*

4. Rather, the males are left to pasture until they suffer blemishes, and the owner shall eat them with their blemishes.

W. *[As to] two sheep, one that had already given birth and one that had not before given birth, and they gave birth to two males, one [is given] to him [the owner] and the other to the priest.*

X. *R. Tarfon says, "The better of them."*

Y. *R. Aqiva says, "The weaker of them."*

Z. *The second is left to pasture until it suffers a blemish.*

AA. *And it is subject to [Priest's] dues.*

BB. 1. *R. Yose exempts,*

2. *for R. Yose used to say, "[As to] all [animals] whose substitute the priest has, it [the other beast] is exempt from [Priest's] dues."*

CC. 1. *But R. Meir declares liable,*

2. for he used to say, "If it is a firstling, give
it to me; and if [it is] not, give me the dues."

DD. *[If] one of them died--*

EE. *R. Tarfon says, "They divide [the value of the
living one]."*

FF. *R. Aqiva says, "The burden of proof lies on him
who would exact something from his fellow."*

GG. 1. *[If the offspring were] a male and a female,*

2. and it is not known [which came out first],

3. *the priest [can claim] nothing.*

4. Rather, the male is left to pasture until it
suffers a blemish, and the owner [then] eats it with its
blemish.

> Tos. Bekh. 2:7-10, ed. Zucker-
> mandel, p. 536, lns. 3-20

Comment: Tos. comments upon M. L2, V2 and GG2 of Tos. explicitly state that it is not known which animal came first. M.
presupposes, but does not state, this detail. In relation to these
cases, i.e., those in which one of the animals may be a firstling,
M. simply states that the priest receives nothing. We explained
that this ruling is in agreement with Aqiva's view. Tos., however,
prescribes in L4, V4 and GG4 that the animals must be treated as
doubtful firstlings, they must be left to pasture until they suffer
blemishes. These rulings agree in principle with Tarfon's view
that when an animal may be a firstling, it must at least be treated
as a doubtful firstling. Yose's opinion in Tos. is identical to
his view in M. Meir's saying, like Yose's in M. and in Tos., contains an explanatory clause, CC2.

The sayings of Tarfon and Aqiva regarding which animal the
priest receives differ from their sayings in M. Tarfon's opinion
in M. reads, "The priest chooses the better for himself." In Tos.
Tarfon's opinion is, "The better of them." Aqiva's opinion in
Tos. reads, "The weaker of them." This forms a neatly balanced
dispute with Tarfon's opinion. Moreover, in Tos. the meaning of
Aqiva's statement is not unclear as it is in M. Thus as we have
noted in our previous discussion, Tos. comments upon M. by clarifying the dispute between the two masters.

A.   [If the first born of an animal] was extracted
from the side [of the mother by Caesarean section] and [the
mother gave birth in the normal manner to] the one [born]
after it--

B.   1.   R. Tarfon says, "Both are left to pasture until
they suffer blemishes,

2.   "and they shall be eaten by their owner after
they have suffered the blemishes."

C.   1.   R. Aqiva says, "Both are not firstlings;

2.   "the first because it is not such that 'opens
the womb' [Exod 13:12], the second in that another came
before it."

M. Bekh. 2:9

Comment: A gives us an intermediate case. The first born
animal was not born in the normal manner; therefore, it does not
meet the requirements set in Exod 13:12 for a firstling. Exod
13:12 states, "You shall set apart to the Lord all that first open
the womb; all the firstlings of your cattle that are males shall
be the Lord's." It is, however, the first born animal. The second born animal was born in the normal manner; therefore, it is
the first to open the womb. Tarfon classifies both animals as
doubtful firstlings; they must be left to pasture until they suffer blemishes. Aqiva claims that neither of the animals is a
firstling. The opinions of the masters in this dispute are consistent with their views in the preceding pericope. Aqiva rules that
in cases of doubt we presume the animal is not a firstling. Tarfon
holds the opposite view.

The opinions in B1 and C1 are phrased in a similar manner:

ŠNYHN YR'W 'D ŠYŚT'BW
ŠNYHN 'YNN BKWR

B2 and C2 gloss the respective sayings.

The firstlings...are lesser holy [sacrifices]...and
they are eaten...within two days and one night.

M. Zev. 5:8

A.   TNW RBNN: From what verse [do we learn] that a
firstling is eaten within (L) two days and a night?

B.   For it is written, "And their [the firstlings']
flesh shall be yours [the priests'] like the wave breast
and the right thigh" [Num 18:18].

C. Scripture has compared it [the firstling] to the breast and the thigh of peace-offerings.

D. Just as peace-offerings are eaten within two days and one night, so too a firstling is eaten within two days and one night.

E. 1. And

2. this [the following] question was asked before the sages in Kerem BeYavneh:

F. The firstling [within] how many [days] is it eaten?

G. Answered R. Tarfon saying, "Within two days and one night."

H. There was one student there who had come to the *Bet Midrash* before the sages for the first time, and his name [was] R. Yose the Galilean.

I. He [Yose] said to him, "Master, how do you know [that this is the rule regarding the firstling]?"

J. He [Tarfon] said to him, "My son, peace-offerings [are] lesser holy offerings, and firstlings [are] lesser holy offerings.

K. "Just as peace-offerings are eaten within two days and one night, so too a firstling is eaten within two days and one night."

L. He [Yose] said to him, "Master, a firstling [is] a gift for a priest, and a sin-offering and a guilt-offering [are] a gift for a priest; [whereas peace-offerings belong to the owners].

M. "Just as a sin-offering and a guilt-offering [are eaten] within a day and a night, so too a firstling [should be eaten] within [only] a day and a night."

N. He [Tarfon] said to him, [M, V, and D.S. XI, p. 107: "My son] Let us deduce one thing from another thing, and let us learn one thing from another thing.

O. "Just as peace-offerings are not offered [as a sacrifice] for a sin (ḤT'), so too a firstling is not offered [as a sacrifice] for a sin.

P. "Just as peace-offerings are eaten within two days and one night, so too a firstling is eaten within two days and one night."

Q. He [Yose] said to him, "Master, let us deduce one thing from another thing, let us learn one thing from another thing.

R. [M and other Mss. lack R and "just as" in S, see
D.S. XI, p. 106] "A sin-offering and a guilt-offering
[are] a gift for the priest, and the firstling is a gift
for the priest.

S. "Just as a sin-offering and a guilt-offering are
not offered as a vow or as a free-will offering, so too a
firstling is not offered as a vow or as a free-will offering.

T. "Just as a sin-offering and a guilt-offering are
eaten within one day [M and other Mss. add: and a night],
so too a firstling is eaten within one day [M: and a night]."

U. R. Aqiva jumped in and R. Tarfon withdrew.

V. He [Aqiva] said to him, "Lo, it [Scripture] says,
'And its flesh shall be yours [like the wave breast and the
right thigh' (Num 18:18)].

W. "Scripture compared them [the firstlings] to the
breast and the thigh of peace-offerings.

X. "Just as peace-offerings are eaten within two days
and one night, so too a firstling is eaten within two days
and one night."

Y. He [Yose] said to him, "You compared it [the
firstling] to the breast and thigh of peace-offerings and
I compare it to the breast and thigh of a thank-offering.

Z. "Just as a thank-offering is eaten within a day
and a night, so too a firstling is eaten within a day and
a night."

AA. 1. He [Aqiva] said to him, "Lo, it [Scripture]
says, 'And its flesh shall be yours' [M and various Mss.
add: etc.].

2. "Thus it need not state, 'It shall be yours'
[which appears both at the beginning and at the end of
Num 18:18].

3. "What is the reason it [Scripture] states,
'It shall be yours'?

4. "[By adding these words] Scripture prolonged
the existence of the firstling [i.e., you may eat it an
extra day]."

BB. And when [these] matters were reported before
R. Ishmael, he said to them,

CC. "Go out and tell him, R. Aqiva, you have erred
[in accepting the validity of Yose's analogy in Y-Z].

DD.   "[For] on what basis have we learned the rule
concerning [the breast and the thigh] of a thank-offering?
[We have learned it] from [the rules governing] peace-
offerings.

EE.   "And does something which is derived by means of
an analogy go and teach by means of an analogy?

FF.   "Hence, you must not determine it by means of
the latter version [i.e., by means of a comparison with a
thank-offering]; rather, [you must derive the rule] by
means of the first version [i.e., by a comparison with a
peace-offering]."

                                    b. Zev. 57a (Sifre Num. 118,
                                    ed. Horowitz, p. 141)

Comment: The opinions in this pericope relate to a very
fundamental issue of sacrificial law, one not prescribed in Scripture, the number of days within which a firstling is eaten.
Sacrifices must be eaten within the permitted time-period, otherwise they become *notar* and then must be destroyed. The view of
Tarfon, Aqiva, and Ishmael is that a firstling is eaten within two
days and a night. They agree with the anonymous law of M. Zev.
5:8. Yose, however, limits the consumption to a day and a night.
The analysis which follows discusses the structure of the pericope,
and also presents the reasons for these authorities' opinions.

This pericope is an example of a well-constructed discussion
on a single topic. We analyze it in terms of its various sections,
A-D, E-T, U-AA and BB-FF. A-D are an autonomous tradition. They
are attributed in U-X to Aqiva. A asks a question which B answers.
C-D spell out how B responds to A. According to A-D, the mentioning in the same verse of the wave breast and the right thigh together with the firstling indicates that these items' are analogous.
Now the wave breast and right thigh are also mentioned with regard
to peace-offerings. Accordingly, just as the wave breast and the
right thigh of peace-offerings are eaten within two days and a
night, so too a firstling is eaten within the same period.

E2 is formulaic language which introduces the remainder of
the pericope. E1 joins E2 and what follows to A-D. F-G consist
of a question and an answer attributed to Tarfon. It can stand
alone. H introduces Yose into the discussion. The author of the
pericope has not created an opinion for Yose which he could place
in a dispute with F-G. He rather has built upon the motif of the
Bet Midrash and has formulated a debate. It is only in M that we

learn Yose's view. Since no opinion attributed to Yose appears
immediately after G, it is not clear whether Yose simply wants a
proof text in support of Tarfon's opinion, or whether he holds a
view different from that of Tarfon and, therefore, challenges it.
The remainder of the pericope indicates that the latter is the case.

J-T are the arguments assigned to Tarfon and Yose. Yose has
the last say and wins the debate. J-T are extremely well balanced.
Both parties are assigned two arguments, Tarfon J and O, Yose L and
S, in which they draw analogies between firstlings and some other
item. These analogies are spelled out in K and P, and M and T respectively. Since each party in his analogies compares for different reasons the firstling to the same item, the sections, K and P
for Tarfon, M and T for Yose, which draw the conclusions from each
authority's analogies, are identical. As to the content of J-T,
Tarfon treats the firstling as comparable to a peace-offering.
According to J, both types of sacrifices are lesser holy offerings;
according to O, neither is offered as an atonement for sins. Since
a peace-offering is eaten within two days and one night, a firstling is consumed within the same period. Tarfon thus agrees with
the rule in A-D. Yose, in both L and S, compares the firstling to
sin- and guilt-offerings. The latter, as well as firstlings, are
gifts for the priest, L, and neither is offered as a free-will
offering, T. Since sin and guilt-offerings are eaten within a day
and a night, a firstling is eaten within the same period. Yose
thus disagrees with Tarfon and with A-D.

We briefly summarize the remainder of the pericope, for Tarfon
does not appear again. U introduces Aqiva into the discussion.
An exchange, V-AA, between him and Yose follows. As noted, V-X,
Aqiva's first argument, is identical to A-D. We have explained
the latter above. V-X differ in form from the arguments attributed
to Tarfon. Tarfon argues from logic; Aqiva on the basis of Scripture. Perhaps this difference accounts for the switch in names
from Tarfon to Aqiva in U-AA.

Y-Z, which responds to U-X and is assigned to Yose, is another
argument based on an analogy between the firstling and some other
item. In this case the firstling is compared to a thank-offering.
In AA, a final argument is assigned to Aqiva. Aqiva does not reject Yose's contention in Y-Z but instead switches grounds, and by
using a new exegesis, argues that a firstling is eaten within two
days and one night. This is the final argument in the pericope.
Thus the opinion of Aqiva and Tarfon is upheld. Unlike Aqiva,
however, Tarfon does not offer a decisive defense of his view.

BB introduces Ishmael into the discussion. BB-FF is simply a challenge to Aqiva's lack of response to Yose's argument, Y-Z. It is not a new opinion or argument. Ishmael claims that Yose's reasoning is flawed. DD-FF spell out the error in Y-Z. Let us now review E-BB by means of the following chart in which we summarize its various sections.

Tarfon and Yose

1. Tarfon's opinion phrased as an answer to a question.

2. Yose's question, how do we know this. It is unclear whether he merely seeks an argument in support of Tarfon's view, or whether he challenges it.

3. Tarfon compares the firstling to peace-offerings. They are both lesser holy sacrifices.

4. Yose compares the firstling to sin-offerings and guilt-offerings. They are all gifts for the priest.

5. Tarfon again compares the firstling to peace-offerings, but for a reason different from that in 3. Neither is offered as a purification from sin.

6. Yose again compares the firstling to sin-offerings and guilt-offerings, but for a reason different from 4. Neither comes as a vow or as a free-will offering.

Aqiva and Yose

7. Aqiva draws an analogy (*heqesh*) between the firstling and the breast and the thigh of peace-offerings. The argument is based on the identical language in the biblical verses which refer to these sacrifices.

8. Yose responds by comparing the firstling and the breast and thigh of thank-offerings. His argument is of the same type as Aqiva, but in fact is faulty.

Aqiva

9. Aqiva's argument on the basis of a *ribbui*.

10. Ishmael responds to 7-9 by criticizing the need for 9, as 8 is faulty.

The author has done a masterful job. There are no repetitions. In 2 he does not formulate an opinion for Yose but instead
ascribes a question to him. This creates suspense. It is only in
4 that we learn Yose's view. 7-8 present fresh material which
differ from 3-6 in their mode of argumentation. As we have noted,
perhaps for this reason 3-6 are attributed to Aqiva and not to
Tarfon.

    A. "[Everything that opens the womb of all flesh,
whether man or beast, which they offer to the Lord shall
be yours.] Nevertheless, you shall surely redeem [the
first born of man, and the firstling of unclean beasts
you shall redeem]" [Num 18:15].
    B. This is a question which was asked before the
sages at Kerem BeYavneh:
    C. [As to] a firstling which died, what is it [the
law with regard to its] owner['s rights] to redeem it and
to feed it to the dogs? [GRA: What is (the law) with
regard to redeeming it and to feeding it to the dogs?]
    D. 1. Expounded R. Tarfon, "'Nevertheless you
shall surely redeem,'
        2. "[this teaches that] you redeem the one which
is alive, but you do not redeem the one which is dead.
        3. "You redeem the one which is unclean, but you
do not redeem the one which is clean."

                    Sifre Num. 118, ed. Horowitz,
                    p. 138, lns. 13-15

Comment: This is a further example of an exegesis of Tarfon
preserved outside of M.-Tos. Tarfon's exegesis, D, can stand
alone. The redactor has introduced D by means of B+C. The introduction, however, is not appropriate for the following reasons: D
contains two rulings, D2 and D3, only the first of which is relevant to the present context. Second, expressions similar to B are
generally followed by the opinions of several masters. But in
this pericope only Tarfon's saying appears.
    Although the technique of Tarfon's exegesis is unclear,[10]
there is no problem as to its content. One does not redeem either
dead unclean animals or any clean animals. One redeems only living
unclean animals. The ruling regarding alive clean animals agrees
with Num 18:17 which states, "The firstling of a cow, or the firstling of a sheep, or the firstling of a goat, you shall not redeem,

they are holy." But Tarfon's opinion regarding dead animals appears to disagree with the anonymous ruling of Tos. Tem. 4:11:

>   A. [As to] all sanctified [animals] which became
> *ṭerefah* after their sanctification, and afterwards they
> died, they have a redemption.
>   B. But [if they became *ṭerefah*] after their sanctifi-
> cation, and [then] they died, they do not have a redemption.
>   C. For they do not redeem sanctified [foods] in order
> to feed them to the dogs.
>   D. The firstling and tithe have a redemption.
>
>   Tos. Tem. 4:11, ed. Zuckermandel,
>   p. 556, lns. 13-15

If we treat this pericope as a unitary text, then D rules that one
does redeem a dead firstling. This opposes Tarfon's opinion. We
may explain Tarfon's ruling in terms of C of Tos. Tem. When the
firstling dies, it still is holy. A redeemed dead animal can be
used for a very common purpose, such as feeding it to dogs. Tarfon's ruling prevents a person from treating previously sanctified
food in this manner.

Tarfon's ruling in this pericope seems to be based on reasoning identical to that in M. M̊.S. 2:4. In that pericope Tarfon
states that one does not redeem unclean vetches of second-tithe.
Unclean vetches, like a dead animal, can be used for little more
than animal fodder. Thus we have an example of the application of
a principle of Tarfon to identical legal problems. Furthermore,
Tarfon's opinion that one may not redeem unclean vetches of
second-tithe, like his ruling about dead firstlings, disagrees
with D of Tos. Tem. Tos. rules that one may redeem tithes.

>   A. *R. Judah Nesiah had a first-born ass.*
>   B. *He sent it before R. Tarfon.*
>   C. *He [Judah] said to him, "How much am I required
> to give the priest?"*
>   D. *He said to him,* "Lo, they have said, 'A [person]
> liberally [redeems] with a *sela* [= four *zuz*], [a person]
> miserly [redeems] with a *sheqel* [= two *zuz*], on the
> average, [a person redeems] with a *rigia*.'"
>   E. Said Rava, "*The law* [requires redemption] *with
> a rigia.*"
>   F. How much [is a *rigia*]?
>   G. *Three zuz.*
>
>   b. Bekh. 11a

Comment: A-D are a narrative which lacks the term M'SH. A-C, as well as the attributive formula in D, are in Aramaic. The lemma in D is in Hebrew and looks like a citation of a law. But no such law appears anywhere.

The pericope is an example of the breakdown of the Tarfon-tradition in the amoraic stratum. Tarfon renders a decision for Judah Nesiah. The latter generally is identified as the grandson of Judah the Patriarch. But even if we assume that pericope refers to Judah the Patriarch, Tarfon still is portrayed as rendering a decision for someone who lived two generations after him. Moreover, this is the only tradition of Tarfon is which he is associated with either Judah the Patriarch or Judah Nesiah. We can, however, account for the choice of Tarfon's name. The laws regarding firstlings are an important element of the corpus of Tarfon-traditions. Furthermore, Tarfon is depicted as a priest; therefore, it is logical for someone to enquire of him concerning the laws of firstlings. We thus have another tradition of Tarfon, that first appears in the later strata of the corpus, in which he simply supplies a name.

The context of this pericope is a discussion concerning the value of the lamb with which one redeems an ass. The amoraim treat D as an opinion which specifies the required value of the lamb. But if we read A-D without referring to the context, it relates that according to Tarfon one may redeem an ass with money. It says nothing about the value of the redemption-lamb. Albeck ("Qodashim," p. 153, lns. 1 and 3) points out that Tarfon's ruling opposes the mishnaic law regarding the redemption of an ass. M. and the halakhic midrashim interpret W'RPTW in Exod 13:13 and Exod 34:20, which state that one must either redeem a first-born ass with a sheep or W'RPTW, to mean that one must break the neck of the ass. According to this interpretation of the verses, one, therefore, must either redeem the ass with a sheep or break its neck. No one in M. knows anything about exchanging the ass for money. Albeck, however, cites the following saying which indicates that some authorities hold that one may redeem an ass with money.

> Said R. Isaac, Said Resh Laqish, "Whoever has a first-born ass and does not have a lamb [with which] to redeem it, he redeems it with its equivalent value [in money]." (b. Bekh. 11a)

Resh Laqish, like Tarfon, does not require redemption with a sheep but allows the use of money. This view may be based upon a definition of 'RP which means to "change for small coin" or "to change

into small coins."[11] Someone could therefore interpret Exod 13:13
and Exod 34:20, "And if you do not redeem it [with a sheep], you
shall exchange it for coins."[12]

> A.   [As to] one who is not an expert (MMḤH), and he
> examined the firstling, [and he declared it blemished], and
> it was slaughtered on his authority, lo, it [the firstling]
> shall be buried, and he shall pay [a restitution] from his
> own property (MBYTW).
> B.   1.   [If] he judged a matter of law, [and] declared
> innocent the guilty, or declared guilty the innocent, or
> declared unclean what was clean, or declared clean what
> was unclean, what he has done is done, but he pays [a
> restitution] from his own property.
>   2.   But if he was an expert [approved by] the
> court, he is exempt from paying.
> C.   1.   M'SH B: A cow which had its womb removed,
> [was brought before Tarfon], and R. Tarfon fed it to the
> dogs [since he declared the cow *terefah*],
>   2.   and the matter (M'SH) came before sages, and
> they permitted it [to be eaten].
> D.   Said Todos, the doctor, "There is neither cow nor
> sow that leaves Alexandria until they cut out its womb so
> that it cannot give birth."
> E.   Said R. Tarfon, "There goes your ass, Tarfon."
> F.   1.   Said to him R. Aqiva, "R. Tarfon, you are
> exempt, for you are an expert [approved by] the court,
>   2.   "and any expert [approved by] the court is
> exempt from paying."

> M. Bekh. 4:4 (C-F = b. Sanh. 33a)

Comment: The Aqivan circle of redactors responsible for this
pericope have paid attention to only what Tarfon did, that he
erred in a legal decision, but have disregarded the legal issue
discussed in C. Tarfon's actions, as E-F indicate, serve as an
illustration for the law of B. An expert approved by the court
does not have to pay a restitution if he makes an erroneous decision. Aqiva again is depicted as more versed in the law than
Tarfon. Not only does Tarfon rule incorrectly with regard to the
status of the cow, but he also does not know, as E demonstrates,
that an expert is exempt from paying the restitution.

If we treat C as a M'SH from which we may derive a legal
opinion, then according to Tarfon, a cow with its womb removed is
deemed unfit. Sages, however, declare it fit. C could be placed
after M. Ḥul. 3:2 which states, "And these are fit animals...[one
which] had its womb removed." Thus sages in C agree with the
anonymous law of M. Ḥul. 3:2.

We have two traditions of Tarfon, the present and Tos. Ḥul.
3:7, relating to the status of animals with defects. In both
cases Tarfon rules that the animal is unfit. Furthermore, both
traditions are not transmitted in the form of either a simple
declarative sentence or of a dispute. Tos. Ḥul. 3:7 is a testimony form; the present pericope a M'SH.

1. [If a priest has] extra [fingers] on his hands
and extra [toes] on his feet;

2. [namely], six [fingers on each hand] and six
[toes on each foot, such that they make up a total of]
twenty-four--

3. R. Judah declares fit.

4. But sages declare unfit.

M. Bekh. 7:6

A. [*If a priest has*] extra [*fingers or extra toes*]

B. such as [the one about whom Scripture] said,
"[And there was again war with Gath, and there was a
champion whose] fingers on his hands and toes on his
feet were six and six. [Twenty-four was the (total)
number]" [2 Sam 21:20]--

C. *R. Judah declares fit.*

D. But R. Yose declares unfit.

E. 1. Said R. Judah,

2. "M'SH: [An individual] came before R. Tarfon,
and he said,

3. "'May there be more high priests like him in
Israel.'"

F. 1. Said to him R. Yose, "He [Tarfon] said the.
following,

2. "'Like him, may there be fewer *netinim* [and]
mamzerim in Israel.'"

Tos. Bekh. 5:6-7, ed. Zuckermandel, p. 540, lns. 5-8

Comment: Tos. A-D parallel M. B of Tos. gives a Scriptural
verse, and not simply a description as in M.1-2. In Tos., sages'
opinion is attributed to Yose. Tos. E adds new material. The
M'SH is very elliptical. The context must supply the information
about the individual's physical condition. Judah and Yose agree
about the story line, E2, but disagree about Tarfon's response.
According to Judah, Tarfon wishes that the number of priests with
twenty-four digits would increase. Tarfon's saying thus implies
that a priest with extra fingers and toes is fit. But Yose's
version of Tarfon's saying has nothing to do with priests. According to Yose, Tarfon said merely that there should not be many
mamzerim and *netinim* in Israel, just as there should not be many
people with extra fingers and toes. From this we may infer that,
since Tarfon did not want there to be many people with twenty-four
digits, this indicates that this is an abnormality which dis-
qualifies a priest.

    A. 1. TNY': Said R. Judah, "M'SH B: *An individual*
came before R. Tarfon [and had] additional fingers and
toes, six on each [hand and foot making altogether]
twenty-four [digits].
        2. "*He [Tarfon] said* to him,
        3. "'*May there be more like you in Israel.*'"
    B. 1. Said R. Yose to him, "Do you bring proof from
that incident?
        2. "[It is in fact the case that] *he* [Tarfon]
said to him *the following, 'Like* you, *may there be fewer*
mamzerim *and* netinim *in Israel.*'"

                    b. Bekh. 45b

Comment: The wording of the baraita differs from that of Tos.,
but the tradition is still very elliptical. The storyline now contains the information that the person has twenty-four digits. But
Tarfon in A3 does not say anything about priests. It is only on
the basis of the context that we assume the pericope concerns
priests with defects. Thus perhaps the tradition has nothing to
do with priests, but merely considers whether or not it is good
for people to have extra fingers and toes.

    A. [If] the father gave five *selas* to five priests,
his son is redeemed.
    B. [If] he gave them [the *selas*] to him [a priest]
one after another, his son is redeemed.

C. If he gave them to him [the priest], and he [the father] came back and took them from him [the priest], his son is redeemed.

D. 1. Thus (KK HYH) R. Tarfon used to do;

2. he took them [the *selas*] from him [the father], and he [the father] came back, and he [Tarfon] gave [the money] to him.

> Tos. Bekh. 6:14, ed. Zucker-
> mandel, p. 541, lns. 12-14
> (b. Bekh. 51b)

Comment: A-C is a scenario of anonymous laws. D serves the function of a M'SH. It has been formulated together with C. D2 is redundant, for it merely spells out that which D1 implies.

A. R. Aqiva declares [a man] liable [to bring] a suspensive guilt-offering for doubtfully committed sacrileges.

B. But sages exempt.

C. But R. Aqiva admits that he does not bring the restitution for his sacrilege until he is certain [that he did in fact accidentally commit the sacrilege], and [then] he shall bring with it, [the restitution], an unconditional guilt-offering.

D. 1. Said R. Tarfon,

2. "Why does this one bring two guilt-offerings? Rather,

3. "he should bring [a fine equal to the value of] his sacrilege plus one-fifth [the combined value of the sacrilege and the fine], and he shall bring a guilt-offering [costing] two *selas* and he shall say, 'If I have surely committed a sacrilege, this is my [restitution for] the sacrilege, and this is my guilt-offering, and if it is un-certain [that I have committed the sacrilege], the coins are a free-will offering and the guilt-offering is sus-pensive.'

4. "[He may do this], for he brings the same [offering] for that which is certain as for that which is uncertain." [Both the suspensive guilt-offering and the guilt-offering for the sacrilege are a ram worth at least two *selas*.]

E. 1. Said to him R. Aqiva,

2. "Your words make sense with regard to a small sacrilege.

3. "[But] lo, [if it] happens that a doubt shall
occur [concerning] a sacrilege of one hundred *maneh*s, is it
not better for him to bring a guilt-offering worth two
*sela*s and not bring for a doubtfully committed sacrilege
[a restitution] worth one hundred *maneh*s?"

F. Lo, R. Aqiva agrees with R. Tarfon with regard
to a small sacrilege.

M. Ker. 5:2-3

Comment: A-B are a dispute in which the superscription appears
in A. The dispute relates to the following biblical laws. Lev 5:
17-19 mandate that if there is uncertainty about whether or not a
person has accidentally transgressed a commandment, he must bring
a suspensive guilt-offering. Lev 5:15-16 detail what one does if
he commits a sacrilege. He brings an unconditional guilt-offering
worth two *sheqal*s and a restitution equal to 125% of the value of
the desecrated object. A-B discuss whether or not the law of Lev
5:17-19, that regarding a doubtfully committed transgression, applies to the case of an accidental sacrilege. Does one bring a
suspensive guilt-offering for a doubtfully committed sacrilege?
Sages rule that one does not bring the offering; Aqiva rules one
brings it.[13] C expands Aqiva's saying, detailing how one acts
after there is no longer any doubt concerning his having committed
a sacrilege. One then brings the sacrifices ordained in Lev 5:15-
16. But if the transgressor brings these offerings only after
there is no longer any doubt, then he ends up offering two guilt-
offerings, one suspensive and one unconditional.

D has Tarfon respond to Aqiva's position. Thus as the pericope now reads, Tarfon could not have ruled without knowing Aqiva's
view on the question of the procedure for rectifying a doubtfully
committed sacrilege. But if we drop D2, D1+3 could respond to a
superscription such as, "As to a doubtfully committed sacrilege."
The redactor has neatly worked Tarfon's saying into the present
pericope by means of adding C, which could have been generated from
A.[14] Tarfon's ruling offers an alternative means for the person to
right his wrong. His solution avoids the economic problem of
bringing two sacrifices. Tarfon, like Aqiva, rules that one brings
a suspensive guilt-offering for a doubtfully committed sacrilege.
But since the person must bring this offering when he is uncertain,
he has the option which Tarfon lays out in D3. If the uncertainty
persists, then the guilt-offering is suspensive, and the money is
a free-will offering. If, however, the doubt is removed, the

guilt-offering becomes unconditional while the money serves as a
restitution for the sacrilege. Tarfon and Aqiva thus do not disagree about any laws. They simply offer different solutions to a
practical problem. E indicates that Tarfon's proposal is viable
only for cases involving a sacrilege of an object of little value.
But if one follows Tarfon's procedure for cases involving sacrileges of large amounts, and the doubt persists, then he has un-
necessarily given a very substantial free-will offering.

> A.   "And if" [Lev 5:17]. [These are the opening
> words of the section in the Bible which contains the law
> for a suspensive guilt-offering. This section immediately
> follows Lev 5:15-16 which detail the law regarding a
> sacrilege.]
> B.   "Lo, this adds to the first matter [the laws
> about sacrilege] so as to say that a sacrilege that is
> in doubt [requires] a suspensive guilt-offering," the
> words of R. Aqiva.
> C.   Said to him R. Tarfon, "Why...[identical to M.
> Ker. 5:2-3D-F]."
>
>   Sifra Vayiqra' Parashata 12:1,2,
>   ed. Weiss, 26b-c

Comment: Sifra connects M. to a Scriptural proof text. It
revises Aqiva's saying so that it reads as an exegesis. Sifra,
however, omits C of M. and as a result Tarfon's statement in C is
out of place. One must, therefore, read Sifra with M.

Aqiva's exegesis is based on a *ribbui*. The inclusion of the
words "and if" at the beginning of 5:17 indicates that the laws of
the suspensive guilt-offering mentioned in verses 17-19 apply to
cases of sacrilege mentioned in 5:15-16. Thus Scripture supports
the view of Aqiva and Tarfon.

CHAPTER V

[1]The redactor of M., as well as Nathan in Tos. (see p. 132),
treat the dispute as concerned with the question of whether or
not one must scour and rinse a pot on a festival in order to avoid
the problem of "remnant" (*notar*). According to Exod 29:34 and Lev
7:17, one must burn those portions of sacrifices which have not
been eaten once the prescribed period allowed for their consumption has expired. Anyone who eats these remnants, *notar*, sins.
Lev 6:21 mandates that a pot in which one cooks a sin-offering
must be scoured and rinsed. The rabbis explain that this pre-
scription is to avoid the creation of *notar*. The traditional explanation of our pericope treats the saying of Tarfon and sages
as concerned with the problem of "remnant" caused by cooking
sacrifices on the festival. Tarfon, according to this explanation,
rules that if a pot is used from the beginning of a festival, one
may use it, without scouring and rinsing, the entire festival.
Bert. and TYY explain that on each day of the festival, a peace-
offering is cooked in the pot. The sacrifice cooked in the pot on
the second day of the festival has the effect of scouring and
rinsing the pot, and thereby removes any residue from the previous
day's sacrifice. Since peace-offerings may be consumed within a
period of two days and one night, then even on the second day the
residue of the sacrifice from the first day has not become *notar*.
This explanation of Tarfon's opinion, however, eliminates the
whole problem of *notar*. To claim that by cooking in the pot the
residue disappears means that in effect one need not ever scour
and rinse his pots.

The various commentators disagree about the time the sages
prescribe for scouring and rinsing. One view is that these actions must be performed before the expiration of the period allowed
for consumption of the sacrifice, while the second view is that one
must scour and rinse the pot at the time he eats the sacrifice (see
TYT). The former interpretation treats sages' opinion as an illustration of the laws of *notar*. But the second interpretation, which
claims that one must scour and rinse the pot at the time of eating,
in effect avoids the problem of *notar*. The problem of *notar* arises
only after the expiration of the time allowed for consumption.

The traditional explanation of the dispute, besides in effect
eliminating its basis, also reads a great deal into the pericope.
First, we must assume that the opinions deal with the cooking of
sacrifices. Second, we must add to Tarfon's saying the words
"without scouring and rinsing." Third, unless we treat C as part
of sages' saying, then neither Tarfon nor sages mention scouring
and rinsing. Fourth, the above explanation does not account for
the inclusion of the words "from the beginning of" in Tarfon's
saying. Would not the logic given by Bert. to explain Tarfon's
saying still apply even if one began cooking in the pot on the
second day of the Festival? Fifth, Tarfon's saying makes no sense
unless we assume the sacrifices cooked in the pot are peace-
offerings. But if a sin-offering which must be consumed during
the first day and night is cooked in the pot, the alleged reasoning behind Tarfon's statement does not hold up. By the next day,
when a new sacrifice would be cooked in the pot, the residue of
the sin-offering will have already become "remnant."

[2]To treat B-C as the sages' opinion involves reading a great
deal into both it and Tarfon's saying. B and C are elliptical
sayings, and there are several ways of filling in the missing
ideas. One way of reading B+C is, "Until the time of eating [he
may cook therein without] scouring and rinsing." Such a saying
responds to A2-3 and thus is in dispute with A4. But treating B+C
in this manner, in addition to the problem of reading in the above
words, causes the following difficulties. First, B+C and A4 are
not balanced. Second, in order to treat A4 and B+C as a dispute
requires the addition to A4 of the words "without scouring and
rinsing." A second alternative for reading B+C is the following:
"Until the time of eating [one is not required to perform] scouring and rinsing." Such a saying responds to A2. But besides the
lack of balance between A3-4 and B+C, the two sayings appear to
address different issues. A3-4 deal with the time permitted for
cooking. B+C are concerned with the time one must scour and rinse
the pot. A further reason for limiting sages' opinion to B is
that C-D are an intelligible pericope.

[3]In light of the traditional explanation of M. Zev. 11:7, I
can account for Tos. B only if I read Tarfon's comment along with
both Tos. C, and a saying of Simeon in M. Zev. 11:7a. Simeon's
saying appears with an anonymous law in a pericope which reads
(M. Zev. 11:7a):

> 1. It is the same whether [one cooks in the pots]
> more holy sacrifices or less holy sacrifices, they [the
> pots] require scouring and rinsing.
> 2. R. Simeon says, "[For] less holy sacrifices [the
> pots] do not require scouring and rinsing."

Simeon does not require the scouring and rinsing of pots in which
lesser holy sacrifices are cooked. If Tarfon's opinion, as Nathan
in C asserts, applies only to lesser holy sacrifices, and Tarfon
agrees with Simeon, then it follows that one need not scour and
rinse the pots after the festival. But if pots in which lesser
holy sacrifices are cooked never require scouring and rinsing,
then why, as Tarfon's saying implies, must one cook in the pots
every day of the festival?

[4]Only this reading makes sense, for that of Ms. M and of N
does not provide a basis for the analogy drawn between oil and wine.

[5]I treat Tos. Men. 12:10b, in line with Lieberman's emendation,
as a comment upon M. Men. 12:4; therefore, I do not present it.

[6]This agrees with GRA who omits H-L.

[7]Rashba offers the following reconstruction. He contends that,
according to Tarfon, the fact that there is a distinction with regard to the commoner's right to eat the new produce is irrelevant
to the law regarding the use of the new grain in the meal-offerings.
Tarfon argues Scripture explicitly states that one must bring a new
meal-offering on Pentecost. This is a commandment in its own right
and is independent of the laws pertaining to the commoner's right
to eat the new grain. According to Rashba, Tarfon's argument is:

> R. Tarfon says, There is no difference between the
> laws regarding meal-offerings made from new produce which
> were offered prior to the bringing of the 'omer, and those
> which pertain to meal-offerings brought prior to the
> bringing of the bread-offering. Both are unfit. Scrip-
> ture states that on Pentecost one must bring a new

meal-offering. This means that if a meal-offering made
from new grain was brought any time prior to Pentecost
[i.e., even after the '*omer* has been presented], it is
unfit.

Tarfon's opinion thus disagrees with that of M. Judah b. Nehemiah,
however, contends that there is a distinction in the other laws
relating to the two periods; therefore, the distinction in M. is
valid.

[8]Maim. and TYY, based upon b. Bek. 18b-19a, give essentially
the same explanation for the need for citing the three cases A, M,
and W. Maim. and TYY agree with regard for the need for A and M.
They explain that, regarding the case described in A, Aqiva claims
we cannot be certain that the better came out first. The priest,
therefore, receives the weaker of the two animals since he must
supply proof to substantiate his claim. But in the second case,
M, we would assume that the better of the two animals was born
from the animal which gave birth to only one animal. Aqiva would,
therefore, agree that the priest receives the better of the two
animals. It is, therefore, necessary to give M and Aqiva's opinion. Maim. explains the need for W as follows: We would assume
that the better animal was the offspring of the animal which had
already given birth. A second or third child is larger than a
first child. We would, therefore, think that Tarfon agrees that
the weaker of the two animals belongs to the priest. As a result,
M. cites W and Tarfon's opinion in order to teach us that even in
this case, Tarfon claims that the priest is entitled to the better
animal. This explanation of the need for all three cases supports
our explanation of Tarfon's opinion. Tarfon's opinion cannot be
based upon the assumption that the better of the two animals is
the firstling. His ruling, rather, seems to rest upon the notion
that the priest receives the benefit of the doubt. TYY explains
that we need W, since we would think that in this case the better
animal was born from the sheep which had not previously given
birth. Aqiva would, therefore, admit the better animal belongs to
the priest. It is for this reason that it is necessary to give
Aqiva's opinion with regard to this case.

[9]The first explanation is based upon the standard meaning of
the verb ŠMN. The second derives the verb from ŠMN, fat, and
treats MŠMNYM as a *pi'el* with the meaning, "to place the fat between them."

[10]Malbim and Nesiv explain Tarfon's exegesis as a *miyyut*.
The word "nevertheless" teaches that only certain animals may be
redeemed, in this case only alive, unclean animals. Dead or clean
animals may not be redeemed. But why should we interpret "nevertheless" to exclude *these* cases? According to R. Hillel, Tarfon's
exegesis is based upon a *heqesh*. The mention of the first born of
man and the firstling of unclean animals in the same verse teaches
that, just as we do not redeem a dead, first born human, so too we
do not redeem a dead, first born, unclean animal. But M. Bekh.
8:6 preserves the anonymous ruling that one does redeem a human
who dies after reaching the age of redemption, thirty days.

[11]See Jastrow, p. 1122. Sifre Deut. testifies to this usage
of 'RP.

> Another interpretation [of], "May my doctrine drop
> (Y'RWP) like dew" [Deut 32:2].
> R. Nehemiah used to say, "...And Y'RWP is nothing
> but [a word from the] Canaanite language. A parable:

A man does not say to his friend [in Canaanite] change
(PWRṬ) this *sela* into small coins; rather, [he says]
'RWP [change] this *sela* [into small coins]. (Sifre Deut.
306, ed. Finkelstein, p. 336)

This tradition clearly shows that some rabbis knew the usage of
'RWP which means to exchange for small coins. In the Palmyrene
Tarrif (in Cooke, p. 329, ln. 8) we find: 'DT' '(R)PN YH' GB'.
Cooke translates this, "It is a custom to levy in small coin."
Furthermore, Payne Smith (p. 429) translates 'RP "to change
money." Thus this data shows that there is a semitic root 'RP
which means to change into small coin, or to exchange for small
coin.

[12]Albeck offers the following alternative explanation for the
opinion which allows the exchange of coins for the ass: Josephus
and Philo note two means for redeeming an ass. One may either exchange it for a sheep or "redeem it." "Redeem it" probably means
that one gives the priest money equal to the value of the ass.
Thus both Josephus and Philo know nothing of killing the ass.
Albeck claims that Josephus and Philo base their statements on the
Septuagint's translations of Exod 13:13 and Exod 34:20. These
read: "Every firstling of an ass, you shall exchange for a sheep,
and if you will not exchange it, you must redeem it [translation
to Exod 34:20 adds: for its equal amount]." There is clearly an
exegetical tradition which does allow redemption of the ass with
money.

[13]Sages' opinion agrees with the rule of M. Ker. 1:2 that one
brings a suspensive guilt-offering only for those sins for which
one brings a sin-offering if it is certain that the person accidentally transgressed the law. Now since one does not bring a sin-
offering but a guilt-offering for an accidental sacrilege, one does
not bring a suspensive guilt-offering for a doubtfully committed
sacrilege. Maim. explains that Aqiva requires the suspensive
guilt-offering for any transgression for which one brings any type
of sacrifice when certain that he has transgressed.

[14]The option of placing Tarfon's ruling D1+3 in a dispute
with Aqiva's sayings A+C is not very viable. Such a dispute would
read:

    A. As to a sacrilege that is in doubt--
    B. R. Aqiva says, "He shall bring a suspensive
guilt-offering, and if it is made known to him that he
did accidentally commit the sacrilege, he shall then
bring a restitution and an unconditional guilt-offering."
    C. R. Tarfon says, "He shall bring a fine equal to
the value of the sacrilege plus one-fifth and a guilt-
offering worth two *sela*s, and he shall say...[remainder
of D3]."

This proposed dispute is problematic on both formal and literary
grounds. The sayings, contrary to their normal form in a dispute,
are very long. The two sayings, moreover, are not contradictory;
they simply offer different alternatives to a practical but not to
a legal problem.

CHAPTER VI

ṬOHOROT

A. A door bolt (QLSṬR') is susceptible to uncleanness.

B. And one which is plated [wood plated with metal] is clean.

C. The clutch (PYN) and the cross-piece (PRNH) are susceptible to uncleanness.

D. And the door bolt--

E. R. Joshua says, "One separates it (ŠWMṬH) from this door (PTḤ) and suspends it on another (BḤBYRW) on the Sabbath."

F. 1. R. Tarfon says,

2. "Lo, it is like all utensils

3. "and is moved about in a courtyard."

> M. Kel. 11:4 (b. Shab. 124a,[1]
> y. Shab. 17:1 16a)

Comment: A-C discuss the cleanness of certain parts of the door. The general principle which applies is, if a metal object is an autonomous object, it is susceptible to uncleanness. But if it is part of another utensil, it is not susceptible. D appears because of the mention of the door bolt in A, but it concerns the issue, which is entirely unrelated, whether or not one may carry the door bolt on the Sabbath.

The opinions of Tarfon and Joshua are presented in a dispute form. But both formal and literary considerations suggest that D-F are an artificial dispute. The opinions lack balance. The subject in the two sayings differ; in E it is the anonymous "one," and in F it is the "door bolt." Finally, the operative words in the two sayings, ŠWMṬH WṬWLH vs. MṬLṬLT BḤSR, are unrelated.

Our interpretation of these sayings, based on an analysis of the above operative words, shows that the opinions deal with different issues. Joshua's ruling relates to the issue of whether or not on the Sabbath one may use a door bolt in its normal manner.[2] Joshua rules one may do so.[3] Tarfon's saying deals with the issue of whether or not one may carry a door bolt on the Sabbath. Tarfon considers the door bolt an autonomous object, a KLY, and this is sufficient reason to allow one to move it about on the Sabbath. One does not necessarily have to intend to use the door bolt in order to carry it on the Sabbath. The laws relating to carrying objects on the Sabbath seem to be based on the assumption that one

183

may carry an object if it *could* serve a permitted function on the
Sabbath. In light of this fact we may offer an explanation for
the inclusion of the words "in a courtyard" in Tarfon's saying.
One may carry about the door bolt on the Sabbath only in a domain
in which it is possible to use it.[4]

Lying behind these opinions are the assumptions that, for
Joshua, the bolt is an autonomous object when it serves its function. For Tarfon, it is the form of the door bolt which qualifies
it as an autonomous object.[5] In light of this explanation, we
also may conclude that the ruling of A could, under the appropriate circumstances, agree with either Joshua or Tarfon. For Tarfon
the object is always an autonomous utensil, and hence, always unclean. For Joshua, when in use, the object is susceptible to
uncleanness.

>   A. A door bolt--
>   B. R. Tarfon declares susceptible to uncleanness.
>   C. But sages declare clean.
>   D. And Beruria says, "One separates it from this
> door and suspends it on another on the Sabbath."
>   E. When these things were reported before R. Judah
> [alternatively, R. Joshua; see Lieberman, *T.R.* III, p. 35],
> he said, "Beruria ruled beautifully."
>
>   Tos. Kel. B.M. 1:6, ed. Zucker-
>   mandel, pp. 578-79, lns. 40-42

Comment: The anonymous rule of A of M. is now attributed to
Tarfon. In our explanation of M. we noted that under certain conditions Tarfon would concur with this anonymous ruling. Joshua's
saying in M. is cited in Beruria's name. Tos. also knows nothing
of Tarfon's opinion in M. M. and Tos., therefore, are probably
two independent traditions.[6]

>   A. 1. A curved horn is susceptible to uncleanness.
>   2. And a flat one is clean.
>   B. If its mouthpiece was [made] of metal, it is
> unclean.
>   C. Its wide [metal end (QB)]--
>   D. R. Tarfon declares susceptible to uncleanness.
>   E. And sages declare clean.
>   F. And when they are joined, the whole is susceptible
> to uncleanness.
>   M. Kel. 11:7

Comment: The superscription, C, in the dispute between Tarfon
and sages depends upon A. The sayings in D-E use the fixed opposites clean/unclean.

The horn discussed in A is made of bone. A1 follows the rule
of M. Kel. 2:1; 15:1 a flat bone object is insusceptible to uncleanness; a curved one, A2, one shaped like a receptacle, is susceptible to uncleanness. B and C discuss two other parts of the
horn, its mouthpiece and its QB, its wide metal end. The issue is
whether these parts of the horn are objects with a name of their
own, autonomous objects, or whether they are merely parts of the
horn. The metal mouthpiece is an autonomous object and, therefore,
following the ruling of M. Kel. 11:2, is unclean. Sages and Tarfon, however, disagree concerning the QB. Bert., TYY, and Maim.
explain that the QB is made of metal. Tarfon considers it an object with its own name and, therefore, declares it unclean; while
sages hold the opposite opinion. In F sages are brought over
to Tarfon's view. F follows the ruling of M. Kel. 12:2, that what
is joined to something unclean is unclean. F thus presupposes
that one part of the horn, the wide end, is unclean.

> A. All utensils have an outer part and an inner
> part, and they [also] have a part by which they are held
> (BYT ṢBY'H) [a finger hole sunk into the edge which does
> not become unclean if the outside is, and which, when
> unclean, does not render the rest unclean].
> B. R. Tarfon says, "[This distinction in the outer
> parts applies] to a large wooden trough."
> C. R. Aqiva says, "To cups."
> D. R. Meir says, "To the unclean and the clean hands."
> E. Said R. Yose, "They have spoken exclusively about
> clean hands."

M. Kel. 25:7 (Tos. Kel. B.B.
3:8,11, y. Ḥag. 3:1 78d)

Comment: The anonymous rule, A, serves as a superscription for
two sets of disputing opinions, B-C and D-E. These two sets of
opinions discuss different issues. B-C, the dicta with which we
are concerned, list objects to which the rule of A applies.

M. Kel. 25:1 states that all utensils are divided into inner
and outer parts. The effect of this division is that if the outer
part of the vessel is unclean, the inner part still is clean. If,
however, the inner part of the vessel is unclean, the outer part

also is unclean. A of our pericope tells us that we must distinguish among three and not two parts of a vessel. In addition to
inner and outer parts, all utensils have a holding place. Tarfon
and Aqiva gloss this ruling by giving the names of specific vessels to which it applies. The force of these glosses is to limit
A's rule only to the vessels mentioned in the respective opinions.

> A.   [Concerning] a clump of earth from a clean land,
> and a clump of earth from a grave area (BYT HPRŚ), and a
> clump of earth from a clean land, and a clump of earth
> from a [foreign] land, their measure [in order to convey
> uncleanness is the size of] a large stopper of sacks
> (KPYWH GDWLH ŠL ŚQ'YN), and which is [the same size as]
> the upper part of the stopper [used in] a Lachmeite barrel.
> B.   R. Tarfon says, "[The amount of] earth from a
> grave area [which renders unclean must be] enough to cover
> a barleycorn's bulk of bone."

> Tos. Kel. B.M. 7:1, ed. Zucker-
> mandel, p. 585, lns. 37-39

Comment: Our first problem is to determine the proper context
for this pericope. The preceding one, Tos. Kel. B.M. 7:1, is a
dispute between Meir and sages concerning the size of a ladleful
of corpse-mould and is cited here because M. Kel. 17:12 states,
"Sometimes they have prescribed a large measure, thus a ladleful
of corpse-mould is according to the big ladle of physicians...."
M. Kel. 17:12, however, makes no mention of earth from a foreign
country or of earth from a grave-area. The identical dispute between Meir and sages, however, also appears in Tos. Ah. 2:2. In
that location, the dispute comments upon M. Ohal. 2:1 (and possibly
upon M. Ohal. 2:2) which state the rule concerning the uncleanness
of a ladleful of corpse-mould. M. Ohal. 2:3 reads:

> A.   These convey uncleanness by contact and by
> carrying but not by overshadowing:
> B.   (1) a barleycorn's bulk of bone, (2) earth
> from a foreign land, (3) earth from a grave area....

Thus, just as Meir and sages prescribe the measure for the ladleful
of corpse-mould mentioned in M. Ohal. 2:1,2, the opinions in our
pericope supply measures for the amount of earth from a foreign
country or from a grave area which convey uncleanness by contact
or by carrying.

Tarfon requires enough earth to cover a barleycorn's bulk of
bone as the amount of earth from a grave area which conveys uncleanness. The reason earth from a grave area conveys uncleanness
is that it may contain a barleycorn's bulk of bone. Maim., TYY,
MA, and Tosafot Anshé Shem, explaining M. Ohal. 2:3, give this as
the reason that earth from a grave area renders unclean. Sages
give a measurement in terms of stoppers, probably larger than a
barleycorn.

M. Ohal. 17:5 contains the following dispute which may presuppose sages' opinion in our pericope:

> A. "[As to] soil from a grave area or [as to] soil
> from a foreign land which was brought in with vegetables,
> [the several pieces of soil] are included together [to
> make up the bulk] equal to the seal of packing bags
> (KHWTM HMRSWPYM) [which suffices to convey uncleanness],"
> the words of R. Eliezer.
> B. But sages say, "[It conveys uncleanness] only
> if in one place there was a bulk equal to the seal of
> packing bags."

The dispute of Eliezer and sages concerns the question of joining
together (ṣeruf), not the question of the amount of earth which
conveys uncleanness. But both Eliezer and sages presuppose that
the measure for earth from a grave-area which conveys uncleanness
is the size of the seal of packing bags. GRA and TYT equate the
seal of packing bags, the large stopper of sacks, and the upper
part of the stopper used in a Lachmeite barrel. If this equation
is correct, then both Eliezer and sages in M. Ohal. 17:5 agree
with the opinion of sages in Tos. Kel. B.M. 7:1, rejecting Tarfon's
measure.

1. [As to] one who makes a light hole in the first
instance [a new one], its measure [which suffices to give
passage to uncleanness] is that of the breadth of a hole
made by the drill in the chamber of the Temple....

2. [If] water or creeping things bored it [the
hole], or if saltpetre ate it through, its measure is
the size of a fist.

3. [If] one gave thought to it to make use of it,
its measure is a square handbreadth.

4. [If] to make use of it as a light hole, its
measure is the breadth of the hole of the drill.

M. Ohal. 13:1

    A. [As to] a hole that is in the door [which
suffices to allow uncleanness to pass through], its
measure [is]--

    B. "the size of a fist," the words of R. Aqiva.

    C. R. Tarfon says, "A square handbreadth."

M. Ohal. 13:3

Comment: A-C are in a chiastic dispute, "ruling, words of R.
x; R. y says + ruling." Tarfon's opinion employs the ŠYWR B-
formula. The opinions may be reduced to the balanced words
'GRWP vs. ṬPḤ.

According to biblical law, Num 19:14, if a person dies in a
tent, everyone who is in the tent, or who comes into the tent, is
unclean for seven days. A tent under which a corpse or corpse
matter is found thus transfers uncleanness to other things and
persons under it. Underlying the Oral Law of M.-Tos. Ohal. is the
view that a surface the size of a square handbreadth is a tent.
A surface of this size, therefore, can transfer uncleanness to
items under it and, at the same time, prevents the passage of uncleanness to objects outside the tent. Conversely, M.-Tos. assume
that corpse uncleanness passes through an opening of a square
handbreadth, the standard measure. In relationship to M. Ohal.
13:1-3, Neusner therefore notes, "When we come to the history,
within the Mishnaic law, of the prior conception of the standard
measure for the Tent, we find no development, but a major and, to
me, ultimately insoluble problem. Whether man or utensils give
passage to uncleanness is made to depend upon whether we have the
standard measure, the hole sufficient for the passage of corpse-
uncleanness. The Houses assume that corpse-uncleanness will pass
only through a space at least as large as a handbreadth. 13:1-3,
[however], distinguish between various holes by the criteria of
intention, function, and origin, i.e., whether made by man or
whether made by nature and, as a result, the Houses and Aqiva contradict their views in the remainder of the tractate" (*HMLP* V, pp.
250-51). Thus 1-2 of M. Ohal. 13:1 differentiate between holes
made by man and those made by nature. According to 1, if a hole
is deliberately made so as to admit light, then even a hole the
size of a drill suffices to allow for the passage of uncleanness.
But according to 2, a hole made by nature must be larger, the size
of a fist, in order to allow for the passage of uncleanness. 3-4
of M. modify 2. 3 brings the ruling of 2 in line with the law
assumed throughout the remainder of the tractate. A hole must be a

square handbreadth in order to allow for the passage of uncleanness. 4 brings 2 over to the view of 1. A light hole the size of
a drill allows for the passage of uncleanness.

The rulings of Tarfon and Aqiva in 13:3 relate to the laws
of 13:1. Aqiva treats the hole in the door as one made by nature,
not purposely by man. A hole in a door the size of a fist allows
for the passage of uncleanness. Tarfon, however, classifies it as
one purposefully used (3 of M. 13:1). Accordingly, it must be a
square handbreadth to allow for the passage of uncleanness. As we
have noted, these rulings, in light of the remainder of the tractate, are perplexing. Neusner suggests that "perhaps the construction of M. 13:1ff., even including Tarfon's and Aqiva's item,
is wholly Ushan, with its stress on intention, on the one hand,
function (of the hole) on the second, and the distinction between
man and nature, on the third" (*HMLP* V, pp. 250-51).

> A. "And any open vessel [which does not have a seal,
> (and which is in a tent in which a person dies) is unclean]"
> [Num 19:16].
> B. [As to] a hole that is in the door, its measure
> [is]--
> C. "the size of a fist," the words of R. Tarfon.
> D. R. Aqiva says, "A square handbreadth."

> Sifre Zuṭṭa Ḥuqat 19:16-17,
> ed. Horowitz, p. 311, lns. 5-6

Comment: Sifre connects the dispute of M. Ohal. 13:3 to a
verse. "Any open vessel" of Scripture applies to any opening,
even one in a door. The attributions of the opinions are reversed.
Sifre thereby corrects M. so that Aqiva does not contradict his
view in the remainder of Ohal. Tarfon's ruling is also now in
agreement with a principle found through his traditions, i.e., a
person's intentions, in this case to use the hole, are inconsequential. The hole simply must meet the requirements of the form
of a hole in order to allow for the passage of uncleanness.

> 1. And these are [the instances in] which they have
> spoken of a large measure...
> 2. And the light hole not made by the power of man,
> its measure [in order to allow uncleanness to pass through
> it] is that of a large fist.
> 3. This is the fist of Ben Baṭṭiah.

4.   Said R. Yose, "That is the size of a large head
of man."

M. Kel. 17:2

A.   The fist of which they spoke:

B.   R. Tarfon spreads (PWŠT) out the tips of his
fingers and shows [the size].

C.   R. Aqiva closes (QWPṢ) the tips of his fingers
and shows [the size].

D.   R. Judah places his fingers on his big thumb
and brings it down [around it].

E.   R. Yose says, "YŠNW BR'Š KRYM GDWL ŠL ṢYPWRY."

F.   Others say in his name, "A handbreadth and a
third of a handbreadth."

G.   And so did they measure before Ben Baṭṭiaḥ came.
[After that time they measured according to his fist.]

Tos. Kel. B.M. 7:2, ed. Zucker-
mandel, p. 586, lns. 1-4

Comment: The ruling of 2 of M. Ohal. 13:1 = 2 of M. Kel. 17:2
now appears in a catalogue which gives various large measurements.
3-4 of M. Kel. 17:2 gloss 2 by defining the size of the fist. B-F
of Tos. Kel. B.M. 7:2 give five more measurements for the fist.
B-C are neatly balanced descriptions of the actions of Tarfon and
Aqiva. They employ the opposites of PWŠT vs. QWPṢ. Similarly, D
describes the actions of the Ushan, Judah. E's version of Yose's
saying, which is incomprehensible (see Lieberman, *T.R.* III, p. 55),
differs from 4 of M. Kel. 17:12D. The attributive formula in
Tos. is also not the same as that in M. F attributes an alternative saying to Yose. G brings the ruling of Tos. in line with B
of M. Kel. 17:12. If we separate the opinions according to those
of Yavneans and those of Ushans, we see that the descriptions of
the actions of the Yavneans are neatly formulated. But for the
Ushans we have a description of Judah's action, three different
sayings attributed to Yose, using different attributive formulae,
and finally, a simple statement that the fist is the size of that
of Ben Baṭṭiaḥ. I cannot determine, except for F, the exact size
of the proposed measurements for the fist. Tarfon's measurement
clearly is larger than that of Aqiva.

A.   All movables bring uncleanness [as tents if they
are] as thick as an ox-goad [which is a handbreadth in
circumference, a finger and a third in breadth (M. Kel.
17:8)].

B. 1. Said R. Tarfon,

2. "May I bury my sons, for this is a ruined
law (HLKH MQPHṬ), which the hearer heard and erred, that

3. "the farmer passes [by the tomb] with the
ox-goad on his shoulder, and one side of it [the ox-goad]
overshadowed the tomb, and they declared him unclean,

4. "because of [the law governing] utensils
which overshadow the corpse."

C. 1. Said R. Aqiva,

2. "I shall rectify [the law] so that the words
of the sages may endure. Thus:

D. 1. "all movables bring the uncleanness on the
man who carries them [if they are as] thick as an ox-goad,

2. "and to themselves if they are any measure
at all,

3. "and on another man and on [other] utensils
[if they are] a square handbreadth."

M. Ohal. 16:1 (b. Shab. 16b-17a)

Comment: The pericope, as presently formulated, consists of
three elements, an anonymous law phrased as a simple declarative
sentence, A, and two comments upon it, B and C+D. Both comments
claim that A is erroneous. Tarfon's sole contribution is to say
that A is the result of an error in the transmission of a precedent, B3. It is Aqiva who is credited with rectifying this incorrect law. D gives us Aqiva's restatement of A. Thus the pericope,
as presently formulated, is another example of the use of Tarfon
to set up Aqiva. Tarfon merely points out a problem which not he,
but Aqiva, solves. We can, however, isolate elements of what may
lie behind the pericope as it now stands. B3 and D are intelligible on their own. B3 is a precedent which merely lacks the formula M'SH B. The parallel in Tos. supplies this language. D is a
restatement and modification of A. A pericope consisting of A,
B1+3, C1+D thus gives us an anonymous law (A), a precedent (B1+3),
and a reformulation of A (D). With the addition of B2, which
carries in its wake B4 and C2, the pericope has the entirely different structure which we have explained above.

The precedent (B3) attributed to Tarfon, and the rulings (D)
assigned to Aqiva, except for one of their details, are in agreement with the laws assumed throughout Ohal. Thus an object of any
size which overshadows a corpse contracts uncleanness (M. Ohal.
15:10). Anyone who touches such an object, is rendered unclean.

This is the reason the farmer in B3 was declared unclean. Finally, an object must be a square handbreadth in order to bring uncleanness as a tent (M. Ohal. 12:6-7). Only the detail that a movable object must be as thick as an ox-goad in order to convey uncleanness to the person carrying it (D1) is not found in the remainder of the tractate. On the other hand, A, as interpreted by the redactor, does not agree with the presuppositions of the rest of Ohal. The redactor who added B2+4 and C2 thus takes A to mean that an object as thick as an ox-goad, an object which is only one-third of a handbreadth in diameter-width, can convey uncleanness as a tent. But as noted, the standard rule is that an object must be a handbreadth in width in order to transfer uncleanness in this manner. Accordingly, the present version of the pericope has been formulated so that Tarfon and Aqiva declare that A is incorrect and that the latter rectifies it.

> A. *All movables bring uncleanness [as tents if they are as] thick as an ox-goad.*
>
> B. *Said R. Tarfon, "May I bury my son, that this is a ruined law.* I do not know what is the nature of the case, but *the one who heard, heard but erred.*
>
> C. "And M'SH B: One was passing *[by a tomb] with an ox-goad on his shoulder, and one side of it overshadowed the tomb, and they declared him unclean*
>
> D. *"because [of the utensils that] overshadowed the corpse.*
>
> E. "And the one who heard, heard but erred."
>
> F. Said R. Judah, "M'SH B: One was ploughing and shook the plough, and it came out that a [whole] skull of a corpse was cleaving to the plough, and they declared him unclean because it overshadowed the corpse.
>
> G. "And the one who heard, heard but erred."
>
> H. Said R. Judah, "M'SH B: One was ploughing and shook the plough, and it came out that a [whole] skull of a corpse was cleaving to the plough, and they declared him unclean because he [actually] moved the corpse.
>
> I. "And the one who heard, heard but erred."
>
> Tos. Ah. 15:12, ed. Zuckermandel, p. 613, lns. 22-29

Comment: Tos. comments upon M. It adds a phrase in B, and as the following chart indicates, it assimilates to the precedents attributed to Judah, the one attributed to Tarfon.

Tos. Ah. 15:12

1. Said R. Tarfon,

2. May I bury my son, that this is a ruined law. I do not know what is the nature of the case,

3. but the one who heard, heard but erred.

4. And M'SH B: One was passing [by a tomb] with an ox-goad on his shoulder,

5. and one side of it over-shadowed the tomb,

6. and they declared him un-clean because [the utensils] overshadowed the corpse.

7. And the one who heard, heard but erred.

Tos. Ah. 15:13a

1. Said R. Judah,

2. - - -

3. - - -

4. M'SH B: One was ploughing and shook the plough,

5. and it came out that a [whole] skull of a corpse was cleaving to the plough

6. " " "
   " " "
   " " "

7. " " "
   " " "

Tos. Ah. 15:13b

1. Said R. Judah,

2. - - -

3. - - -

4. " "
   " "

5. " " "
   " " "
   " " "

6. " " "
   he [actually] moved the corpse.

7. " " "
   " " "

The report, 4 (which in M is introduced by Š), in Tos. has the
formula M'SH B. The two traditions attributed by Judah also use
this formula. 7 of 15:12, which is redundant--for 3 already states
that the hearer erred--is paralleled by 7 of 13a and 13b. Tos.,
therefore, contains three *ma'asim* which have been erroneously
transmitted.

> A. Hyssop which is fit for the purification-rite is
> fit for the leper.
> B. [If] he sprinkled with it for the purification-
> rite, it is fit for the leper.
> C. R. Eliezer says, "Cedarwood, and hyssop, and
> scarlet wool mentioned in the Torah [Lev 14:4, refer to
> materials] with which work has not been done [which·have
> not been used]."
> D. Said R. Judah, "It was my turn to lecture,[7] and
> I went [to visit] R. Tarfon at his home.
> E. "He said to me, 'Judah, my son, give me my
> sandal,' and I gave it to him.
> F. "He stretched out his hand to the window and he
> took a staff (MQL) from there [Sifra, y.: he gave me a
> staff from there].
> G. "He said to me, 'My son, with this I have
> declared clean three lepers,
> H. "'and I have taught with it seven laws which are:
> (1) [it must be made from] cypress wood (ŠL 'BRYT), (2)
> and its top is smoothed and planed (WR'ŠH ṬRWP) [Sifra:
> on its head is a leaf], (3) and its length [is] a cubit,
> (4) and its thickness is like [that of] one-quarter of
> the thickness of the leg of the bed, one divided into two,
> and [then] two into four, (5) they sprinkle [once], they
> do it twice, they do it three times [with the same piece
> of cedarwood], (6) [they declare clean] both while the
> House [the Temple] is standing and not while the House
> is standing, (7) and they purify in the outer districts
> [Lieberman: outside the Land of Israel].'"

Tos. Neg. 8:2 (D-H = y. Soṭ.
2:12 18a, Sifra Meṣora'
Parashata 1:13, ed. Weiss, 70a)

Comment: This pericope consists of three independent traditions (A-B, C, D-H) which address slightly different issues. A,

which also appears in M. Par. 11:6, speaks only of hyssop. In C
Eliezer mentions cedarwood, hyssop, and scarlet wool. Tarfon's
saying concerns only cedarwood. But there is a certain common
ground among the traditions. A states that hyssop which is fit
for the purification rite (Numbers 19) is fit for the purification
of a leper. By itself A may mean either the same type, but not the
same piece, of hyssop may be used in both rites, or the same piece
of hyssop may be used in both rites. B glosses A by showing the
second interpretation is correct. B also joins A to C. In C
Eliezer claims that one must take an unused piece of hyssop. Thus
A and C disagree, at least concerning hyssop.

Tarfon's tradition consists of two elements: D-F (a narrative
prologue) and G-H (rulings of Tarfon). E-F are the setting for a
walk.[8] The mention of the staff in F sets up Tarfon's statement
(G-H) in which he claims that he both purified lepers with the
staff and taught seven laws by means of its use. Tarfon's rulings
in G-H relate to several different aspects of the cedarwood used
in the purification rite of the leper described in Leviticus 14.

In G Tarfon asserts that he used the same piece of cedarwood
three times. H5 lists this as one of the laws which Tarfon taught.
The only opinion in M.-Tos. which opposes this view is Eliezer's
in C. MB explains that Eliezer treats the cedarwood, hyssop, and
scarlet wool like the water used for making the purification ashes.
One may use only water with which work has not been done.

According to H1, Tarfon rules that the stick must be made of
cypress wood. Cypress wood is a type of cedarwood. The only
opinion related to H1 is preserved in Sifra Meṣora' Parashata 1:12,
Sifre Num. 124, and Sifre Zuṭṭa 19:6. It explains that the
Torah says "one should take a tree [of] cedarwood" in order to
teach us that it must be a cedar tree and not some other type of
tree. Whether or not this conflicts with Tarfon's view is unclear.

The reading of H2 is problematic, and I have followed Lieberman's suggestions. If the correct interpretation of H2 is that
the stick must be planed and smoothed, then Tarfon agrees with the
anonymous ruling found in the above sections of Sifra, Sifre, and
Sifre Zuṭṭa. These sources state that the cedarwood should not be
an uneven branch but a smoothed, planed piece of wood taken from
the heart of the tree. The other reading for H2 is "on its head
there is a leaf." In Sifra Meṣora' Parashata 1:12, which immediately follows the statement just cited, we find the following
saying of Haninah b. Gamaliel, a contemporary of Tarfon.

R. Haninah b. Gamaliel says, "On its head [there is]
a leaf."

If the second interpretation of Tarfon's statement is correct,
then Ḥaninah and Tarfon agree.

H3-4 give the dimensions of the stick. These are identical
to those found in M. Neg. 14:6. The wording of the two sources
is essentially the same.

> Tos. Neg. 8:2: 'RKH 'MH W'BYYH KRBW' KR' HMṬH ḤLWQ 'ḤD
> LŠNYM WŠNYM L'RB'H

> M. Neg. 14:6: (MṢVT 'Ṣ 'RZ) 'RKW 'MH W'BYW KRBY' KR'
> HMṬH 'ḤD LŠNYM WŠNYM L'RB'H

We have already discussed H5. H6-7 detail the time and place
in which one may purify a leper. According to Tarfon, one may
purify a leper whether or not the Temple is standing, and both
inside and outside the Land of Israel (so Lieberman).[9] Thus we
have another ruling ascribed to Tarfon which relates to priestly
functions which could be performed even after the destruction of
the Temple.

Our review of H shows that two of its laws (H3 and H4) also
appear in M. in almost identical language. The remainder of the
laws have no exact parallels, although some may be associated with
other rules in either M.-Tos. or halakhic midrashim. It seems,
therefore, that the issues of H were not of great interest to the
redactors of M.-Tos. and its related literature. But it is not
surprising that these concerns are part of the agendum of Tarfon,
the priest.

> A.   [Whenever the Torah speaks of lambs], the lambs
> must be no more than one year old, and [whenever it speaks
> of rams], the rams [must be no more than] two years old.
> B.   And all [the years are reckoned] from the day [of
> birth until the corresponding] day [of the next year].
> C.   A [sheep] thirteen months old is not fit either
> for [offerings which require] a ram, or for [those which
> require] a lamb.
> D.   1. R. Tarfon calls it [a sheep in its thirteenth
> month] a *palgēs*.
>   2. Ben Azzai calls it *noqed*.
>   3. R. Ishmael calls it *parakharygma*.
> E.   1. [If] someone sacrificed it, he brings with
> it a drink offering for a ram,

2. but this does not count for his sacrifice.

F. [If it was] thirteen months and a day old, lo,
this is a ram.

> M. Par. 1:3 (C-D = Sifre Zuṭṭa
> Shelaḥ 15:6, ed. Horowitz, p.
> 281, ln. 20)

Comment: A-C and E-F are a scenario of laws relating to the
classification and use of lambs and rams as sacrifices. According
to A, a sheep under a year of age is considered a lamb. One which
is thirteen months and a day is a ram, E. But one of thirteen
months counts as neither a lamb or a ram, C. The three masters in
D assign names to such a sheep. Tarfon calls it a *palgês*, which
in Greek means a maiden or youth, someone of an age between child-
hood and adulthood. *Noqed*, the name given by Ben Azzai, appears
in Amos 1:1 and 2 Kgs 3:4 and refers to a herdsman. Maim. explains
that just as a herdsman leads his pack, so too a sheep of thirteen
months leads a pack of sheep. Ishmael calls the thirteen-month-old
a *parakharyma*, which in Greek is the term for a coin issued by a
previous king and annulled by a later king, a useless coin.

This is the only Tarfon-tradition in which Ben Azzai appears.
In b. Pes. 74a and parallels, however, Ishmael and Tarfon assign
names to the paschal offering. Thus these two masters are depicted
as showing some interest in the proper designation of sacrificial
animals.

1. Whoever [is unclean and] requires immersion in
water, whether because of [uncleanness] declared by the
Torah, or whether because of [uncleanness] declared by
the Scribes, renders unclean, through contact and through
carrying, the water of purification, and the ashes of the
purification-offering, and the one who sprinkles the
water of purification.

2. "[He renders unclean] the hyssop that has been
rendered susceptible [to uncleanness, i.e., it has been
made wet], the water which has not yet been sanctified,
and the empty vessel that is clean [and which has been
set aside to hold] the [water] of the purification-
offering, through contact and through carrying," the
words of R. Meir.

3. But sages say, "[He renders these unclean]
through contact but not through carrying."

> M. Par. 11:6

A. *Whoever [is unclean and] requires immersion in*
water, whether because of [uncleanness] declared by the
Torah, or whether because of [uncleanness] declared by the
Scribes, before his immersion in the water, *renders un-*
clean, through contact and through carrying, the water
of purification, and the ashes of the purification-
offering, and the one who sprinkles the water of purifi-
cation.

B. R. Eleazar says in the name of R. Tarfon, "The
one unclean by [virtue of] corpse uncleanness carries,
on a yoke (B'YŚL) on his shoulder, the clean vessels
[which have been set aside] for the purification-offering,
and there is no concern [that they will become unclean]."

> Tos. Par. 11:5, ed. Zucker-
> mandel, p. 639, lns. 34-37

Comment: Tos. comments upon M. A of Tos. adds to M.1 the
words, "before his immersion," and thereby indicates that a *ṭebul*
yom, one who has immersed and is waiting for the setting of the
sun, no longer renders the objects unclean. B of Tos., as we shall
see, gives us a saying of Tarfon which supports the view of sages
in M.3. This is the only Tarfon-tradition for which Eleazar is the
tradent.

According to M. Par. 10:1, the objects used in the
purification-rite are susceptible to *maddaf*-uncleanness. They
thus are rendered unclean by indirect carrying and by indirect
contact. The objects listed in 1 of M. have already become part of
the paraphrenalia used in the ceremony of the red heifer--they
have been sanctified; therefore, the stringent rules apply to them.
But the objects mentioned in 2 of M., the ruling to which Tarfon's
saying relates, although capable of contracting uncleanness, have
merely been set aside for use in the rite of the red heifer. They
have not yet been sanctified. The dispute between Meir and sages
concerns whether or not these objects are subject to the stringent
rules which apply to those items used during the ceremony Meir
rules that even these objects fall into the category of articles
which can be rendered unclean by indirect carrying and by indirect
contact. According to sages, however, these objects are rendered
unclean only by contact. This is the normal rule which applies
for conveying uncleanness. But the stringent rule, that objects
used in the ceremony of the red heifer may be rendered unclean by
indirect carrying, does not apply to these items. The future

function of the objects thus does not affect their present status.
GRA and Lieberman explain that Tarfon's saying concurs with the
ruling of sages. Tarfon describes a case in which a man unclean
with a virulent type of uncleanness, corpse-uncleanness, moves in
an indirect manner--on a yoke--a vessel set aside for use in the
rite of the red heifer. According to B, Tarfon states that we
need not be concerned about the vessel becoming unclean. Thus, as
sages rule, the object is not subject to the laws which apply to
those items used in the ceremony. We, therefore, have another
ruling of Tarfon which is based on the principle that the future
function of an object is irrelevant in determining its present
status.

>A. [As to] all handles of vessels which are [too]
>long, and one is going to cut them off--
>
>B. one immerses them up to the place of [their
>proper] measure.
>
>C. R. Judah says, "[They are not clean] until one
>immerses the entire [handle]."
>
>D. [The proper measure of] a chain of a large
>bucket is four handbreadths, and [that of] a small
>[bucket] is ten handbreadths [= M. Kel. 14:3].
>
>E. One immerses them up to the place of [their
>proper] measure.
>
>F. R. Tarfon says, "[They are not clean] until one
>immerses the entire ring [in the chain, if only part of
>it comes within the appointed length]."

M. Miq. 10:5

Comment: The pericope consists of two units, A-C and D-F.
The following chart demonstrates that the same apodoses, 2-3, respond to different protases, 1.

1. [As to] all handles of vessels which are [too] long, and one is going to cut them off--	1. [The proper measure] of a chain of a large bucket is four hand-breadths, and [that of] a small [bucket] is ten handbreadths.
2. one immerses them up to the place of [their proper] measure.	2. " " " " " "
3. R. Judah says, [They are not clean] until one immerses the entire [handle].	3. R. Tarfon says, " " " " ring.

The key words in the opposing opinions in 2 and 3 are MQWM HMDH
vs. KL. We discuss only the section relevant to Tarfon.

This pericope, like M. Miq. 10:1-4, relates to the issue of
interposition. The general principle is that those parts of a
utensil, which are not integral, interpose when the utensil is immersed in a ritual pool. Tarfon's saying glosses the anonymous
law of E. According to E, one immerses the chain of a bucket only
until that point which is essential in its use. Tarfon adds that
if part of the ring is within the specified point, one immerses
the entire ring.

> 1. And so did R. Judah say in the name of R. Tarfon,
> "One has to immerse *the entire ring*."

> Tos. Miq. 7:3, ed. Zucker-
> mandel, p. 660, lns. 1-2

Comment: Tos. adds to the attributive formula of M. 10:5E.

> A. 1. [*As to*] *an immersion pool which was measured
> and was found lacking* [*the required amount of forty* seahs
> *of water*],
>   2. *all the acts requiring cleanness which were
> carried out depending upon it,*
>   3. *whether this immersion pool was in a public
> domain or whether this immersion pool was in a private
> domain,*
>   4. *are retroactively unclean* [b. V omits 4].
> B. R. Simeon says, "[Those done in an immersion
> pool] in a private domain are unclean, [those done in
> one] in a public domain are clean."
> C. Said R. Simeon,
> D. "M'SH B: The water reservoir of Discus in Yavneh
> was measured and was found lacking [water],
> E. 1. "and R. Tarfon did declare [the previous
> purifications] clean,
>   2. "and R. Aqiva did declare [them] unclean.
> F. "Said R. Tarfon, 'Since an immersion pool is
> presumed to be in a state of cleanness, it remains per-
> petually [in this status] of cleanness until it will be
> known that it is unclean.'
> G. "Said R. Aqiva, 'Since this immersion pool [b.,y.,
> Sens: unclean person] is presumed to be in a state of

uncleanness, he remains perpetually [in this status] of
uncleanness until it will be known that he is clean.'

H.   "Said R. Tarfon, 'To what may this be compared?
[This case is comparable] to one [a priest] who stands
and offers [sacrifices] on the altar, and it becomes
known that he is a son of a divorcee or a son of a
haluṣah, for his [previous] service is [still] valid.'

I.   "Said R. Aqiva, 'To what may this be compared?
To one who stands and offers [sacrifices] on the altar,
and it becomes known that he is disqualified by reason
of a blemish, for his [previous] service is invalid.'

J.   1.   "Said R. Tarfon, 'You draw an analogy to
one who is blemished, and I draw an analogy to the son
of a divorcee or of a *haluṣah*.

2.   "'Let us see to what matter it is appropriately likened.

3.   "'If it is [analogous] to a blemished
[priest], let us learn the [present] law from the case
of a blemished [priest]. If it is [analogous] to a son
of a divorcee [add: or to the son of a *haluṣah*], let us
learn the law from the case of a son of a divorcee, or
of a *haluṣah*.'

K.   1.   "R. Aqiva says, 'The unfitness affecting
an immersion pool affects [the immersion pool] itself,
and the unfit aspect of a blemished [priest] affects
[the blemished priest] himself.

2.   "'But let not the case of a son of a
divorcee or of a son of a *haluṣah* prove the matter, for
his matter of unfitness depends upon others [his parents].

L.   1.   "'An immersion pool's unfitness [depends]
upon one, and the unfitness of a blemished [priest depends]
upon an individual only.

2.   "'But let not the case of a son of a divorcee
or of a son of a *haluṣah* prove the matter, for the unfitness of this one [depends] upon a court [Lieberman deletes
HYRW].'

M.   "They were polled about this case, and they declared it unclean.

N.   "Said to him R. Tarfon, 'Aqiva, anyone who
separates himself from you is as if he separates himself
from his life.'"

202 Rabbi Tarfon

>   Tos. Miq. 1:16-19, ed. Zucker-
>   mandel, pp. 653-654, lns. 27-37,
>   1-3 (A = M. Miq. 2:1; A-B = b.
>   Qid. 79a, b. Nid. 2b; D-N = y.
>   Ter. 8:2 45b, b. Qid. 66b)

Comment: The pericope consists of A-B, a dispute between the anonymous law (A), a citation of M., and Simeon; and D-N, a M'SH containing a dispute (D-E) and a debate (F-N) involving Tarfon and Aqiva. We discuss these items separately.

According to A, all items purified in a ritual pool that was measured and found lacking the required amount of water are deemed retroactively unclean. A makes no distinctions on the basis of the pool's location. Simeon in B disagrees with A by differentiating between immersions performed in pools in the public domain and those done in pools in the private domain. Immersions done in pools in the private domain, as A claims, are deemed retroactively unclean. But purifications performed in those in the public domain are not deemed retroactively unclean. We now expect Simeon to cite a precedent which supports his view with regard to the issue under dispute between himself and the anonymous law, i.e., with regard to the cleanness of items previously immersed in a pool in the public domain. But D-N apparently deal with an immersion pool in the private domain, the immersion pool of Discus at Yavneh. Even if we assume that the exchange in D-N relates to a *miqveh* in a public domain, it does not support Simeon's view. Aqiva, who rules that the previously performed purifications are retroactively unclean, wins the debate. Finally, as Neusner notes (*HMLP* XIII, p. 51), "Even if all Simeon introduced were the dispute in D-E, without the debate, he still finds himself invoking the name of Tarfon against that of Aqiva, and at Usha it is difficult to see how much he would have gained thereby."

The dispute + debate in D-N are set within the framework of a M'SH. As to its literary traits, D serves the function of a superscription. The opinions of the two masters in E use the fixed opposites ṬHR vs. ṬM'. In F-G the two authorities offer reasons for their respective opinions. H-I continue the debate with a new set of arguments. In J Tarfon indicates that he and Aqiva use different comparisons. Up until now we have had a fair debate for both authorities are assigned good analogies. But in K-L, Aqiva is given two arguments in support of his comparison, I. Tarfon is not assigned either an argument which rejects K-L, or one which supports his own analogy, H. Thus we again have a debate which is

unfairly formulated, to Aqiva's advantage. The vote in M is
curious, for Aqiva obviously has won the debate. N is the standard
conclusion to exchanges between Tarfon and Aqiva.

This pericope is another dispute between Tarfon and Aqiva
regarding a case involving doubt. Since the immersion pool now
lacks the required amount of water, we are not sure whether or not
it previously contained the required forty *seahs* of water. Tarfon
declares retroactively clean all items previously immersed in such
a pool. Aqiva rules that these items are retroactively unclean.
We may explain these rulings in terms of the arguments in F-G.
Both of the masters agree that we confirm the status of one of the
parties involved in the purification. They disagree about which
item this is. Thus Tarfon asserts (F), we always assume that,
until definitely proven otherwise, an immersion pool is clean.
The present doubt concerning the past status of the pool is not
sufficient to have us override our presumption and to cause us to
declare retroactively unclean all the previous purifications performed in it. Aqiva contends that, since an unclean person is
presumed to be unclean until it is certain that he has been purified, the present doubt concerning the past status of the pool is
sufficient reason to cause us to declare the previously immersed
items unclean. Furthermore, as in M. Yev. 15:6-7 and M. Bekh. 2:
6-8, Tarfon's opinion is in accord with the principle that in
cases of doubt we may act leniently even if this involves a possible transgression--declaring clean an unclean person. For Aqiva
the possible transgression is of concern; therefore, one must act
stringently.

In the debate H-L, each party compares the immersion pool to
priests with different statuses. Tarfon thus draws an analogy between the immersion pool discussed in our pericope and a priest
who discovers that he is the offspring of a priest and a woman
forbidden to the latter. Aqiva compares the immersion pool to a
priest who finds out that he is blemished. As noted, only Aqiva
is assigned reasons to support his argument. Both immersion pools
and blemished priests have defects which only affect themselves.
Thus, unlike a priest who is the son of a divorcee, their defects
are not because of others. Similarly, the unfitness of blemished
priests and immersion pools depend only upon an individual. Those
of a priest who is the son of a divorcee depend upon a court.

The analogies cited in H and I are drawn from a dispute between Joshua and Eliezer. In M. Ter. 8:1, Joshua and Eliezer

disagree concerning the retroactive validity of the service performed by a priest found to be the son of a ḥaluṣah. Joshua says
that the previous service is valid, while Eliezer says it is not.
H of our pericope assumes that the priest's previous service is
fit; therefore, it agrees with Joshua's opinion. The ruling to
which Aqiva appeals in I appears anonymously in M. Ter. 8:1.

> A. 1. *Any hand which makes many examinations* [*to*
> *see whether or not there has been an emission*]--
>   2. *in the case of women, lo, it is to be praised.*
>   3. *but in the case of men, it is to be cut off*
> [= M. Nid. 2:1].
>   B. R. Tarfon says, "It should be cut off [while
> lying] upon his belly button."
>   C. He [read: they] said to him, "Lo, his belly will
> be split open."
>   D. He said to them, "Indeed, I intended exactly that."
>   E. They drew a parable. To what is the matter com-
> pared? To one who puts his finger in his eye, for all the
> time that he exerts pressure, he brings forth a tear.
>   F. Under what circumstances [does the ruling in A3
> apply]? With regard to [one who checks for] a seminal
> emission. But with regard to [one who checks for] a flux,
> any hand which makes many examinations, lo, it is to be
> praised.
>
>   Tos. Nid. 2:8, ed. Zuckermandel,
>   p. 643, lns. 3-7

Comment: Tos. comments upon M. Nid. 2:1. A cites M. Tarfon's
comment glosses A3 by indicating where the man's hand is to be cut
off, on the person's belly. A man who checks frequently for seminal emissions may masturbate. Accordingly, his hand should be cut
off. C-D point out that adherence to Tarfon's ruling will cause
the man's death. The parable in E spells out A3; F modifies it.

> A. *Any hand which makes frequent examinations, in*
> *the case of women is to be praised.*
>   B. KNY MTNYT': Anyone who often puts his hand in
> his eye will bring forth an abundance of tears.
>   C. R. Tarfon says, "It should be cut off on his
> belly button."
>   D. They said to him, "But lo, his belly will be
> split open."

E. He said to them, "I said that this one's death
is better for him than his life."

F. The colleagues say, "R. Tarfon curses him [with]
a curse that afflicts his body."

G. Said R. Yose, "He [Tarfon] intended to indicate
only that it is forbidden [for a man] to feel from his
belly button downwards."

H. This [the above] is said [only] with regard to
[one who checks for] a flux, anyone who makes many exami-
nations is praised by his friends.

y. Nid. 2:1 2d

Comment: The numbers refer to the chart of pp. 207-208.
5-8 of y. parallel 6-8, 16 of Tos. 8 of y. gives a different
saying for Tarfon, but its force is the same as Tos. 8.
9-10 of y., unlike 7-8, treat Tarfon's comment figuratively.

A. *But in the case of men, it is to be cut off.*

B. *It was asked of them: Have we here learned a law
or merely an execration? [If] we have learned a law,
then it is like the time that R. Huna cut off someone's
hand. Or is it merely an execration?*

C. Come and hear, DTNY': R. Tarfon says, "[If] a
hand [touches] the membrum, it should be cut off upon
his belly button."

D. They said to him, "But lo, his belly will be
split open."

E. He said to them, "It is preferable that his
belly be split open than that he should go down into
the pit of destruction."

F. [The *gemara* discusses whether or not Tarfon
means his comment to be taken as a law, and concludes
that he did not. It continues:] R. Tarfon said the
following, "Whoever puts his hand below his belly button, it should be cut off."

G. They said to R. Tarfon, "If a thorn stuck in
his belly, should he not remove it?"

H. He said to them, "No."

I. [They said to him,] "But lo, his belly will
be split open?"

J.   He said to them, "It is preferable that his
belly be split open than that he should go down into
the pit of destruction."

b. Nid. 13b

Comment: The following chart (p. 207) indicates that b. is
the most elaborate version of this tradition. 4 of b. asks the
question implicit in the other two versions of this tradition.
b.6 has an expanded version of Tarfon's saying. The meaning of 8
is the same as that of the parallel sections in the other versions;
Tarfon meant his comment to be taken literally. 11-15, however,
revise Tarfon's saying and his exchange with the anonymous "they,"
6-8, so that Tarfon's statement means that a person's hand should
be cut off if he puts it in the area of his genitals. Furthermore,
Tarfon's remark about the person's belly being split open was not
said with regard to the issue of cutting off the person's hand but
with regard to the thorn stuck in the person's belly.

Tos. Nid. 2:8	y. Nid. 2:1	b. Nid. 13b
1. Any hand which makes many examinations—	1. " " "	1. - - -
2. in the case of women, lo, it is to be praised,	2. " " "	2. - - -
3. in the case of men, it is to be cut off.	3. - -	3. " " "
4. - - -	4. - - -	4. *It was asked of them: Have we here learned a law or merely an execration? [If] we have learned a law, then it is like the time R. Huna cut off someone's hand. Or is it merely an execration?*
5. See below #15.	5. KNY MTNYT': Anyone who often puts his hand in his eye will bring forth an abundance of tears.	5. - - -
6. R. Tarfon says, It should be cut off on his belly button.	6. " " "	
7. They said to him, Lo, his belly will be split open.	7. " " " "	7. " " " "
8. He said to them, Indeed, I intended exactly that.	8. " I said that this one's death is better for him than his life.	8. " It is preferable that his belly be split open than that he should go down into the pit of destruction.
9. - - -	9. The colleagues say, R. Tarfon curses him [with] a curse that afflicts his body.	9. - - -
10. - - -	10. Said R. Yose, He [Tarfon] intended to indicate only that it is forbidden [for a man] to feel from his belly button downwards.	10. - - -

Tos. Nid. 2:8	y. Nid. 2:1	b. Nid. 13b
11. - - -	11. - - -	11. R. Tarfon said the following: Whoever puts his hand below his belly button, it should be cut off.
12. - - -	12. - - -	12. They said to R. Tarfon, If a thorn stuck in his belly, should he not remove it?
13. - - -	13. - - -	13. He said to them, No.
14. - - -	14. - - -	14. [They said to him,] But lo, his belly will be split open.
15. - - -	15. - - -	15. He said to them, It is preferable that his belly be split open than that he should go down into the pit of destruction.
16. They gave a parable. To what is the matter compared? To one who puts his finger in his eye, for all the time that he exerts pressure he brings forth a tear.	16. See above #5.	16. - - -

A. 1. *How long can labor be protracted,*

2. and it [the blood which she sees] shall be
assumed [to be caused] by the child [and not be that of
a *zabah*]?

B. *"Even forty or fifty days," the words of R. Meir.*

C. *R. Judah says* in the name of R. Tarfon, *"Sufficient for her is her ninth month."*

D. How so? [If she had labor pains] two [days] of
the eighth [month] and [one day] of the ninth, she has not
given birth as a *zabah*. [If] three [days] of the eighth
and [one] of the ninth, she has given birth as a *zabah*.

E. 1. *R. Yose and R. Simeon say, "Fourteen [days],*

2. "like one who has given birth to a female
[child];

3. "therefore, if [she was in] labor seventeen
[days before giving birth], the first three are fitting
for flux, and she has [in consequence] given birth as a
zabah."

> Tos. Nid. 5:9, ed. Zuckermandel,
> p. 646, lns. 11-15 (M. Nid. 4:5)

Comment: Tos. comments upon M. Nid. 4:5. A1 is a citation
from M. A2 spells out the issue under discussion. A woman can be
rendered unclean by menstrual blood and by fluxes, the flow of
blood for three successive days not during her period. A woman
who suffers a flux is known as a *zabah*. Blood produced in labor
leading to a viable birth, however, is not unclean. But how long
prior to giving birth is the blood emitted by a woman who has con-
tinuous labor pains[10] assumed to be associated with the birth and
not with a flux? B, C, and E give us the opinions of three Ushans--
two weeks, one month, forty or fifty days. These sayings also appear in M. Tos., however, adds Tarfon's name to the attributive
formula in C. Tos. D and E3 give illustrations for the respective
rulings in C and E1. Both D and E3 indicate that the blood is
assumed to be that of a *zabah* only if the three successive days of
flow occur prior to the period allotted for hard labor.

A. TNY': *R. Judah says in the name of R. Tarfon,
"Her [ninth] month is sufficient."*

B. In this there is an aspect of leniency and an
aspect of stringency. How so? [*If*] *she had hard labor
for two* [*days*] *at the end of her eighth* [*month*] *and one*

210   Rabbi Tarfon

[*day*] *at the beginning of her ninth* [*month*], and even if
she gave birth at the beginning of the ninth [month], lo,
this is one who has given birth as *zabah*. But [if] she
had hard labor for one [day] at the end of her eighth
[month] and two [days] at the beginning of her ninth
[month], and even if she gave birth at the end of her
ninth [month], this is not one who has given birth as a
zabah.

Comment: B of b. introduces a principle, that of the majority
of the days, and thereby modifies Judah's opinion. Thus if two
of the three days of flow occur prior to the period associated
with the birth of the child, i.e., during the final two days of
the eighth month, then the blood is deemed that of a *zabah*.

        A.   [As to] one who measures a cistern--
        B.   "[the water which comes up upon the measuring
rod] whether [the rod was used for measuring] the depth,
or whether [it was used for measuring] the width, [falls]
within [the category of] 'if water be put on'" [Lev 11:38],
the words of R. Tarfon.
        C.   R. Aqiva says, "[That which comes up when the
rod is used to measure] the depth [falls under the laws
of] 'if water be put on.' But [that which comes up when
measuring] the width does not [fall under the law of]
'if water be put on.'"

Comment: A-B are apocopated. They contain the superscription
for the dispute. The opinions B+C are well balanced.
     Lev 11:38 which reads, "But if water be put on the seed, and
anything of their carcass falls thereon, it is unclean for you,"
underlies the tractate of Maks. From this verse the principle is
deduced that water detached and intentionally put on dry foodstuff
renders it susceptible to uncleanness (M. Maks. 1:3). This law is
referred to by the phrase, "if water be put on." The disagreement
between Tarfon and Aqiva centers upon what we count as intentionally
"put on water." Does intention apply to only that water essential to
the performance of a task, or also to water inadvertently put on
while performing the action? Aqiva holds the former position, while
Tarfon adheres to the latter. Thus, according to Aqiva, only when
the person measures the cistern's depth does he want the water on

the rod, only that water falls under the law of "if water be put
on." Tarfon, however, asserts that even the water which comes up
while measuring the cistern's depth falls under this rule, for it
is irrelevant that this water is not essential to carrying out the
procedure. By extending intention to encompass both the water the
person wants and that which he does not want, Tarfon in essence
evacuates this concept. According to his view, we determine a
person's intentions not from any prestated volition, but from his
actions. This line of reasoning ultimately eliminates the basis
for the entire tractate of Maks. Aqiva's view, in fact, underlies
the unfolding of this tractate.[11]

> A. [As to] one who measures a cistern, whether its
> depth or its width, the [water which comes up] does not
> [fall] within [the law of] "if water be put on."
>
> B. Said to him R. Tarfon, "What is the difference
> between when he measures it for its depth and when he
> measures it for its width?"
>
> C. He [Aqiva] said to him, "When he measures it for
> its depth, he wants [finds acceptable] the liquid that is
> at the mark [the point up to which the water reaches.
> But when he measures it] for its width, he does not want
> the liquid that is at the mark."
>
> D. He [Tarfon] said to him, "If so, let the liquid
> at the mark be unclean, [and let] the liquid below the
> mark [see Lieberman, T.R. IV, p. 114] be clean."
>
> E. 1. He said to him, "Do you not admit that,
> [concerning] one who fills a bucket, the water
> which is brought up on its outside, [and] on the rope
> which is wound around the neck, and on the rope which is
> necessary for its use that they [fall into the category
> of] 'if water be put on' [= M. Maks. 4:1]?
>
> 2. "For the water does not fall into it [the
> bucket] until it touches the outside [of the bucket].
>
> 3. "If so, [then similarly] it is impossible
> for water [to reach] the mark [on the measuring rod]
> until it has [touched the surface] below the mark."
>
> F. R. Tarfon changed his mind and [began] to teach
> according to the words of R. Aqiva.

> Tos. Maks. 2:14, ed. Zucker-
> mandel, p. 675, lns. 1-8

Comment: This is another typical debate between Tarfon and
Aqiva. Tarfon's questions serve merely as a device which enable
Aqiva to spell out his view. Tarfon never offers the reasoning
behind his own opinion.

A, according to Lieberman, is a shortened citation of M. It
leaves out everything in M. from the word "lo" in M. until "does
not" in M. B. Tarfon's question in Tos. B sets up Aqiva's answer,
C, which presents the reason behind Aqiva's ruling. According to
C, only the water which the person wants renders foods susceptible
to uncleanness. In D Tarfon attempts to draw out the conclusion
to which Aqiva's reasoning, in C, leads. Tarfon notes that if
Aqiva uses the person's intention as the determinative factor,
then only the water at the uppermost point should be unclean. The
person does not want any of the water below this point. In E
Aqiva appeals to a law with which Tarfon must agree, and thereby
refutes Tarfon's challenge, D. The point of E1, as E2-3 indicate,
is that any water which the person knows will come up, not just
the uppermost drop of water, falls within the category of "if
water be put on." Thus "intention" applies both to the water
which is wanted and to that which the person knows will inadvertently come up. The debate closes with Tarfon accepting Aqiva'a
view.

    A. On that day they said,

    B. What of Ammon and Moab in the Sabbatical year?

    C. Decreed R. Tarfon [that they give] poorman's-tithe.

    D. And decreed R. Eleazar b. Azariah [that they give]
second-tithe.

    E. 1. Said R. Ishmael, "Eleazar b. Azariah, you must
bring forth proof since you give a stringent ruling;

        2. "for every one that gives a stringent ruling
must bring forth proof."

    F. 1. Said to him R. Eleazar b. Azariah, "Ishmael,
my brother, I have not changed the order of the years.

        2. "Tarfon, my brother, changed it, and he must
bring forth proof."

    G. Answered R. Tarfon, "Egypt is outside the Land
[of Israel], and Ammon and Moab are outside the Land [of
Israel]; therefore [just as in] Egypt poorman's-tithe
[must be given] in the Sabbatical year, so [in] Ammon and
Moab poorman's-tithe [must be given] in the Sabbatical
year."

H.   Answered R. Eleazar b. Azariah, "Babylonia is
outside the Land [of Israel], and Ammon and Moab are outside the Land [of Israel]; therefore, [just as in] Babylonia second-tithe [must be given] in the Sabbatical year,
so [in] Ammon and Moab second-tithe [must be given] in
the Sabbatical year."

I.   Said R. Tarfon, "Egypt, which is near [the Land
of Israel], they have made [liable for] poorman's-tithe,
that the poor of Israel may rely upon it [for sustenance]
in the Sabbatical year, so too, Ammon and Moab, which are
near [the Land of Israel], they have made [liable for]
poorman's-tithe, that the poor of Israel may rely upon
it in the Sabbatical year."

J.   1.   Said to him R. Eleazar b. Azariah, "Lo, you
are like one that would bestow [on them] worldly gain,
yet you are like one that would cause their lives to perish.

2.   "You would prevent (QWB') the heavens from
sending down both dew and rain,

3.   "for it is written, 'Will a man rob God? Yet
you rob me.' But you say, 'Wherein have we robbed you?'
In tithes and heave-offering. Bring the tithes into the
storehouse, that there may be food in [my house, and
thereby put me to the test, says the Lord of Hosts, if I
will not open the windows of heaven for you...'"] [Mal
3:8,10].

K.   [K,L,P,Pb,N,M,Pr.: Answered R. Tarfon.]

L.   1.   Said R. Joshua,

2.   "Lo, I am like one who will respond on behalf
of Tarfon my brother, but not according to the subject of
words.

3.   "[The rule concerning] Egypt is a new decision,
and [the rule concerning] Babylonia is an old decision, and
the argument which is before us is a new decision. Let
[the rule concerning] a new decision be derived from [the
rule concerning] a new decision, but do not let [the rule
concerning] a new decision be derived from [the rule con-
cerning] an old decision.

4.   "[The rule concerning] Egypt is the decision
of the elders. But [the rule concerning] Babylonia is the
decision of the Prophets, and the issue before us is the
decision of the elders. Let [the rule concerning] a decision of the elders be derived from [the rule concerning]

a decision of the elders, but do not let [the rule con-
cerning] a decision of the elders be derived from [the
rule concerning] a decision of the Prophets."

    M. They were polled and decided:

    N. Ammon and Moab give poorman's-tithe in the
Sabbatical year.

    O. And when R. Yose the son of the Damascene came to
R. Eliezer at Lydda, he said to him, "What new thing did
you [hear] in the *Bet HaMidrash*?"

    P. 1. He said to him, "They were polled and decided,

        2. "Ammon and Moab give poorman's-tithe in the
Sabbatical year."

    Q. 1. R. Eliezer wept and said, "'The secret of the
Lord is with those who fear Him, and He will show them His
covenant' [Ps 25:14]. Go and tell them, Do not be anxious
about your voting; I have received a tradition from Rabban
Yoḥanan b. Zakkai, who heard it from his teacher, and his
teacher from his teacher, as a *halakhah* given to Moses at
Sinai, that,

        2. "Ammon and Moab give poorman's-tithe in the
Sabbatical year."

M. Yad. 4:3

Comment: A is redactional language which joins the pericope
to a series of other independent traditions (M. Yad. 3:5-4:3).[12]
The remainder of the pericope consists of the following units:
B-D, E-F, G-K, L, M-N, and O-Q. Our discussion focuses upon the
sections relevant to Tarfon.

    B-D are a well-balanced dispute between Tarfon and Eleazar.
The attributive formula for the sayings is GZR (decreed) and not
'WMR (says), the only use of this formula in M.-Tos. The brief
debate, E-F, which interrupts the dispute and debate between Tarfon and Eleazar, consists of a challenge, E, to the opinion attributed to Eleazar in D, and F1, a response to this question.
The appearance of Ishmael in E is odd, for generally the parties
to a debate are the same as those in the preceding dispute. F2
returns us to the exchange between Tarfon and Eleazar.

    The debate, G-J, opens with extremely well-balanced arguments,
G and H, and continues with supporting arguments in I and J. Yose
has the last word. K is no more than an attributive formula which
introduces an argument. Either the saying which follows K has been
lost, or it is simply a scribal error. The fact that L presupposes

that Eleazar wins the debate suggests that K is a mistake. L reopens the discussion. It is an argument in support of Tarfon's
analogy, G, and thereby it reverses the outcome of the debate, G-J.
The attribution of L to Joshua, like that of E to Ishmael, is odd.
N, a ruling in the form of a simple declarative sentence, has been
joined to the above by M. M also links the pericope to its larger
context, M. Yad. 3:5-4:3. M. Yad. 3:5 and 4:1 contain expressions
similar to M. O-Q comment upon M-N by supporting this decision.
The climax of the pericope, therefore, comes at N. A-L lead up to
it; O-Q reinforce it.

The question discussed in the dispute, B-D, that of the tithes
which the people in Ammon and Moab give during the Sabbatical year,
is an intermediate case. The obligation to tithe crops and to observe the Sabbatical year generally applies to what, according to
the rabbis, is considered the Land of Israel. In the opinion of
all of the authorities mentioned in this pericope, although the
Jewish inhabitants of Ammon and Moab do not observe the Sabbatical
year, they still should give tithes during this year. Ammon and
Moab thus are sufficiently part of the Land of Israel so that the
laws of tithing apply there, but are sufficiently not part of the
Land of Israel so that the laws of the Sabbatical year do not apply
there.

The masters in this pericope disagree about the type of tithes
these people must give during the Seventh year. The reason for
this disagreement is that, since the inhabitants of the Land of
Israel do not tithe during the Sabbatical year, there is no precedent for deciding what the people in Ammon and Moab should give.
Tarfon and all the other authorities in the pericope, except for
Eleazar, rule that the inhabitants of these lands give poorman's-
tithe during the Sabbatical year. Poorman's-tithe is normally set
aside during the third and sixth years of the Sabbatical cycle.
In all other years, except the seventh itself, one gives second-
tithes. Tarfon apparently treats the Sabbatical year as an extension of the sixth year; accordingly, the inhabitants of Ammon and
Moab set aside poorman's-tithes. Tarfon's ruling may also be based
upon the fact that Ammon and Moab are an intermediate case; one,
therfore, may apply a more lenient ruling to them. It is easier to
give poorman's-tithe than second-tithe. The former may be eaten
anywhere, while second-tithe must be consumed in Jerusalem.

Eleazar rules that these people give second-tithe during the
Sabbatical year. He reasons that poorman's-tithe is set aside only

in a year following one in which second-tithe is given. Since in
the sixth year the inhabitants of Ammon and Moab give poorman's-
tithe, they must set aside second-tithe during the Sabbatical year.

As noted, E-F are an intrusion between the dispute + debate
of Tarfon and Eleazar. Ishmael argues that, since--as we have
explained--Eleazar rules more stringently than Tarfon, he must
supply a proof for his opinion. Eleazar responds in F1 that he
does not have to prove his point, for it is based on the regular
sequence of years for tithing. Rather, as F2 states, Tarfon, who
changes the sequence, must present evidence in support of his view.
F2 thus provides a bridge to Tarfon's argument in G. But on the
basis of F1 we do not expect any further arguments by Eleazar in
support of his view. In H and J, however, Eleazar gives such
arguments in his debate with Tarfon. Thus E-F1 presuppose the
dispute, B-D, but not the debate, G-J.

In the debate, G-J, Tarfon compares Ammon and Moab to Egypt,
while Eleazar draws an analogy between the former and Babylonia.
Tarfon in I spells out the appropriateness of his analogy. Egypt,
like Ammon and Moab, but unlike Babylonia, is near the Land of
Israel. Eleazar responds not by offering an argument similar to I
but by pointing out the implications of Tarfon's ruling. Adherence
to Tarfon's opinion does not allow the inhabitants of these lands
to fulfill the obligation of offering second-tithe. Eleazar thus
has the last say. Joshua, however, reopens the issue and demonstrates on grounds different from those in I, the appropriateness
of Tarfon's analogy, G.

NOTES

CHAPTER VI

[1]The version recorded in b. is identical to that in M. except
for its superscription. The superscription in b. reads: "A QLWSTR',
DTNN: [As to] a door bolt which has on its top a fastening contrivance (QLWSTR')." Ms. M, however, lacks the words "DTNN...con-
trivance"; hence, its reading is identical to that in M. (see D.S.
II, p. 281). In M. Eruv. 10:10 we find the clause "a door bolt
with a fastening contrivance on it." This phrase may have led to
the faulty reading in b. Shab.

[2]The following pericopae discuss this issue:

"A man may not stand within a private domain and
open [a door] in the public domain, [or stand] within
the public domain and open [a door] in a private domain
unless he had made a partition ten handbreadths high,"
the words of R. Meir. (M. Eruv. 10:9)

[Pr,M: R. Eliezer] [K,L,P.N,y.: Eleazar] forbids
a bolt with a fastening device (QLSTR') on its end.
But R. Yose permits it. (M. Eruv. 10:10)

They may shut up [the gates] in the Temple with a
bolt that is dragged [on the ground], but not in the
provinces. But one that can be laid apart is forbidden
in either place.
R. Judah says, "One that could be laid apart was
permitted in the Temple, and one that was dragged [on the
ground] was permitted in the provinces." (M. Eruv. 10:11)

They may thrust back [to its socket] the power pivot
[of a door] in the Temple, but not in the provinces.
(M. Eruv. 10:12)

[As to] a bolt (NGR) which is tied and suspended,
they open and close with it. And if [it is] not [tied
and suspended], they do not open and close with it.
A bolt, if it is completely detached (NŠMT), is
forbidden. [If it is] partially detached (NQMZ), it is
permitted. (Tos. Eruv. 11:15)

[3]As noted, our interpretation of Joshua's saying is based
upon an analysis of the words ŠWMT M and ḤBYRW. The simplest
meaning ŠWMT (M) has in M.-Tos. is "to separate one thing from
another" (M. Kil. 9:10; Shab. 20:5, 23:5; Suk. 4:7; Mak. 2:1; Bekh.
6:7; Kel. 10:3, 18:2; Tos. Shab. 13:14; Eruv. 11:17,18; Yev. 12:12;
B.Q. 3:6; A.Z. 3:6; Mak. 2:10,11; Ḥul. 2:4; Kel. B.M. 8:1). The
effect of this separation is that object A no longer touches object
B. Thus Joshua says one moves the door bolt in such a manner that
it no longer touches the door. This does not imply that one must
pick up the door bolt and then either carry it or drag it. Joshua's
saying seems to mean that one can simply use the door bolt in its
normal manner. If we envisage two doors side by side, then one
could move the door bolt from door A to door B by passing it
through brackets. This would be an instance of ŠWMT M. An explanation of the word ḤBYRW supports this interpretation. ḤBYRW often
refers to two objects of the same genus. But there are several

217

places in M. (M. Kel. 2:7, 20:7, 26:7, and possibly M. Ter. 2:6)
in which ḤBYRW refers to not only an object belonging to the same
genus as the previously mentioned item, but also to an object of
the same genus which is situated next to the previously mentioned
item. In our pericope the ḤBR of door A is another door, B, right
next to it.
       The information relating to door bolts supports the above
interpretation. The word *claustra* "is used in a sense as general
and indefinite as our word fastening" (Rich, pp. 171-72). The
word *claustra* thus may refer to different types of door bolts.
The information which I have been able to gather concerning door
bolts indicates that the locking mechanism and the keys used to
open doors changed and developed. The door bolt, however, was
generally a bar which was modified simply by adding notches or
grooves, depending upon the type of lock into which it was inserted. There is, therefore, no reason to rule out the suggestion
that Joshua speaks of a door bolt used to lock two doors side by
side. Furthermore, Krauss (I/ii, pp. 366-67), Bert., Maim., and
TYY suggest that the *claustra* mentioned in our pericope indeed
locks two doors next to each other. (On Greek and Roman door bolts,
see T. K. Derry and Trevor Williams, *A Short History of Technology*
[Oxford, 1961], p. 152; Albert Neuburger, *The Technical Arts and
Sciences of the Ancients* [reprinted; New York, 1969], pp. 336-39;
Hermann Diels, *Parmenides* [Berlin, 1897], pp. 117-51; idem, *Antike
Technik* [reprinted; Osnabrück, 1965], pp. 40-71. Yigael Yadin,
Bar Kokhba [New York, 1971], pp. 197-220, has discovered the Roman
style key in Judaea.)

       [4]Rashi, MA, and GRA, based on the discussion of this pericope
in b. Shab. 124a, offer the following explanation. The word ḤṢR,
when used by itself in M.-Tos., usually means a courtyard without
an '*eruv*. Tos. Eruv. 11:1 states that one may carry objects in a
courtyard which lacks an '*eruv*. Rashi in commenting upon our
pericope notes that a yard without an '*eruv* is still considered a
domain unto itself; therefore, any object within the yard may be
carried within it. A yard lacking an '*eruv*, however, differs from
one which has an '*eruv*, in that one may not take objects into the
yard from the houses which open onto it and vice versa.
       In light of this principle, Rashi, MA, and GRA explain that
Tarfon considers a door between a courtyard and a house to be part
of the yard. The door bolt, therefore, is considered to be in the
yard and, like any other utensil already in the yard, may be moved
about the yard. This interpretation of Tarfon's saying does not
alter our first explanation of his ruling but, in fact, presupposes
it, and then uses it to answer another question. One could not
raise the question of carrying the door bolt in a courtyard without
an '*eruv* unless he already considers the bolt an object which one
may carry on the Sabbath. The addition of the words "in a courtyard" implies that, according to Tarfon, the door is part of the
yard. This interpretation of Tarfon's ruling reads into his saying the location of the door.
       If this explanation of Tarfon's saying is correct, then one
must reconsider the interpretation of Joshua's ruling. We have
explained above that Joshua allows the moving of the door bolt in
any domain only when the bolt is used in its normal manner. But
in light of Tarfon's ruling, MA and Rashi interpret Joshua's saying to mean that, in an area in which carrying is permitted, one
may carry the door bolt. Joshua agrees that an object, so long as
it is an autonomous utensil, may be carried on the Sabbath. It is
only because of the circumstances assumed in the pericope, i.e., a
courtyard which lacks an '*eruv*, that Joshua does not allow one to
carry the bolt. Joshua considers the door to be part of the house.

Since the courtyard does not have an 'eruv, one may not take objects into it from the house. It is for this reason that Joshua
does not allow the person to carry the bolt in the yard.

[5]William Green (Joshua, p. 393) explains the opinions in
this manner.

[6]Green (ibid.) reaches this conclusion.

[7]See Epstein (Mevo'ot, p. 427) who offers this interpretation.

[8]To take one's staff and sandal (or shoe) is a metaphor
which suggests that one is about to take a journey or that one has
come from a journey. Exod 12:11 commands the Israelites in Egypt
to eat the paschal lamb with their shoes on their feet and their
staffs in their hands, i.e., ready to leave. M. Ber. 9:5 and M.
Yev. 16:7 also speak of people having their staffs and their shoes.
Both traditions relate to traveling.

[9]Lieberman claims that H6-7 agree with the anonymous law of
Tos. Neg. 14:1, which reads:

> And the priest who declares [him] unclean is com-
> manded to declare [him] clean, for it is written, "To
> declare him clean or to declare him unclean" [Lev 13:59].
> [He is commanded to do this] both in the Land [of
> Israel] and outside of the Land [of Israel].

[10]The anonymous law in M. Nid. 4:4, that knows of no limit for
the period deemed to be that of hard labor, states that, if there
is a respite from the labor pains, the blood is assumed to be that
of a zabah. Joshua and Eliezer disagree about the duration of the
respite.

[11]See Neusner, HMLP XVII, p. 221 and XXII, p. 151.

[12]Epstein, Mavo, pp. 424-25.

NON-LEGAL MATERIALS

Homiletical-Theological

A. M'SH B: R. Tarfon was sitting in the shade of
of the dovecoat in the afternoon on the Sabbath.

B. They brought before him a bucket of cold [water].

C. He says [first ed., E: said] to his students,

D. "[As to] one who drinks water to quench his
thirst, how does he bless?"

E. They said to him, "Teach us, our master."

F. He said to them, "[He says], 'Who creates living
things and their wants.'"

G. He said to them, "May I inquire?"

H. They said to him, "Teach us, our master."

I. He said to them, "Lo, it [Scripture] says, 'And
they sat to eat bread, and they raised their eyes and
they saw,

        "'and behold a caravan of Arabs was coming from
Gilead with their camels bearing spicery and balm and
ludanum' [Gen 37:25].

J. "And is it not the custom of Arabs to carry only
skins and bad smelling things and *itron*?

K. "Rather, He [God] placed that righteous man
[Joseph], among lovely items.

L. "[And we can learn from this] by means of a *qal
vaḥomer* that

M. "if when [God] is angry [with] the righteous He
has pity on them, how much the more so [does He care for
them] during the time of His compassion."

> [A series of additional biblical verses follow
> which teach the same lesson as M. The pericope
> then returns to the dialogue between Tarfon
> and his students.]

N. He [Tarfon] said to them, "May I inquire?"

O. They said to him, "Teach us, our master."

P. He said to them, "Why did Judah merit Kingship?"

Q. [They said to him], "Because he confessed [his
guilt] regarding Tamar."

R.   1. M'SH B: Four elders who were sitting at the
gatehouse of R. Joshua,

   2. Eleazar b. Matia and Ḥanania b. Kinai, and
Simeon b. Azzai, and Simeon the Temani,

   3. and they were engaged with that which R.
Aqiva taught them. [First ed.: with that which R. Tarfon taught them. Said to them R. Aqiva.]

S.   "Why did Judah merit the Kingship?

T.   "Because he confessed regarding Tamar."

U.   They [the elders], added by themselves, "What
wise men have told, and their fathers have not hidden,
to them alone the land was given," etc. [Job 15:18,19].

V.   He [Tarfon] said to them, "And do they reward
[people] because of sins?

W.   "Rather, why did Judah merit Kingship?"

X.   "Because he saved his brother from death.

Y.   "As it is written, 'And Judah said to his
brothers, What profit [us if we slay our brother]'"
[Gen 37:26].

Z.   He said to them, "The saving [of Joseph] is
sufficient only to atone for the sale.

AA.   "Rather, why did Judah merit Kingship?"

BB.   They said to him, "Because of his humility.

CC.   "For it is written, 'Now please let your servant
remain instead of the lad'" [Gen 44:33].

>   [A statement follows which claims that even
>   Saul merited Kingship only because of his
>   humility. A discussion ensues,and then the
>   text returns to the dialogue between Tarfon
>   and the students.]

DD.   He [Tarfon] said to them, "But he [Judah] is
the guarantor.

EE.   "And in the end a guarantor must fulfill his
commitment.

FF.   "Rather, why did Judah merit Kingship?"

GG.   They said to him, "Teach us, our master."

HH.   He said to them, "Because he sanctified the name
of the Holy One, Blessed be He, at the Sea.

II.   "[For] when the tribes came and stood by the Sea,

JJ.   "this one says, 'I will go down,' and this one
says, 'I will go down.'

KK.   "The tribe of Judah jumped in first and sanctified
the name of God at the Sea.

LL. "And it [Scripture] says in relation to that
hour,

MM. "'Save me, O God, for the waters have come up
to my neck. I sink in the deep mire where there is no
foothold,' etc. [Ps 69:2-3]. 'Let not the flood [sweep
over me, or the deep swallow me up' [Ps 69:15]. And
it says, 'Judah was His sanctuary,' etc. [Ps 114:2].

NN. "Judah sanctified the name of the Holy One,
Blessed be He, at the Sea.

OO. "Therefore, 'Israel was his kingdom'" [Ps
114:2].

> Tos. Ber. 4:16-18, ed. Lieberman,
> pp. 22-24, lns. 61-94

Comment: The editor of this pericope places Tarfon's legal
saying D+F (= M. Ber. 6:8) into the setting of a dialogue between
master and students and utilizes this setting to append two exegeses, I-M and P-Q + V-OO. I-M contend that if God has pity on the
righteous when he is angry, he surely has pity on them during the
hour of his compassion. Thus, God aids the righteous in their
hour of need. P-Q + V-OO teach the reason that Judah merited the
Kingship. To merit self-rule, an issue of great importance to
first- and second-century Judaism, it is not enough to confess
one's sins (V), to atone for one's sins (Z), or to fulfill one's
duty of acting humbly (EE). One rather must sanctify the name of
God by plunging into danger only with complete faith in Him (GG).
Heinemann (*Aggadah*, p. 82) states with regard to P-Q + V-OO, "Just
as in the past Judah merited the Kingship because of its daring
plunge into the Sea, so in the future the nation of Judah will
again merit rulership and independence because of heroic and
mighty actions, and because of the sanctification of God's name.
The political independence of Judah will not be renewed by those
who stand helplessly around and simply discuss matters, but by
those who dare to make the great leap, that of raising the banner
of rebellion and martyrdom." Thus two teachings appropriate for
the period after the destruction of the Temple have been assigned
to Tarfon. I-M proclaim that God remembers the righteous when
they are in distress. P-Q + V-OO are an activist call to fight for
the independence of the nation, and to sanctify the name of God.

R-U is an independent tradition. According to Aqiva, Judah
merited Kingship because he confessed with regard to Tamar. In the
tradition ascribed to Tarfon (P-Q + V-OO), this reason is rejected.

A. WKBR HYH: R. Tarfon and his students were sitting
at Kerem BeYavneh.

B. Said R. Tarfon to his students,

C. "May I ask a question of you?"

D. They said to him, "Teach us."

E. [He asked, "As to] one who drinks water to quench
his thirst, how does he bless?

F. "For I say [he should say],

G. "'Who creates living things and their wants.'"

H. They said to him, "You have taught us, our master."

I. [Epstein and Melamed add: He said to them,] "Lo,
it [Scripture] says, 'And they sat to eat bread, [and
they raised their eyes and they saw, and behold, a caravan
of Arabs were coming from Gilead with their camels bearing
spicery and balm and ludanum]' [Gen 37:25].

J. "This is to proclaim the extent of the merit of
the righteous.

K. "For if Joseph, the dear one (ḤBB HW'), had gone
down to Egypt with [ordinary] Arabs, would they not have
killed him with their bad odor?

L. "Rather, the Holy One, Blessed be He, prepared
for him sacks full of spices, and the wind blew within
them so as [to counteract] the smell of the Arabs."

M. He said to them, "Through what merit did Judah
take Kingship?

N. "If it is because it is written [with regard to
Tamar], 'She is more righteous than I [inasmuch as I did
not give her my son Shelah]' [Gen 38:26],

O. "the confession is sufficient only to atone for
the cohabitation.

P. "If because it is written [with regard to
Joseph], 'What profit is it if we slay our brother' [Gen
37:26],

Q. "the saving [of Joseph] is sufficient only to
atone for the sale.

R. "If because he said [with regard to Benjamin],
'For your servant became surety for the lad [to my
father]' [Gen 44:32],

S. "behold, he is the guarantor,

T. "and in every case the guarantor pays."

U. They said to him, "Teach us."

V. He said to them, "[It is] because when the tribes came and stood by the sea,

W. "this one says, 'I will go down,' and this one says, 'I will go down.'

X. "Naḥshon b. Aminadab [of the tribe of Judah] jumped and fell into the sea,

Y. "as it is written above. [The section which describes the actions at the sea appears in the exegesis which precedes our pericope. I fill in Z-GG on the basis of that pericope.]

Z. "For it is written, 'And Judah is not wayward toward God' [Hos 12:1]. Do not read [the words as] 'wayward toward (RD 'M)' but [as] 'goes down into the sea [(RD YM) with God].'

AA. "And it is explicitly [written] in the tradition (BQBLH) with regard to him, 'Save me, O God, for the waters have come up [to my neck]. I sink in the deep mire [where there is no foothold]' [Ps 69:2-3]. 'Let not the flood [sweep over me, or the deep swallow me up]' [Ps 69:15].

BB. "The Holy One, Blessed be He, said to Moses, 'My beloved is sinking in the Sea and you stand reciting long prayers. "Why cry unto me, [speak unto the children of Israel that they go forward], and lift up your rod [and stretch out your hand over the Sea and divide it]"' [Exod 14:15-16].

CC. "What did the tribes say at the Sea?

DD. "'Your hands have established the sanctuary of the Lord' [Exod 15:17].

EE. "At that very hour the Holy One, Blessed be He, said to Moses, 'He who sanctified my name at the Sea shall rule (MWŠL) over Israel.'

FF. "For it is written, 'When the Israelites came forth from Egypt [...Judah became His sanctuary]' [Ps 114:2].

GG. "Judah who sanctified my name at the Sea will rule over Israel."

Mekh. Sim., Exod 14:22, ed.
Epstein and Melamed, pp. 63-64,
lns. 3-18, Z-GG = pp. 63-64,
lns. 20-25, 1-3

Comment: As the synoptic chart below indicates, the major difference between this version of the tradition and that of Tos. is linguistic. The formulaic language of the dialogue between Tarfon and his students thus is not as elaborate here as in Tos. For example, in Mekh., Tarfon himself rejects his own hypothetical answers to the question, why Judah merited the Kingship. In Tos., the students suggest their answers which Tarfon dismisses.

I have noted in my translation that Z-GG have been filled in on the basis of the pericope which precedes the one under discussion. I assume that this is what is meant in Y by, "as it is written above." There is, however, no way to determine whether or not what originally followed Y is identical to Z-GG. We must keep this in mind when we compare the various versions of the pericope.

A. KBR HYH: R. Tarfon and the elders were sitting in the shade of the dovecoat at Yavneh, and this question was asked before them:

B. [Why does Scripture say], "With their camels bearing spicery and balm and ludanum?" [Gen 37:25].

C. [This is] to proclaim the extent to which the merit of the righteous helps them.

D. For if this beloved friend [Joseph] had gone down with [ordinary] Arabs, would they not have killed him with the smell of the camels and with the smell of the *itron*?

E. Rather, the Holy One, Blessed be He, prepared for him sacks full of spices and all [kinds of] good-smelling balms so that he would not die from the smell of the camels and from the smell of the *itron*.

F. They said to him, "You have taught us, our master." [Ms. O and first ed. of Yalkut Shimoni lack the sayings and skip from the attributive formula in F to the saying in G.]

G. They said to him, "Master, teach us.

H. "[As to] one who drinks water to quench his thirst, how does he bless?"

I. He said to them, "Who creates many living things and their wants."

J. They said to him, "You have taught us, our master."

K. They said to him, "Master, teach us.

L. "By what virtue did Judah merit Kingship?"

M.   He said to them, "You tell [me]."

N.   They said, "By virtue of his having said, 'What profit is it if we slay [our brother]?" [Gen 37:26].

O.   He said to them, "[His] saving [of Joseph's life] is sufficient only to atone for the sale."

P.   [First ed. Yalkut Shimoni, Midrash Hakhamim: They said to him], "If so, by virtue of his having said, 'And Judah acknowledged them and said, She [Tamar] is more righteous than I'" [Gen 38:26].

Q.   He said to them, "The confession is sufficient only to atone for the cohabitation [with her]."

R.   "If so, by virtue of his having said, 'Now, therefore, please let your servant remain instead of the lad'" [Gen 44:33].

S.   He said to them, "We find in every case that the guarantor must pay."

T.   They said to him, "Master, teach us.

U.   "By what virtue did Judah merit the Kingship?"

V.   He said to them, "When the tribes stood by the Sea,

W.   "this one says, 'I will go down [to the Sea] first,' and this one says, 'I will go down [to the Sea] first,'

X.   "as it is written, 'Ephraim surrounds me with lies [and the house of Israel with deceit]' [Hos 12:1].

Y.   "While they were standing and deliberating with one another,

Z.   "Nahshon b. Aminadab and his tribe following [after] him jumped into the waves of the Sea.

AA.   "Therefore, [Judah] merited Kingship,

BB.   "as it is written, 'When the Israelites came forth from Egypt, the house of Jacob from the people of strange tongues, Judah was his sanctuary'; therefore, 'Israel was his [Judah's] kingdom' [Ps 114:1-2].

CC.   "Said the Lord (MQWM), 'Whoever sanctified my name at the Sea shall come and rule over Israel.'"

> Mekh. Ish. Beshalah 6, ed.
> Lauterbach, pp. 235-37, lns.
> 44-71

Comment: The order of the three major units differs in this version of the tradition from that in Tos. and in Mekh. Sim. The exegesis about the merit of the righteous precedes both the legal

tradition and the exegesis about Judah and kingship. The editor
marks off these sections by means of the formulaic language at F
and J. In this version, as in Tos., the students propose answers
to the question about Judah and the kingship which Tarfon then
rejects.

      A. Another interpretation [of] "God is known in
Judah" [Ps 76:2].

      B. Why did [Judah] merit kingship?

      C. The students asked this question before R. Tarfon
[who was sitting] in the shade of the dovecoat at Yavneh--

      D. "Why did Judah merit the kingdom"?

      E. He said to them, "Because he confessed in the
incident [involving] Tamar."

      F. They said to him, "The confession is sufficient
only to atone for the cohabitation [with her]."

      G. He said to them, "Because he said, 'What profit
is it if we slay our brother?'" [Gen 37:26].

      H. They said to him, "The saving [of Joseph] is
sufficient only to atone from the sale."

      I. He said to them, "By means of his having said,
'Now please let your servant remain instead of the lad'"
[Gen 44:33].

      J. They said to him, "*It is required of a guarantor
that he fulfill his commitment.*"

      K. He said to them, "If so, by what virtue did
Judah merit [kingship]?"

      L. They said to him, "By virtue of having jumped
into the waves at the Sea.

      M. "For all the tribes were standing and not one
[of them] went down into the Sea.

      N. "Rather, this one says, 'I will go down first,'
and this one says, 'I will go down first,'

      O. "[and the tribe of] Judah sanctified the name
of the Holy One, Blessed be He, and went down into the Sea.

      P. "For it is written, 'And Judah is yet wayward
toward God' [Hos 12:1].

      Q. "He [Judah] reconciled himself with the Holy One,
Blessed be He, and sanctified the name of the Holy One,
Blessed be He and went down [into the Sea].

      R. "And by virtue of this he merited kingship.

S.   "For it is written, 'Judah was His sanctuary'
[Ps 114:2].

T.   "Because Judah was His sanctuary,

U.   "therefore, 'Israel was His kingdom' [Ps 114:2].

V.   "Lo, 'God is known in Judah'; therefore, 'his
name,' that of Judah, 'is great in Israel'" [Ps 76:2].

Mid. Ps. 76:2, ed. Buber, p. 341

Comment: The redactor has placed the tradition about Judah
meriting the kingship within the redactional setting of A and V.
B is redundant, since the same question appears in D. Mid. Ps.
clearly is a secondary version of the pericope, for P-Q is unintelligible unless the reader knows the exegesis of Hos 12:1. The
major difference between this version and the others is that here
Tarfon proposes the answers which the students reject. The students in L give the correct response.

Let us now compare the four versions of this tradition by
means of a synoptic table.

Tos. Ber.	Mekh. Simeon	Mekh. Ish.	Mid. Ps.
1.	1. - - -	1. - - - -	1. Another interpretation [of] "God is known in Judah."
2.	2. - - -	2. - - - -	2. Why did Judah merit the kingdom?
3. M'SH B R. Tarfon was sitting in the shade of the dovecoat	3. WKBR HYH R. Tarfon and his students were sitting at Kerem beYavneh.	3. KBR HYH R. Tarfon and the elders were sitting in the shade of the dovecoat at Yavneh and this question was asked before them:	3. The students asked this question before R. Tarfon [who was sitting] in the shade of the dovecoat at Yavneh.
4. in the afternoon on the Sabbath.	4. - - -	4. - - - -	4. - - -
5. See below #20-23.	5. See below #20-23.	5. [Why does Scripture say] "With their camels bearing spicery and balm and ludanum?"	5. - - -
6. - - -	6. - - -	6. This is to proclaim the extent to which the merit of the righteous helps them.	6. - - -
7. - - -	7. - - -	7. For if this beloved friend had gone down with [ordinary] Arabs, would **they** not have killed him with the smell of the camels and with the smell of the *itron*?	7. - - -

Tos. Ber.	Mekh. Simeon	Mekh. Ish.	Mid. Ps.
8. - - -	8. - - -	8. Rather, the Holy One, Blessed be He, prepared for him sacks full of spices and all good smelling balms, so that he would not die from the smell of the camels and from the smell of the *itron*.	8. - - -
9. - - -	9. - - -	9. They said to him, You have taught us, our Master.	9. - - -
10. They brought before him a bucket of cold [water].	10. - - -	10. - - -	10. - - -
11. He said to his students,	11. Said R. Tarfon to his students,	11. - - -	11. - - -
12. - - -	12. May I ask a question of you?	12. - - -	12. - - -
13. - - -	13. They said to him, Teach us.	13. They said to him, Master, teach us.	13. - - -
14. As to one who drinks water to quench his thirst, how does he bless?	14. " " " " " " " " "	14. " " " " " " " " " " " "	14. - - -
15. They said to him, Teach us, our master.	15. - - -	15. - - -	15. - - -
16. He said to them, [He says] Who creates living things and their wants.	16. For I say [he should say] " " " " " "	16. He said to them " " " " " " " " "	16. - - -

Tos. Ber.	Mekh. Simeon	Mekh. Ish.	Mid. Ps.
17. - - -	17. They said to him, You have taught us, our master.	17. " " " " " "	17. - - -
18. He said to them, May I inquire?	18. - - -	18. - -	18. - - -
19. They said to him, Teach us, our master.	19. - - -	19. - -	19. - - -
20. He said to them, Lo, it Scripture says, "And they sat to eat bread, and they raised their eyes and they saw, [and behold a caravan of Arabs was coming from Gilead with their camels bearing spicery, and balm, and ludanum]."	20. "	20. See above #5-9.	20. - - -
21. - - -	21. This is to proclaim the extent of the merit of the righteous.	21. - -	21. - -
22. And is not the custom of Arabs to carry only skins and bad smelling things and *itzron*?	22. For if Joseph, the dear one, had gone down to Egypt with [ordinary] Arabs, would they not have killed him with their bad odor?	22. - -	22. - -
23. Rather, He placed that righteous man, [Joseph], among lovely items.	23. Rather, the Holy One, Blessed be He, prepared for him sacks full of spices, and the wind blew within them so as [to counteract] the smell of the Arabs.	23. - - -	23. - - -

	Tos. Ber.	Mekh. Simeon	Mekh. Ish.	Mid. Ps.
24.	[And we can learn from this] by means of a *qal vaḥomer* [that]	- - -	- - -	- - -
25.	if when God is angry [with] the righteous He has pity on them, how much the more so [does He care for them] during the time of His compassion.	- - -	- - -	- - -
26.	[Interpolation: More examples of the same lesson.]	- - -	- - -	- - -
27.	He said to them, May I inquire?	- - -	- - -	- - -
28.	They said to him, Teach us, our master.	- - -	They said to him, Master, teach us.	- - -
29.	He said to them, Why did Judah merit kingship?	He said to them, Through what merit did Judah take the kingship?	By what virtue did Judah merit kingship?	Why did Judah merit kingship?
30.	- - -	- - -	He said to them, You tell [me].	- - -
31.	See below #37-39.	See below #37-39.	They said to him, By virtue of his having said "What profit is it if we slay, [our brother]."	See below #37-39.
32.	- - -	- - -	He said to them, [His] saving [of Joseph] is sufficient only to atone for the sale.	- - -

Tos. Ber.	Mekh. Simeon	Mekh. Ish.	Mid. Ps.
33. Because he confessed regarding Tamar.	33. If it is because it is written, "She is more righteous than I,"	33. They said to him, If so, by virtue of his having said, "And Judah acknowledged them and said, She is more righteous than I."	33. He said to them, Because he confessed in the incident [involving] Tamar.
34. [Interpolation: Four sages discussing Aqiva's teaching.]	34.	34.	34.
35. He [Tarfon] said to them, And do they reward [people] because of sins?	35. - - - the confession is sufficient only to atone for the cohabitation.	35. He said to them, the confession " " " " " " "	35. They said to him, the confession " " " " " " "
36. Rather, why did Judah merit kingship?	36. - - -	36. - - -	36. He said to them
37. Because he saved his brother from death,	37. If because	37. See above #31-32.	37. Because
38. as it is written, "And Judah said to his brothers, 'What profit,'" etc.	38. it is written, "What profit is it if we slay our brother."	38. - - -	38. he said, What profit is " " "
39. He said to them, The saving [of Joseph] is sufficient only to atone for the sale.	39. - - - " " " "	39. - - -	39. They said to him, " " " " " "
40. Rather, why did Judah merit kingship?	40. - - -	40. - - -	40. - - -
41. They said to him, Because of his humility.	41. If because	41. If so by virtue of	41. He said to them, By means of

Tos. Ber.	Mekh. Simeon	Mekh. Ish.	Mid. Ps.
42. For it is written, "Now please let your servant remain instead of the lad."	42. he said, "For your servant became surety for the lad," etc.	42. his having said, "Now therefore, please let your servant remain instead of the lad."	42. his having said, " " " " " " - - -
43. [Interpolation: Comment about Saul and humility.]	43. - - -	43. - - -	43.
44. He said to them, but he is the guarantor,	44. Behold, he is the guarantor	44. He said to them,	44. They said to him,
45. and in the end the guarantor must fulfill his commitment.	45. and in every case the guarantor pays.	45. We find in every case that the guarantor pays.	45. *It is required of a guarantor that he fulfill his commitment.*
46. Rather why did Judah merit kingship? They said to him, Teach us, our master.	46. They said to him, Teach us.	46. They said to him, Master, teach us, by what virtue did Judah merit kingship.	46. He said to them, If so by what virtue did Judah merit the kingship?
47. He said to them,	47. " "	47. " "	47. They said to him,
48. - - -	48. - - -	48. - - -	48. By virtue of having jumped into the waves at the Sea.
49. Because he sanctified the name of the Holy One, Blessed be He, at the Sea,	49. - - -	49. - - -	49. - - -
50. for when the tribes came and stood by the Sea,	50. it is [because] " " " " " "	50. " " " " " "	50. For all the tribes were standing and not one [of them] went into the Sea.

Tos. Ber.	Mekh. Simeon	Mekh. Ish.	Mid. Ps.

51. this one says, I will go down, and this one says, I will go down.	51. " "
	  " "
	  " "
	  " "
		51. this one says, I will go down first, and this one says, I will go down first,	51. " "
			  " "
			  " "
			  " "

52. - - -	52. - - -	52. as it is written, "Ephraim surrounds me with lies," etc.	52. - - -
53. - - -	53. - - -	53. While they were standing and deliberating with one another,	53. - - -
54. The tribe of Judah jumped in first and sanctified the name of God at the Sea.	54. Nahshon b. Aminadab jumped and fell into the Sea,	54. Nahshon b. Aminadab and his tribe following [after] him jumped into the waves of the Sea.	54. [and the tribe of] Judah sanctified the name of the Holy One, Blessed be He, and went down into the Sea.
55. - - -	55. as it is written above.	55. - - -	55. - - -
56. - - -	56. For it is written, "And Judah is yet wayward toward God." Do not read "wayward toward" but "goes down into the Sea."	56. - - -	56. for it is written, "And Judah is yet wayward toward God." He reconciled himself with the Holy One, Blessed be He, and sanctified the name of the Holy One, Blessed be He, and went down [into the Sea].

57. And it [Scripture] says in relation to that very hour, "Save me, O God, for the waters have come up to my neck. I sink in the deep mire where there is no foothold." "Let not the flood," etc.	57. And it is explicitly [written] in the tradition with regard to him, " "
	  " "
	  " "
	  " "
		57. - - -	57. - - -

Tos. Ber.	Mekh. Simeon	Mekh. Ish.	Mid. Ps.
58. - - -	58. The Holy One, Blessed be He, said to Moses, My beloved is sinking in the Sea and you stand reciting long prayers, "Why cry unto me," etc. "Lift up your rod," etc.	58. - - -	58. - - -
59. - - -	59. What did the tribes say at the Sea? "Your hands have established the sanctuary of the Lord."	59. - - -	59. - - -
60. - - -	60. At that very hour, the Holy One, Blessed be He, said to Moses, He who sanctified my name at the Sea, shall rule over Israel.	60. See below #65.	60. - - -
61. - - -	61. - - -	61. Therefore, [Judah] merited kingship,	61. And by virtue of this he merited the kingship.
62. And it says, "Judah was His sanctuary," etc.	62. For it is written, "When the Israelites came forth from Egypt," etc. ["..Judah was his sanctuary"].	62. as it is written, "When the Israelites came forth from Egypt, the house of Jacob from the people of strange tongues, Judah was His sanctuary."	62. For it is written, "Judah was his sanctuary."
63. Judah sanctified the name of the Holy One, Blessed be He, at the Sea.	63. Judah who sanctified My name at the Sea,	63. - - -	63. Because Judah was His sanctuary.
64. Therefore, "Israel was his kingdom."	64. will rule over Israel.	64. therefore, "Israel was his kingdom."	64. " " " " " "

Tos. Ber.	Mekh. Simeon	Mekh. Ish.	Mid. Ps.
65. - -	65. See above #60.	65. Said the Lord, Whoever sanctified my name at the Sea shall come and rule over Israel.	65. - - -
66. - -	66. - - -	66. - - -	66. Lo, "God is known in Judah"; therefore, "his name," that of Judah, "is great in Israel."

Tos. gives us the most heavily interpolated and elaborate
version of the item. But this does not indicate that it is dependent on the other versions; rather, they may derive from a non-
extant common source. Besides the interpolations at 26, 34 and 43,
Tos. contains the additional details of 4 and 10. The formulaic
language of the dialogue is additionally repeated at 18, 19, and
27. 36 and 40 repeat the question, "Why did Judah merit the kingship?" 33, 37, and 41 give statements of the proposed reasons,
thereby introducing the Scriptural proof texts. Similarly, 49
introduces the evidence which demonstrates that Judah sanctified
the name of God at the Sea. 49, 54, and 63 all emphasize the notion of the sanctification of God's name. None of these details,
however, proves that Tos. is dependent upon the versions in the
Mekh.

Regarding Mekh. Simeon we first recall that we have filled in
56-63 of it on the assumption that 55 refers to the pericope which
precedes the tradition of Tarfon. We restrict our comparison of
Mekh. Simeon with the other versions to 1-54. Mekh. Simeon is the
most compact version of the item. This is most evident in 29-48,
in which Tarfon simply gives hypothetical answers which he then
rejects. In Mekh. Ish. and in Tos., the students propose the
answers and Tarfon then dismisses them. Mekh. Ish. is very similar in content to Mekh. Simeon. It does, however, contain some
elaborations. Aside from the differences between 29-48 of the two
versions which we have just noted, 7-8 of Mekh. Ish. is more detailed than 22-23 of Mekh. Simeon. Thus Mekh. Simeon speaks only
of the smell of the Arabs, while Mekh. Ish. mentions that of the
itron and the camels. Furthermore, 8 of Mekh. Ish. also includes
"and all good smelling balms."

Mid. Ps. takes part of the tradition and places it in the redactional setting 1-2, 66. 56 indicates that Mid. Ps. presupposes
some other version of the item, for otherwise the verse is unintelligible. Mid. Ps. seems closest to Mekh. Ish. for the following reasons: 3 of both versions mentions both the dovecoat and·
Yavneh. In 28 of Ish. and in 3 of Mid. Ps. the students, and not
Tarfon, ask why Judah merited the kingship. Finally, 51 of Mid.
Ps. and 51 of Mekh. Ish. differ from the parallel item in the
other two versions. The major difference between Mid. Ps. and the
other versions is that in it Tarfon gives the incorrect answers
to the question regarding Judah while the students give the right
reply.

The comparison of the different versions of the pericope
indicates that Tos., the Mekhiltot, and probably Mid. Ps. appear to derive from a non-extant common source. They are close to
each other but sufficiently different to make direct literary
dependence unlikely.

> A. A Sanhedrin that puts one person to death in a
> week [of years] is called destructive (HBLNYT).
> B. R. Eleazar b. Azariah says, "[One that puts] one
> person to death in seventy years [is so called]."
> C. R. Tarfon and R. Aqiva say, "If we were in the
> Sanhedrin, no one would ever have been put to death."
> D. Rabban Simeon b. Gamaliel says, "Even they
> [would have] increased the shedders of blood in Israel."

M. Mak. 1:10

Comment: A-B disagree about the definition of HBLNYT. A supplies the protasis for B. C, an independent saying, makes the
same point as A-B. It expresses opposition to capital punishment.
C is one of three sayings which have the attributive formula, "R.
Tarfon and R. Aqiva say." D responds to C and asserts that murder
would increase if there were no capital punishment.

> A. R. Tarfon says, "(1) The day is short, (2) and
> the work is abundant, (3) and the workers are lazy, (4)
> and the reward is great, (5) and the owner is [demanding]
> (DWHQ)."
> B. He used to say, "It is not incumbent upon you to
> finish the work, but you are not free to desist from it.
> C. "If you have learned a great deal of Torah,
> they give you a great reward.
> D. "[L: And] faithful is your taskmaster to pay
> you the reward for your labor.
> E. "[L,N.Pr,Pc,Maim.,Romm: And] know that the
> rewarding of the righteous is in the age to come
> (L'TYD LB')."

M. Avot 2:15,16 (ARN B Ch. 35,
ed. Schechter, p. 84)

Comment: Tarfon's saying differs in form from those which
precede and follow it.[1] A is a general statement which B-D gloss.
B fills out A1 by stating that, even though there is a great deal
of work, one may not desist from his labors. C relates to A4 and

connects it with the study of the Torah. D repeats A4. The inclusion of E, which glosses D, is supported only by some of the
Mss. It appears in ARN, its primary location, in place of A5.

The message of this pericope is straightforward. One receives a reward for whatever amount of work he does. According to
C this work is Torah-study, and one need not complete the task in
order to receive his just due.

> A. *R. Tarfon says, "(1) The day is short, (2) and*
> *the work is abundant, (3) and the workers are lazy, (4)*
> *and the reward is great,* (5) and know that the rewarding
> of the righteous is in the age to come."
>
> B. He used to say, "Do not remove yourself from
> the measure which has no limit and from the work which
> does not have an end.
>
> C. "A parable, to what may this be likened?
>
> D. "To one who used to take sea water and pour it
> on the land.
>
> E. "The sea does not diminish, and the land does
> not become full.
>
> F. "If he became impatient, they said to him,
> 'Wretch, why do you become impatient? Every day take
> your reward of gold.'"
>
> > ARN A Ch. 27, trans. Goldin,
> > p. 115

Comment: ARN supplements M. Avot 2:15-16A-B. A of ARN is
identical to M. 2:15A, except for 5. B restates B of M. The
parable's message is the same as that of M.A-B. One receives a
reward as long as he does his job, but one need not complete an
endless task. ARN knows nothing of Torah-study.

> A. ["And the dew went up, and there was on the
> face of the wilderness] a fine [flake-like thing (DQ
> MḤŚPŚ), fine as hoarfrost (DQ KKPWR), on the ground]"
> [Exod 16:14].
>
> B. "Fine" teaches that it used to come down from
> heaven,
>
> C. as it says, "That stretches the heaven like a
> thin curtain (KDWQ)" [Isa 40:22].
>
> D. And since it used to come down from heaven, [one]
> might [think] that it came down cold.

E.   It says, "Warm (HM)."

F.   [One] might [think] it came down with noise.
[Mekh. Sim.: Since it came down from above to below,
[one] might [think] it came down with noise. How do we
know it came down quietly?]

G.   It says, "Silent (ḤŚ)."

H.   1.   [One] might [think] it came down upon the land,

     2.   from where [do we know that] it fell only
into vessels?

I.   It says, "Like a lid (KKPWR)." [If one reads
KKPWR as KKPWRT, the word has this meaning.]   [Mekh. Sim.;
Mekh. Ish., Ms. Oxford II: It says, "A bowl (ŚP)."]

J.   R. Tarfon says, "It fell only upon [Mekh. Ish.:
those who gathered it (H'WŚPYM); Mekh. Sim.: the thresh-
holds (H'WŚPYYM); Mekh. Ish., ed. Horowitz: the palms of
the hands (H'WPŚYM); Mid. HaGadol: the branches (HŚ'PYM);
Yalkut Shimoni: the box (HQWPŚ').]

> Mekh. Ish. Vayassa 4, ed.
> Lauterbach, p. 112, lns. 66-71
> (Mekh. Sim. Exod 16:14, ed.
> Epstein and Melamed, p. 110,
> lns. 25-5, Mid. HaGadol, Exod
> 16:14)

Comment: The exegesis in this pericope explains by means of
notariqon, rearranging the letters in a word to form new words,
the *hapax legomenon* MḤŚPŚ. Tarfon's comment, which is phrased
like the second clause in D and F, offers a different exegesis
from H2-I to show that the *manna* did not fall upon the land. His
point is that God performs a miracle in a manner advantageous to
His beneficiaries. There is no firm tradition concerning the
exact content of Tarfon's saying, for there are the following readings: (1) 'WŚPYM, (2) 'WŚPYYM, (3) QWPS', (4) 'WPŚYM, and (5)
Ś'PYM. All of these words, like the term MḤŚPŚ, contain the con-
sonants ŚP. The differences between the words are in the vowels
', ', W, and Y.

A.   KBR HYH: R. Tarfon [b. adds: R. Ishmael] and the
elders [Mekh. Sim.: and his students] were seated, and R.
Eleazar of Modin was seated before [Mekh. Sim.,b.: among]
them.

B.   Said to them R. Eleazar of Modin,

C.   "The *manna* which came down for Israel was sixty
cubits high."

D.   They said to him, "Modiite, [Mekh. Sim.:
Eleazar, our brother] How long will you continue to
astonish us [i.e., make astonishing statements]? [Mekh.
Sim., b.: How long will you gather and bring (words)
against us?"]

E.   He said to them, "It is [on the basis of] a
Scriptural verse [that I make this statement]." [The
pericope then cites Eleazar's exegesis. There is no
further comment by the elders.]

> Mekh. Ish. Vayassa 4, ed.
> Lauterbach, pp. 113-14, lns.
> 74-89 (Mekh. Sim. Exod 16:14,
> ed. Epstein and Melamed, pp.
> 110-11, lns. 7-19, b. Yoma 76a)

Comment: A and D provide a setting for Eleazar's exegesis.
It allows Eleazar to appear wiser than Tarfon and the elders for,
by means of his exegesis, he refutes their accusation, D. The
setting given in A probably is generated from two sources: (1)
those units of traditions which describe Tarfon and the elders as
sitting and discussing questions, (2) the item just analyzed,
which contains an exegesis, ascribed to Tarfon, dealing with *manna*.

A.   KBR HYH: R. Eliezer was sick and four elders came
in to visit him.

B.   [They are] R. Tarfon, and R. Joshua, and R.
Eleazar b. Azariah, and R. Aqiva.

C.   1.   Answered R. Tarfon and he said, "Master,
you are more precious to Israel than the globe of the sun.

2.   "For the globe of the sun sheds light in this
world, and you shed light for us in this world and for the
world to come" [b. assigns the saying in C to Joshua].

D.   1.   Answered R. Joshua and he said, "Master,
you are more precious to Israel than a day of rain.

2.   "[For] the rain gives life in this world,
and you give us life in this world and for the world to
come" [b. assigns D to Tarfon].

E.   1.   Answered R. Eleazar b. Azariah and he said,
"Master, you are more precious to Israel than a father
and a mother.

2.   "For a father and a mother bring man into
life of this world, and you have brought us into life of
the world to come."

F.   Answered R. Aqiva and he said, "Master, chastisements are precious."

G.   Said R. Eliezer to his students, "Help me up."

H.   R. Eliezer sat up, he said, "Speak, Aqiva."

I.   He [Aqiva] said to him, "Lo, it [Scripture]
says, 'Menasseh was twelve years old when he began to
reign; and he reigned fifty-five years in Jerusalem.
And he did that which was evil in the sight of the Lord,'
etc. [2 Chr 33:1-2].

J.   "And it says, 'These also are proverbs of
Solomon, which the men of Hezekiah, king of Judah,
transcribed' [Prov 25:1].

K.   "And could the thought enter your mind that
Hezekiah, king of Judah, taught Torah to all of Israel,
and to Menasseh, his son, he did not teach the Torah?

L.   "You must, therefore, say that all the instructions which he taught him, and all the trouble which he
took with him did not help him at all.

M.   "And what did help him?

N.   "Lo, you must say the chastisements:

O.   "For it says, 'And God spoke to Menasseh and to
his nation, and they did not listen. And the Lord brought
[upon them] the captains of the host of the king of
Assyria, who took Menasseh with hooks and bound him with
fetters, and carried him to Babylon. And when he was in
distress, he besought the Lord his God, and humbled himself greatly before the God of his fathers. And he
prayed unto Him, and He was entreated by him and heard
his supplication, and brought him back to Jerusalem
into his kingdom' [2 Chr 33:10-13].

P.   "Thus you learn that chastisements are precious."

> Mekh. Ish. Baḥodesh 10, ed.
> Lauterbach, pp. 280-82, lns.
> 58-86 (Sifre Deut. 32, ed.
> Finkelstein, pp. 57-58, lns.
> 12-16, 1-13, b. Sanh. 101a-b)

Comment: This is another unit of tradition built upon the
motif of four elders gathering at a fifth sage's sickbed or his
house of mourning. y. Yev. 1:6, a unit of tradition which does not
utilize a setting similar to that of A, places together the four
sages mentioned in this pericope (Tarfon, Joshua, Eleazar b.
Azariah, and Aqiva). The other items which have a setting like A

have Yose the Galilean instead of Joshua. The names in this unit
of tradition appear in the usual order.

Tarfon, Joshua, and Eleazar all make the same point: the
centrality of the rabbi. The rabbi is the key and the way to the
world to come. Aqiva, however, teaches a lesson different from
that of the other three sages: chastisements are precious for they
can accomplish even what learning cannot at times do. Chastisements can lead to repentance. Thus, unlike other similar stories,
this one does not assign the same message to all four rabbis.
A, therefore, provides a framework for two lessons: (1) the importance of the rabbi in providing the way to the world to come, (2)
the preciousness of chastisements. The editor highlights Aqiva's
saying, for he places it last, and also has Eliezer (G-E) sit up
to hear it.

     A. R. Tarfon says,

     B. "The Holy One, Blessed be He, said, 'It is clear
and evident to me that Israel is worthy to leave Egypt
and to be given over to Ammon and Moab and Amaleq.'

     C. "But I swore to fight their wars and to save them,

     D. "as it is written, 'A hand upon the banner of
the Lord [the Lord will have war with Amaleq from generation to generation]' [Exod 17:16].

     E. "And it says, 'But I acted [in Egypt] for the
sake of my name so that it would not be profaned [in the
sight of the nations among whom they dwelt]' [Exod 20:9].

     F. "And lo, I want to take them out from Egypt and
you say to me, 'Send [by the hand of him whom you will
send]'" [Exod 4:13].

                         Mekh. Sim. Exod 6:2, ed.
                         Epstein and Melamed, p. 5,
                         lns. 12-16

Comment: This is one of nine consecutive exegeses, assigned
to Yavneans and to Ushans, which deal with the same issue. God
tells Moses that he is about to redeem Israel, and Moses shirks
his responsibility by asking God to send someone else to lead
them. Our pericope illustrates by means of a *qal vaḥomer* the in-
appropriateness of Moses' response. God, who should be reticent
to redeem Israel, is not; yet Moses who should not be reticent to
fulfill his mission, is. This premise also points to God's faith-
fulness to his promises of redemption.

A.   Said R. Tarfon, "[I swear by] the Temple-service,
if there is anyone in this generation who is able to
reprove."

B.   Said R. Eleazar b. Azariah, "[I swear by] the
Temple-service, if there is anyone in this generation
who can accept reproof."

C.   Said R. Aqiva, "[I swear by] the Temple-service,
if there is anyone in this generation who knows how to
reprove."

D.   1.   Said R. Yoḥanan b. Nuri,

2.   "I call upon heaven and earth as my witnesses,

3.   "that more than four or five times Aqiva was
flogged on account of me before Rabban Gamaliel,

4.   "for I used to complain about him [Aqiva]
to him [Gamaliel],

5.   "and I knew so well that he [Aqiva] would
shower more love upon me."

> Sifra Qodashim Pereq 4:9,
> ed. Weiss, 89b

Comment: A-C are a thematic and formal unit. The names of
the three sages appear in the standard order. All three sayings
illustrate the deficiency of the period; no one knows how to give,
or to receive reproof, or is able to reprove. D, which can stand
alone, demonstrates that Aqiva knows how to accept reproof.

A.   Said R. Tarfon, "[I swear by] the Temple-service,
if there is anyone in this generation who is able to
reprove."

B.   Said R. Eleazar b. Azariah, "[I swear by] the
Temple-service, if there is anyone in this generation who
can accept reproof."

C.   Said R. Aqiva, "[I swear by] the Temple-service,
if there is anyone in this generation who knows how to
reprove."

D.   1.   Said R. Yoḥanan b. Nuri,

2.   "I call upon heaven and earth as my witnesses,

3.   "that more than five times Aqiva was chided
on account of me before Rabban Gamaliel at Yavneh,

4.   "for I used to complain about him [Aqiva],
and he [Gamaliel] used to chide him,

5. "and I know so well that because of each
one [of my complaints], he used to shower more love
upon me

6. "in order to fulfill that which is written,
'Reprove not a scorner lest he hate you; reprove a wise
man, and he will love you'" [Prov 9:8].

> Sifre Deut. 1, ed. Finkelstein,
> pp. 3-4, lns. 9-11, 1-3

Comment: Sifre tones down the punishment that Aqiva received
at the hands of Gamaliel. Aqiva was chided, not flogged. D6 adds
a proof-text to Yoḥanan b. Nuri's account.

A.   TNY': Said R. Tarfon, "I wonder whether there is
anyone in this generation who accepts reproof [M: who is
able to reprove].

B.   "[For] if [one says to him], 'Remove the chip
from between your eyes,' he answers him, 'Remove the plank
from between your eyes.'"

C.   Said R. Eleazar b. Azariah, "I wonder whether
there is anyone in this generation who knows [how] to
reprove."

D.   [M:] Said R. Aqiva, "I wonder whether there is
anyone in this generation who accepts reproof."

E.   1.   And said R. Yoḥanan b. Nuri,

2.   "I call upon heaven and earth as my witnesses,

3.   "that Aqiva was flogged many times on
account of me,

4.   "for I used to complain about him before
Rabban Simeon b. Rabbi [M: Rabban Simeon b. Gamaliel],

5.   "and all the more so I showered more love
upon him,

6.   "in order to fulfill that which is written,
'Reprove not a scorner lest he hate you; reprove a wise
man, and he will love you'" [Prov 9:8].

> b. Arak. 16b

Comment: This version of the unit of tradition is slightly
garbled. There is some uncertainty regarding the assignment of
the sayings, as well as the name of the authority before whom
Yoḥanan complained. B, which glosses A, is taken from its proper
context in b. B.B. 15b-16a.

A. WKBR: R. Tarfon was late in coming to the
Bet Midrash.

B. Said to him Rabban Gamaliel, "Why did you see
[fit] to be late?"

C. He said to him, "[I was late] because I was
performing Temple-service."

D. He said to him, "Indeed all your words are
mysteries; for is there now [after the destruction of
the Temple] Temple-service?"

E. He said to him, "Lo, it [Scripture] says, 'I
give you the priesthood as a service of gift ('BWDT
MTNH)'" [Num 18:7].

F. [Scripture says this] so as to make the eating
of heave-offering within the boundaries [of the Land of
Israel] equivalent to service in the Temple.

> Sifre Qoraḥ 116, ed. Horowitz,
> p. 133, lnṡ. 16-19

Comment: Tarfon's exegesis, E, which indicates that eating
heave-offering after the destruction of the Temple is equivalent
to performing Temple-service, is based on the word MTNH. The
MTNH, the gift, which the priest receives, the heave-offering, is
called 'BWDT MTNH. *'Avodah* is the word which designates Temple-
service. The eating of the gift, the heave-offering, therefore,
is equivalent to performing service in the Temple. Thus there is
a substitute for the cult after the Temple's destruction. F
glosses the teaching of E by specifying that it applies to heave-
offering eaten within the boundaries of the Land of Israel.

A. *Where is heave-offering designated as Temple-
service* ('BWDH)?

B. DTNY': M'SH B: R. Tarfon did not come to the
Bet Midrash the previous evening.

C. In the morning Rabban Gamaliel met him and said
to him, "Why did you not come to the *Bet Midrash* last night?"

D. He said to him, "I performed Temple-service ('BWDH
'BDTY)."

E. 1. He said to him,

2. "All your words are only mysteries to me,

3. "for whence [do you learn that] there is Temple-
service nowadays [i.e., after the destruction of the Temple]?"

F. He said to him, "Lo, it [Scripture] says, 'I
give you the priesthood as a service of gift ('BWDT MTNH),
and the common man that draws near shall be put to death'"
[Num 18:7].

G. They made [Ms. Oxford: Scripture made] the eating
of heave-offering within the border [of Israel] equivalent
to the Temple-service on the Day of Atonement.

b. Pes. 72b-73a

Comment: There are several differences between this version
of the unit of tradition and that recorded in Sifre. b., unlike
Sifre, specifies when Tarfon was late in coming to the *Bet Midrash*.
Gamaliel's question, E3, "from whence," is phrased so as to anticipate an answer which appeals to a Scriptural proof-text. Finally,
G lacks the joining language found in Sifre, "so as," and thus
clearly stands separate from the M'SH.

A. 1. They said, [As to] everyone who gives heave-
offering to anyone who eats it according to its commandment [i.e., properly],

2. they credit him as if he performed Temple-
service.

B. 1. And a priest who eats heave-offering according
to its commandment,

2. they credit him as if he performed Temple-
service.

C. 1. They said about R. Tarfon that he used to
eat heave-offering in the morning,

2. and he [would] say, "I have sacrificed the
daily morning offering."

3. And he [would] eat heave-offering at dusk,

4. and he [would] say, "I have sacrificed the
daily afternoon offering."

D. And from where [do we know] that the eating of
sanctified [food by] the priests [within] the boundaries
is equivalent to Temple-service?

E. For it says, "I give you the priesthood as a
service of gift" [Num 18:7].

Sifre Zuṭṭa Qoraḥ 18:7, ed.
Horowitz, p. 293, lns. 6-10

Comment: Sifre Zuṭṭa gives us an allusion to Tarfon which draws out the implications of the other versions. Tarfon regularly ate heave-offering at the time of the daily sacrifices. The redactional setting in Sifre Zuṭṭa also claims that the giving of heave-offering, as well as the eating of it, is equivalent to service in the Temple. Thus every man in Israel can act as a priest; he can perform Temple-service.

> A. WKBR HYH: R. Tarfon and the elders were assembled in the upper chamber of the house of Nitzeh [Aggadot HaTalmud: Arza] in Lydda.
> B. The following question was asked before them:
> C. Is learning greater or is deed greater?
> D. Answered R. Tarfon saying, "Deed is greater."
> E. Answered R. Aqiva saying, "Learning is greater."
> F. They all answered saying, "Learning is greater,
> G. "for learning leads to [the performance of] deeds."

> b. Qid. 40b (C.R. 2:14)

Comment: A-B provide a framework for the well-balanced dispute, C-E. The item as usual is formulated to favor Aqiva, for sages support his opinion. This pericope focuses upon the universal question of whether study or action is supreme. The discussion of this issue would be particularly appropriate immediately after the destruction of the Temple. In the Temple one served God through actions, through the cult. The center piece of rabbinism, as exemplified in the teachings of Yoḥanan b. Zakkai, is study of Torah. But is study of Torah more important than the performance of deeds? The answer deemed correct in our pericope effects a compromise between the two values. Study is of supreme value; but it has this distinction because it leads to action.

Our pericope centers upon a recurrent issue in rabbinic Judaism. The saying attributed to Hillel, that an *'am-ha'areṣ* cannot be righteous (Avot 2:5), is in line with the decision of E-F. ARN A Ch. 22, however, preserves the following comment of Ḥanina b. Dosa which seems to give a different solution to the dilemma. It reads:

> He [Ḥanina] used to say, "He whose works exceed his his wisdom, his wisdom shall endure. But he whose wisdom exceeds his works, his works shall not endure."
>
> ARN A Ch. 22, trans. Goldin, p. 99

This tradition implies that one needs both works and wisdom, but the priority should be given to actions. Avot. 1:17 contains a saying attributed to Simeon b. Gamaliel which also favors actions. It reads:

> Not the study (MDRŠ) but the performance [of the law] is essential.

Similarly, b. A.Z. 17b preserves the following dialogue between Eleazar b. Peraṭa and R. Ḥanina b. Teradion which indicates that it is not enough to study Torah; one must also perform deeds.

> When R. Eleazar b. Peraṭa and R. Ḥanina b. Teradion were arrested, Eleazar said to Ḥanina, "Happy are you that you have been arrested on one count; whereas I have been arrested on five."
> Ḥanina answered, "Happy are you, who will be set free; woe is me, who will not be delivered. You occupied yourself with the study of the Law, and with deeds of charity, whereas I occupied myself with the study of the Law only."
> Ḥanina said this according to the teaching of R. Huna who declared, "He who occupies himself with the study of the Law only, is as if he has no God."
>
>> b. A.Z. 17b, trans. in Monte-
>> fiore and Loewe, *A Rabbinic
>> Anthology*, pp. 174-75

(See also the sayings of Elisha b. Abuya in ARN A Ch. 24 which express the identical idea.)

    A. WKBR HYW: R. Tarfon and R. Aqiva and R. Yose the Galilean were assembled in the upper chamber of the house of Ares in Lydda.

    B. The following question was asked before them:

    C. Which is greater, learning or deed?

    D. Said R. Tarfon, "Deed is greater."

    E. R. Aqiva says, "Learning is greater."

    F. They all answered, "Learning is greater,

    G. "for learning leads to action."

    H. R. Yose the Galilean says, "Learning is greater,

    I. "for [the giving of the Torah occurred] forty years before the [obligation to separate] dough-offering [was applicable], and fifty-four [years] before tithe, and sixty-one years before the Sabbatical year, and one hundred and three years before Jubilees."

> Sifre Deut. 41, ed. Finkelstein,
> p. 85, lns. 13-17 (Mid. Tan.
> Deut. 11:13, ed. Hoffmann, p. 34)

Comment: This version integrates the story involving Tarfon and Aqiva with a saying of Yose the Galilean. The redactor has simply added Yose's name to A to enable him to append H-I. Yose concurs with the opinion of Aqiva and the elders. The attributive formula in D-E are not matched.

    A.   TNW RBNN: Who is wealthy?

    B.   "Everyone who has pleasure with his wealth," the words of R. Meir.

    C.   [Mneumonic] MṬQS

    D.   R. Tarfon says, "Everyone who possesses a hundred vineyards, and a hundred fields, and a hundred slaves working in them."

    E.   R. Aqiva says, "Everyone who has a wife [who is] pleasant in her deeds."

    F.   R. Yose says, "Everyone who has a toilet near his table."

                          b. Shab. 25b

Comment: The sayings of the Yavneans, Aqiva and Tarfon, break up those of the Ushans, B and F. The association of Tarfon with material goods, particularly slaves and fields, is a motif in several of the traditions about him (b. Ned. 49b, b. Ned. 62a, Lev. R. 34:16).

    A.   TNW RBNN: When the sons of R. Ishmael died, four elders came in to comfort him.

    B.   [They are] R. Tarfon, and R. Yose the Galilean, and R. Eleazar b. Azariah, and R. Aqiva.

    C.   Said to them R. Tarfon, "Know that he is a great sage and an expert in homilies.

    D.   "None of you should interrupt his fellow."

    E.   Said R. Aqiva, "And I am last."

    F.   Began (PTḤ) R. Ishmael saying, "His sins are many, his bereavement came in close succession, he bothered his masters one time and then a second."

    G.   Answered R. Tarfon saying, "[It is written], 'But your brethren the whole House of Israel bewail the burning which the Lord has kindled' [Lev 10:6].

    H.   "And we may learn by means of an argument *a fortiori*.

I. 1. "And if [the whole House of Israel mourned
for] Nadab and Abihu who performed only one commandment,

2. "as it is written, 'And the sons of Aaron
presented the blood unto him' [Lev 9:9],

3. "how much the more so [should they mourn
for] the sons of R. Ishmael."

J. Answered R. Yose the Galilean saying, "[It is
written], 'And all Israel shall lament for him [Abiyah]
and bury him' [1 Kgs 14:13].

K. "And we can learn by means of an argument
a fortiori.

L. 1. "And if [the whole House of Israel mourned
for] Abiyah, the son of Jerobam, who did only one good
thing,

2. "as it is written, 'Because in him there
is found some good things [toward the Lord God of Israel]'
[1 Kgs 14:13],

3. "how much the more so [should they mourn
for] the sons of R. Ishmael."

[A discussion follows between R. Zeira and
R. Papa concerning the one good thing Abiyah
did.]

M. Answered R. Eleazar b. Azariah saying, "[It is
written], 'You [Zedekiah] shall die in peace, and with
the burnings of your fathers, the former kings who were
before you; so shall they make a burning for you' [Jer
34:5].

N. "And we may learn by means of an argument
a fortiori.

O. 1. And if [there was such a treatment for]
Zedikiah, the king of Judah, who fulfilled only one
commandment,

2. "[which is] that he lifted Jeremiah from
the mire [Jer 38:6],

3. "how much the more so [should there be
such a treatment] for the sons of R. Ishmael."

P. Answered R. Aqiva saying, "[It is written], 'In
that day there shall be a great mourning in Jerusalem as
the mourning of Haddrimmon in the valley of Megiddo'"
[Zech 12:11].

Q. And said R. Joseph, *"If it were not for the*
Targum to this verse I would not know [what it means]."

R. [The Targum translates the verse as follows:]
In that time the mourning at Jerusalem will be as great
as the lament over Ahab son of Omri, whom Haddrimmon son
of Tabrimmon killed [1 Kgs 22:34], and as the lament over
Josiah son of Amon whom Pharoh Neho killed in the valley
of Megiddo" [2 Sam 4:4, 9:3; 2 Kgs 23:29-30; 2 Chr 35:20].

S. "And we may learn by means of an argument
a fortiori.

T. 1. "And if [there was such mourning for] Ahab,
the king of Israel, who did only one good thing,

2. "as it is written, 'And the king stayed up
in his chariot against the Armeneans' [1 Kgs 22:35],

3. "how much the more so [should there be such
mourning for] the sons of R. Ishmael."

b. M.Q. 28b

Comment: This is another chria in which Tarfon and the three
elders mentioned in B give discourses after the death of a sage
(see Tos. Git. 9:1). The order of the names in this pericope is
identical to that in Tos. Git. Tarfon speaks first; Aqiva has the
last say. Q-R interrupt Aqiva's argument and supply the information required for T. All four sages proclaim the same rabbinic
message: All of Israel should mourn for Ishmael's sons because
they performed many *misvot*.

A. TN'Y HY' DTNY': Said R. Meir, "Watch me because
of (HZHRW BY) my daughter."

B. Said R. Tarfon, "Watch me because of my daughter-
in-law."

C. A disciple ('WTW TLMYD) scoffed at him.

D. Said R. Abbahu in the name of R. Hanina b.
Gamaliel, "It did not take long before that disciple
was led to sin through his mother-in-law."

b. Qid. 81b

Comment: A+B are two identically formulated sayings. Because
of chronological and logical considerations, B should precede A.
If the order were B-A, then it would appear that Meir, the younger
of the two masters, extends Tarfon's comment. His students should
guard him because of his daughter, not just because of his

daughter-in-law. The message of the two sayings is that great
authorities have strong desires for their close relatives.

   C-D are an addition to A-B. No mention previous to C is made
of "that student." C is a stock phrase which appears two other
times in b. (Shab. 30b, B.B. 75a [Sanh. 100a]). In our pericope,
C-D build upon A-B and teach that one who scoffs at sages falls
victim to his own words. Abbahu clearly relies upon and attests
to A-B. Thus this pericope is similar to b. Ned. 62a which also
contains a story involving Tarfon upon which Abbahu comments.

   A. 1. *R. Ḥanina b. Dosa was sitting, eating*
       2. on the Sabbath eve
       3. [and suddenly] *the table* (PTWR') *broke*
   before him.
   B. *They said to him,* "What is this?"
   C. *He said to him, "I borrowed* [some] spice from
   my neighbor, and I did not tithe it."
   D. 1. He recalled the teachings [regarding food
   that was found on the Sabbath not to have been tithed],
       2. and the table rose by itself.
   E. *R. Tarfon was sitting, eating, and* his bread
   (PYTWT') *fell* from him.
   F. *They said to him* [V: *He said to her*], *"What
   is this?"*
   G. *He said to him* [V: *She said to him*], "I borrowed
   an ax [from my neighbor], and I used it upon food [requir-
   ing] cleanness.

                        y. Demai 1:3 22a

Comment: A-C and E-G are two structurally identical stories
with different details. One (A-C) deals with tithing, the other
(E-G) with cleanness, the usual pair in Demai. In both stories, a
"negative" miracle occurs for a sage when he is about to eat (A and
E). The anonymous "they" ask him what is wrong (B and F). The
sage, recognizing that he was about to sin, states his oversight
(C and G). Thus divine providence keeps the righteous from sin.
The story about Ḥaninah includes an additional action, a miracu-
lous conclusion. Ḥaninah, the miracle worker, takes the necessary
halakhic action (D1), and the situation returns to normal (D2).

A.   Two pregnant women came before R. Tarfon [to
ask him whether or not they may eat on Yom Kippur].

B.   *He sent two of his students to them. He said
to them, "Go and tell them it is the Great Fast* [Yom
Kippur today]."

C.   *They spoke to the first, and she was put at
ease. They* [then] *recited* [the following about her],
"Thou art my God from my mother's womb" [Ps 22:11].

D.   *They spoke to the second, but she was not put
at ease. They recited* [the following about her], "The
wicked are estranged from the womb. The speakers of
lies go astray as soon as they are born" [Ps 58:4].

y. Yoma 8:4 45a

Comment: This pericope is a homiletical story. Its message
is that a mother's religious actions determine her child's nature.
Tarfon is peripheral to the story; the story-teller merely utilizes his name. b. Yoma 82b-83a preserves the following stories
which are very similar to the one involving Tarfon.

A pregnant woman who had smelled [some food] *came to
Rabbi. He said to them* [his students], *"Go and whisper
to her that it is Yom Kippur." They whispered to her*
[that it was Yom Kippur], *and she was put at ease. They
recited about her,* "Before I formed you in the belly,
I knew you" [Jer 1:3]. *R. Yoḥanan came forth from
her* [the woman].

*A pregnant woman who had smelled some food came
before R. Haninah. He said to them, "Whisper to her*
[that it is Yom Kippur]." *But she was not put at ease.
They recited about her,* "The wicked are estranged from
youth" [Ps 58:4]. *From her came forth Shabbetai the
hoarder of provisions* [for speculation, a most detest-
able act]."

The core of these stories are the same as that found in the
incident involving Tarfon. The major difference is in the name of
the authorities before whom the women appear. There thus is only
one story into which the names of different authorities have been
placed. I cannot account for the choice of Tarfon's name.

A.   *R. Judah was sitting before R. Tarfon.*

B.   *Said to him R. Tarfon,* "Today your face is shiny."

C.   *He said to him,* "Yesterday your servants went
out to the fields and they brought us beets, and we ate
them without salt.

D. "And if we had eaten them with salt, how much more would our faces be shiny."

b. Ned. 49b

Comment: This pericope appears among several other items which describe the effects of Judah's eating habits upon his regularity. The pericope which follows the one under discussion indicates that a shiny face testifies to regularity. This explains C-D. This unit of tradition includes the motifs that (1) Judah is Tarfon's student and (2) Tarfon has slaves and fields.

A. TN': [If] the majority of the mats upon which figs are dried have been folded (HWQPLW RWB HMQSW'WT),[2] they [the figs] are permitted [to strangers] as far as theft is concerned [i.e., one may take them and it is not considered stealing], and they are exempt from tithes.

> [A series of statements follow which detail the observance by certain rabbis of this law.]

B. *A man found R. Tarfon*

C. at the time that the mats upon which the figs are dried had been folded,

D. *eating.*

E. *He* [the man] *threw him* [Tarfon] *in a sack, and carried him, and brought him* [to a river] *in order to throw him into the river.*

F. He [Tarfon] said, "Woe to Tarfon, for this [man] is going to kill him."

G. *The* [man] *heard, he released him* [Tarfon], *and fled.*

H. Said R. Abbahu in the name of R. Ḥananiah b. Gamaliel, "All the days of that righteous man['s life] he was grieved about this.

I. "He [Tarfon] said, 'Woe is me, that I used the crown of the Torah [for my profit].'"

> [The *gemara* continues with a discussion about using the crown of the Torah for various purposes. It then returns to the story about Tarfon.]

J. [Now] *since R. Tarfon ate* [when] *most of the mats used for drying figs were folded, why did the man ill-treat him?*

K. *Because this man had grapes stolen from him
all year, and when he found R. Tarfon, he thought that
it was he who had stolen them.*

L. *If so, why was he* [Tarfon] *so grieved* [at
revealing his identity? He had no choice but to identify himself, otherwise, he would have had to pay for
a whole year's crops].

M. [He was grieved] *because R. Tarfon was very
wealthy, and he* [Tarfon] *could have paid him off with
money.*

N. Said Rava, "*A man is permitted to reveal his
identity in a place in which he is unknown, as it is
written,* 'But I [Elijah], thy servant, fear the Lord
from my youth' [1 Kgs 18:12].

O. "*But* [as far as] *the difficulty of R. Tarfon,*
[this does not apply], *because he was very wealthy, and
he should have pacified him with money.*"

b. Ned. 62a

Comment: B, D-G are a story about Tarfon which shows that a
sage saved his life by mentioning his own name. The story points
to the common man's fear of the rabbi; people run away upon hear-
ing his name. In the present narrative Tarfon merely supplies a
name. The editor's choice of Tarfon may be based upon the traditions in which he mentions his own name. C, an interpolation,
links the story to A. Abbahu, a third-generation Palestinian
amora, attests the story. He interprets it as an example of the
misuse by a sage of his reputation. H-I, the comments following
H-I which deal with the misuse of the crown of the Torah, and the
story, B + D-G, are a unit. The redactor adds C and inserted the entire unit into the present context. M and O assert that Tarfon
was wealthy, a common motif in stories about him.

A. 1. R. Tarfon went [during the Sabbatical year]
to eat figs (QSY'WT)

2. from his [from the stores of another person]
without his permission,

3. according to the words of the House of
Shammai. [The House of Shammai rule in M. Shev. 4:2
that one may eat food during the Sabbatical year from
the stores of another person only without the owner's
permission.]

B. *The watchmen and the guards saw him* [Tarfon].
They beat him.

C. *When he* [Tarfon] *saw that he was in danger* [of
dying], *he said to them, "Swear that you will tell the*
[members] *of the house of Tarfon to prepare his funeral
garments."*

D. *When they heard this, they fell on their faces.
They said to him, "Rabbi, forgive us."*

E. *He said to them, "Let them* [the strokes] *come
upon me, for as soon as one stroke comes upon me, I
have already forgiven you for the previous one."*

F. *In regard to these two things R. Tarfon acted
according to* [the opinion of] *the House of Shammai,
and he endangered himself;* [that is in] *this* [incident],
and with [regard to] *the recitation of the Shema'*
[M. Ber. 1:3].

G. R. Abbahu [said] in the name of R. Ḥananiah
b. Gamaliel, "All the days of R. Tarfon's life, he
[Tarfon] was grieved (MT'NH) about this one thing and
he said, 'Woe is me, that I have honored myself with
the crown of the Torah.'"

y. Shev. 4:2 36b

Comment: The following chart shows that the same story underlies y. Shev. and b. Ned. y.'s version is slightly more elaborate
and connects Tarfon's action with a Shammaite ruling.

b. Ned. 62a	y. Shev. 4:2
1. *A man found R. Tarfon,*	1. R. Tarfon went
2. at the time that the mats upon which the figs are dried had been folded,	2. - - -
3. *eating.*	3. to eat
4. - - -	4. figs
5. - - -	5. from his, without the owner's permission, according to the words of the House of Shammai.
6. *He* [the man] *threw him* [Tarfon] *in a sack, and carried him, and brought him in order to throw him into the river.*	6. *The watchmen and the guards saw him. They beat him.*

b. Ned. 62a	y. Shev. 4:2
7. He [Tarfon] said, Woe to Tarfon, for this [man] is killing him.	7. *When he* [Tarfon] *saw that he was in danger* [of dying], *he said to them, Swear that you will tell the* [members] *of the house of Tarfon to prepare his funeral garments.*
8. *The man heard, he released him* [Tarfon] *and fled.*	8. *When they heard this, they fell on their faces.*
9. - - -	9. *They said, Rabbi, forgive us.*
10. - - -	10. *He said to them, Let them* [the strokes]...
11. - - -	11. *In regard to these two things R. Tarfon acted according to* [the opinion of] *the House of Shammai...*
12. R. Abbahu said in the name of R. Ḥananiah b. Gamaliel,	12. R. Abbahu [said] in the name " " "
13. All the days of that righteous man['s life] he was grieved about this.	13. All the days of Tarfon's life he was grieved about this one thing,
14. He [the righteous man] said, Woe is me, that I used the crown of the Torah.	14. and he said, Woe is me, that I have honored myself with the crown of the Torah.

1-3 set the story. 2 of b. is an interpolation. 4-5 of y. correspond to 2 of b. 2, 4-5 link the versions of this story to their respective contexts. 6-10 of y. are more elaborate than b. 6 of b. speaks of a man. In y. we have watchmen and guards. Tarfon's monologue in 7 of b. is a dialogue in 7-10 of y. 11 develops the claim of 2. It points out that two times Tarfon endangered himself by acting according to the ruling of the House of Shammai. 14 of y. explicitly mentions Tarfon's name.

We may now summarize our remarks about the history of this tradition. The simplest story (1+3, 7-10 of b.) shows that by mentioning his name a sage saved his life. Abbahu redirects the story to teach that it is wrong for a sage to take advantage of his reputation. His comments and the story form a unit. The redactor of b. expanded this unit by inserting C, in order to serve as an illustration for the law of b. Ned. In Palestine the tradition had a different history. A redactor added details to the story and also connected Tarfon's actions with a ruling of the House of Shammai. He built upon M. Ber. 1:3, which alleges that

Tarfon once acted according to the words of the House of Shammai and endangered himself. Both items thus show that it is deadly to adhere to the Shammaite position.

     A.   1. *R. Tarfon had a* [Asher, Alfasi: *an old*] *mother.*

           2. *Whenever she wanted to climb into bed,*

           3. *he* [Tarfon] *bent down and she* [M: *stood upon him and*] *ascended.*

           4. [Vilna, V 111:] *and whenever she descended, she stepped down upon him.*

     B. *She came and praised him at the Bet Midrash.*

     C. *They said to him,* "You have not fulfilled even half of the honor [demanded by the Torah].

     D. "Has it yet [happened that she has] thrown a [M, V 111: your] purse before you into the sea, without you rebuking her?"

b. Qid. 31b

Comment: A can stand alone. C, which is joined to A by means of B, uses A to illustrate the magnitude of the honor to one's parents the Torah demands. D glosses A-C. We shall presently see that this item is one of several similar stories.

     A.   1. R. Tarfon's mother went down to walk in her yard on the Sabbath.

           2. [y. Qid: and her sandal broke] [Pes. Rab.: What did R. Tarfon do?]

           3. And R. Tarfon went and put his two hands under her feet,

           4. and she continued to walk upon them,

           5. until she reached her bed.

     B.   1. One time he [Pes. Rab.: R. Tarfon] became ill [V omits],

           2. and the sages came to visit him.

     C.   1. She said to them, "Pray for my son, R. Tarfon,

           2. "because he gives me too much honor."

     D. They asked her, *"What does he do for you*?"

     E. *She repeated to them the incident* [noted in A].

     F. They said to her, "Even if he did this thousands and thousands [of times], he has not reached even half of the honor that the Torah demands."

G.   R. Ishmael's mother came and complained about him to the rabbis.

H.   She said to them, "Rebuke my son Ishmael, [for] he does not act with honor toward me."

I.   At that instance the rabbis' faces grew pale.

J.   They said, "Is it possible that R. Ishmael did not act with honor toward his parents?"

K.   They said to her, *What does he do for you?*"

L.   She said, "*When he leaves the Bet HaVa'ad, I want to wash his feet and* [then] *drink from it* [the water], *and he does not allow me.*"

M.   They said to him, "Since this is her desire, this is the way to honor her."

N.   Said Mana, "The millers speak correctly [when they say that] *everyman's merit is within his own fist,* [i.e., one gets what he wants].

O.   "[For] R. Tarfon's mother spoke to them thusly, and they answered her accordingly. Ishmael's mother spoke to them thusly, and they answered her accordingly."

P.   *R. Zeira was* [always] *sad and said,* "*Would that I have a father and a mother* so that I could honor them [in order that I could receive] beams from the candle in the Garden of Eden."

Q.   *When he heard these two incidents, he said,* "*Blessed is God that I do not have either a father or a mother*; neither like R. Tarfon's [mother whom] I would have been unable to serve, nor like Ishmael's [mother whom] I would have had to endure."

> y. Peah 1:1 15c (y. Qid. 1:7
> 61b, Pes. Rab. 23-24)

Comment: In our discussion we first compare b. Qid. 31b to A-F of y., and then discuss y. as a whole. The following synoptic table demonstrates that y. and b. are two independent stories on the same theme.

b. Qid. 31b	y. Peah 1:1 15c
1. *R. Tarfon had a mother*	1. R. Tarfon's mother
2. - - -	2. went down
3. - - -	3. to walk in the yard on the Sabbath,
4. - - -	4. and her sandal broke.

b. Qid. 31b	y. Peah 1:1 15c
5. - - -	5. and R. Tarfon went and put his hands under her feet,
6. - - -	6. and she used to walk upon them
7. *that whenever she wanted to climb into bed, he bent down and she ascended,*	7. until she reached her bed.
8. *and whenever she descended, she stepped down upon him.*	8. - - -
9. *She came*	9. One time he [R. Tarfon] became ill, and the sages came to visit him.
10. *and praised him at the* Bet Midrash.	10. She said to them, Pray for my son, R. Tarfon, because he gives me too much honor.
11. - - -	11. They said to her, *What does he do for you?*
12. - - -	12. *She repeated to them the incident.*
13. *They said to him,* - - -	13. They said to her, Even if he did this thousands and thousands of times,
You have not fulfilled even half of the honor [demanded in the Torah].	" " "
	" " "

The two versions of the story share the apothegm, 13, and the motifs of (1) Tarfon bending down for his mother, (2) the bed, and
(3) a meeting between Tarfon's mother and the sages. They have
filled in in different ways the remainder of the stories. Neither
version is dependent upon the other.

G-M contrast with the story about Tarfon. Ishmael does not
allow his mother to humiliate herself before him. The rabbis,
therefore, rebuke Ishmael for not honoring his mother. The dominant motifs of this story are the same as those which appear in
A-F. L, like A3, centers upon feet. Thus A-F and G-M are two
similarly formulated stories which deal with the issue of honoring
parents.

> A. *Rabbi happened to come to the town of R. Tarfon.*
> B. 1. Said he to them, "Does that righteous man,
> 2. who used to [swear that he would] bury his
> children,
> 3. have a son?"
> C. They said to him, "He has [left] no son, but he
> has [left] a [grand]son from a daughter.

D.   "And every harlot who is hired for two [*zuz*]
hires him for eight."

E.   *They brought him* [the son] *before him* [Rabbi].

F.   *He* [Rabbi] *said to him, "Should you repent, I
will give you my daughter."*

G.   *He repented.*

H.   *Some say he married her* [Rabbi's daughter],
and divorced her.

I.   *Others* [say] *that he did not marry her at all,*

J.   so that they [people] will not say he repented
for this reason.

K.   *And why did he* [Rabbi do] *all this for him*?

L.   1.   Because said R. Judah, said Rav;

     2.   others say, Said R. Ḥiyya b. Abba said
R. Yoḥanan;

     3.   others say, Said R. Samuel b. Naḥmani
said R. Yoḥanan,

M.   "Whoever teaches Torah to his neighbor's son is
privileged and will sit in the Heavenly Academy,

N.   "for it [Scripture] says, 'If you will [cause
Israel to] repent, then I will return you, and you shall
stand before me' [Jer 15:19].

O.   1.   "And whoever teaches Torah to the son of an
'*am-ha'areṣ*,

     2.   "even [if] the Holy One, Blessed be He,
makes a decree, He annuls it for his sake,

P.   "for it says, 'And if you shall take forth the
precious from the vile, you shall be as My mouth'" [Jer
15:19].

b. B.M. 85a

Comment: A-G are the core of the story. It demonstrates the
concern of sages for the wayward children of their colleagues, and
the effect of that concern. A sage can bring about the repentance
of even the most lowly character.

H-I gloss A-G. K-O are amoraic comments which derive an
additional rabbinic message from the story. One who teaches Torah
receives the reward of a seat in the Heavenly Academy. Moreover,
if one teaches Torah to an '*am-ha'areṣ*, he causes God to change
His will.

b. B.M. 85a contains a story about Rabbi and the son of
Eleazar b. Simeon which is structurally similar to A-G. It reads:

A. *Rabbi happened to come to the town of R. Eleazar b. R. Simeon.*

B. He said to them, "Does that righteous man have a son?"

C. They said to him, "He has a son,

D. "and every harlot who is hired for two [*zuz*] hires him for eight."

E. 1. They brought him [to Rabbi].

2. He [Rabbi] ordained him a rabbi,

3. and he entrusted him to R. Simeon b. Issi b. Lakonia, his mother's brother [to teach him].

F. *Every day he* [Eleazar's son] *would say, "I am going* [back] *to my town."*

G. He [Simeon] said to him, "*They made you a sage, and they spread a gold cloak over you, and they called you rabbi, and you say, I am going* [back] *to my town?"*

H. He said to him, "My weakness [my desire for women] has gone."

A. *The sons of R. Tarfon's sister were sitting before R. Tarfon.*

B. He began to expound, saying (PTH), "And Abraham took another wife, and her name was Yoḥani" [Gen 25:1]. [This is an incorrect citation of the verse.]

C. *They said to him*, "Qeturah is written."

D. He [Tarfon] dubbed them (QRY 'LYHM) the children of Qeturah [i.e., ignoramuses].

b. Zev. 62b

Comment: This pericope follows a story in which R. Joseph dubs people who ridicule him "the children of Qeturah," i.e., ignoramuses who are descendants of Abraham's non-Jewish concubine. Similarly in our pericope, Tarfon's nephews do not know how to correct properly a rabbi's error; therefore, Tarfon calls them the children of Qeturah. This is the only mention in the Tarfon-corpus of his sister and her children.

A. Abba Saul was the tallest man in his generation, and R. Tarfon reached to his shoulders.

B. R. Tarfon was the tallest man in his generation, and R. Meir reached to his shoulders.

C. R. Meir was the tallest man in his generation, and Rabbi reached to his shoulders.

D. Rabbi was the tallest man in his generation, and R. Ḥiyya reached to his shoulders.

E. R. Ḥiyya was the tallest man in his generation, and Rav reached to his shoulders.

F.   Rav was the tallest man in his generation, and R. Judah reached to his shoulders.

G.   R. Judah was the tallest man in his generation, and his waiter Adda reached to his shoulders.

H.   1.   *Pushtabna of Pumbeditha reached to half of the height of the waiter Adda,*

2.   *and everybody else reached only to the loins of Pushtabna of Pumbeditha.*

b. Nid. 24b (Num. R. 9:24)

Comment: A-G are a unit. H, although formally different from A-G, continues their message. The assertion that there is a continual decline in the height of people is a metaphor for the continual decline in the knowledge of people. I cannot account for the choice of the names.

A.   Said Rabbah, [As to] *slander, though one should not believe it,* [yet] *one should take it into account.*

B.   *There were certain Galileans about whom a rumor was spread that they killed a person.*

C.   *They came to R. Tarfon and said to him, "Will the master hide us?"*

D.   He said to them, "How shall I act?

E.   1.   *"If I do not hide you, they* [the avengers of the blood] *will see you.*

2.   *"If I do hide you, Lo, it is said by the rabbis,*

3.   "'[As to] slander, though one should not believe it, one should take it into account.'

F.   *"Go and hide yourselves."*

b. Nid. 61a

Comment: The story, B-F, illustrates the proper fulfillment of the rabbis' advice, E3 = A. Tarfon does not believe the slander, for he does not hide the suspected murderers. He neither ignores the slander, for he does answer their question. Tarfon notes the rumor and, accordingly, advises the suspected convicts. I again cannot account for the use of Tarfon's name.

A.   A man is duty bound to attend upon four scholars.

B.   Such as, R. Eliezer, and R. Joshua, and R. Aqiva, and R. Tarfon.

C. For it is written, "Happy is the man who listens to me, watching daily at my gates (DLTWTY), waiting at my doors" [Prov 8:34].

D. Read not "my gates" (*daltotai*) but "my four gates" (*dalet daltotai*).

ARN A Ch. 3, trans. Goldin,
pp. 28-29

Comment: This is another tradition in which Tarfon supplies a name. A gives the "rabbinic" maxim. C-D provide the exegetical basis for A. Gate, *delet*, can be read as four, *dalet*.

A. Concerning them [those who study with a teacher], Scripture says, "Happy is the man who listens to me, watching daily at my gates, waiting at my doors" [Prov 8:34].

B. What four?

C. R. Eliezer, and R. Joshua, and R. Tarfon.

D. Said R. Aqiva, If you...

ARN B Ch. 18, ed. Schechter,
p. 39

Comment: The version in ARN B appears after the comment of Netai the Arbelite that one must provide himself with a teacher. Accordingly, ARN B lacks the maxim, A of ARN A. C of ARN B contains only three names. Saldarini (p. 121 n. 12) suggests that, because of an haplography with D, Aqiva's name does not appear in C.

A. R. Tarfon says, "Even the Holy One, Blessed be He, did not cause his *Shekhinah* to rest upon Israel before they did work.

B. "For it is written, 'And let them make me a sanctuary, and [then] I shall dwell among them'" [Exod 25:8].

ARN A Ch. 11, trans. Goldin,
pp. 60-61

Comment: Tarfon's saying appears in a comment upon Shemaiah's statement that one should love work. A-B extol the virtues of work by pointing out that God caused his *Shekhinah* to rest upon Israel only after they built Him a sanctuary. In ARN B Ch. 21, Tarfon's saying is attributed to Yose. It reads:

A. R. Yose says, "Work is great, for

B. "the *Shekhinah* did not rest upon Israel until they did work.

C. "For it is written, 'And let them make me a sanctuary, and [then] I shall dwell among them'" [Exod 25:8].

> ARN B Ch. 21, ed. Schechter,
> p. 44

Mekh. Sim. 20:9 assigns the remark to Eleazar b. Azariah.

A. M'SH B: R. Tarfon was sitting and teaching his students,

B. and a bride passed before him.

C. He ordered that she be brought into the house.

D. And he said to his mother and to his wife,

E. "(1) Wash her, (2) anoint her, (3) have her outfitted, (4) dance before her until she goes onto her husband's house."

> ARN A Ch. 41, trans. Goldin,
> p. 173

Comment: The story appears in the context of statements of the form, "Five things were said with regard to x." Goldin (p. 220) cites Ginzberg's suggestion that our story should be preceded by the statement:

> Five things were said with regard to a bride: (1) she is to be bathed, (2) anointed, (3) outfitted, (4) danced with, (5) and have her praises sung.

Tarfon's saying would then provide an illustration for this law.

A. "And they that shall be from you shall build the old waste places" [Isa 58:12].

B. *R. Tarfon gave R. Aqiva six centenaria of silver.*

C. *He [Tarfon] said to him, "Buy for us an estate, and we shall be supported from it, and the two of us shall labor in [the study of the] Torah."*

D. *He [Aqiva] took them [the coins] and distributed them among scribes, and those who repeat Mishnah, and those who study Torah.*

E. *After some time R. Tarfon met him [Aqiva].*

F. *He [Tarfon] said to him, "Did you buy that estate [about] which I told you?"*

G. *He said to him, "Yes."*

H. *He said to him, "And is all well?"*

I. *He said to him, "Yes."*

J. *He said to him, "And will you not show it to me?"*

K. *He* [Aqiva] *took him and showed him the scribes,*
and those who repeat Mishnah, and those who study Torah,
and the Torah which they treasure.

L. *He said to him, "Is there a man who labors*
for nothing?

M. *"And where is the writ?"*

N. *He said to him, "It is with David, the king;*

O. *"as it is written,* 'He [the one who fears God]
has scattered abroad, he has given to the needy, his
righteousness (SDQTW) endures forever'" [Ps 112:19].

Lev. R. 34:16, ed. Margoliot,
pp. 812-13, lns. 3-5, 1-5

Comment: The point of the "rabbinical" story B-O is that the
soundest possible "investment" is to give money for Torah study.
David, the author of Psalms, is the one who has informed us of
this; he is the guarantor of the writ (M-N). If one donates money
for the study of Torah, his righteousness endures forever. Margoliot explains that by joining B-O to A the redactor teaches that
those who study Torah are the ones who build and uphold the world.

This unit of tradition is built upon several elements found
in other stories about Tarfon. Tarfon is wealthy (b. Ned. 62a),
and he thinks of wealth in terms of estates (b. Shab. 25b). Aqiva
is wiser than Tarfon; accordingly, Aqiva invests Tarfon's money in
a manner the latter did not consider.

A. M'SH B: R. Tarfon gave R. Aqiva one hundred and
eighty *centenaria* of gold.

B. He said to him, "Buy us an estate."

C. R. Aqiva went and performed many deeds (MSWT)
with it [the money].

D. After some time, he came to R. Tarfon.

E. He [Tarfon] said to him, "What have you accom-
plished [with the money]?

F. "Is the estate which you bought nice?"

G. He said to him, "Yes, and there is nothing as
excellent as it in the world."

H. [He said to him], "And where is the writ?"

I. He said to him, "Lo, it is in the hand of David;

J. "[for it is written], 'He has scattered abroad,
he has given to the needy, his righteousness [charity]
endures forever, his horn shall be exalted in honor'"
[Ps 112:19].

K. 1. "His horn shall be exalted" in this world,

    2. "and his righteousness endures forever" in
the world to come.

Pes. Rab. 25:2

Comment: The redactor of Pesikta uses the story involving
Aqiva and Tarfon, A-J, to teach an additional lesson, K. Investing money in charitable deeds guarantees a person life in the
world to come.

This version of the story is clearly dependent on another
version of the item, for Aqiva's answer in I to Tarfon's question
would be unintelligible to Tarfon. This version lacks the line
that Aqiva took to Tarfon and showed him how he spent the money.
We shall compare below all versions of the story.

A. One time *R. Tarfon gave R. Aqiva six hundred*
centenaria *of silver.*

B. *He said to him, "Go and buy that estate so we
can toil with the Torah and be supported from it."*

C. *R. Aqiva went* [and] *gave a third to the poor,
and two-thirds he distributed to those who repeat Mishnah,
and to those who deal with the Torah, and to scribes.*

D. *When he* [Tarfon] *found him he said to him,
"Where is the estate?"*

E. *He said to him, "I have bought it with it*
[the money]."

F. *He said to him, "And is all well with it?"*

G. *He said to him, "It is well, infinitely good."*

H. *He brought him to the* Bet Midrash.

I. *He said to him, "Where is it* [the writ]?"

J. *He said, "It is with David, the king of Israel;*

K. *"as it is written,* 'He has scattered abroad,
he has given to the poor'" [Ps 112:19].

L. *He said to him, "Why did you do this?"*

M. 1. *He said to him, "And did you know that*

    2. "when Naqdimon b. Gorion used to go from
his house to the *Bet Midrash*, fine woolen clothes were
spread beneath him and the poor of Israel used to take
them,

    3. *"and even so, since he did not act as was
required of him, he was punished."*

N. *He* [Tarfon] *said to him, "This is what I said to
you, Why did you not act as I desired?"*

O. *He said to him, "Did I not act on your behalf?"*

P. *He said to him,* "For I say that the one who
causes (M'SH) someone to act is greater than the one
who acts;

Q. "for it is written, 'And the effect [*ma'aseh*
to be read *me'aseh*--the one who causes charity to be
given] of the righteous is peace'" [Isa 32:17].

> Kallah Rab. 2:13, ed. Higger,
> pp. 208-09, lns. 2-17 (M = b.
> Ket. 66b-67a; P-Q = b. B.B. 9a)

Comment: Kallah Rabbati builds upon the story involving
Tarfon and Aqiva, A-K, and teaches that one who causes someone to
give charity, reading *ma'aseh* as *me'aseh*, is greater than the one
who gives charity. P-Q, this secondary maxim, appear in b. B.B.
9a in the name of R. Eliezer.

A. They said concerning R. Tarfon that he was very
wealthy, and that he did not give [K.R. adds: many] gifts
to the poor.

B. One time R. Aqiva met him.

C. He [Aqiva] said to him, "Master, is it your
desire that I purchase for you one or two cities?"

D. He said to him, "Yes."

E. Immediately, Tarfon stood up and gave him four
thousand *denar*s of gold.

F. R. Aqiva took them [the coins] and distributed
them to the poor.

G. After some time R. Tarfon met him.

H. He said to him, "Aqiva, where are the cities
which you purchased for me?"

I. He [Aqiva] took him by the hand and brought him
to the *Bet Midrash*,

J. and he brought a book of Psalms, and placed it
before them, and they read it until they reached the
following verse:

K. "He has scattered abroad, he has given to the
poor, his righteousness endures forever, his horn shall
be exalted in honor" [Ps 112:19].

L. R. Tarfon stood up and kissed him [Aqiva] on
the head.

M. He said to him, "Master, my Prince, my master
in wisdom and my prince in comportment (DRK 'RṢ)."

> Kallah 21, ed. Higger, pp.
> 157-59, lns. 50-60 (A-K =
> Kallah Rab. 2:13, ed.
> Higger, p. 207, lns. 94-100)

A. *And did not R. Tarfon* [fulfill the commandment
of] "Open your [hand to the poor"] [Deut 15:11]?
B. *Rather, he did give.*
C. *Buy why did R. Aqiva pressure him?*
D. *He said to him, "Go like a camel according to
its burden* [i.e., you should give commensurate with
your ability]."

> Kallah Rab. 2:13, ed. Higger,
> pp. 207-08, lns. 1-2

Comment: A, L-M utilize the story involving Tarfon and Aqiva,
B-K, to formulate a pro-Aqivan, anti-Tarfon tradition. In this
version of the story, Tarfon is totally passive. Aqiva proposes
to Tarfon that he should invest his money. Kal. Rab. A-D, the
gemara upon Kallah 21, tones down the claim of Kallah A by assert-
ing that Tarfon gave money to the poor but not according to his
ability. This version of the story deals with charity in general
and not with charity for Torah-study.

Let us now compare the four versions of the story.

Lev. Rab. 34:16	Kal. Rab. 2:13	Pes. Rab. 25:2	Kallah 21
1. - - -	1. - - -	1. - - -	1. They said concerning R. Tarfon that he was very wealthy and that he did not give gifts to the poor.
2. *R. Tarfon gave R. Aqiva six centenaria of silver.*	2. *One time " six hundred " "*	2. M SH B: R. Tarfon gave R. Aqiva one hundred and eighty *centenaria* of silver.	2. One time R. Aqiva met him.
3. *He said to him, Buy us an estate and we shall be supported from it, and the two of us shall labor in [the study of] Torah.*	3. *" " " Go buy that estate so we can toil with the Torah and be supported from it.*	3. " " " Buy us an estate.	3. " " " Is it your desire that I purchase for you one or two cities?
4. - - -	4. - - -	4. - - -	4. He said to him, Yes.
5. - - -	5. - - -	5. - - -	5. Immediately R. Tarfon stood up and gave him four thousand *denars* of silver. [See #2 of other versions.]
6. *He [Aqiva] took them [the coins] and distributed them among scribes, and those who repeat Mishnah, and those who study Torah.*	6. *R. Aqiva went [and gave one third to the poor and two-thirds he distributed " " " "*	6. R. Aqiva went and performed many deeds (MSWT) with it [the money].	6. R. Aqiva took them [the coins] and distributed them to the poor.
7. *After some time R. Tarfon met him.*	7. *When he [Tarfon] found him*	7. After some time he [Aqiva] came to R. Tarfon.	7. After some time R. Tarfon met him.
8. *He said to him, Did you buy that field [about] which I told you?*	8. " " " *Where is the estate?*	8. " " " What have you accomplished? Is the estate which you bought nice?	8. " " " Aqiva, where are the cities you purchased for me?

Lev. Rab. 34:16	Kal. Rab. 2:13	Pes. Rab. 25:2	Kallah 21
9. He said to him, Yes.	9. " " " I have bought it with it.	9. " " " Yes.	9. – – –
10. He said to him, And is all well?	10. " " " " with it?	10. – – –	10. – – –
11. He said to him, Yes.	11. " " It is well, infinitely good.	11. and there is nothing as excellent as it in the world.	11. – – –
12. He said to him, And will you not show it to me.	12. – – –	12. – – –	12. – – –
13. He took him and showed him the scribes, and those who repeat Mishnah, and those who study Torah, and the Torah which they treasure.	13. He brought him to the Bet Midrash.	13. – – –	13. He took him to the Bet Midrash, and brought him a book of Psalms, and placed it before them, and they read it until they reached the verse:
14. He said to him, Is there a man who labors for nothing?	14. – – –	14. – – –	14. – – –
15. And where is the writ?	15. He said to him, Where is it [the writ]?	15. " " " And where is the writ?	15. – – –
16. He said to him, It is with David, King of Israel.	16. " " "	16. " " " Lo, it is on the hand of David.	16. – – –
17. As it is written, "He has scattered abroad..."	17. " " "	17. for it is written, " " "	17. "He has..."
18. – – –	18. [Continues with the dialogue between Tarfon and Aqiva which culminates in the lesson that one who causes someone to give charity is more meritorious than one who gives charity.]	18. "He has scattered abroad"--in this world. "And his charity endures forever"--in the world to come.	18. [Tarfon then kisses Aqiva and praises him. Kal. Rab. 2:13 comments on the above by toning down the claim in #1.]

The version in Kal. Rab. 2:13 is very close to that of Lev. Rab.
The only major difference between the two is in 6, in which Kal.
Rab. adds, "the poor." Pes. Rab. gives a more condensed version,
omitting 12-14. But we have noted that this omission renders unintelligible, to Tarfon, Aqiva's answer in 16. This indicates that
Pes. Rab. is dependent on an earlier version of the story. 6 of
Pes. does not mention those who study Torah but only deeds, *miṣvot*.
Kallah 21 is the most embellished version of the story as it contains very large figures, e.g., one or two cities, four thousand
denars of gold. 6 of Kallah mentions only the poor. Thus the
later versions of the story generalize its message by indicating
that charity for the poor, and not just charity for Torah-study,
is the best investment.

A.   Another comment on "*Shiggayon* of David which he
sang unto the Lord concerning the matter of Cush the
Benjamite" [Ps 7:1].
B.   R. Tarfon said, "David praised the Holy One,
Blessed be He [with] many praises.
C.   1.   "Said David, 'Master of the universe, [Just
as] Israel whom you took out of Egypt and brought up
from the Red Sea sing unto You.
2.   "'So too I, even though Saul pursues me;
my song of praise shall not cease.'"

Mid. Ps. 7:13

Comment: This is one of several comments upon the rare biblical word *shiggayon*. The word appears only here in Psalms and in
the plural in Hab 3:1. All of the comments in Mid. Ps. are
phrased differently and are attributed to both tannaim and amoraim.
Tarfon's saying is probably based upon reading *shiggayon* as
siggayon. SGY' means "many." Tarfon's exegesis indicates that
Israel should praise God even when they are persecuted (C2).

A.   "Happy are they that keep justice, that do
righteousness at all times" [Ps 106:3].
B.   R. Tarfon's students asked him,
C.   "Who is it that does righteousness at all times?"
D.   He said to them, "It is he that transcribes
books and lends them to others."
E.   They said to him, "And are the instructors of
the young ever idle?

F. "And is he that raises an orphan in his house
ever idle?"

G. They said, "[But is it not true] *that he* [the
orphan] *goes naked*?"

H. They said, "We need the Modiite."

I. For said R. Eleazar of Modin, "Even though [the
orphan at times] stands naked, nevertheless, it is the
portion of bread which he eats [which] is [the act that
entitles his provider to be called] the one who does
righteousness at all times."

Mid. Ps. 106:3

Comment: Buber notes that the text of this tradition is cor-
rupt, for in G the students reject the proposal of F, but then in
H call for the Modiite, who in turn validates F. G should therefore probably read, "he said to them." The parallel version of
this tradition in Esther Rab. supports this emendation. The dialogue between Tarfon and his students now has the following order.
Tarfon in E answers the students' question, D. The students in F
and G counter Tarfon's answer by suggesting two further candidates
for the title of him that does righteousness at all times. Tarfon
in G rejects their proposal of F. The students then call for
Eleazar's saying which supports their answer of F. F-H thus set
up Eleazar's teaching. It probably has been added on to A-E.
This is the second unit of tradition in which Eleazar is pictured
as wiser than Tarfon. The other is Mekh. Ish. Vayassa 4.

b. Ket. 50a preserves a tradition parallel to our pericope.
It reads:

A. "Happy are they that keep justice, that do
righteousness at all times" [Ps 106:3].
B. And is it possible to do righteousness at
all times?
C. Our rabbis expounded at Yavneh.
D. And there are those who say R. Eliezer [V 130,
V 113, V 487, Leningrad, *Haggadot Ḥazal*: said]
E. "This is the one who feeds his sons and
daughters when they are young."
F. Samuel b. Naḥmani said, "This is the one who
raises in his house male and female orphans and arranges
for their marriages.

b. Ket. 50a, like Mid. Ps. 106:3, places at Yavneh the discussion of the verse. E offers a response to the question, different from those given in Mid. Ps. F is thematically but not
formally identical to the students' answer, Mid. Ps. F, and to the
saying of Eleazar the Modiite.

A. "Happy are they that keep justice, that do righteousness at all times" [Ps 106:3].

B. They were polled in the upper chamber [of the house of] R. Tarfon, and they said,

C. "Who is it that does righteousness at all times?"

D. 1. If you say, these are the scribes and those who repeat Mishnah,

2. do they not eat and drink and sleep?

E. 1. Rather, these are the ones who write phylacteries and *mezuzot*.

2. Do they not eat and drink and sleep?

F. Rather, who is it that does righteousness at all times?

G. I say, it is he who raises orphans in his house.

H. Will you say that he [the orphan] does not lie naked at night?

I. They said to him, "We still need the Modiite."

J. Eleazar the Modiite came and taught:

K. The Torah applied these words [to the one who feeds orphans] only because of the bread which he [the orphan] eats in his [the donor's] house.

Esther R. 6:1

Comment: This version does not have in the dialogue all the attributive formulae. As in Mid. Ps., Tarfon in H rejects the students' proposal about the one who feeds orphans. The students then call for Eleazar whose teaching is appended. Esther R. places the discussion between Tarfon and his disciples in the upper chamber of Tarfon's house; it is the only item that speaks of Tarfon's house.

A. "And the Lord had prepared (WYMN) a great fish to swallow up Jonah" [Jonah 1:17].

B. R. Tarfon says, "That fish was set aside from the six days of creation to swallow up Jonah;

C. "for it is said, 'And the Lord had prepared a great fish to swallow up Jonah.'"

Pirqé de R. Eliezer, Ch. 10,
trans. Friedlander, p. 69

A. R. Yoḥanan said, "The Holy One, Blessed be He, made a stipulation with the sea that it should divide before Israel."

B.   R. Jeremiah b. Eleazar said, "Not with the sea
alone did God make a stipulation, but with everything
that was created in the six days of creation....[A list
follows which details what God commanded].
C.   "I commanded the fish to vomit forth Jonah."

Gen. R. 5:5

Comment: This saying indicates that miracles are ordained at
the time of creation. The exegesis is based upon the past tense
of the verb, "to prepare." C of Gen. R. is thematically related
to Tarfon's comment. It, however, speaks of vomiting forth, and
not of swallowing Jonah. Hyman (II, p. 814) dates Jeremiah as a
fourth-generation Palestinian amora, and notes that all of his
materials are aggadic.

A.   R. Joshua b. Qorḥah [rehearsed] before R. Tarfon.
B.   1.   "Whatever Pharaoh gave, he gave to Sarah.
     2.   "Whatever Abimelekh gave, he gave to Abraham,
C.   "as it is said, 'And Abimelekh took sheep and
oxen [and gave them to Abraham]'" [Gen 20:14].

Pirqé de R. Eliezer, Ch. 26,
trans. Friedlander, p. 192

Comment: This is the only item in which Joshua b. Qorḥah is
depicted as a disciple of Tarfon.

A.   R. Tarfon said, "The Holy One, Blessed be He, rose
and came from Mount Sinai and was revealed unto the sons of
Esau, as it is said, 'And he [Moses] said, "The Lord came
from Sinai, and rose from Seir unto them"' [Deut 33:2].
B.   "And 'Seir' means only the sons of Esau, as it
is said, 'And Esau dwelt in Mount Seir' [Gen 36:8].
C.   "The Holy One, Blessed be He, said to them,
'Will you accept for yourselves the Torah?'
D.   "They said to Him, 'What is written therein?'
E.   "He said to them, 'It is written therein, "Thou
shalt not murder"' [Exod 20:18].
F.   "They said to Him, 'We are unable to abandon
the blessing with which Isaac blessed Esau, for he said
to him, "By thy sword shalt thou live"' [Gen 27:40].
G.   "Then He turned and was revealed unto the chil-
dren of Ishmael, as it is said, 'He shined forth from
Mount Paran' [Deut 33:2].

H. "'Paran' means only the sons of Ishmael, as it is said, 'And he [Ishmael] dwelt in the wilderness of Paran' [Gen 21:21].

I. "The Holy One, Blessed be He, said to them, 'Will you accept for yourselves the Torah?'

J. "They said to Him, 'What is written therein?'

K. "He said to them, 'Thou shalt not steal' [Exod 20:15].

L. "They said to Him, 'We are not able to abandon the usage which our fathers observed, for they brought Joseph down into Egypt, as it is said, "For indeed I was stolen away out of the land of the Hebrews"' [Gen 40:15].

M. 1. "Then He sent messengers to all the nations of the world.

2. "He said to them, 'Will you receive for yourselves the Torah?'

N. "They said to Him, 'What is written therein?'

O. "He said to them, 'Thou shalt have no other gods before me' [Exod 20:3].

P. "They said to Him, 'We have no delight in the Torah; therefore, let Him give His Torah to His people, as it is said,   Lord will give strength unto His people; the Lord will bless His people with peace"' [Ps 29:11].

Q. "Then He returned and was revealed unto the children of Israel, as it is said, 'And he came from the ten thousands of holy ones [at His right hand was a fiery law unto them]' [Deut 33:2].

R. "The expression 'ten thousands' means the children of Israel, as it is said, 'And when it rested, he said, "Return, O Lord, unto the ten thousands of the thousands of Israel"'" [Num 10:36].

> Pirqé de R. Eliezer, Ch. 41,
> trans. Friedlander, pp. 318-20

Comment: Only PRE assigns this frequently cited item to Tarfon. In b. A.Z. 2b it is attributed to R. Yoḥanan, while Pes. Rab. 21 gives it in the name of Joshua b. Ḥananiah. All other versions (see Finkelstein, Sifre Deut., p. 395) are anonymous.

A.   Said R. Simeon b. Laqish, "Do not say, if R.
Zeira were alive, I would learn Torah in his presence;
if R. Tarfon were alive, I would learn Torah in his
presence.

B.   "You have only the sage of your generation."

Midrash Samuel 15:2,
ed. Buber, p. 92

A.   R. Abba b. Kahana said, and there are some who
say [he said] in the name of R. Adda b. Ḥunia,

B.   "The coming generation should be esteemed by
you like the generation which has passed;

C.   "Such that you will not say, If R. Aqiva were
alive, I would recite before him; if R. Zeira and R.
Yoḥanan were alive, I would repeat before them.

D.   "Rather, the generation which comes in your day
and the sage of your day [should be] like the generation
which passed, and [like] the former sages which preceded
you."

Mid. Qohelet R. I 4:4

Comment: This item appears only in this late midrashic com-
pilation. Tarfon simply supplies a name. The version in Qohelet
R. contains Aqiva's name and not that of Tarfon.

A.   M'SH HYH B: R. Gamaliel, in whose presence the
elders assembled, and Ṭabi his slave stood and waited
upon him.

B.   Said R. Eleazar b. Azariah, "Whence do you
[claim] that Canaan is required to [serve] your sons
whether they are righteous or wicked? By right Ṭabi
should recline and I should serve him."

C.   Said R. Ishmael, "We have found something greater
than this. Abraham, the great one of the world, waited
upon the Canaanites."

D.   Said R. Tarfon, "We have found something greater
than this. The High Priest waits upon Israel on the Day
of Atonement."

E.   Said to them R. Gamaliel, "You have neglected
the honor of the King of Kings, of Kings of the Holy One,
Blessed be He, and you are occupied with the honor of
flesh and blood.

F. "The Holy One, Blessed be He, created His
world, causes winds to blow, causes the sun to shine,
brings down rain, causes dew to fall, causes plants to
grow, and prepares a table before each and every one;

G. "for it is written, 'You prepare a table before
me' [Ps 23:5].

H. "And why [does he] do this?

I. "Because of the merit of the Torah.

J. "Therefore, Solomon prophesied and said, 'She
[Wisdom = Torah] has also set her table'" [Prov 9:2].

Midrash Mishlé, Ch. 9,
ed. Buber, pp. 62-63

Comment: In this Torah-centered tradition, Eleazar b. Azariah,
Ishmael, and Tarfon are depicted as colleagues of Gamaliel. This
is only the second mention of Gamaliel in all of Tarfon's traditions. A parallel version of this story, with different details,
omits Tarfon, and assigns sayings similar to those of Eleazar,
Ishmael and Gamaliel to Eliezer, Joshua and Ṣadoq, respectively.
We present the parallels in a synoptic chart:

Mid. Mishlé 9	Sifre Deut. 38, Mekh. Sim. 18:12, Mekh. Ish. ʿAmaleq 1, b. Qid. 32b
1. MʿSH HYH B: R. Gamaliel in whose presence the elders assembled,	1. WKBR: R. Eliezer, R. Joshua, and R. Ṣadoq were reclining at the wedding-banquet of the son of Rabban Gamaliel.
2. and Ṭabi his slave stood and waited upon him.	2. Rabban Gamaliel mixed the cup [of wine] for R. Eliezer,
3. - - -	3. but he [Eliezer] did not want to take it.
4.	4. R. Joshua took it.
5. Said R. Eleazar b. Azariah, Whence do you [claim] that Canaan is required to [serve] your sons whether they are righteous or wicked?	5. R. Eliezer said to him, What is this Joshua, Is it right that we should recline and Gamaliel Beribbi should stand over and serve us?
6. By right Ṭabi should recline and I should serve him.	6. - - - - - -
7. Said R. Ishmael, We have found something greater than this. Abraham, the great one of the world, waited upon Canaanites.	7. R. Joshua said to him, Let him do service. Abraham, the great one of the world, served the ministering angels assuming they were Arabs and idolators.

Mid. Mishlé 9	Sifre Deut. 38, Mekh. Sim. 18:12, Mekh. Ish. ʿAmaleq 1, b. Qid. 32b
8. - - -	8. As it is said, "And he lifted up his eyes and he saw, and behold three men" [Gen 18:2].
9. - - -	9. And it is *qal vaḥomer*. If Abraham, the great one of the world, served the ministering angels, [even while] assuming they were Arabs and idolators, should not Gamaliel Beribbi serve us [Mekh. Ish., Mekh. Sim.: serve sages who study Torah].
10. Said R. Tarfon, We have found something greater than this. The High Priest waits upon Israel on the Day of Atonement.	10. - - -
11. Said to them R. Gamaliel, You have neglected the honor of the King of Kings of Kings, of the Holy One, Blessed be He, and you are occupied with the honor of flesh and blood.	11. R. Ṣadoq said to them, You have neglected the honor of the Omnipresent " " " " " " " " "
12. The Holy One, Blessed be He, created His world, causes winds to blow, causes the sun to shine, brings down rain, causes dew to fall, causes plants to grow, and prepares a table before each and everyone,	12. If He who spoke and brought the world into being restores winds, brings up clouds, brings down rains, raises grain, and sets a table for each and everyone,

13. - - -
    - - -
    - - -
	13. should not Gamaliel Beribbi serve us [Mekh. Ish., Mekh. Sim.: serve sages and sons of Torah]?

14. for it is written, "You prepare a table before me."	14. - - -
15. And why does he do this?	15. - - -
16. Because of the merit of the Torah.	16. - - -
17. Therefore Solomon prophesied and said, "She [Wisdom = Torah] has also set her table."	17. - - -

Historical-Biographical

A. 1. [As to] a cow which drank purification-water,

2. and they slaughtered it within the period of twenty-four hours.

B. This incident occurred (ZH HYH M'SH):

C. 1. And R. Yose the Galilean did declare clean,

2. and R. Aqiva did declare unclean.

D. 1. R. Tarfon supported R. Yose the Galilean.

2. R. Simeon b. Nannos supported R. Aqiva.

E. 1. R. Simeon b. Nannos bested R. Tarfon.

2. R. Yose the Galilean bested R. Simeon b. Nannos.

3. R. Aqiva bested R. Yose the Galilean.

F. After some time, he [Yose] found an answer.

G. He [Yose] said to him [to Aqiva], "May I reopen [the issue]?"

H. 1. He said to him, "[I would not allow] any other person [to reopen the issue] but you,

2. "since you are R. Yose the Galilean.

3. "Speak."

I. 1. [He said], "Lo, it [Scripture] says, 'And it shall be kept for the congregation of the children of Israel for a water of sprinkling, it is a purification from sin' [Num 19:9].

2. "When it is watched, [it is] water of sprinkling.

3. "But [it is not water of sprinkling] when a cow drinks it."

J. This was the case and they took a poll of the thirty-two elders in Lydda and they declared it clean.

K. 1. At that very hour

2. R. Tarfon recited the following Scriptural [passage]:

L. 1. "I saw the ram pushing westward and north-ward and southward, and no beasts could stand before him, neither was there any that could deliver out of his hand. But he did according to his will and magnified himself" [Dan 8:4].

2. [This refers to] R. Aqiva.

M. 1. "And as I was considering, behold, a he-goat came from the west over the face of the whole earth and

touched not the ground, and the goat had a conspicuous
horn between his eyes" [Dan 8:5].

        2. This is Yose the Galilean and his answer.

N. 1. "And he came to the ram that had two horns,
which I saw standing before the stream, and ran at him
in the fury of his power. And I saw him come close unto
the ram, and he was moved with choler against him, and
smote the ram and broke his two horns" [Dan 8:6-7].

        2. These are Aqiva and Simeon b. Nannos.

O. 1. "And there was no power in the ram to stand
before him, but he cast him down to the ground and
trampled upon him" [Dan 8:7].

        2. This is Yose the Galilean.

P. 1. "And there was none that could deliver the
ram out of his hand" [Dan 8:7].

        2. These are the thirty-two elders who were
polled in Lydda and declared it clean.

> Tos. Miq. 7:11, ed. Zucker-
> mandel, pp. 660-61, lns. 31-37,
> 1-10

Comment: The editor of this pericope has integrated several
traditions. A+C are a well-balanced dispute form. Yose's opinion
is identical to that of Judah in M. Parah 9:5. The argument
ascribed to Yose in I gives him the last say and thus indicates
that he wins the debate. J, therefore, seems superfluous. The
anti-Aqivan, pro-Yose the Galilean saying attributed to Tarfon in
K2-P has been joined to the remainder of the pericope by Kl and
the formulaic language of C-D. The verses cited in K2-P have been
have been divided so that they refer to all parties mentioned in
the pericope. This is the only item in the Tarfon-corpus which
portrays him as a supporter of Yose.

    Lightstone (p. 260 n. 5) notes that K2-P is the product of a
conscious attempt to divest the passage in Daniel of its apocalyp-
tic force. Thus the processes leading to salvation, once thought
to take place on the level of world history and politics, now occur
within the walls of the House of Study. Rabbinic study and debate
is of cosmic and salvific significance; political activism is not.

A. "And it shall be kept for the congreation of
Israel [for a water of sprinkling]" [Num 19:9].

B. On the basis of this [verse] they said:

C. [As to] a cow which drank the purification-water--

D. its flesh is unclean for twenty-four hours
(M'T L'T).

E. R. Judah says, "It is [immediately] annulled
in her bowels."

C-E = M. Parah 9:5

F. For they said, "It shall be kept," etc. [i.e.,
it is purification-water only when it is watched].

G. WKBR: This law was discussed before the thirty-
eight elders at Kerem BeYavneh, and they declared its
flesh clean.

H. "And it shall be kept for the children of Israel."

I. This is one of the [R. Hillel: five] issues
which R. Yose the Galilean argued before R. Aqiva, and
R. Aqiva defeated (ŚYLQW) him, and afterwards he [Yose]
found a reply.

J. He [Yose] said to him, "Lo, it [Scripture] says,
'It shall be kept for the children of Israel for a water
of sprinkling.'

K. "When they are watched, lo, they are a water
of sprinkling."

L. 1. Said R. Tarfon, "'I saw a ram pushing westward and northward and southward and no beasts could
stand before him, neither was there any that could
deliver out of his hand. But he did according to his
will and magnified himself' [Dan 8:4].

2. "This [refers to] R. Aqiva.

M. 1. "'And as I was considering, behold, a he-
goat came from the west over the face of the whole earth
and touched not the ground, and the goat had a conspicuous
horn between his eyes. And he came to the ram that had
two horns, which I saw standing before the stream, and ran
at him in the fury of his power. And I saw him come close
unto the ram, and he was moved with choler against him and
smote the ram and broke his two horns. And there was no
power in the ram to stand before him, but he cast him down
to the ground and trampled upon him. And there was none
that could deliver the ram out of his hand' [Dan 8:4-7].

2. "This [refers to] Yose the Galilean."

Sifre Ḥuqat 125, ed. Horowitz,
pp. 158-59, lns. 12-20, 1-4

Comment: I, which simply summarizes the nature of the exchange
between Aqiva and Yose but does not present their views, indicates
that Sifre is dependent on an earlier version of the tradition.
There are several other differences between the versions of this
item in Sifre and in Tos. Miq. In Sifre the comments about the
poll of the elders precedes, and is separated by means of H from,
the tradition involving Aqiva and Yose; thus their redundancy is
eliminated. Tarfon's saying is simply appended to the remainder
of the pericope. Nothing in A-K foreshadows his appearance in L.
The verses in L-M are divided so that they refer only to Yose and
Aqiva; no mention is made of the elders or of Ben Nannos.

        A. 1. At first (BR'ŠWNH) he [the priest] would
say it [the divine name] in a loud voice.
           2. After the licentious ones (PRWṢYN) became
numerous, he would say it in a low voice.
        B. 1. Said R. Tarfon, "I was standing in a row
among my brothers, the priests,
           2. "and I cocked my ear toward the high priest,
           3. "and I heard him cause it [the divine name]
to be swallowed up in the singing of the priests."
        C. 1. At first it [the divine name] was passed on
to everyone.
           2. After the licentious ones became numerous,
it was passed on only to those who were fit.

y. Yoma 3:7 40d

Comment: A+C are a unit which deals with the recitation and
transmission of the divine name. The redactor has inserted B, for
he assumes the priest pronounced the divine name so that it would
not be heard, because the licentious ones had already become numerous. Thus he treats B as an illustration of A. Like Tos. Soṭ.
7:16, B is phrased as a recollection relating to Temple-practice.

        A. After the licentious ones became numerous, they
resumed passing it [the divine name] on to only the
virtuous ones (LṢNW'YM) among the priesthood.
        B. 1. Said R. Tarfon, "M'SH W: I was standing in a
row among my brothers the priests,
           2. "and I cocked my ear toward the high priest,

3.   "and I heard him say it [so that it would be lost] in the singing of his fellow priests."

Sifre Zuṭṭa Naso' 6:27, ed.
Horowitz, p. 250, lns. 13-16

Comment: The numbers refer to the chart on p. 288. In Sifre Zuṭṭa 7, Tarfon's saying is introduced by the formula M'SH W. 4 has virtuous priests and not fit priests. The former is preferable since it is the opposite of licentious priests.

A.   1.   TNW RBNN: At first they would pass the name of twelve letters on to everyone.

2.   After the licentious ones became numerous, they would pass it on only to the virtuous ones in the priesthood.

3.   And the virtuous ones in the priesthood [when pronouncing it] would cause it to be swallowed up in the singing of their fellow priests.

B.   1.   TNY': Said R. Tarfon, "One time I followed my maternal uncles onto the platform (LDWKN),

2.   "and I cocked my ear to the high priest,

3.   "and I heard [him pronounce] the name so that it was swallowed up in the singing of his fellow priests."

b. Qid. 71a

Comment: 3 of b. specifies which divine name was passed on. 5 sets up Tarfon's comment that follows. In 7 of b., Tarfon's "brothers" become his "maternal uncles." The parallels to Tos. Soṭ. 7:16 speak of Tarfon's maternal uncle, Simeon.

y. Yoma 3:7[3]	Sifre Zuṭa 6:27	b. Qid. 71a
1. At first he would say it in a loud voice.	1. - - -	1. - - -
2. After the licentious ones became numerous, he would say it in a low voice.	2. - - -	2. - - -
3. At first it was passed on to everyone.	3. - - -	3. " they would pass the name of twelve letters on to everyone.
4. After the licentious ones became numerous, it was passed on only to those who were fit.	4. " " " " they resumed passing it on to only the virtuous among the priesthood.	4. " " " " they would pass it on " " "
5. - - -	5. - - -	5. And the virtuous ones in the priesthood [when pronouncing it] would cause it to be swallowed up in the singing of their fellow priests.
6. Said R. Tarfon,	6. " " ".	6. " " " "
7. I was standing in a row among my brothers, the priests,	7. M'SH W " " "	7. One time I followed my maternal uncles onto the platform,
8. and I cocked my ear toward the high priest,	8. " " " "	8. " " " "
9. and I heard him cause it to be swallowed up in the singing of the priests.	9. " say it [so that it would be lost] " " " his fellow priests.	9. " [him pronounce] the name so that it was swallowed up in the singing of his fellow priests.

A.   DTNY': 'Issi b. Judah used to enumerate the
merits of sages:

B.   R. Meir: a sage and a scribe.

C.   R. Judah: a sage when he wants to be.

D.   R. Tarfon: a heap of nuts.

E.   R. Ishmael: a well-stocked shop.

F.   R. Aqiva: a well-packed storehouse.

G.   R. Yoḥanan b. Nuri: a peddler's basket.

H.   R. Eleazar b. Azariah: a basket of spices.

I.   The teaching of R. Eliezer b. Jacob: little
[lit.: a *qab*] but spotless.

J.   R. Yose: he has his reasons.

K.   R. Simeon: grinds much and produces little.

b. Giṭ. 67a

Comment: This tradition, like M. Avot 2:8, contains descriptions of various sages. M. Avot 2:8 consists of Yoḥanan b.
Zakkai's comments about his disciples. The present pericope is
comprised of descriptions attributed to an Ushan. Yavneans (D-H)
are sandwiched between Ushans (B-C, I-K). Tarfon's name again
appears first among those of the Yavneans. After we cite the
parallel version of this pericope, we shall discuss the meaning
of D.

A.   In like manner Judah the Patriarch used to
enumerate the merits of sages:

B.   of R. Tarfon, of R. Aqiva, and of R. Eleazar
b. Azariah, and of R. Yoḥanan b. Nuri, and of R. Yose
the Galilean.

C.   R. Tarfon he called a heap of stones.

D.   And there are some who say, a heap of nuts.

E.   For when a person removes one of them, all of
them go tumbling down over each other.

F.   1.   This is what R. Tarfon was like.

2.   When a disciple came to him and said to
him, "Teach me,"

3.   he cited for him Scripture, and mishnah,
midrash, halakhot, and aggadot.

G.   When he [the disciple] departed, he would leave
filled with blessing and good.

H.   R. Aqiva he called a well-packed storehouse.

I.   1.   To what may R. Aqiva be compared?

    2.   To a worker who took his basket and went
forth. He found wheat, he put that in; he found barley,
he put that in; spelt, he put that in; lentils, he put
that in.

    3.   When he returned to his house, he sorted
out the wheat by itself, the barley by itself, the beans
by themselves, the lentils by themselves.

J.   This is how R. Aqiva acted, and he arranged the
whole Torah in rings.

K.   R. Eleazar b. Azariah he called a peddler's
basket.

L.   1.   To what may Eleazar b. Azariah be compared?

    2.   To a peddler who took his basket and went
into a city, and the people of the city came and said to
him, "Do you have good wine with you? Do you have oint-
ment with you? Do you have balsam with you?"

    3.   They find he has everything with him.

M.   1.   Such was R. Eleazar b. Azariah when disciples
came to him.

    2.   [If] they asked him about Scripture, he
answered them; on mishnah, he answered them; on
midrash, he answered them; on halakhot, he answered
them; on aggadot, he answered them.

N.   When he [the disciple] departed, he would leave
filled with blessing and good.

        [A story about R. Joshua follows. The text
        then returns to the merits of the sages.]

O.   And R. Yoḥanan b. Nuri he called a basket of
halakhot.

P.   And R. Yose the Galilean: gathers well without
arrogance.

Q.   For he held fast to the quality of the sages
[imposed upon all] at Mount Sinai, and he used to praise
all the sages of Israel for the same quality.

R.   'Issi b. Judah used to assign epithets (ŠMWT)
to sages:

S.   R. Meir: a sage and a scribe.

T.   R. Judah: a sage when he wants to be.

U.   R. Eliezer b. Jacob: little but spotless.

V.   R. Yoḥanan b. Nuri: a basket of halakhot.

W.   R. Yose the Galilean: gathers well without arrogance.

X.   R. Simeon b. Gamaliel: a shopfull of precious purple.

Y.   R. Simeon: studies much [and] forgets little.

ARN A Ch. 18, trans. Goldin,
pp. 90-92

Comment: Let us compare ARN A with b. Giṭ. 67a.

b. Git. 67a	ARN A Ch. 18	ARN A Ch. 18
1. 'Issi b. Judah used to enumerate the merits of sages:	1. In like manner Judah the Patriarch used to enumerate the merits of sages:	1. 'Issi b. Judah used to assign epithets to sages:
2. R. Meir: a sage and a scribe.	2. - - -	2. - - -
3. R. Judah: a sage when he wants to be.	3. - - -	3. - - -
4. - - -	4. of R. Tarfon, of R. Aqiva, and of R. Eleazar b. Azariah, and of R. Yohanan b. Nuri, and of R. Yose the Galilean.	4. - - -
5. R. Tarfon: a heap of nuts.	5. R. Tarfon he called a heap of stones.	5. - - -
6. - - -	6. And there are some who say, a heap of nuts.	6. - - -
7. - - -	7. For when a person removes one of them, all of them go tumbling down over each other.	7. - - -
8. - - -	8. This is what R. Tarfon was like. When a disciple came to him and he said, teach me, he cited for him Scripture...	8. - - -
9. - - -	9. When he departed, he would leave filled with blessing and good.	9. - - -
10. R. Ishmael: a well-stocked shop.	10. - - -	10. - - -
11. R. Aqiva: a well-packed storehouse.	11. R. Aqiva he called a well-packed storehouse.	11. - - -
12. - - -	12. To what may R. Aqiva be compared. To a worker...This is how R. Aqiva acted, and arranged the whole Torah in rings.	12. - - -
13. R. Yohanan b. Nuri: a peddler's basket.	13. See below #17.	13. See below #22.

b. Git. 67a	ARN A Ch. 18	ARN A Ch. 18
14. R. Eleazar b. Azariah: a basket of spices.	14. R. Eleazar b. Azariah he called a peddler's basket.	14. - - -
15. - - -	15. To what may R. Eleazar b. Azariah be compared? To a peddler....They find he has everything with him.	15. - - -
16. - - -	16. Such was R. Eleazar b. Azariah when disciples came to him. If they asked him....When he departed he would leave filled with blessing and good.	16. - - -
17. See above #13.	17. R. Yohanan b. Nuri he called a basket of halakhot.	17. See below #22.
18. - - -	18. R. Yose the Galilean: gathers well without arrogance.	18. See below #23.
19.	19. For he held fast to the quality of the sages....	19.
20. The teachings of R. Eliezer b. Jacob: little but spotless.	20. - - -	20. R. Eliezer b. Jacob " " "
21. R. Yose: he has his reasons.	21. - - -	21.
22. See above #13.	22.	22. R. Yohanan b. Nuri: a basket of halakhot.
23. - - -	23. See above #18.	23. R. Yose the Galilean: gathers well without arrogance.
24. - - -	24. - - -	24. R. Simeon b. Gamaliel: a shop full of precious purple.
25. R. Simeon: grinds much and produces little.	25. - - -	25. R. Simeon: studies much [and] forgets little.

The important point for us is that Judah the Patriarch's version of the catalogue fills in with rabbinic content the descriptions of several of the Yavneans (7-9, 12, 15-16). Tarfon, according to E (7), is called a heap of nuts because, although he
has a great deal of knowledge, it is not systematically organized.
Tarfon thus is the exact opposite of Aqiva, I-J (12), whose learning is well ordered. I cannot account for this description of
Tarfon. G (9) is not an appropriate summation to the description
of Tarfon, for it, unlike E (7) and F (8), portrays him in a positive light. G (9) appears verbatim in N (16) and belongs there.

A. He [Dosa] said, "May my two eyes remain so that
I can see the sages of Israel."

B. He saw R. Joshua and recited about him, "'To
whom will he teach knowledge [and to whom will he explain
the message? Those who are weaned from milk and taken
from the breast]' [Isa 28:9].

C. "[For] I remember that his mother would bring
his crib to the synagogue in order to atune his ears to
words of the Torah."

D. [He saw] R. Aqiva and recited about him, "'The
young lions suffer want and hunger, [But those who seek
the Lord lack no good]' [Ps 34:10].

E. "I recognize him, that he is a great man of Torah."

F. He saw R. Leazar b. Azariah and recited about him,
"'I have been young and now am old [yet I have not seen the
righteous forsaken]' [Ps 37:25].

G. "I recognize him that he is [a descendant of] the
tenth generation from Ezra, *and his eyes are like his*
[those of Ezra. This is how he recognizes him]."

H. Said R. Ḥaninah of Sepphoris, "Even R. Tarfon
was among them.

I. "And he recited [the verse] for him just as he
recited about Eleazar b. Azariah."

y. Yev. 1:6 3a-b

Comment: Ḥaninah of Sepphoris, an amora of the final generation of Palestinian amoraim (so Hyman II, pp. 497-98) adds Tarfon
to Dosa's list, thereby giving us a list of four sages: Aqiva,
Joshua, Eleazar b. Azariah, and Tarfon. Mekh. Ish. Baḥodesh 10
also contains this grouping.

A. "And he said, 'My son shall not go down with you'" [Gen 42:38].

B. R. Ḥaninah [ARN B: Nehemiah] and R. Marinos say in the name of Abba [Mss. Oxford, Paris, M, V, Adler; ARN B: R. Nehorai],

C. "When someone would make a cogent remark in the presence of R. Tarfon, he would say, 'Well spoken' [lit.: a capital and a blossom] [Exod 25:39, 37:19].

D. "But when someone would make a meaningless statement, he would say, 'My son (BNY) shall not go down with you'" [Gen 42:38].

> Gen. R. 91:9, ed. Theodor and
> Albeck, p. 1133, lns. 1-3
> (B-D = ARN B Ch. 40)

Comment: The tradition reports that Tarfon responded to comments by citing biblical phrases. The force of the biblical citation in D is unclear. Saldarini (p. 241 n. 18) interprets D as follows. Jacob's answer to Reuben, Gen 42:38, does not respond to Reuben's statement. This is a form of a rejection. Alternatively, BNY, *benī*, may be read *bēnī*, my understanding does not agree with you.

A. "The Lord has swallowed up unsparingly all the habitations of Jacob" [Lam 2:2].

B. [This refers to] all the glorious ones of Jacob.

C. Such as (1) R. Ishmael, (2) and R. Simeon b. Gamaliel, (3) and R. Yeshobat, (4) and R. Ḥuspit, (5) and R. Ḥaninah b. Teradion, (6) and R. Judah, the baker, (7) and R. Judah b. Baba, (8) and R. Simeon b. Azzai, (9) and R. Aqiva, (10) and R. Tarfon.

D. And there are some who exclude R. Tarfon and include R. Eleazar b. Ḥarsum.

> Lam. R. II 2,4

Comment: This is the only unit of tradition about the ten martyrs that lists Tarfon. D indicates the uncertainty about the inclusion of Tarfon. For a more complete discussion of these lists, see S. Buber (*Schoḥar Tov*, p. 88 n. 89) and L. Zunz (*HaDerashot BeYisrael*, pp. 312-14 nn. 97-99).

A.   Said to him [i.e., to Aqiva] R. Tarfon, "Aqiva,
the [following] verse refers to you.

B.   "'He binds the streams that they trickle not,
and the thing that is hidden he brings to light' [Job
28:11].

C.   "Things concealed from men R. Aqiva did bring
forth to light."

ARN A Ch. 6, trans. Goldin,
p. 42.

Comment: This is another one of the items in which Tarfon
praises Aqiva. It appears after a story which relates how Aqiva,
after having studied first with Eliezer and Joshua and then by
himself, returned and reduced to silence his two teachers. In ARN
B 12 the comment is attributed to Eliezer.

CHAPTER VII

[1]Tarfon's saying appears after a section that contains apothegms attributed to the five students of R. Yoḥanan b. Zakkai. The section consists of (1) the superscription, "They said three things," and (2) three lemmas attributed to each authority. Chapter Three opens with individual sayings by various authors.

[2]My translation is based on Lieberman's interpretation of these words in Tos. Demai 1:3 (*Zeraim*, p. 62). Jastrow (p. 832) gives two other translations. They are, "until they fold the knives used for cutting figs," "until they lay the figs in layers." Thus in any case the words relate to figs.

[3]In y., 3-4 appear after 6-9. For the sake of comparison, I place them before Tarfon's saying.

PART TWO

ANALYSIS

CHAPTER VIII

THE CORPUS AS A WHOLE: ITS STRATA

The Corpus as a Whole: Its Strata

In Part One we examined from various perspectives each of the
128 discrete units of tradition. Their formal, literary, and substantive traits have been noted. We now may synthesize these data
in order to yield their history, and perhaps a picture of the
historical Tarfon. Our first task is to gain some perspective on
the corpus as a whole, that is, to note its general patterns.
To do this we list the items, first legal (Nos. 1-88), and then
non-legal (homiletical-theological, Nos. 89-121; historical-
biographical, Nos. 122-128), in the order of their appearance in
the following five strata: M.-Tos., halakhic midrashim, beraitot,
amoraic materials, and later compilations. For our purposes,
M.-Tos. are compiled around 200 A.D. Halakhic midrashim and
beraitot come later. Amoraic materials and later compilations
range from the fifth century until medieval times.

Item	M.-Tos.	Halakhic Midrashim	Baraita-Stratum	Amoraic Materials	Later Compilations
1. Saying the *Shemaʿ*	M. Ber. 1:3				
2. Blessing over water	M. Ber. 6:8 (Tos. Ber. 4:16)		b. Eruv. 14b		Deut.R. 3:8
3. Land liable for *Peʾah*	M. Peah 3:6				
4. Untithed crops mixed with already tithed crops	Tos. Demai 5:22		b. Men. 31a y. Demai 5:9		
5. Crops deposited with a gentile			y. Demai 3:4		
6. Hemp: diverse kinds in a vineyard	M. Kil. 5:8				
7. Cuscuta: diverse kinds in a vineyard	Tos. Kil. 3:16				
8. Arum and the Sabbatical year	Tos. Shev. 4:4		b. Shab. 139a		
9. Balsam and the Sabbatical year	Tos. Shev. 5:12				
10. Increase heave-offering	M. Ter. 4:5				
11. Field sown with heave-offering	M. Ter. 9:2		y. Ter. 9:2		
12. Vine in a yard	M. Ma. 3:9				
13. Unclean vetches of second-tithe	M. M.S. 2:4				
14. Second-tithe money in Jerusalem	M. M.S. 2:9				
15. Dough mixed with oil	M. Ed. 1:10		y. Hal. 2:3		

Item	I	II	III	IV	V
16. Oil for lamp	M. Shab. 2:2 Tos. Shab. 2:3		b. Shab. 26a	y. Shab. 2:2	
17. Perforated eggshell as lamp			b. Shab. 29b		
18. Linen covering on the Sabbath	Tos. Shab. 5:13b				
19. Scrolls of sectarians	Tos. Shab. 13:5		b. Shab. 116a y. Shab. 16:1		
20. Entering town on the Sabbath	M. Eruv. 4:4		b. Eruv. 45a y. Eruv. 4:4		
21. Prayer of redemption at the Seder	M. Pes. 10:6				
22. Fourth cup of wine			b. Pes. 118a		
23. Roasting Passover-offering		Mekh. Simeon 12:9 Mekh. Ish. Pisḥa 6	b. Pes. 74a	y. Pes. 7:1	
24. Women and children on Passover				y. Pes. 10:1	
25. Broken off myrtles	M. Suk. 3:4	Sifra 'Emor 16:7	b. Suk. 34b y. Suk. 3:1		
26. Length of palm	Tos. Suk. 2:8		b. Suk. 32b y. Suk. 3:1		
27. Palm in a bunch		Sifra 'Emor 16:4	b. Suk. 31a,32a y. Suk. 3:1		
28. Animal died on a festival	M. Beṣ. 3:5				
29. Sanhedrin which observed a murder			b. R.H. 25b b. B.Q. 90b		
30. Fasting for rain	M. Ta. 3:9				
31. Minor reading the *Megillah*	Tos. Meg. 2:8		b. Meg. 20a	y. Meg. 2:4	

Item	I	II	III	IV	V
32. Stripes for those liable to *karet*			y. Meg. 1:8 y. Ket. 3:1		
33. Eulogizing on a festival	Tos. Ḥag. 2:13		b. Ḥag. 18a		
34. Receiving heave-offering from anyone	Tos. Ḥag. 3:33				
35. Marrying daughter's co-wife	Tos. Yev. 1:10		b. Yev. 15a y. Yev. 1:6		
36. Married sister-in-law				y. Yev. 4:11	Sem. 7:15
37. Insufficient evidence	M. Yev. 15:6-7 Tos. Yev. 14:2		b. Yev. 118b y. Yev. 15:9 b. B.Q. 103b b. B.M. 37a,b	b. B.Q. 103b	
38. *Ḥaliṣah*-ceremony	Tos. Yev. 13:15	Sifre Deut. 291	b. Yev. 101b,106b b. Qid. 14a		
39. Cross-examine witnesses	Tos. Yev. 14:10		b. Yev. 122b	y. Yev. 16:5	
40. Food given to woman betrothed to a priest	M. Ket. 5:2 Tos. Ket. 5:1		b. Ket. 58a y. Ket. 5:3		
41. Betrothed three hundred women	Tos. Ket. 5:1H			y. Ket. 4:12	
42. Scolding woman	M. Ket. 7:6				
43. Distribution of husband's property	M. Ket. 9:2-3				
44. Forbidden to eat eggs	M. Ned. 6:6		b. Ned. 52b		
45. Conditional Nazirite vow	M. Naz. 5:5 Tos. Nez. 3:19		b. Eruv. 82a b. Ḥag. 10a b. Ned. 19b,21a b. Naz. 34a,62a b. Sanh. 25a y. Naz. 5:6		

Item	I	II	III	IV	V
46. Cutting of hair for unclean Nazirite	M. Naz. 6:6	Sifra Mesora 2:7			
47. Nazirite in cemetery				y. Naz. 3:5	Sem. 4:10
48. Memory-offering of suspected adulteress	Tos. Soṭ. 1:10	Sifre Num. 8	y. Soṭ. 3:4		Num. R. 9:34
49. One witness and *ketubah* of suspected adulteress				y. Soṭ. 6:2	
50. Lame priest blowing horn	Tos. Soṭ. 7:16	Sifre Num. 75	y. Yoma 1:1 y. Meg. 1:12 y. Hor. 3:5		
51. Four sages on Eliezer's opinion regarding conditional divorce	Tos. Giṭ. 9:1	Sifre Deut. 269	b. Giṭ. 83a	y. Giṭ. 9:1	
52. Use of gentile courts			b. Giṭ. 88b		Tanḥuma Mishpaṭim 6
53. Purification of *mamzerim*	M. Qid. 3:13				
54. Writ for injured slave			b. Qid. 24b b. Giṭ. 42b		
55. Ox causing damage in domain of the injured party	M. B.Q. 2:5 Tos. B.Q. 1:9b Tos. B.Q. 5:12		b. B.Q. 26a		
56. Coins received for selling lost animal	M. B.M. 2:7			y. B.M. 2:9	
57. Defrauding	M. B.M. 4:3	Sifra Behar 3:5			
58. Cooking in pot on festival	M. Zev. 11:7 Tos. Zev. 10:13	Sifra Ṣav 7:2	b. Zev. 97a		

Item	I	II	III	IV	V
59. Sprinkling and receiving blood	Tos. Zev. 1:8	Sifra Vayiqra' 4:4-5		b. Zev. 13a	
60. Free-will offerings of oil	M. Men. 12:5 Tos. Men. 12:10a M. Zev. 10:8	Sifra Vayiqra' 8:7	b. Zev. 91b		
61. Bread-offering and lambs		Sifra 'Emor 13:4	b. Men. 45b		
62. Meal-offering made from new grain		Sifre Num. 148		b. Men. 68b	
63. Animal stripped of its hide	Tos. Hul. 3:7			b. Hul. 55b	
64. Uncertainty about birth of firstlings	M. Bekh. 2:6-8 Tos. Bekh. 2:7-10				
65. Firstling born Caesarean	M. Bekh. 2:9				
66. Period for consumption of a firstling		Sifre Num. 118	b. Zev. 57a		
67. Redemption of dead and unclean firstlings		Sifre Num. 118			
68. Redemption price of an ass				b. Bekh. 11a	
69. Cow with womb removed	M. Bekh. 4:4			b. Sanh. 33a	
70. Individual with extra digits	Tos. Bekh. 5:6-7		b. Bekh. 45b		
71. Priest returns redemption-money	Tos. Bekh. 6:14		b. Bekh. 51b		
72. Doubtfully committed sacrilege	M. Ker. 5:2-3	Sifra Vayiqra' 12:1-2			

Item	I	II	III	IV	V
73. Door bolt	M. Kel. 11:4 Tos. Kel. B.M. 1:6		b. Shab. 124a y. Shab. 17:1		
74. Wide end of a horn	M. Kel. 11:7				
75. Holding place	M. Kel. 25:7 Tos. Kel. B.B. 3:8,11		y. Ḥag. 3:1		
76. Earth from a grave area	Tos. Kel. B.M. 7:1	Sifre Zuṭṭa 19:16-17			
77. Hole in a door	M. Ohol. 13:1				
78. Size of fist	Tos. Kel. B.M. 7:2				
79. Movables bring uncleanness	M. Ohol. 16:1 Tos. Ah. 15:12		b. Shab. 16b		
80. Cedarwood	Tos. Neg. 8:2	Sifra Mesora 1:13			
81. Thirteen-month-old lamb	M. Par. 1:3	Sifre Zuṭṭa 15:6	y. Soṭ. 2:12		
82. Paraphernalia set aside for purification-rite	Tos. Par. 11:5				
83. Ring in chain	M. Miq. 10:5 Tos. Miq. 7:3				
84. Immersion-pool lacking water	Tos. Miq. 1:16-19		b. Qid. 66b		
85. Male who checks for seminal emissions	Tos. Nid. 2:8		b. Nid. 13b y. Nid. 2:1	y. Ter. 8:2	
86. Duration of protracted labor	Tos. Nid. 5:9		b. Nid. 38a		
87. Water on measuring rod	M. Maks. 5:4 Tos. Maks. 2:14				
88. Ammon and Moab in Sabbatical year	M. Yad. 4:3				

Item	I	II	III	IV	V
89. God's compassion; kingship	Tos. Ber. 4:16-18	Mekh. Ish. Beshalaḥ 6 Mekh. Simeon 14:22			Mid. Ps. 76:2
90. Capital punishment	M. Mak. 1:10				ARN A 27 ARN B 35
91. Reward for study	M. Avot 2:15,16				
92. God's providence (Exod 16:14)		Mekh. Ish. Vayassa 4 Mekh. Simeon 16:14	b. Sanh. 101a	b. Yoma 76a	Mid. HaGadol Exod. 16:14
94. Rabbi brings into world to come		Mekh. Ish. Baḥodesh 10 Sifre Deut. 32			
95. Moses shirks his duty (Exod 4:13)		Mekh. Simeon 6:2			
96. Reproof		Sifra Qodashim 4:9 Sifre Deut. 1	b. Arak. 16b		
97. Eating heave-offering		Sifre Num. 116 Sifre Zuṭṭa 18:17	b. Pes. 72b		C.R. 2:14
98. Learning vs. action		Sifre Deut. 41	b. Qid. 40b		
99. Who is wealthy			b. Shab. 25b		
100. Mourn for those who perform *miṣvot*			b. M.Q. 28b		
101. Urges of sages			b. Qid. 81b		
102. Pernicious signs guard sages				y. Demai 1:3	
103. Children and parents' actions				y. Yoma 8:4	
104. Regularity				b. Ned. 49b	
105. Fear of sage				b. Ned. 62a y. Shev. 4:2	
106. Honoring parents				b. Qid. 31b y. Peah 1:1 y. Qid. 1:7	Pes. Rab. 23-24

Item	I	II	III	IV	V
107. Sage causes repentance				b. B.M. 85a	
108. Response to a sage				b. Zev. 62b	
109. Decline in knowledge				b. Nid. 24b	Num. R. 9:24
110. Slander				b. Nid. 61a	
111. Attend upon sages					ARN A 3 ARN B 18
112. Work for *Shekhinah*					ARN A 11
113. Bride					ARN A 41
114. Torah: best investment					Lev. R. 34:16 Pes. Rab. 25:2 Kal. Rab. 2:13 Kal. 21
115. Persecution (Ps 7:1)					Mid. Ps. 7:13
116. He who does righteousness (Ps 106:3)					Mid. Ps. 106:3 Esther R. 6:1
117. Miracles ordained at creation (Jonah 1:17)					PRE 10
118. Gifts for Abraham and Sarah (Gen 20:14)					PRE 26
119. Torah and the nations					PRE 41
120. Sage of your generation					Mid. Sam. 15:2
121. Serve others as God does					Mid. Mishlé 9
122. Praise of Yose the Galilean		Tos. Miq. 7:11 Sifre Num. 125			
123. Recitation of divine name		Sifre Zuṭṭa 6:27	b. Qid. 71a	y. Yoma 3:7	

Item	I	II	III	IV	V
124. A heap of nuts			b. Giṭ. 67a		ARN A 18
125. Described in terms of Ps 37:25				y. Yev. 1:6	
126. Response to remarks					Gen. R. 91:9
127. One of ten martyrs					Lam. R. II 2:4
128. Praise of Aqiva (Job 28:11)					ARN A 6

Legal materials predominate in the corpus as a whole and also in its earliest stratum, M.-Tos. Eighty-eight items (69% of the total corpus) are legal in nature; only forty units of tradition (31% of the entire corpus) are non-legal. Of the seventy-three items in M.-Tos., sixty-nine (94.5%) have legal content. These sixty-nine units of tradition constitute 78% of the entire legal corpus. An additional 16% of the legal items (fourteen) first surface in halakhic midrashim and beraitot; six items in the former, eight in the latter. Of these fourteen items, seven are related in their themes and in their principles to materials in M.-Tos. (No. 5 to No. 4, No. 17 to No. 16, Nos. 22-23 to No. 21, No. 27 to Nos. 25-26, and Nos. 66-67 to Nos. 64-65). Only five legal units (6% of the total legal corpus) first appear in the amoraic stratum. But four of these items (5% of the total legal agendum) are closely related to units of tradition in M.-Tos. (No. 24 to No. 21, No. 47 to No. 46, No. 49 to Nos. 42 and 37, and No. 68 to Nos. 64-65). 91% of the legal units of tradition, therefore, either first appear in M.-Tos. or are related in their themes and in their principles to items in these documents. 94% of the legal materials are located in the three earliest strata.

Most of the non-legal materials by contrast appear in documents of the fourth and fifth strata. Only four items (10% of the non-legal units of tradition) can be dated by their location in M.-Tos. The halakhic midrashim add eight items (20%) and the beraitot four items (10%). Only 40% of the non-legal materials thus appear in the first three strata. This is in sharp contrast to the 94% of the total legal agendum preserved in these strata. Of the 60% of the non-legal units of tradition first surfacing in the two latest strata, 25% (ten items) are in the amoraic stratum, 35% (fourteen items) in later compilations. Furthermore, as we shall see in our detailed discussion of these materials, in the later levels of the corpus, few of these pericopae bear any relationship to legal or non-legal units of tradition first appearing in strata I-III.

Let us now summarize our findings by means of three charts. (We add the data presently available for the corpora of other Yavneans.)[1] In Figure 1 we list for each master the number of legal and non-legal units of tradition, and the respective percentages these represent of the entire corpus. Figures 2 and 3 then break down these numbers. In Figure 2 we divide the legal traditions by strata, giving the raw numbers and percentages for how

much of all legal materials first appear within each stratum.
Figure 3 does the same for the non-legal data.

Fig. 1. Total Corpus

Name	legal %	#	non-legal %	#
Tarfon	69	(88)	31	(40)
Eliezer	71	(229)	29	(93)
Eleazar	57	(68)	43	(52)

Fig. 2. Distribution of Legal Materials by Strata

Name	I %	#	II %	#	III %	#	IV %	#	V %	#
Tarfon	78	(69)	7	(6)	9	(8)	6	(5)	0	(0)
Eliezer	91.2	(209)	3	(7)	4.4	(10)	1.3	(3)	0	(0)
Eleazar	71	(48)	11.5	(8)	11.5	(8)	3	(2)	3	(2)

Fig. 3. Distribution of Non-Legal Materials by Strata

Name	I %	#	II %	#	III %	#	IV %	#	V %	#
Tarfon	10	(4)	20	(8)	10	(4)	25	(10)	35	(14)
Eliezer	11	(10)	27	(26)	21	(20)	15	(14)	25	(23)
Eleazar	12	(6)	28	(15)	8	(4)	27	(14)	25	(13)

The figures for the three masters are very close. In all cases
the legal materials predominate and appear in documents redacted
earlier than the compilations in which the non-legal items are
found. Legal data comprise 71% of the Eliezer-corpus; 69% of that
of Tarfon, and 57% of that of Eleazar. Strata I-III account for
94% of Tarfon's legal materials, 98.7% of those of Eliezer, and
94% of those of Eleazar. By contrast, only 40% of Tarfon's non-
legal units of tradition, 48% of those of Eleazar, and 59% of
those of Eliezer are in these strata. The greatest differences
between the distribution of legal and non-legal items occur at the
ends of the chart. While the percentage of legal materials in all
cases first occurring in stratum V, later compilations, is null or
negligible, at least a quarter of the non-legal materials are in
this stratum. Stratum I gives us the opposite picture. 70% or
more of the legal materials first appear here. But M.-Tos. account
for only 10% of the non-legal units of tradition.

The above data point to the greater *prima facie* reliability of
the legal materials. That is, we assume that units of tradition
which first appear in earlier strata are apt to preserve more

reliable information than those which first surface in later levels
of the corpus. In the Tarfon-corpus these are the legal materials.
We do not of course assert that an item which first appears in a
later stratum could not have originated with either Tarfon himself
or his immediate circle of disciples. Such an item, however, has
no *prima facie* claim to early origins. On the other hand, we do
not have any basis for claiming that even our "earliest materials"
are the *ipsissima verba* of Tarfon.[2] In fact, the data in the next
chapter support the contrary position.

Attestations

The identification of attested units of tradition allows us
to further stratify the corpus by isolating materials which probably were known prior to A.D. 200. We have an attestation if,
within rabbinic literature, the comments of a master, standing outside the structure of a pericope in which a unit of tradition attributed to Tarfon appears, refer to this item.[3] For example, if an
Ushan authority modifies a ruling assigned to Tarfon, or gives a
new ruling which is based upon and extends an opinion attributed
to Tarfon, we have grounds for assuming that the substance of this
ruling was known at the latest in Ushan times.[4] The following
chart lists and briefly discusses all attested items.

Attestations--Legal Materials

I   Yavneh: There are no Yavnean attestations.
II Usha: Ushans attest five units of tradition of Tarfon.

1. *Tos. Ket. 5:1/M. Ket. 5:2* (No. 40)
In M., Tarfon and Aqiva gloss an anonymous law, which
states that a man who is betrothed to a woman and has not
performed *nissu'in* with her within the allotted twelve
months, must provide her with sustenance. If he is a
priest, he may feed her heave-offering. Tarfon and Aqiva
disagree about the amount of heave-offering he may give
her. It is cheaper for a priest to provide her with this
consecrated produce. Tarfon rules the woman may receive
all her provisions as heave-offering. According to Aqiva,
only half may be heave-offering. Tos. revises Tarfon's
ruling in accordance with the opinion that the daughter
of an Israelite betrothed to a priest may not eat heave-
offering prior to performing *nissu'in*. Judah, who agrees
in principle with this modification, asserts in Tos. that
the bride-to-be sells the heave-offering she receives.
Judah, therefore, glosses the anonymous law of M. Ket.
5:2D2, and possibly the opinions of Tarfon and Aqiva.

2. *Tos. Giṭ. 7:1* (No. 51)
The pericope contains four objections attributed to
Yavneans to Eliezer's view that a divorce is valid even
if it contains the stipulation that the woman may not

marry a certain person. Yose interrupts the responses
of the Yavneans, and asserts that he agrees with the
opinion of Eleazar b. Azariah. Zahavy notes that this
is not a strong attestation, for Yose's saying could
appear after any of Eleazar's rulings.

3. *Tos. B.Q. 1:9b/M. B.Q. 2:5* (No. 55)
In M., Tarfon and sages disagree about the amount of the
restitution the owner of an ox, which causes damage in the
domain of the injuried party, pays. An anonymous gloss
specifies that the ox causes damage by goring, pushing,
biting, laying down, or kicking. In Tos., the opinions
have been revised by Simeon and Eleazar so that sages and
Tarfon disagree only about cases in which the above-
mentioned types of damage are caused by a harmless ox.

4. *Tos. Zev. 10:13/M. Zev. 11:7* (No. 58)
Tarfon in M. rules that one may cook in a pot during the
entire festival. His opinion is opposed by sages who
state that one may cook in the pot only until the time of
eating. The dispute originally is about Sabbath and
festival law. The redactor of M., however, relates the
sayings to the issue of scouring and rinsing pots in
which sacrifices are cooked on the festival. Nathan
attests this use of the pericope by commenting upon
Tarfon's saying. He states that it applies only to pots
in which lesser holy sacrifices are cooked. The reasoning behind Tarfon's ruling does not apply to pots in
which one cooks more holy sacrifices.

5. *y. Nid. 2:1/Tos. Nid. 2:8* (No. 85)
Tarfon in Tos. glosses the ruling of M. Nid. 2:1, which
states that the hand of a man who checks for seminal
emissions should be cut off. Tarfon says that it should
be cut off upon his belly. The discussion following this
comment treats it literally. In y.'s version of the
tradition, however, Yose and an anonymous saying revise
Tarfon's statement so that it no longer is taken literally. Yose states that Tarfon meant only that it is
forbidden for a man to feel below his belly button.
Since Yose's saying is preserved in a baraita, it does
not have the same *prima facie* strength as an attestation
found in M.-Tos.

III   Bet Shearim: One item is attested by a contemporary of R.
      Judah the Patriarch.

1. *Tos. Yev. 14:2/M. Yev. 15:6-7*
Simeon b. Eleazar in Tos. revises the protasis of the
dispute between Tarfon and Aqiva. This dispute concerns
whether or not in cases of doubt we act stringently in
order to avoid any possible transgression. Aqiva rules
we do; Tarfon rules we do not. M. has two types of
cases, each of which is spelled out in two examples.
The examples which illustrate the second type of case
are not similar. In one of these examples a crime has
been committed. In the other, no one has violated any
laws. Simeon revises the dispute so that Tarfon and
Aqiva disagree only about cases in which some law has
been broken. Simeon's revision is in opposition to an
anonymous statement in Tos., which asserts that the dispute concerns two cases in which no transgressions has
occurred.

The attestations are few (six) and episodic. There are no
Yavnean attestations. Only five legal items can be dated to Ushan
times, one to the time of Judah the Patriarch. Except for Yose,
each of the other authorities attest one unit of tradition. Yose
comments upon two items. In all, only 7% of the legal units of
tradition can be dated to before 200 A.D.[5] The sample is too
small to speak of another layer of the corpus. The best units of
tradition, therefore, are those first appearing in M.-Tos.

CHAPTER VIII

[1]For Eliezer, see Neusner (*Eliezer* II, pp. 1-17); for Eleazar, Zahavy (p. 224). As of yet we do not have studies of the complete corpora of other masters.

[2]Neusner, *Eliezer* II, pp. 87-88.

[3]It now seems we are begging the question; for if we do not necessarily accept the veracity of the attribution which assigns a teaching to Tarfon, why should we accept the attribution of the other saying to the Ushan? Why should we question the attribution of the primary saying to Tarfon but accept at face value the attribution of the secondary saying to the Ushan? We may answer this question as follows: Our acceptance of the attestation attributed to an Ushan is based upon the fact that it, along with other Ushan attestations, give us a coherent and limited agendum of items known in Ushan times. We claim no more than that Ushans know materials appropriate to a specific limited range of topics. Two tacit assumptions lie behind this claim. First, we take for granted that the production of materials attributed to various masters is not one great pseudepigraphic enterprise, but that different circles, at different times, and at different places, produced and preserved materials. Second, we postulate that these circles were not in collusion with each other, and again pseudepigraphically produced all items assigned to an earlier authority. Thus to review, if it can be shown that the attestations from a given period of Tarfon-materials add up to a coherent and limited agendum, we may accept their reliability.

[4]We do not discuss here tradental evidence (defined below, p. 332), e.g., chains of tradition, because they provide no substantive evidence external to the tradition itself which indicates knowledge of it. The evidence is only formal, an attributional formula. On the basis of this type of data, we therefore cannot claim that a given unit of tradition was known at a particular time. We thus may not use tradental evidence in order to stratify *chronologically* the corpus. Chains of tradition, however, do provide precise information about the circles responsible for the transmission of materials.

[5]The figure for attested items, 7%, is very low when compared with those for the corpora of Eliezer, 40% (91/228), and the Houses, 62% (140/227). But it is in line with the percentages for other Yavneans: Eleazar, 12% (8/68); Joshua, 11% (19/177); Ishmael, 3% (4/152); Yose, 2% (1/42); Aqiva in Zera'im, 2% (1/64). The fact that a small number of units of tradition are commented upon by later authorities suggests merely that either because of their tradental history, the Tarfon-materials were not known, or that although they may have entered, at an early date, the mainstream of transmission, they were ignored. Attestations in fact may indicate very little about the history of materials. Lack of attestations does not mean that later authorities did not know or were not interested in these items. We assume that attestations point to the centrality of a corpus only because of the high figures for the corpora of the Houses and Eliezer.

CHAPTER IX

LITERARY TRAITS

The Issues and Definitions

Description and analysis of the literary characteristics of
units of tradition enable us to discuss the history of their formulation, transmission, and redaction.[1] In particular, we are
interested in how and when these processes took place and in those
responsible for their occurrence. To answer these questions, we
compare the individual units of tradition with each other, as well
as with data available from analyses of corpora attributed to
other Yavnean masters. We also note relevant substantive and
chronological features in order to determine significant correlations between these and the formal aspects of the materials.

All of the units of tradition belong to one of two large
literary types or categories--sayings (61% of the whole) and narratives (39%), an exceptionally high proportion. The latter needs no
definition. A saying is a lemma joined fore or aft to an attributive formula (e.g., "X says"). The materials that fall into both of
these categories exhibit varying degrees of disciplined formulation. Some of the items belonging to a particular category have
in common only the most general literary traits. For example,
many of the stories can be grouped together because they use the
narrative technique of brief dialogue. Other units of tradition,
on the other hand, have been phrased in accord with an established,
disciplined, and recurrent arrangement of words, in accord with a
formulary pattern.[2] The words and frequently the formulas (e.g.,
"X says," *ma'aseh*) used in these items and the pattern in which these
words are put together have been determined by the imposition of a
particular formulary pattern. In what follows we define and discuss these patterns as well as the more varied structures in which
the materials appear. We analyze the sayings first and then the
narratives.

The Sayings

Two-thirds of the sayings are in one of two patterns, the
dispute (64% of all sayings) and the gloss (3%). The remaining
items, independent sayings (33%), are less structured. As to the
definitions of these categories: A saying attributed to Tarfon appearing with and formulated in close literary relationship to an

opposing opinion is in the dispute form. In a true dispute the
opinions respond to a common problem and to each other. Moreover,
in the most tightly formulated disputes, the sayings contain a
balanced number of syllables, use fixed opposites (e.g., liable
vs. exempt), or constitute a mnemonic. There are three major
variations of the dispute. Most of the items are in the pattern:

>   statement of problem (= protasis)
>   X says...
>   Y says...

A minor variation of the above is the use of an intensive transi-
tive verb, e.g., "declares clean," "permits," instead of "X says +
lemma." In some disputes the statement of the problem is contained
within the saying of the first master. This yields the second
variation of the dispute:

>   X says + statement of problem + apodosis
>   Y says + apodosis

In both variations of the dispute, the first opinion sometimes has
the attributive formula, "words of X" in place of "X says."

In the third variation of the dispute, a saying of Tarfon
follows, and has been formulated in close literary relationship
to an anonymous law with which it disagrees. This yields the
pattern:

>   anonymous law + X says

The anonymous law in this case is formally identical to the opinion
of the first master in the preceding variation of the dispute. All
disputes are listed under letter A. Debates are not catalogued by
themselves. We have shown in Part One that they are secondary developments of disputes. We, therefore, record them together with
the latter.[3]

The gloss form is identical in formulation to the third variation of the dispute, "anonymous law + X says." This form, however,
differs functionally from the dispute in that Tarfon's comment
glosses but does not disagree with the anonymous law. The two
items in this pattern appear under letter B.

A saying attributed to Tarfon, that is a lemma joined fore or
aft to an attributive formula, not standing in close literary relationship to either another assigned or anonymous saying, and intelligible on its own, belongs to the broad category, independent sayings. The pattern of words in the various lemmas greatly differ;
they therefore cannot be treated as a single form. We can, however,

break down the lemmas into three well-disciplined patterns: (1)
rulings or sayings phrased as simple declarative sentences, (2)
exegeses (verse + interpretation or saying + verse), and (3) first
person sayings. The attributive formula in half of the cases is
"X says." Other formulae, such as, "Said X, X said, words of X,
testified X and expounded X," are used much less frequently. Most
of the independent sayings stand alone. But in a number of instances someone has juxtaposed an independent saying attributed to
Tarfon with either an anonymous law or a saying assigned to another
master, thereby creating the semblance of a dispute. All items
belonging to the category of independent sayings are listed under
letter C.

In the following charts, we list and describe the sayings.
Within each category and subcategory we first catalogue the legal
and then the non-legal units of tradition. These items are presented in the order in which they first appear in the various
strata.

A

Dispute

Statement of problem--X says...Y says... Thirty (Nos. 1-30)
legal and two (Nos. 31-32) non-legal units units of tradition are
in this variation of the dispute form. Those pericopae in M.-Tos.
containing only two opposing opinions are listed in Nos. 1-20;
those with more than two opinions in Nos. 21-26. Nos. 27-30 are
disputes that first appear in later strata. In many of the disputes the opinions are well balanced or use mnemonic elements.
These features are noted in the parentheses within the descriptions.

1. M. Kil. 5:8--Hemp--Tarfon vs. sages (+/-).

2. Tos. Kil. 3:16--Cuscuta--Tarfon vs. sages (+/-) + said Tarfon;
    no response attributed to sages.

3. M. Ma. 3:9--Vine in a yard--ruling + words of Tarfon + Aqiva
    says. The apodoses mention grapes, pomegranates, and water-
    melons. Aqiva's saying uses technical language, which also
    appears in M. Ma. 3:6, and this may account for the mention
    of the other crops. Tarfon's saying is glossed to balance
    Aqiva's.

4. M. M.S. 2:4--Unclean vetches of second tithe--Tarfon vs.
    sages, balanced rulings (YPDW vs. YTHLQW).

5. M. Pes. 10:6--Houses dispute + gloss (conclude with prayer of
    redemption)--Tarfon, Aqiva.

6. M. Suk. 3:4--Ishmael says + ruling + gloss vs. Tarfon says +
    Aqiva says. The dispute between Tarfon and the gloss is
    inserted into that between Ishmael and Aqiva.

7. M. Yev. 15:6-7--A collection of four disputes, all illustrat-
    ing the same problem: insufficient evidence. Each consists
    of: protasis--ruling + words of Tarfon + Aqiva says.

8. M. Ket. 5:2--Woman betrothed and not married within twelve
    months--Tarfon vs. Aqiva (KL vs. MḤṢH).

9. M. Ket. 9:2,3--A collection of two disputes illustrating the
    same principle, inheritance of property. Protasis--Tarfon
    vs. Aqiva, balanced rulings (KLWSL vs. LYWRŠYN).

10. M. B.Q. 2:5--Ox does damage in domain of injured party +
    gloss--Tarfon vs. sages (KL vs. ḤṢY) + debate.

11. Tos. B.Q. 5:12--Ox brought into yard without owner's
    permission--ruling + words of Tarfon + Aqiva says (ḤYYB vs.
    PṬWR).

12. M. B.M. 2:7--Found animal + gloss phrased as a question--
    Tarfon vs. Aqiva (+/-).

13. M. Bekh. 2:6-8--A set of anonymous laws, consisting of three
    examples which illustrate the same principle, provide the
    superscriptions for disputes between Tarfon and Aqiva.

14. M. Bekh. 2:9--First born Caesarean, second in normal manner--
    Tarfon vs. Aqiva (similarly formulated sayings).

15. M. Kel. 11:4--Door bolt--Joshua, Tarfon; an artificial dispute.

16. M. Kel. 11:7--Wide metal end of a horn--Tarfon vs. sages
    (clean vs. unclean) + gloss.

17. M. Ohal. 13:3--Hole in door--ruling + words of Aqiva + Tarfon
    says (fist vs. handbreadth).

18. Tos. Miq. 1:16-19--Said Simeon + M'SH B + setting (water
    reservoir measured and found lacking required amount of
    water) + Tarfon declared clean + Aqiva declared unclean +
    debate. The M'SH is not appropriate for Simeon's purposes.

19. M. Maks. 5:4--Rod to measure cistern--ruling + words of
    Tarfon + Aqiva says (+/-).

20. M. Yad. 4:3--Question (Ammon and Moab in Sabbatical year)--
    decreed Tarfon, decreed Eleazar b. Azariah + debate between
    Ishmael and Eleazar + debate between Tarfon and Eleazar +
    Joshua supports Tarfon + they were polled + anonymous law +
    story about Eliezer.

21. M. Ter. 4:5--Increase heave-offering--Eliezer + gloss,
    Ishmael, Tarfon and Aqiva.

22. M. M.S. 2:9--Second-tithe money in Jerusalem--Houses
    (balanced rulings), they that made argument vs. Aqiva
    (balanced rulings, but in terms different from those of the
    Houses), Tarfon, Shammai.

23. M. Naz. 5:5--Six persons on a journey--Houses, Tarfon (all
    vs. none).

24. Tos. Kel. B.M. 7:2--Fist of which they spoke = M. Kel. 17:12--
    Tarfon spreads, Aqiva closes (PWRŠ vs. QWPṢ), Judah places,
    Yose says, others say in his name.

25. M. Par. 1:3--Thirteen month old lamb--Tarfon, Ben Azzai,
    Ishmael.

26. Tos. Nid. 5:9--Question (length of protracted labor)--
    ruling + words of Meir, Judah says in name of Tarfon, Yose,
    and Simeon.

27. y. Suk. 3:1--"Palm branches"--Tarfon vs. Aqiva + Judah says;
    the dispute is intelligible only when read with Judah's
    saying.

28. y. Pes. 7:1--How do they roast the Passover-offering (= M. Pes. 7:1)--ruling + words of Tarfon + Ishmael says. This is a poorly preserved unit of tradition, for the parallel versions have different attributions and different sayings.

29. b. R.H. 25b--Sanhedrin which observed a murder--ruling + words of Tarfon + Aqiva says (KL vs. MḤṢH). A different version of Aqiva's saying appears in Tos. Mak. 3:7 without that of Tarfon.

30. b. Qid. 24b--Injured slave goes free + words of Simeon, Meir vs. Eleazar, Tarfon vs. Aqiva (+/-).

31. Sifre Deut. 41--KBR HYH + setting (sages gathered together) + question (action vs. study) + answered Tarfon + lemma + answered Aqiva + lemma + they all answered + lemma. The question and the two responses are a good dispute.

32. b. Shab. 25b--Question (who is wealthy)--lemma + words of Meir, Tarfon, Aqiva, Yose.

Statement of problem in the first opinion. Nos. 1-5 have legal content; Nos. 6-7, non-legal. Of the legal materials, only No. 1 contains more than two opinions.

1. M. Peah. 3:6--Eliezer + statement of law (land liable to *pe'ah*), Joshua, Tarfon, Judah b. Bathyra + gloss + Aqiva says (an independent saying).

2. Tos. Soṭ. 1:10--Tarfon says + lemma + verse + Aqiva says + lemma + verse (KL ḤWṢ MN vs. 'P ZW), re: memory-offering of women suspected of adultery.

3. M. Zev. 11:7--Tarfon says + statement of law (cooking in pot on a festival) + sages say (KL vs. 'D).

4. M. Men. 12:5--Ruling (free-will offering of oil) + words of Aqiva + Tarfon says + debate (+/-).

5. y. Soṭ. 6:2--Tarfon says + saying (one witness and *ketubah* of women suspected of adultery) + Aqiva says + saying (+/-) + debate + Aqiva began to teach like Tarfon (names have been reversed).

6. Sifra Qodashim 4:9--Said Tarfon, Eleazar b. Azariah, Aqiva about reproof; three sayings formulated together.

7. b. Qid. 81b--Said Meir, said Tarfon + gloss + said Abbahu, re: sexual urges of sages.

Anonymous law + X says

1. M. Ber. 6:8--Drinks water to quench thirst + Tarfon says.

2. M. Ter. 9:2--Field mistakenly sown with heave-offering + said Tarfon (and vs. only) + said Aqiva (*reductio ad absurdum*).

3. Tos. Suk. 2:8--Length of palm + Tarfon says (saying uses *b*).

4. M. Kel. 25:7--Holding place + Tarfon says, Aqiva says. Two sayings of the two masters gloss and limit the anonymous law. They are similarly formulated, *l* + name of object.

5. M. Ohal. 16:1--Movables bring uncleanness + said Tarfon + precedent + said Aqiva + saying which modifies the anonymous law. These are the elements which lie behind the current formulation of the pericope. As it now stands, Tarfon and Aqiva both claim that the anonymous law is incorrect. Only Aqiva, however, is assigned a corrected version of the ruling. Tarfon, therefore, serves as a literary device.

6. M. Miq. 10:5--Chain of a bucket + Tarfon says (balanced).

7. Sifre Num. 148--Tarfon's ruling, phrased as an argument,
    glosses and disagrees with an anonymous law = M. Men. 10:6,
    re: meal-offerings made from new grain. An argument attribu-
    ted to Judah b. Naḥman, in support of the anonymous law,
    responds to Tarfon's saying.

8. y. Demai 3:4--Simeon says in name of Tarfon + saying about
    crops deposited with a gentile. Simeon's ruling appears in
    M. Demai 3:4 and glosses an anonymous law with which it
    disagrees.

9. y. Naz. 3:5--Person who vows while in a cemetery to become a
    Nazirite = M. Naz. 3:5--Tarfon vs. Aqiva (liable vs. exempt)
    + debate.

Use of Tarfon's name as a literary device. In the following
instances, Tarfon's question in a debate serves as a means for
explicating Aqiva's rulings. His query implies that he holds a
contrary opinion. But no such ruling is attributed to him. The
formulation of these items has been influenced by the dispute
form. Accordingly, I list them together with the latter.

1. M. Naz. 6:6--Ruling attributed to Aqiva + said to him Tarfon
    + he said to him. The answer attributed to Aqiva explains
    his ruling.

2. Tos. Zev. 1:8--An objection assigned to Tarfon joins together
    two Aqivan rulings on sprinkling and receiving blood. A de-
    bate between the two masters serves as the framework for the
    second of Aqiva's teachings.

B

Gloss

1. M. Ket. 7:6--Women do not receive *ketubah* + gloss with four
    examples + gloss with three examples + Abba Saul says +
    Tarfon says.

2. Tos. Nid. 2:8--Hand of man who checks for seminal emissions
    + Tarfon says + debate.

C

Independent Saying

Stand alone
    a. A ruling or a saying phrased as a simple declarative
sentence. Five legal and one non-legal independent sayings are
phrased in this manner.

1. Tos. Shev. 5:12--Testified + authority (Judah b. Isaiah the
    spice maker) + before x (Aqiva) + in the name of y (Tarfon)
    + that (Š) + ruling (balsam in the Sabbatical year).

2. Tos. Ḥul. 3:7--Same as above except it has "concerning" ('L)
    instead of Š; animal stripped of its hide.

3. Tos. Par. 11:5--Eleazar says in name of Tarfon + ruling about
    uncleanness of objects used in the purification ceremony.

4. b. Pes. 118a--Saying + words of Tarfon, re: fourth cup of
    wine.

5. b. Giṭ. 88b--Tarfon did say + lemma + exegesis; gentile
    courts.

6. M. Avot 2:15,16--Tarfon says + lemma + he used to say +
    lemma, re: work.

    b. Exegetical. Most, ten (Nos. 1-4, legal; Nos. 5-10, non-
legal), of the independent sayings which stand alone are exegeses.

1. Sifra 'Emor 13:4--Verse (bread-offering) + exegesis + words
    of Tarfon.

2. Sifre Num. 118--Expounded Tarfon + verse + ruling, re:
    redemption of unclean and dead firstlings.

3. y. Hal. 2:3--Simeon b. Yoḥai, Tarfon say + exegesis, based on
    gezerah shavah, dealing with dough mixed with oil.

4. y. Meg. 1:8--Simeon, Tarfon say + exegesis, same as above,
    on subject of stripes.

5. Mekh. Simeon Ex. 6:2--Tarfon says + exegesis (Moses shirks
    his responsibility).

6. ARN A 6--Said Tarfon to Aqiva + verse + exegesis (praise
    of Aqiva).

7. ARN A 11--Tarfon says + lemma + verse, re: work for *shekhinah*.

8. Mid. Ps. 7:13--Verse + Tarfon said + exegesis--interpretation
    of *shiggayon*.

9. PRE 10--Verse + Tarfon says + lemma + verse--miracles
    ordained at time of creation.

10. PRE 41--Tarfon said + exegesis, re: nations reject Torah.

    c. First person saying

1. Tos. Yev. 1:10--Said Tarfon + first person saying about
    marrying co-wife of his daughter; a gloss of Houses' dispute
    M. Yev. 1:3.

2. Sifre Zuṭṭa 6:27--Said Tarfon + first person report about
    recitation of the divine name.

    Juxtaposed independent sayings
    a. A ruling or saying phrased as a simple declarative
sentence. Four legal and one non-legal sayings of this type have
been juxtaposed in the semblance of a dispute with other dicta.

1. M. Shab. 2:2--Anonymous law (lighting lamp on holiday) +
    Ishmael says (lighting on Sabbath) + sages + Tarfon (olive
    oil).

2. M. Qid. 3:13--Tarfon says + lemma + joining language + anony-
    mous law + gloss + Eliezer says. Tarfon's saying about the
    purification of *mamzerim* is joined to a dispute between
    Eliezer and the anonymous law.

3. M. Ker. 5:2-3--Dispute of Aqiva vs. sages + Aqiva admits +
    said Tarfon + lemma + response attributed to Aqiva. By
    glossing the dispute of Aqiva vs. sages, the redactor joins
    it to Tarfon's saying about a doubtfully committed sacrilege.

4. Tos. Kel. B.M. 7:1--Anonymous law about the amount of dirt
    from various locations, including a grave area, which convey
    uncleanness + Tarfon says + ruling on land from a grave area.

5. M. Mak. 1:10--Dispute between Eleazar b. Azariah and an
    anonymous law + Tarfon and Aqiva say + Simeon b. Gamaliel
    says; all sayings relate to capital punishment.

    b. Exegetical

1. Mekh. Ish. Vayassa 4--Verse + exegesis + Tarfon says + exe-
    gesis; alternative explanations of MḤŚPŚ.

    c. First person saying

1. M. Ber. 1:3--Houses' dispute + glosses + said Tarfon + first
    person saying + gloss + they said to him. Tarfon's saying
    and the opinions attributed to the Houses deal with different
    aspects of the recitation of the Shema'.

2. Tos. Shab. 13:5--Yose the Galilean says + saying + said Tarfon
    + first person saying + gloss. Yose and Tarfon disagree about
    cutting out the divine names from the books of sectarians. An
    independent saying attributed to Ishmael on the same subject
    follows these statements.

To summarize these data, we first divide them by their content,
legal and non-legal. In Figure 1 we give the raw numbers and corresponding percentages for how many legal and non-legal sayings are
cast in each of the patterns.

Fig. 1. Distribution of Legal and Non-legal Sayings by Patterns

Pattern	Legal		Non-legal		Total	
	%	#	%	#	%	#
Dispute	72	(46)	29	(4)	64	(50)
Gloss	3	(2)	0	(0)	3	(2)
Independent Saying	25	(16)	71	(10)	33	(26)
TOTAL	100	(64)	100	(14)	100	(78)

The legal and non-legal materials exhibit opposite formal preferences. 72% of all legal sayings are cast in the dispute form. By
contrast, almost the same percentage of non-legal dicta are independent sayings. A division of the sayings by the strata in which
they first appear shows that in M.-Tos., the earliest stratum, and
therefore our best data, most of the dicta with legal substance
are in the dispute form. Furthermore, these units of tradition
account for nearly all of the legal sayings. Most of the non-
legal items, on the other hand, first appear in later strata and
are formulated as independent sayings. (Figs. 2 and 3 give the
raw numbers for legal and non-legal units of tradition respectively.)

Fig. 2. Legal Sayings by Strata (Raw Numbers)

Pattern	I	II	III	IV	V	Total
Dispute	38	2	4	2	0	46
Gloss	2	0	0	0	0	2
Independent Saying	10	1	5	0	0	16
TOTAL	50	3	9	2	0	64

Fig. 3. Non-legal Sayings by Strata

Pattern	I	II	III	IV	V	Total
Dispute	0	2	2	0	0	4
Independent Saying	2	3	0	0	5	10

Sayings in disputes account for 76% (thirty-eight of fifty items)
of the sayings with legal content first appearing in M.-Tos. These
items constitute 83% (thirty-eight of forty-six) of all legal disputes. Only 20% of the items in M.-Tos. are formulated as independent sayings. But six (M. Shab. 2:2, M. Qid. 3:13, M. Ker. 5:2-3,
Tos. Kel. B.M. 7:1, M. Ber. 1:3, and Tos. Shab. 13:5) of these ten
items (= 12% of all legal sayings in M.-Tos.) are juxtaposed with
other independent dicta, thereby creating the semblance of a dispute. 88% of all legal sayings in M.-Tos. (forty-four of fifty
items), therefore, are phrased as disputes or in a semblance
thereof. We may accordingly say that the earliest level of the
corpus consists of highly formalized legal items.

The thirty-eight disputes in M.-Tos. are carefully formulated.
They exhibit features found in the best constructed items in this
form, the disputes of the Houses.[4] First, thirty-seven of the
items are true disputes, for in these instances the opinions respond to a common problem and to each other. The one exception is
M. Kel. 11:4. Second, thirty-one of these units of tradition (the
exceptions are: M. Ter. 4:5, M. M.S. 2:9, M. Naz. 5:5, Tos. Kel.
B.M. 7:2, M. Par. 1:3, Tos. Nid. 5:9, M. Peah 3:6) contain only
two opposing opinions. Third, in only two disputes (Tos. Kel.
B.M. 7:2, Tos. Nid. 5:9), Tarfon disagrees with an Ushan. In the
former, however, the opinion attributed to Tarfon also opposes a
ruling assigned to Aqiva. Fourth, as the following charts indicate, mnemonic elements (e.g., balanced or similarly formulated
opinions, fixed opposites) are found in two-thirds of the materials.[5] In a number of disputes the names of the disputants consistently are in the same order, a further highly stylized trait
of these materials. (In Fig. 4 we list those items which contain

mnemonic elements and in Fig. 5 those in which they are not present. We note these features as well as the order of the names of
the disputants.)

Fig. 4. Disputes with Mnemonic Elements

Pericope	Element	Order of Names
1. M. Kil. 5:8	+/-	Tarfon, sages
2. Tos. Kil. 3:16	+/-	Tarfon, sages
3. M. M.S. 2:4	balanced rulings	Tarfon, sages
4. M. Suk. 3:4	two vs. three	Ishmael, Tarfon (Aqiva)
5. M. Ket. 5:2	KL vs. MḤŠH	Tarfon, Aqiva
6. M. Ket. 9:2-3	balanced rulings	Tarfon, Aqiva
7. M. B.Q. 2:5	KL vs. ḤṢY	Tarfon, sages
8. Tos. B.Q. 5:12	liable/exempt	Tarfon, Aqiva
9. M. B.M. 2:7	+/-	Tarfon, Aqiva
10. M. Bekh. 2:9	similar formulation	Tarfon, Aqiva
11. M. Kel. 11:7	clean/unclean	Tarfon, sages
12. M. Ohol. 13:3	fist vs. handbreadth	Aqiva, Tarfon
13. Tos. Miq. 1:16-19	clean/unclean	Tarfon, Aqiva
14. M. Maks. 5:4	+/-	Tarfon, Aqiva
15. M. Yad. 4:3	balanced rulings	Tarfon, Eleazar
16. M. Naz. 5:5	all vs. none	Houses, Tarfon
17. Tos. Kel. B.M. 7:2	balanced rulings	Tarfon, Aqiva, Judah, Yose
18. Tos. Sot. 1:10	KL ḤWŠ MN vs. 'P ZW	Tarfon, Aqiva
19. M. Zev. 11:7	KL vs. 'D	Tarfon, sages
20. M. Men. 12:5	+/-	Aqiva, Tarfon
21. M. Ter. 9:2	x and y vs. only x	anonymous law, Tarfon (Aqiva)
22. Tos. Suk. 2:8	gloss with b, four vs. five	anon. law, Tarfon
23. M. Kel. 25:7	similar formulation	Tarfon, Aqiva
24. M. Miq. 10:5	balanced rulings	anon. law, Tarfon

Fig. 5. Disputes without Mnemonic Elements

1.	M. Ma. 3:9	Tarfon, Aqiva
2.	M. Pes. 10:6	Tarfon, Aqiva
3.	M. Yev. 15:6-7	Tarfon, Aqiva
4.	M. Bekh. 2:6-8	Tarfon, Aqiva
5.	M. Kel. 11:4	Joshua, Tarfon
6.	M. Ter. 4:5	Eliezer, Ishmael, Tarfon + Aqiva
7.	M. M.S. 2:9	Houses, Aqiva, they made argument Tarfon, Shammai
8.	M. Par. 1:3	Tarfon, Ben Azzai, Ishmael
9.	Tos. Nid. 5:9	Meir, Judah + Tarfon, Yose + Simeon
10.	M. Peah 3:6	Eliezer, Joshua, Tarfon, Judah b. Bathyra, Aqiva
11.	M. Ber. 6:8	anonymous law, Tarfon
12.	M. Ohal. 16:1	anonymous, Tarfon, Aqiva

Twenty-four of thirty-six items (two-thirds) are formulated to
facilitate memorization. This figure is lower than that for the
Houses' disputes (98%). The strictness of the formulation of the
dispute thus has loosened, a finding reached in studies of the corpora of other Yavnean masters, as well as in those of the Order of
Purities.[6]

Of the twenty-four items that are neatly balanced, fourteen
are disputes between Tarfon and Aqiva, six between Tarfon and
sages. In both of these groups of disputes, the names of the authorities consistently appear in the same order. Tarfon's ruling
precedes that of Aqiva, in all but two of the units of tradition:
M. Ohal. 13:3 (for which there is contrary evidence), and M. Men.
12:5. The same pattern is present in their four disputes that
lack balance. Similarly, Tarfon's opinion comes before that of
sages in all six of their disputes. Disputes between Tarfon and
authorities other than sages and Aqiva generally lack balance.
Only M. Yad. 4:3 (Tarfon vs. Eleazar) and M. Naz. 5:5 (Tarfon vs.
Houses) contain balanced dicta. There is also no pattern to the
order of the names in these other disputes. There thus is a quali-
tative difference between the disputes of Tarfon and masters other
than Aqiva and sages, and those in which Tarfon disagrees with these
latter authorities. Furthermore, as the following summary indicates, there is also a quantitative difference between the disputes
of Tarfon and Aqiva and Tarfon and sages, and those containing rulings of masters other than Aqiva.[7] (In Fig. 6 we note the number
of times opinions attributed to the various authorities appear in
disputes with dicta assigned to Tarfon.)

Fig. 6. Frequency of Appearance of Masters in Disputes with Tarfon

Aqiva	24
Sages	6
Ishmael	4
Joshua	3
Eliezer	2
Houses	2
Eleazar	1
Judah b. Bathyra	1
Shammai	1
They made argument	1
Ben Azzai	1
Judah	1
Yose	1
Simeon	1
Meir	1

Aqiva appears in disputes with Tarfon four and one-half more times
than does Ishmael, the next most frequently cited master. The figures for authorities other than Aqiva are even misleading, for half
(five of ten: M. Suk. 3:4, M. Ter. 4:5, M. Peah 3:6, M. M.S. 2:9, Tos.
Kel. B.M. 7:2) of their disputes with Tarfon contain as well an opinion attributed to Aqiva. Only in M. Par. 1:3 (Ben Azzai, Ishmael),
M. Naz. 5:5 (Houses), M. Kel. 11:4 (Joshua), M. Yad. 4:3 (Eleazar)

and Tos. Nid. 5:9 (Meir, Yose, Simeon) do authorities other than
Aqiva disagree with Tarfon. By contrast to the number of disputes
between Tarfon and Aqiva, in four (M. Shab. 2:2 [Ishmael, sages],
Tos. Shab. 13:5 [Yose, Ishmael], M. Ber. 1:3 [Houses], M. Qid.
3:13 [Eliezer]), of the five instances of juxtaposed independent
sayings an opinion of a master other than Aqiva is placed with
Tarfon's dictum. Only in M. Ker. 5:2-3 has Aqiva's saying been
juxtaposed with a view assigned to Tarfon. From the above data we
see that at some point in the transmission of Tarfon's dicta, someone brought a sizeable portion of them together with rulings attributed to Aqiva and formulated these materials in a highly disciplined and formalized manner.

     An examination of the formulation of these items indicates
that Aqivan circles are responsible for their construction. The
wording of a number of the disputes favors Aqiva. This strongly
suggests that they are the products of circles for whom his opinion is normative. In three traditions (M. Yev. 15:6-7, M. Ket.
9:2-3 and Tos. Soṭ. 1:10), Aqiva's saying responds to that of Tarfon, giving the former the final say. In the three debates between these masters found in M.-Tos. (Tos. Miq. 1:16-19, Tos. Maks.
2:14 [M. Maks. 5:4] and M. Men. 12:5), Tarfon is not an equal partner. For example, in Tos. Miq. 1:16-19 Aqiva is assigned two arguments in support of his analogy, while none is attributed to Tarfon.
Tarfon's contention in Tos. Maks. 2:14 and in M. Men. 12:5 sets up
Aqiva's justification of his own opinion. In two pericopae (M.
Naz. 6:6 and Tos. Zev. 1:8), Tarfon serves as a literary device
for explicating rulings of Aqiva. Similarly, Aqivans have reworked
M. Ohal. 16:1 so that in its present formulation Tarfon's comment
points out a problem which Aqiva then solves. M. Ter. 9:2 also
seems to have been tampered with by Aqivans. This pericope consists of a well-formulated dispute between the anonymous law and
Tarfon, and an appended comment attributed to Aqiva which tries to
show that Tarfon's view leads to an absurd position. In the case
of all ten of the above disputes favorable to Aqiva, we may conclude that they derive from his and not Tarfon's circles of disciples. These ten items provide a basis for identifying the circle
of formulators responsible for the remaining disputes of Tarfon
and Aqiva. Since the formal traits of these ten units of tradition and those of the other Tarfon-Aqivan materials are the same,
specifically, the order of the names and the preference for well-
balanced, highly formalized apodoses, both these segments of the
disputes are the products of the same pro-Aqivan formulary process.

In M.-Tos. Aqiva appears in a significant number of legal
disputes with four other masters: Ishmael (twenty-six items),
Eliezer (twenty-three), Yose (sixteen), and Joshua (eleven).
The formal characteristics of these four groups of disputes, as
well as those of Tarfon and Aqiva, are essentially identical.
In all cases there is a propensity to place Aqiva's name last
and to construct well-balanced lemmas. Aqiva's ruling follows
Tarfon's in 92% of their units of tradition (twenty-two of
twenty-four; exceptions are: M. Ohal. 13:3, M. Men. 12:5);
Ishmael's in 85% (twenty-two of twenty-six; exceptions: M. Ber.
7:3, Tos. Meg. 3:11, M. Ohal. 3:5, M. B.M. 6:4); Eliezer's in 87%
(twenty of twenty-three; exceptions: M. Par. 2:5, M. Ber. 5:2,
M. Pes. 9:2); Yose's in 88% (fourteen of sixteen; exceptions:
Tos. Sheq. 1:7 and M. Ḥul. 8:4); and Joshua's in 91% (ten of
eleven; exception: M. Yev. 4:13). In each instance approximately
60% of the disputes contain balanced dicta: Tarfon 58% (fourteen
of twenty-four), Ishmael 61% (sixteen of twenty-six), Eliezer 65%
(fifteen of twenty-three), Yose 63% (ten of sixteen), Joshua 55%
(six of eleven).[8] By contrast, in all of the corpora except
Yose's, there are few juxtaposed independent sayings in the semblance of a dispute; one each in Tarfon's (M. Ker. 5:2-3) and
Joshua's (M. Shev. 1:8), two each in Eliezer's (M. Ber. 4:3, M.
Shab. 19:1), and Ishmael's (M. Bekh. 6:6, M. Kel. 2:2), five in
Yose's (M. Ḥul. 8:4, M. Ber. 7:3, M. A.Z. 3:5, Tos. Men. 10:12
and Tos. Par. 12:17). Furthermore, as in the Tarfon-material, the
wording of these other masters' pericopae often favors Aqiva.
M. Peah 7:7, M. Yev. 12:3, M. Me. 11:2, Tos. R.H. 2:10, M. Ned.
10:6 highlight Aqiva's and not Eliezer's ruling. M. Pes. 7:1,
Tos. Sheq. 1:7, M. Ber. 7:3, M. A.Z. 3:5 and Tos. Men. 10:12 focus
upon Aqiva and not Yose. The above data strongly suggest that the
same pro-Aqivan process of formulation lies behind all of these
groups of disputes.

The formal traits of the Aqivan disputes are also found in
the two other large corpora of disputes involving Yavneans (Eliezer
vs. Joshua) and pre-Yavneans (the Houses). In both of these instances there is a consistent pattern to the order of the names:
Eliezer, Joshua (seventy of seventy-four items [95%]; exceptions:
Tos. Zev. 1:1, Tos. Ed. 3:1, M. Ed. 6:2, M. Ed. 7:6); House of
Shammai, House of Hillel (two hundred and nineteen of two hundred
and twenty-seven [96%[9]]). The lemmas in 67%[10] of the disputes
(fifty of seventy-four) between Eliezer and Joshua, and in 98%[11]

of the Houses' disputes are balanced. The presence of the same
types of features in all three groups of disputes (the Aqivan, the
Houses', and those of Joshua and Eliezer) suggests that they all
are the products of the same formulary process; a process that may
be characterized as pro-Hillelite, pro-Joshua, and pro-Aqivan.[12]

Units of tradition assigned to Tarfon other than the dispute
also have passed through Aqivan hands. Two independent sayings
(Tos. Shev. 5:12 and Tos. Ḥul. 3:7), according to their attributive formula, were recited before Aqiva by Judah b. Isaiah the
spicemaker. We may assume that they owe their preservation to
Aqivan circles. Furthermore, one *ma'aseh* (M. Bekh. 4:4), to be
discussed below, has passed through Aqivan hands.

By use of "chains of tradition" we may isolate other stemma
of the corpus, other groups responsible for the materials. A chain
of tradition, an attributive formula such as, "R. X says in the
name of R. Y," pretends to relate that the first authority, R. X,
transmits the words of the second, and usually earlier master,
R. Y. Now an attributive chain is no more reliable than any other
attribution. But we may use chains for what they purport to be,
that is, as tradental evidence. We assume merely that materials
for which R. X is the alleged tradent are the products of circles
of that master.

Three sayings, first appearing in M.-Tos., have chains indicating that they are the products of the circle of Judah. All
three dicta are in disputes. They are the following:

1. *Tos. Nez. 3:19/M. Naz. 5:5*
   Tarfon appears in M. in a tripartite dispute with
   the Houses. In Tos., Judah is the tradent for a
   glossed version of his saying. The opinions are
   carefully formulated, using mnemonic elements.

2. *Tos. Miq. 7:3/M. Miq. 10:5*
   M. contains two disputes, one between an anonymous
   law and Judah, the second between an anonymous law
   and Tarfon. The pericopae have been formulated as
   a unit, for the opposing balanced apodoses in the
   two disputes are identical. Tos. gives a glossed
   version of Judah's saying and adds his name as the
   tradent for Tarfon's dictum.

3. *Tos. Nid. 5:9/M. Nid. 4:5*
   M. contains a dispute among Meir, Judah, and Simeon.
   Tos. glosses the rulings and assigns Judah's opinion
   to Tarfon, with Judah serving as the tradent.

In these three similar units of tradition, Tos. glosses M. and has
Judah as the tradent for Tarfon's opinion. The opposing dicta in
the first two of these disputes are balanced. Three items do not

allow us to establish a Judah-stemma of the corpus. But we see
below that a significant portion of the narratives are products of
his circle. This stemma will be discussed below in greater detail
when we introduce this other evidence. We presently note that,
like Tarfon's materials, those of Eliezer are the products of two
distinct circles, the Aqivan and that of Judah. The former tends
to cast dicta into disputes. Aqiva rarely is the tradent in a
standard chain of tradition. On the other hand, chains are the
distinguishing characteristic of Judah-tradents.[13]

One further saying in M.-Tos. (Tos. Par. 11:5) has an attributive chain. This dictum, the tradent of which is Eleazar, has
not been placed in a dispute. (M. does contain rulings on the
matter dealt with in this saying.) Without further evidence we
cannot postulate that Eleazar's circles had a significant role in
the formulation and transmission of Tarfon-materials.

One final aspect of the Tarfon-sayings, their relationship to
their larger redactional contexts, remains to be explored. We
want to know whether the syntax or the word choices of these sayings correspond to those of their larger redactional settings, or
whether the sayings, on formal grounds, do not belong to larger
complexes of traditions. We limit our discussion to the items in
M., for Tos. does not consist of large blocks of similarly formulated materials.[14] In any case, 70% (thirty-five of fifty) of the
sayings appear in M. The following chart (Fig. 7) presents the
results of our analysis. Items marked with an asterisk stand
apart from their redactional contexts.

Fig. 7. Relationship of Units of Tradition to Redactional Context

Disputes

1.	M. Kil. 5:8	Part of a unit consisting of two other similarly formulated items: crop-- +/- diverse kinds in a vineyard. Chapter One of M. Kil. uses the identical pattern for diverse kinds among crops.
2.	M. Ma. 3:9	Protasis has same pattern as those of 3:8-10. All the apodoses use third person singular present participles; severe apocopation.
3.	M.S. 2:4	The protases of M. 2:3-6 have the same pattern: X of second-tithe (that + niph'al perfect).
4.	M. Pes. 10:6	A gloss of a Houses' dispute serves as the superscription for this dispute. The superscription of the Houses' dispute presupposes the conclusion of M. 10:5.
*5.	M. Suk. 3:4	Inserted into M. 3:1-3 + 5.

6. M. Yev. 15:6-7   15:1-16:2, a major unit of tradition.
                           Use complex protases beginning with the
                           words "he who" and have same key words;
                           simple sentences.

7. M. Ket. 5:2   Dispute glosses anonymous law of 5:2.
                           The latter belongs to the larger unit
                           5:1-3; simple sentences. The apodoses
                           of the dispute, like 5:1-3, use present
                           participles.

*8. M. Ket. 9:2-3   Glossed internally and thereby joined
                           to the larger setting.

9. M. B.Q. 2:5   Apodoses same as those of M. 1:5-2:6:
                           complete damage vs. half damages; severe
                           apocopation throughout the unit.

10. M. B.M. 2:7   Gloss of the anonymous law of 2:7 serves
                           as the protasis for this dispute. 2:7-8
                           are similarly formulated, simple sen-
                           tences.

11. M. Bekh. 2:6-8   The disputes are inserted into a major
                           unit of anonymous law. M. Bekh. 1:3-4
                           and 8:3-6 parallel the latter. 2:1,4-8:
                           mild apocopation.

12. M. Bekh. 2:9   Formulated with the preceding item.
                           Parallels M. 8:2.

13. M. Kel. 11:4   Protasis has same formulary pattern as
                           the rest of the chapter: name of an ob-
                           ject. Tarfon's ruling is a simple sen-
                           tence like those in the remainder of the
                           chapter.

14. M. Kel. 11:7   Same formulation as chapter: name of
                           object--clean/unclean.

15. M. Ohal. 13:3   Same formulation as disputes in its
                           context 13:1-4: object--fist vs. square
                           handbreadth; simple sentences.

16. M. Maks. 5:4   Uses apodoses found throughout Maks. +/-
                           if water be put on. Like 5:1-2,4-6, it
                           is in the "he-who-it is" pattern of
                           apocopation.

*17. M. Yad. 4:3   Joined to larger context by "on that day."
                           It is, however, a major unit of tradition
                           consisting of several discrete items.

18. M. Ter. 4:5   Same formulation as 4:1-5: simple sen-
                           tences opening with "he who."

19. M. M.S. 2:9   M. 2:7-10 is a major unit. The pericopae
                           share the same key word, *sela*, and all
                           are simple sentences.

20. M. Naz. 5:5   Has same apodoses as 5:4-7, protasis
                           similar to that of 5:7.

21. M. Par. 1:3   The anonymous law which serves as the
                           statement of the problem for this dispute
                           is part of its larger context, Ch. 1;
                           simple sentences.

22. M. Peah 3:6   M. 3:2-6 all are simple declarative
                           sentences.

23. M. Zev. 11:7	M. 11:6 supplies the protasis for this dispute. The rulings contain same key words found in remainder of 11:7 and in 11:8, "cooked in it." 11:4-7 are simple sentences.
24. M. Men. 12:5	12:3-13:10, a major unit consisting of simple, declarative sentences.
25. M. Ber. 6:8	Remainder of 6:8, as well as 6:2,5-6, are simple, declarative sentences.
26. M. Ter. 9:2	The anonymous law with which Tarfon disagrees belongs to the major unit, 9:1-3. Entire chapter is composed of simple declarative sentences.
27. M. Kel. 25:7	The anonymous law, which is glossed, has the same formulation as rest of chapter, simple sentences.
28. M. Ohal. 16:1	Uses same key words found in M. Ohal. 15:10-16:2, and like them is a simple sentence.
29. M. Miq. 10:5	Formulated with 10:5a, a dispute between Judah and an anonymous law. 10:1 and 10:5 have same protasis.
30. M. Naz. 6:6	Same formulation as 6:7. The latter consists of a dispute between Judah and Eleazar

Juxtaposed independent sayings

31. M. Shab. 2:2	M. Shab. 2:1-3 all use the construction: +/- they light with x. Entire chapter consists of simple declarative sentences.
*32. M. Qid. 3:13	This saying has been glossed and thereby juxtaposed with a ruling of Eliezer. Does not share formal traits of the chapter.
*33. M. Ker. 5:2-3	The saying has been juxtaposed with a dispute between Aqiva and sages. The remainder of the chapter shares the formal characteristics of this dispute, simple sentences.
*34. M. Ber. 1:3	Same key words as are in the larger unit in which this first person saying appears. It however is cast in a different formulary pattern.

Gloss

35. M. Ket. 7:6	The anonymous law which Tarfon's saying glosses uses same key words as are found in the redactional context. 7:1-6 simple declarative sentences.

The formulation of 83% of the sayings in M. (twenty-nine of thirty-five items) corresponds to that of their larger contexts. In most cases (the exceptions are Nos. 1, 10, 29) the context is an entire chapter or a significant portion thereof. The sayings,

therefore, have been formulated within the mainstream of M.'s
redactional process.[15]

*Summary of sayings in M.-Tos. and comparisons with those
first appearing in later strata:* The formal traits of the sayings
first found in M.-Tos. suggest that their attribution to Tarfon is
not random. A limited number of features and patterns can be discerned in these items: the predilection to formulate the dicta in
highly formalized and well-constructed disputes, the centrality of
Aqiva and the virtual absence of other authorities, the formulation
of the disputes (in some cases by pro-Aqivan circles), as well as
the other sayings within the mainstream of the mishnaic redactional
process. In light of the consistent use of these features, we conclude that the sayings in M.-Tos. constitute a formally coherent
tradition. The legal sayings first found in the later strata of
the corpus have the same traits. Figure 2 (above, p. 327) indicates that a majority, 57% (eight of fourteen), of the sayings are
in the dispute form.[16] As the following chart (Fig. 8) shows, the
traits of these disputes are similar to those of the disputes of
the earliest stratum, M.-Tos. (We divide the disputes by strata,
and note the order of the masters and any mnemonic elements.)

Fig. 8. Legal Disputes First Appearing in Strata II-IV

II (halakhic midrashim)

1. Sifre Num. 148	Anonymous law + gloss of Tarfon + Judah b. Naḥman	Gloss in the form of an argument, same key words as the anonymous law

III (beraitot)

1. y. Suk. 3:1	Tarfon, Aqiva	balanced
2. b. R.H. 25b	Tarfon, Aqiva	KL vs. MḤSH
3. b. Qid. 24b	Simeon, Meir, Eleazar, Tarfon, Aqiva	+/-
4. y. Pes. 7:1	Tarfon, Ishmael	poorly preserved
5. y. Demai 3:4	Anonymous law, Simeon in the name of Tarfon	not balanced

IV (amoraic)

1. y. Soṭ. 6:2	Tarfon, Aqiva	+/-
2. y. Naz. 3:5	Tarfon, Aqiva	liable/exempt

Five of these eight items contain an opposing opinion attributed to
Aqiva. All five have mnemonic elements, and in all five, Tarfon's
name comes first. Other masters appear only once in the disputes
first found in later strata. The formal characteristics of the

disputes first found in M.-Tos. thus are also present in the items
cast in this form that surface only in later strata.[17]

The Narratives

Four types of narratives together account for 39% of the
corpus: (1) the *ma'aseh*, (2) the homiletical story, (3) the saying
or dialogue set in a stereotyped narrative framework, and (4) the
allusion. These categories, as our definitions indicate, vary in
their degree of formal discipline. We catalogue and discuss each
type of story separately.

A. The *Ma'aseh*

The *ma'aseh* is the most disciplined of all types of narratives.
A *ma'aseh* is a narrative consisting of three literary elements, a
brief statement of the setting, a subject, a description of his action or his ruling.[18] It is generally introduced by the formula
M'SH (B, W, or Š). The order of the three literary elements varies. The most common pattern is *setting + subject + action or
ruling*. The setting details a specific set of operative conditions, e.g., a rainy Sabbath (Tos. Shab. 5:13), mourners on a festival (Tos. Ḥag. 2:13), or a specific question (untithed crops
mixed with already tithed crops; Tos. Demai 5:22) that presents
the occasion for Tarfon's decision or action. Without these operative conditions, Tarfon's action or ruling is unintelligible. To
put it differently, one cannot state the message of the story without mentioning the specific operative conditions. *Ma'asim* contain
no more dialogue than a question (= setting) and a response.
Opinions attributed to masters other than Tarfon are not included.
If other characters do appear, they serve as literary devices to
accentuate Tarfon. The purpose of the *ma'aseh* is to report Tarfon's authoritative action or decision from which one may derive
a specific rule for conduct.

Five items not catalogued with the *ma'asim* are introduced by
the formula M'SH: Tos. Miq. 1:16-19, Tos. Miq. 7:11, Tos. Ber. 4:
16-18, Tos. Ḥag. 3:33, and Midrash Mishlé 9). I omit the first two
items (Tos. Miq. 1:16-19 and Tos. Miq. 7:10) because in these instances a dispute which is intelligible on its own has had the
structure of the *ma'aseh* imposed upon it. In the case of Tos. Ber.
4:16-18 and Tos. Ḥag. 3:33, a saying attributed to Tarfon that is
intelligible on its own, appears within the framework of a *ma'aseh*.
Finally, Midrash Mishlé 9 is a homily. Parallel versions of this

tradition (Sifre Deut. 38 and Mekh. Simeon Ex. 18:12) lack the
formula M'SH. The structure of each of the above items differs
from those listed in the following catalogue; therefore, I do not
classify them as *ma'asim*.

One non-legal and seventeen legal units of tradition are
formulated as *ma'asim*. In our descriptions of these items we list
their literary elements and, in parentheses, give more detailed
substantive information. We also note the function the unit of
tradition serves in its context.

1. Tos. Demai 5:22--Said Simeon Shezuri + M'SH Š + setting (came
    to ask Tarfon) + subject + Tarfon's advice, re: untithed
    crops mixed with tithed crops.

2. Tos. Shev. 4:4--Said Judah + M'SH W + setting (Judah and
    others ate arum) + on the authority of Tarfon. A challenge
    attributed to Yose questions Judah's presentation of the
    facts. This M'SH serves as a precedent for Judah's opinion
    in M. Shev. 5:5, which deals with eating arum at the end of
    the Sabbatical year. The clause about Tarfon was probably
    inserted when the M'SH was joined to Judah's opinion.

3. Tos. Shab. 5:13--Said Judah + M'SH B + Tarfon + action +
    setting. The M'SH contains several unnecessary details, re:
    wearing linen on the Sabbath.

4. M. Eruv. 4:4--Said Judah + M'SH HYH W + action + Tarfon +
    incomplete setting. The M'SH is cryptic, as the context sup-
    plies the setting. It serves as a precedent for Judah's
    opinion in the dispute between him and Meir. It has been
    formulated together with that dispute.

5. M. Beṣ. 3:5--M'SH W + setting (they asked Tarfon about x and
    he went into *Bet Midrash*) + subject (they said to him) +
    ruling. The M'SH, which deals with the subject of *muqṣeh*,
    serves as an illustration for the anonymous law preceding it.
    It, however, was originally formulated independent of the
    anonymous law.

6. M. Ta. 3:9--M'SH Š + setting (decreed a fast for rain) + said
    to them Tarfon + ruling + gloss detailing adherence to Tar-
    fon's view. The M'SH serves as an illustration for Eliezer's
    ruling presented in the first part of this *mishnah*.

7. Tos. Meg. 2:8--Said R. Judah + setting (while a minor, Judah
    read the *megillah* before Tarfon) + Tarfon's reaction; a prece-
    dent for Judah's opinion in M. Meg. 2:4.

8. Tos. Ḥag. 2:13--M'SH Š + setting (came to eulogize on a festi-
    val) + said to them Tarfon + ruling.

9. Tos. Yev. 12:15--Said Judah + (Vienna: M'SH W) (first ed.:
    M'SH, E: One time) + setting (*ḥaliṣah*-ceremony) + Tarfon said
    + ruling; precedent for Judah's opinion in preceding part of
    the pericope.

10. Tos. Yev. 14:10--M'SH B + setting (witness testifies in behalf
    of woman that her husband has died) + action of Tarfon. The
    M'SH has been expanded by its assimilation to one found in the
    pericope preceding it. Precedent for opinion attributed to
    Tarfon and to Aqiva in a dispute with an anonymous law.

11. Tos. Ket. 5:1H--Said R. Menaḥem b. Nappaḥ in name of Liezer
     the Qaphar + M'SH B + Tarfon + action (betrothed woman) +
     operative conditions = setting.

12. M. Ned. 6:6--Said Judah + M'SH W + Tarfon + ruling. The M'SH
     lacks a statement of the operative conditions. M. Ned. 6:6
     is not its proper context, but it has been inserted here as a
     precedent for Judah's ruling relating to vows to abstain from
     meat.

13. M. Bekh. 4:4--M'SH B + setting (cow without a womb brought
     before Tarfon) + Tarfon's action + setting (brought before
     sages) + sages' action. The M'SH deals with the fitness of
     a cow without a womb. Aqivan redactors use it to illustrate
     the law that an expert who errs need not pay a fine.

14. Tos. Bekh. 5:6-7--Said Judah + M'SH + incomplete setting (man
     came to Tarfon) + Tarfon + saying. The M'SH is cryptic. The
     context supplies the remainder of the setting; a man with
     extra digits came to Tarfon. Yose disagrees with Judah's
     version of Tarfon's saying.

15. b. Shab. 29b--Said Judah + setting (on the Sabbath used an
     eggshell as a lamp) + Tarfon's reaction. This story serves
     as a precedent for Judah's opinion in M. Shab. 2:4 (Tos.
     Shab. 2:5). In Tos. the story lacks Tarfon's name. It prob-
     ably has been added to b.'s version of the tradition.

16. y. Yev. 4:11--M'SH Š + setting (in cemetery for the burial of
     his wife) + Tarfon's action (proposed to his sister-in-law) +
     gloss; illustration for preceding anonymous law.

17. b. Bekh. 11a--Setting (Judah Nesiah sent a first born ass to
     Tarfon and asked about its redemption price) + Tarfon's
     answer.

18. ARN A 41--M'SH B + setting (Tarfon teaching students and a
     bride passed by) + Tarfon's directives.

Fourteen (Nos. 1-14) of the seventeen *ma'asim* with legal content first appear in M.-Tos. Of the remaining three legal *ma'asim*,
one is a baraita (b. Shab. 29b); two, Nos. 16-17, first occur in
amoraic materials. The one non-legal *ma'aseh* (No. 18) is found in
ARN, a document belonging to stratum V. In the following analysis
we focus upon the fourteen items in M.-Tos., our best data. These
ma'asim are so succinctly formulated that the focus clearly is upon
Tarfon. The setting in nine instances (Tos. Shab. 5:13, M. Eruv.
4:4, M. Ta. 3:9, Tos. Ḥag. 2:13, Tos. Yev. 12:15, Tos. Yev. 14:10,
Tos. Ket. 5:1H, M. Ned. 6:6, M. Bekh. 4:4) consists of a brief·
clause or sentence detailing the specific time, place, or other
operative conditions in which Tarfon is alleged to have ruled or
acted. In three cases a problem posed to Tarfon constitutes the
setting (Tos. Demai 5:22, M. Beṣ. 3:5 and M. Bekh. 4:4). In the
two remaining *ma'asim*, someone acts with Tarfon's approval (Tos.
Meg. 2:8, Tos. Shev. 4:4). The only authorities mentioned in all
of these items are Tarfon and the person who either asks the question of Tarfon (Tos. Demai 5:22), or who is told by him how to act

(Tos. Yev. 12:15, M. Ned. 6:6, Tos. Meg. 2:8 and Tos. Shev. 4:4).
Twelve of the fourteen items contain only rulings assigned to
Tarfon.   (The two exceptions, M. Beṣ. 3:5 and M. Bekh. 4:4 are
discussed below.)   The intent of the *ma'aseh* clearly is to report
Tarfon's view on a particular problem.   The premise of these stories is that his actions are distinctive to him and are prescriptive,
and are not merely pious deeds.   These stories, therefore, are in
essence equivalent to dicta assigned to Tarfon.   By contrast, as
we shall see below, homilies do not focus upon Tarfon, do not contain ideas distinctive to him, and merely report his pious actions.

The purposes of these items in their respective contexts sup-
ports the above observation.[19]   Seven of the *ma'asim* (Tos. Shev.
4:4 [to which Tarfon's name may have been added], M. Eruv. 4:4,
Tos. Meg. 2:8, Tos. Yev. 12:15, Tos. Yev. 14:10, M. Ned. 6:6 and
Tos. Bekh. 5:6-7) function as precedents for opinions attributed
to other masters; in all instances but Tos. Yev. 14:10, Judah.
They thus are like dicta introduced by the attributive formula,
"R. Judah says in the name of R. Tarfon."   Four of the stories
(Tos. Ḥag. 2:13, M. Beṣ. 3:5, M. Bekh. 4:4 and M. Ta. 3:9) serve
as illustrations for laws discussed in their contexts.   Finally,
Tos. Demai 5:22, Tos. Shab. 5:13 and Tos. Ket. 5:1H are juxtaposed
with other anonymous or attributed sayings.   In these cases, as
well as when used as precedents and as illustrations, the *ma'asim*
are treated as equivalent to sayings assigned to Tarfon.

Two pericopae (M. Beṣ. 3:5 and M. Bekh. 4:4) are exceptional,
for they also contain rulings of authorities other than Tarfon.
In M. Beṣ. 3:5 Tarfon is asked a question, but instead of answering it, he goes into the *Bet Midrash* where sages rule on the matter.   Perhaps a *ma'aseh* containing a ruling by Tarfon has been reworked when the item was included in the present context as a
precedent in support of the preceding anonymous law.   M. Bekh. 4:4
contains, in addition to Tarfon's opinion, a ruling attributed to
sages.   The contextual function of this item accounts for the inclusion of this second opinion.   Aqivans utilize this *ma'aseh* to
teach that an expert who errs need not pay a fine.   With the addition of the "correct" ruling assigned to sages, and therefore with
the breakdown of the structure of the *ma'aseh*, Tarfon can play the
role of the sage who rules incorrectly.   Similarly, Tos. Miq. 1:
16-19 shows the effects of Aqivan hands upon the structure of the
ma'aseh.   In this pericope a dispute and debate appear within a
narrative setting.   The entire unit opens with a storyline introduced by the formula M'SH B.   It is the only other narrative unit

of tradition about Tarfon, using this formula, that contains a
ruling contrary to his. The two items that place a dispute within
the structure of the *ma'aseh* thus are products of Aqivan circles.

Nine of the *ma'asim* have chains of tradition through which we
may identify the circles responsible for them. Liezer the Qaphar
(Tos. Ket. 5:1H) and Simeon Shezuri (Tos. Demai 5:22) are each the
tradent for one unit of tradition. Judah is the tradent for the
other seven *ma'asim* with chains = 50% of all *ma'asim* that appear
in M.-Tos. (Tos. Shev. 4:4, Tos. Shab. 5:13, M. Eruv. 4:4, Tos.
Meg. 2:8, Tos. Yev. 12:15, M. Ned. 6:6 and Tos. Bekh. 5:6-7). The
circle of Judah, therefore, is responsible for a considerable portion of the Tarfon-corpus, seven *ma'asim* and three sayings. Additionally, Tos. Neg. 8:2 is preceded by the attributive formula,
"R. Judah says." Eleven items (15% of all materials in M.-Tos.)
thus derive from the Judah-circle. This circle for the most part
has not cast Tarfon's materials into disputes. Eight of the
eleven items rather are stories preceded by chains of tradition.

More than half (nine of fourteen) of the *ma'asim* apparently
have been either formulated (Tos. Shev. 4:4, M. Eruv. 4:4, M. Ta.
3:9, Tos. Neg. 2:8, Tos. Yev. 12:15, Tos. Yev. 14:10 and Tos. Shab.
5:13) or reformulated (M. Ned. 6:6, Tos. Bekh. 5:6-7) with the
materials of their redactional contexts. In all these instances,
the *ma'aseh* uses the same key words and deals with the identical
issue as the surrounding pericopae. Furthermore, four are unintelligible without their contexts (M. Eruv. 4:4, Tos. Meg. 2:8,
M. Ned. 6:6 and Tos. Bekh. 5:6-7). Seven of the nine (exceptions
are M. Ta. 3:9, Tos. Yev. 14:10) are preceded by the attributive
formula, "R. Judah says in the name of R. Tarfon," and six of
these items (Tos. Shab. 5:13 is the exception) serve as precedents
for his opinions. It, therefore, seems that materials serving as
precedents for Judah's view take shape within the mainstream redactional process of M.-Tos. By contrast to the above nine *ma'asim*,
five others are formulated independent of their redactional contexts
(Tos. Demai 5:22, M. Beṣ. 3:5, Tos. Ḥag. 2:13, Tos. Yev. 5:1H and M.
Bekh. 4:4).[20] By this we mean that on a primary level they do not
deal with the issues discussed in the surrounding pericopae, and
that they show no evidence of having been formulated with these
other items. These five units of tradition which have no pattern in
terms of their content or redactional functions indicate that redactors of M.-Tos. had before them completed materials which they
then inserted into those documents. Two of these items have chains

of tradition containing names of masters infrequently cited in
M.-Tos. (Tos. Demai 5:22--Simeon Shezuri, and Tos. Ket. 5:1H--
Liezer the Qaphar). This trait of these items coincides with the
fact that they are not formulated within the mainstream of the
mishnaic redactional process.

The formal traits of the *ma'asim* told about Tarfon are very
similar to those of the same type of narrative relating to Gamaliel, the only other master whose corpus consists of a sizeable
portion of *ma'asim*. Twenty of the twenty-eight items dealing with
Gamaliel contain only his ruling. Eighteen of these units of tradition are succinct and consist of a brief setting and no more
dialogue than found in the comparable stories told about Tarfon.[21]
Only M. Ber. 2:5-7, a highly developed unit, and Tos. Suk. 13:11
are composed of a *setting + Gamaliel's action + question by students + Gamaliel's response*. These added elements, the question
and the response, merely increase the tension in the story. Of
the eight *ma'asim* containing rulings besides Gamaliel's, seven
assign this other opinion to Aqiva.[22] The Gamaliel-corpus of
ma'asim, therefore, in this respect also is comparable to the
Tarfon-materials. All of the above observations show that those
responsible for the formulation of the *ma'asim* about these two
masters adhere to the same structural pattern. The utilization
of this same highly formalized schema suggests that, like the disputes, *ma'asim* do not record the *ipsissima verba* of Tarfon.[23]

B. Homiletical Story

A homily is a story from which one may deduce a general principle for action, or that teaches a lesson. But it does not teach
a concrete rule. b. Nid. 61a, which illustrates the principle
that one should not believe rumors, is an example of a homily
articulating a general principle. y. Demai 1:3, which shows that
bad omens (the collapse of the table at the beginning of a meal)
guard the righteous from sin, is an example of a homily that teaches
a lesson. In the case of a particular homily, other stories with
entirely different details can make the same point. For example,
one can tell many stories which indicate that bad omens guard the
righteous from error. The sign does not have to be the collapse
of a table at the beginning of a meal. In this respect homilies
differ from *ma'asim*, for one can convey the message of a *ma'aseh*
only by mentioning the specific operative conditions contained in
its setting. Homilies differ from *ma'asim* also in that Tarfon is

not always their central figure but may serve as the foil for the
articulation of a point by others. Stories of this type have in
common only the use of narration and dialogue. They, however, are
cast in a broad range of structures, e.g., long story, short story,
mostly narration, mostly dialogue, detailed setting, concise
setting.

1. Mekh. Ishmael Baḥodesh 10--KBR HYH + setting (Eliezer sick) +
   Tarfon, Joshua, Eleazar b. Azariah, Aqiva (centrality of the
   rabbi).

2. b. M.Q. 28b--Setting (death of Ishmael's sons) + Tarfon, Yose
   the Galilean, Eleazar b. Azariah, Aqiva (mourn for those who
   perform miṣvot).

3. y. Demai 1:3--Tarfon + setting (Sabbath eve and the table
   fell) + they said to him + he said to them (pernicious signs
   guard the righteous from sin).

4. y. Yoma 8:4--Setting (pregnant women on Yom Kippur) + Tarfon's
   action and saying + response of women + student's exegesis
   (parents' actions determine character of child).

5. b. Ned. 62a--Setting (man found Tarfon in his field) + action
   + said Tarfon + man's reaction (fear of the rabbi).

6. b. Qid. 31b--Story line (Tarfon had a mother) + description of
   Tarfon's action + mother's action (came to Bet Midrash) + they
   said to her + lemma (difficulty of honoring parents).

7. b. Nid. 61a--Setting (suspected murderers came to Tarfon) +
   Tarfon's advice (do not believe rumors).

8. Lev. R. 34:16--Setting (Tarfon gave Aqiva money) + Aqiva's
   action + extended dialogue ending with exegesis (Torah the
   best investment).

9. Midrash Mishlê 9--M'SH HYH + setting (Gamaliel waited on sages)
   + Eleazar b. Azariah, Ishmael, Tarfon, Gamaliel (in order to
   imitate God, one should wait on his fellow human).

Most of the nine homilies first appear in later strata of the
corpus: Nos. 3-7 in amoraic materials, Nos. 8-9 in later compilations. The stories greatly differ from each other in their structures and show little continuity with the materials found in the
earliest stratum, M.-Tos. y. Demai 1:3 and b. Nid. 61a are brief
stories consisting of a concise setting and dialogue or a saying.
b. Qid. 31b has a detailed setting. y. Yoma 8:4 and b. Ned. 62a
are told mostly through narration. Lev. R. 34:16 is a lengthy
narrative containing narration and dialogue. None of the above
items have structural parallels in the traditions in M.-Tos. The
two homilies that occur in earlier strata (Mekh. Ish. Baḥodesh 10
and b. M.Q. 28b), on the other hand, are very similar to Tos. Giṭ.
9:1. In all three instances the illness or death of a sage serves
as the setting for the comments of four masters. The names of the
rabbis are the same in these three items, except for the change of

Yose to Joshua in Mekh. In all the homiletical stories (except
for y. Demai 1:3, b. Ned. 62a, and b. Nid. 61a), Tarfon is not
the central character. Homilies as opposed to *ma'asim*, therefore,
do not usually derive from circles primarily interested in Tarfon.

C. Saying or Dialogue in Stereotyped Narrative Framework

A number of sayings and dialogues which are intelligible on
their own appear in a narrative framework. In these instances the
setting is not integral, for even when it is omitted, the saying is
comprehensible. The setting in most cases is fairly standardized,
e.g., a gathering of sages at the *Bet Midrash* or a discussion between master and disciple. Both legal and non-legal materials
belong in this category.

a. Legal

In the following four legal units of tradition a saying (Nos.
1 and 3) or a dispute (Nos. 2 and 4) which is intelligible on its
own appears within a narrative framework.

1. Tos. Ḥag. 3:33--M'SH B + Tarfon + setting (old man met him) +
   old man said to him + saying + said R. Tarfon + dicta. This
   unit has been glossed so that Tarfon reverses his ruling and
   accepts the criticism of the old man. Tarfon's ruling about
   receiving heave-offering from anyone, which could stand alone,
   disagrees with the anonymous law of Tos. Ḥag. 3:32.

2. Tos. Giṭ. 9:1--Anonymous law + Eliezer permits + gloss + setting (after death of Eliezer) + said Tarfon + said Yose the
   Galilean + Eleazar b. Azariah says + said Aqiva (alt. Aqiva
   says). Responses of Tarfon and Yose are similarly formulated.
   The pericope is an artificial construction. The storyline
   allows the editor to combine different types of material.

3. Tos. Neg. 8:2--Said Judah + setting (went to visit Tarfon) +
   Tarfon said to him + narration + Tarfon said + ruling about
   the cedarwood used in the purification of a leper.

4. Sifre Num. 118--Setting (*Bet Midrash*) + question + answered
   Tarfon + storyline (Yose the Galilean was there) + asked Yose
   + debate + debate between Aqiva and Yose + comment of Ishmael
   re: period for eating a firstling.

b. Non-legal

1. Tos. Ber. 4:16-18--M'SH B + setting + Tarfon says + lemma +
   dialogue between students and Tarfon which contains two exegeses about the merit of the righteous.

2. Sifre Num. 116--KBR + setting (Gamaliel met Tarfon) + dialogue
   between Gamaliel and Tarfon ending with the citation of a verse
   and an exegesis re: eating heave-offering equivalent to performing service in the Temple.

3. b. Ned. 49b--Setting (Judah seated before Tarfon) + said Tarfon
   + Judah said. Story deals with eating habits and regularity.

4. b. Zev. 62b--Setting (Tarfon's nephews seated before him) +
    Tarfon said + exegesis + they said to him + Tarfon's response
    re: proper conduct before a sage.
5. Mid. Ps. 106:3--Verse + setting (students asked Tarfon) +
    question + answers, students give the correct answer re:
    identification of the one who always does righteousness.

Nos. 1 and 2, items in earlier strata, focus upon Tarfon. In
two of the three units of tradition first appearing in later levels
of the corpus (Nos. 3 and 5) Tarfon is not the central character.

D. The Allusion

Some traditions merely allude to Tarfon or refer to what he
regularly did. The point of these stories is not to report historical or biographical information about Tarfon but to teach some
general lesson. When analyzed not in terms of how they use Tarfon's name, most of the non-legal items are not really narratives
but sayings or exegeses (Nos. 2, 3, 4, 7, 8, 9, 10, 11). Tarfon
occupies the central position in three of the four legal items
(Nos. 2-4), but in only one (No. 7) of the eleven non-legal
allusions.

a. Legal

1. Tos. Soṭ. 7:16--Tarfon + observed a lame priest blowing the
    horn. The redactional context supplies the setting for Tar-
    fon's observation.
2. M. B.M. 4:3--Taught Tarfon at Lydda + ruling (re: defrauding)
    + narrative + dialogue + narrative. This story has been jux-
    taposed and formulated with an anonymous law with which it
    disagrees.
3. Tos. Bekh. 6:14--Scenario of anonymous laws (re: procedure for
    the redemption of a human child) + thus R. Tarfon used to do +
    gloss.
4. y. Pes. 10:1--y. glosses Judah's opinion in Tos. Pisḥa 10:4
    about women and children on Passover and adds, "They say Tar-
    fon used to do this"; an illustration of Judah's view.

b. Non-legal

1. Tos. Miq. 7:11--Statement of legal problem + ZH HYH M'SH +
    dispute between Yose the Galilean and Aqiva + glosses + Yose
    said + exegesis + vote + Tarfon recited verses and interpreted
    them.
2. Mekh. Ish. Vayassa 4--KBR HYH + setting (Tarfon and elders
    seated) + said Eleazar of Modin + lemma + they said to him +
    question + he said to them + exegesis about the height of the
    manna. Eleazar's exegesis can stand alone.
3. b. Giṭ. 67a--Issi b. Judah's descriptions of sages: Meir,
    Judah, Tarfon, Ishmael, Aqiva, Yoḥanan b. Nuri, Eleazar b.
    Azariah, Eliezer b. Jacob, Yose, Simeon.

4. y. Yev. 1:6--Dosa said + lemma + he saw Joshua, Aqiva, Eleazar
    b. Azariah (descriptions of each) + said Ḥaninah of Sephoris +
    even Tarfon.

5. b. B.M. 85a--Setting (Rabbi came to town of Tarfon) + story
    about repentance of Tarfon's grandson.

6. b. Nid. 24b--Catalogue of tallest sages.

7. Gen. R. 91:9--Ḥaninah and Marinos say in name of Abba + lemma
    (description of Tarfon's responses to remarks).

8. Lam. R. II 2:4--Verse + exegesis + list of ten martyrs.

9. ARN A 3--Anonymous saying + gloss + verse + exegesis re: serve
    four sages.

10. Midrash Samuel 15:2--Said R. Simeon b. Laqish + lemma re:
    serve sage of your generation.

11. PRE 26--Setting (Joshua b. Qorḥah rehearsed before Tarfon) +
    lemma + verse.

E. Summary of Narratives

        The following chart, in which we summarize the above four
catalogues (listed under letters A-D), shows that the legal and
non-legal narratives are equivalent in number (twenty-five vs.
twenty-six) but differ in that most of the former belong to the
most disciplined type of narrative, the *ma'aseh*, while the latter
are distributed among types of narratives with varied structures,
and which do not focus upon Tarfon.

Fig. 9. Distribution of Legal and Non-legal Narratives by Types

Type	Legal		Non-legal		Total
	%	#	%	#	#
Ma'aseh	68	(17)	4	(1)	18
Homily	0	(0)	35	(9)	9
Narrative framework	16	(4)	19	(5)	9
Allusion	16	(4)	42	(11)	15
TOTAL	100	(25)	100	(26)	51

The legal materials significantly differ from the non-legal items
in terms of the range of narrative types in which they are regularly cast. 68% of the legal materials are in one pattern, the
ma'aseh. The remaining materials are evenly distributed between
sayings in narrative frameworks and allusions. By contrast, only
one non-legal unit of tradition is a *ma'aseh*, while the other
twenty-five non-legal items belong to the other three types of
stories. The latter have varied structures and do not place Tarfon in the central role. The following charts, in which we divide
the legal and non-legal narratives according to the strata in which

they first appear, indicate that most of the tightly formulated
legal materials, the ones that focus upon Tarfon, first surface in
M.-Tos. Almost all the non-legal materials, on the other hand,
first appear in later strata. The Tarfon corpus thus consists of
two different types of narrative materials. Legal items center
upon Tarfon, cite his actions as precedents for specific rules of
conduct, and generally first appear in the earliest levels of the
corpus. The non-legal items use Tarfon's name for that of a sage,
illustrate general principles, and for the most part first surface
in the latest strata. (In the following charts, containing the
figures for the distribution of the materials by strata, raw numbers are read both up and down and across while percentages are
read only across.)

Fig. 10. Legal Stories by Strata

Type	I %	I #	II %	II #	III %	III #	IV %	IV #	Total #
Ma'aseh	82	(14)	0	(0)	6	(1)	12	(2)	17
Narrative framework	75	(3)	25	(1)	0	(0)	0	(0)	4
Allusion	75	(3)	0	(0)	0	(0)	25	(1)	4
TOTAL	80	(20)	4	(1)	4	(1)	12	(3)	25

Fig. 11. Non-legal Stories by Strata

Type	I %	I #	II %	II #	III %	III #	IV %	IV #	V %	V #	Total #
Ma'aseh	0	(0)	0	(0)	0	(0)	0	(0)	100	(1)	1
Homily	0	(0)	11	(1)	11	(1)	56	(5)	22	(2)	9
Narrative framework	20	(1)	20	(1)	0	(0)	40	(2)	20	(1)	5
Allusion	9	(1)	9	(1)	9	(1)	27	(3)	46	(5)	11
TOTAL	8	(2)	11	(3)	8	(2)	38	(10)	35	(9)	26

Fourteen of the seventeen legal *ma'asim* (82%) first appear in
M.-Tos. These fourteen items constitute more than half (fourteen
of twenty-five), 56%, of all narratives with legal content, and
more specifically, 70% (fourteen of twenty) of the legal narratives
in M.-Tos. We therefore have in these items a sizeable sample
(fourteen items) and a significant portion of all the narratives
with legal content. The legal items found in later strata exhibit
the formal preferences of M.-Tos., for three of the five legal
items in strata II-IV are *ma'asim*. Of the non-legal narratives,
only two of twenty-six (8%) first appear in M.-Tos. 27% of the
non-legal items (seven of twenty-six) are found in the first three

strata. These items are evenly distributed among the categories, homilies, saying in narrative frameworks, and allusions. Strata IV and V respectively account for 38% (ten of twenty-six) and 35% (nine of twenty-six) of all non-legal narratives. The majority of the items in the former are homilies, while in the latter, allusions predominate. In both cases Tarfon usually is not the central character in the narrative. All of the above data show that the legal items are more tightly formulated than their non-legal counterparts, that they tend to focus upon Tarfon, and that a significant portion of them, as opposed to the non-legal items, first appear in M.-Tos.

Summary and Comparisons

We begin our summary by dividing the corpus into its various types and patterns and by noting the number and corresponding percentages of legal and non-legal items cast in each of these categories.

Fig. 12. Distribution by Types and Patterns of the Corpus as a Whole

	Legal %	Legal #	Non-legal %	Non-legal #	Total %	Total #
Sayings						
Dispute	52	(46)	10	(4)	39	(50)
Gloss	2	(2)	0	(0)	2	(2)
Independent saying	18	(16)	25	(10)	20	(26)
Narratives						
Ma'aseh	20	(17)	2.5	(1)	14	(18)
Homily	0	(0)	22.5	(9)	7	(9)
Narrative framework	4	(4)	12.5	(5)	7	(9)
Allusion	4	(4)	27.5	(11)	11	(15)
TOTAL	100	(89)	100	(40)	100	(129)

74% of the legal materials are cast in the most disciplined patterns: the dispute, the gloss, and the ma'aseh. Only 18% of the legal units of tradition stand alone as independent sayings. The remaining 8% of the legal items are narratives with varied structures. The figures for the non-legal units of tradition greatly diverge from the above. The majority (62.5%) of these items appear in narratives with varied structures. In these narratives Tarfon often is only one of several characters and does not occupy the central role. 25% of the non-legal items stand alone as independent sayings. Like the narratives, these materials have diverse

formal traits. Only 12.5% of the non-legal units of tradition are
formulated as disputes or as *ma'asim*.

Let us now divide the legal and non-legal items according to
the strata in which they first appear. We see that most of the
former are tightly formulated and are found in the earliest
stratum, M.-Tos. By contrast, the non-legal items, those that do
not focus upon Tarfon, are loosely structured and first surface in
later strata of the corpus. (In Fig. 13 we give the raw numbers
and corresponding percentages for the legal materials. Fig. 14
contains only the raw numbers for the non-legal items. There are
so few items in most strata that percentages are meaningless.)

Fig. 13. Distribution by Strata of Legal Materials

Pattern or Type	I %	I #	II %	II #	III %	III #	IV %	IV #	Total #
Dispute	55	(38)	40	(2)	44	(4)	40	(2)	46
Gloss	3	(2)	0	(0)	0	(0)	0	(0)	2
Independent saying	14	(10)	40	(2)	44	(4)	0	(0)	16
Ma'aseh	20	(14)	0	(0)	12	(1)	40	(2)	17
Narrative framework	4	(3)	20	(1)	0	(0)	0	(0)	4
Allusion	4	(3)	0	(0)	0	(0)	20	(1)	4
TOTAL	100	(70)	100	(5)	100	(9)	100	(5)	89

Fig. 14. Distribution by Strata of Non-legal Materials (Raw Numbers

Pattern or Type	I #	II #	III #	IV #	V #	Total #
Dispute	0	2	2	0	0	4
Independent saying	2	3	0	0	5	10
Ma'aseh	0	0	0	0	1	1
Homily	0	1	1	5	2	9
Narrative framework	1	1	0	2	1	5
Allusion	1	1	1	3	5	11
TOTAL	4	8	4	10	14	40

About 80% (seventy of eighty-nine items) of all legal units
of tradition first appear in M.-Tos. 78% (fifty-four) of these
seventy items are formulated as disputes, glosses, and *ma'asim*. A
comparison between the percentages in Figures 12 and 13 shows that
roughly the same proportion of items formulated as disputes and as
ma'asim in the earliest stratum, M.-Tos., is found in the legal

corpus as a whole. This means that those responsible for the
formulation of the items of strata II-IV adhered to the same preferences as reflected in the items of M.-Tos. The formal consistency and coherence of the legal materials suggest that they constitute a tradition in that they are a body of materials that has
been formulated within the limits of a clearly delineated set of
formal preferences. We cannot say the same about the non-legal
materials. Most of these items are phrased as narratives that
have varied structures. A clearly defined set of formal traits
does not characterize these materials. Nothing indicates that
they have formulated in relationship to each other. They, therefore, do not constitute a tradition in that no persistent pattern
is found throughout this portion of the corpus.

Two final questions regarding the formulation of the Tarfon-
corpus are left to be answered. How do the formal traits of the
Tarfon-materials compare with those of the units of tradition of
other masters? What do these comparisons suggest? We limit our
discussion to the legal units of tradition in M.-Tos. In the
following chart (Fig. 15), we list the percentage of each master's units of tradition that are cast in the various patterns.
(All narratives are recorded together.)

Fig. 15. Distribution by Patterns of Legal Units of Tradition in
         M.-Tos.

Pattern	Tarfon	Houses	Eliezer	Joshua	Ishmael	Gamaliel	Eleazar	Yose
Disputes	55%	85%	91%	60%	44%	42%	34%	49%
Independent sayings	14%	1%	7%	20%	21%	8%	46%	45%
Narratives	28%	2%	2%	5%	8%	49%	19%	2%

Narratives account for a significant proportion of the materials
of only three authorities: Eleazar (19%), Gamaliel (49%), and Tarfon (28%). Few of the legal items assigned to other masters are
phrased in this manner. The narratives about Tarfon, Gamaliel, and
Eleazar are also comparable in that a sizeable portion of these
stories are in each case *ma'asim*. I have no idea why so many of
the Tarfon-traditions are constructed and preserved as narratives.[24]

Studies of the corpora of other masters have shown a correla-
tion between the substance of units of tradition and their form.
Specifically, a large percentage of disputes and a corresponding
small proportion of independent sayings characterize the materials
of those masters whose rulings deal with matters of central concern

to M. This applies to the dicta assigned to the Houses, Eliezer,
and Joshua. Many of the rulings attributed to Eleazar and to
Yose, on the other hand, are formulated and preserved as independent sayings and do not focus upon the primary legal issues of M.
The formal traits of the Tarfon-corpus suggest that his rulings
deal with central concerns of M. We now turn to this matter.

NOTES

CHAPTER IX

[1] Our analysis of the formal traits of these materials is not
form criticism as that term is generally understood. The classical analyses of this sort seek to identify not only types and
forms but also to determine their history. Günkel, Dibelius, and
Bultmann, for example, try to isolate the actual "setting in life"
which has given rise to a particular formal type. The only setting we can identify for the patterns and types found in M.-Tos.
is that of first and second century rabbinism. There is no history in this sense for these patterns, for they are the common
property of all circles. With regard to the attempt of classical
form critics to identify structures with particular "settings in
life," see the remarks of Rolf Knierim ("Old Testament Form Criticism Reconsidered," *Interpretation* 27 [1973] pp. 435-68), J. Arthur
Baird ("Genre Analysis as a Method of Historical Criticism," *SBL
Papers 1972* II, ed. Lane McGaughy [Cambridge, 1972], pp. 395-411),
and William Doty ("The Concept of Genre in Literary Analysis,"
SBL Papers 1972 II, pp. 413-48).
Our analysis differs from many exercises in form criticism
also in the definition of what constitutes a form or a pattern. A
form according to my definition, taken for the most part from Neusner (*HMLP* III, pp. 192-94; *Phar.* III, pp. 5-42; *Eliezer* II, pp.
18-62), is established on the basis of formal and functional criteria. See the remarks of Edwin Redlich (*Form Criticism* [London,
1939], p. 51), Gene Tucker (*Form Criticism of the Old Testament*
[Philadelphia, 1971], p. 12), W. Sibley Towner (*The Rabbinic Enu-
meration of Scriptural Examples* [Leiden, 1973], pp. 29-30), and of
Wolfgang Richter (*Exegese als Literaturwissenschaft* [Göttingen,
1971]) on the use of various criteria for the definition of forms.

[2] The arrangement of words in the case of a form is also not
determined by what is expressed in it. Its literary traits thus
bear no intrinsic relationship to its content.

[3] Neusner (*Phar.* III, pp. 16-23, and *HMLP* III, p. 197) reaches
the same conclusion.

[4] Neusner, *Phar.* III, pp. 5-14, 119-43.

[5] We omit from these lists M. Naz. 6:6 and Tos. Zev. 1:8, the
two units of tradition in which Tarfon's name serves as a literary
device.

[6] See Neusner (*Eliezer* II, p. 34, and *HMLP* III, pp. 196-97), Porton (diss., pp. 318-46), Zahavy (p. 250), and Lightstone (pp. 287-91).

[7] We now include M. Naz. 6:6 and Tos. Zev. 1:8.

[8] The data for these figures are as follows: *Ishmael--balanced*:
M. Peah 4:10, M. Kil. 3:6, Tos. Kil. 2:12, M. Sheq. 4:4, Tos. Ned.
7:6, M. B.B. 3:1, M. Miq. 8:3, M. Neg. 12:3, Tos. Ed. 1:9, M. Suk.
3:4, M. Ber. 7:3, M. Pes. 10:9, Tos. Meg. 3:11, M. Par. 8:11, M.
Ohal. 3:5, Tos. Ker. 2:16; *Ishmael--unbalanced*: M. Kil. 3:3, M.
Ter. 4:5, M. Bekh. 6:6, M. Shab. 15:3, M. Sheq. 4:3, M. Kel. 2:2,
M. Neg. 1:2, M. Nid. 6:12, M. B.B. 6:4, M. Shev. 2:5; *Eliezer--
balanced*: M. Peah 7:7, M. Ter. 6:6, M. Ma. 4:6, M. Kel. 2:1, M.
Shab. 2:3, M. Pes. 9:2, M. Yev. 12:3, M. Ned. 10:6, M. Sot. 9:3-4,
M. Me. 1:2-3, M. Par. 2:5, M. Kel. 28:2, M. Yev. 16:7, M. B.Q. 6:4,
Tos. Maks. 1:4; *Eliezer--unbalanced*: M. Ber. 4:3, M. Ber. 5:2,

M. Sheq. 8:7, M. Yoma 7:3, Tos. R.H. 2:10, M. Sanh. 1:4, M. Ter.
4:8, M. Shab. 19:1; *Yose--balanced*: M. Shev. 4:6, M. Ket. 3:3,
M. Sanh. 10:6, M. Mak. 2:7, M. Hor. 2:5, Tos. Ḥul. 9:14, Tos. Miq.
7:11, M. Pes. 7:1, M. Par. 3:4, M. Nid. 5:8; *Yose--unbalanced*:
Tos. Sheq. 1:7, M. Ḥul. 8:4, M. Ber. 7:3, M. A.Z. 3:5, Tos. Men.
10:12, Tos. Par. 12:17; *Joshua--balanced*: M. Kel. 28:2, M. Nid.
10:3, M. Ned. 10:6, Tos. B.Q. 6:22, M. Yev. 16:7, Tos. Maks. 1:4;
Joshua--unbalanced: M. Ter. 4:8, M. Shev. 1:8, M. Shev. 3:10, M.
Yev. 4:13, M. Peah 3:6.

[9]See Neusner, *Phar.* II, pp. 344-53.

[10]The following are balanced: M. Shev. 5:3, M. Ter. 4:7, M.
Ter. 4:8, M. Ter. 4:11, M. Ter. 8:1,2,3, M. Ter. 11:2, M. Shab.
12:4, M. Shab. 19:1, Tos. Shab. 1:17, M. Pes. 1:7, M. Pes. 6:5,
M. Sheq. 4:7, M. Ta. 1:1, Tos. Ta. 2:5, Tos. Yev. 13:3-5, M. Sot.
1:1, Tos. Pisha 4:5-6, Tos. Zev. 2:16, M. Zev. 7:4, M. Zev. 8:10,
Tos. Men. 2:16, M. Men. 3:4, Tos. Men. 8:19, M. Ker. 4:2-3, Tos.
Zev. 4:1-2, M. Kel. 14:7, M. Kel. 17:1, Tos. Ah. 9:7, M. Ohal.
12:3, M. Ohal. 12:8, M. Ohal. 14:4, M. Par. 10:1, Tos. Par. 10:4,
M. Ṭoh. 2:2, M. Ṭoh. 8:7, M. Miq. 2:3, M. Miq. 2:8, M. Miq. 2:10,
Tos. Nid. 2:3, Tos. Ed. 1:10, Tos. Ed. 3:1, M. Ed. 6:3, M. Ed.
7:6, M. Ned. 10:6, M. Kel. 28:2, M. Nid. 10:3, M. Shev. 9:5,
M. Ter. 8:5. The following are unbalanced: M. Ter. 4:10, M. Orl.
1:7, M. Eruv. 7:10, Tos. Y.Ṭ. 3:2, M. Soṭ. 6:1, M. B.B. 9:7, Tos.
Zev. 1:1, M. Arak. 6:1, M. Ohal. 2:4, M. Ohal. 9:15, M. Ohal. 14:5,
M. Ohal. 17:2, M. Par. 5:4, M. Par. 9:4, Tos. Ah. 7:11, M. Nid.
1:3, M. Nid. 4:4, M. Ed. 6:2, M. Yev. 16:7, M. Yev. 13:7, M. Ket.
1:6, M. Ket. 1:7, M. Ket. 1:8, M. Peah 3:6.

[11]See Neusner, *Phar.* III, pp. 119-43.

[12]Our findings coincide with the results reached on different
grounds by Neusner in study of the Houses' materials. He argues
(*Phar.* III, p. 209) that, since one-third of the Yavnean attestations of the Houses' disputes are Aqivan, "the use of the Houses-
form [= dispute] was limited to Aqivan circles."

[13]Neusner, *Eliezer* II, pp. 120-27, 368-71.

[14]Neusner, *HMLP* XXI, p. 247.

[15]The use of balanced phrases, fixed opposites, and other
highly stylized elements in the apodoses of the disputes suggests
that they do not preserve Tarfon's *ipsissima verba*. The redactional evidence indicates that the same holds true for the sayings
as a whole. Only two phrases found in all of the sayings are
unique to the Tarfon-corpus (not necessarily spoken by Tarfon himself): the formulae, "May I bury my son" (M. Ohal. 16:1, Tos.
Ohal. 15:12, Tos. Shab. 13:5, Tos. Zev. 1:8, Tos. Ḥag. 3:33, and
Sifre Num. 75), and "Anyone who separates himself from you is as
if he separates himself from his life" (Tos. Zev. 1:8, Tos. Miq.
1:19, Sifra Vayiqra' Parashata 4:4, and Sifre Num. 75).

[16]The six legal independent sayings first surfacing in the
later levels of the corpus are not random. Four (Sifre Num. 118,
y. Ḥal. 2:3, y. Meg. 1:8 and b. Men. 45b) of these traditions are
exegetical. By contrast, none of the legal independent sayings
and only one of the disputes in M.-Tos. deal with the interpretation of Scripture. There thus is a pattern to the independent
sayings first found in the later strata; albeit, it is not that of
the materials that first appear in M.-Tos.

The same is true of the non-legal independent sayings. Seven out of eight are exegetical (Mekh. Simeon Ex. 6:2, Mekh. Ish. Vayassa 4, ARN A 6, ARN A 11, Mid. Ps. 7:13, PRE 10, PRE 41). Sifre Zuṭṭa 6:27 is the only non-exegetical, non-legal independent saying.

[17]The sample of non-legal disputes is too small for meaningful discussion--four items (Sifre Deut. 41, Sifra Qodashim 4:9, b. Shab. 25b, b. Qid. 81b). Aqiva is the disputant in the first three of these traditions.

[18]Our characterization agrees for the most part with Arnold Goldberg's "Form und Funktion des Ma'ase in der Mischna" (pp. 1-38). According to Goldberg, a *ma'aseh* consists of three literary elements: a situation, a question, and a decision. He, however, notes that the question generally is implied in the description of the situation and is not stated separately. For this reason we treat the situation + the question as one element, the setting. On the other hand, working on a man, we emphasize the role of Tarfon as an authoritative figure. Accordingly, we divide the decision into two elements: the subject and his ruling or action.

[19]Our discussion of the history of the *ma'asim* (p. 341) indicates that five of fourteen have been formulated independently of their present contexts. We, accordingly, first characterize the *ma'aseh* and then turn to its redactional purpose.

[20]In the following chart, we list these items and note the reasons for this conclusion. We also state the redactional function of the *ma'aseh* in order to determine any correlations between this aspect of the item and its formulation.

1. Tos. Demai 5:22--The surrounding pericopae discuss whether or not one may separate tithes from one Israelite's crops on behalf of those of another Israelite. This issue must be read into this *ma'aseh* whose primary concern is the problem of how to separate tithes on behalf of untithed crops that have been mixed with already tithed produce. The *ma'aseh* is juxtaposed with sayings attributed to Ushans. It supports the view of Meir and Yose and disagrees with Eleazar's opinion.

2. M. Beṣ. 3:5--The anonymous law of M. 3:5 states that on the festival one may not move an animal that died that day. The *ma'aseh* reports that they asked Tarfon about unclean dough-offering and "about it," (the dead animal). Since the surrounding pericopae do not mention unclean dough-offering, we may conclude that the *ma'aseh* originally stands outside the present context. The *ma'aseh* is inserted here by adding "about it." It now serves as an illustration for the anonymous law of M. 3:5.

3. Tos. Ḥag. 2:13--This *ma'aseh* indicates that one may not mourn on a festival. It appears after a Houses' dispute about how one observes the Day of Slaughter, the day on which the sacrifices are slaughtered, if Passover falls on the Sabbath. It is placed here because the agreement between the Houses that one may mourn on such a Day of Slaughter implies that one normally does not mourn on a festival. The *ma'aseh* serves as an illustration for this implied ruling.

4. Tos. Yev. 5:1H--The context focuses upon the type of
produce one feeds a betrothed woman after the expiration of the twelve-month period of preparation. The
ma'aseh is only thematically related, for it details
that Tarfon immediately fed heave-offering to three
hundred women whom he betrothed. It does not mention
the twelve-month preparation period. It is redacted
with other sayings and anonymous rules and specifically disagrees with the statement that an Israelite
woman may not eat heave-offering until she has performed *nissu'in* with a priest.

5. M. Bekh. 4:4--This *ma'aseh* is taken over by Aqivans,
who ignore its content, in order to illustrate the
view that an expert who errs need not pay a fine.
The *ma'aseh* details that Tarfon fed to the dogs a
cow that had its womb removed.

[21]The data are found in Kanter (Conclusions): M. Ber. 5:7,
M. Shab. 16:8, Tos. Demai 3:15, Tos. Ter. 2:13, Tos. Shab. 13:11,
M. Eruv. 10:10, M. Pes. 7:2, M. Pes. 10:11, M. Suk. 2:1, Tos. Suk.
2:11, M. Beṣ. 3:2, M. Yad. 3:1, M. Ed. 7:7, M. Ber. 1:1, M. Giṭ.
1:5, M. Kel. 5:4, Tos. Nid. 5:5, Tos. Pes. 1:27, Tos. Miq. 2:15,
Tos. Kel. B.M. 11:2.

[22]The following seven items contain opinions attributed to
Aqiva: Tos. Ber. 4:15, M. M.S. 5:9, Tos. Y.T. 2:12, M. Eruv. 4:1,
M. R.H. 1:6, M. R.H. 2:8-9, and Tos. Demai 5:24. The only other
pericope which reports an alternative view is Tos. Miq. 6:3,
Onqelos.

[23]The formal traits of the four *ma'asim* not found in M.-Tos.
are comparable to those of the materials in this earliest stratum.
There thus is no breakdown of this formulary pattern in the later
levels of the corpus.

[24]Neusner and Kanter observe that narratives account for much
of the materials associated with the Patriarch. Nearly half of the
traditions about Gamaliel which first appear in M.-Tos., and nearly
all of the materials about the pre-70 Pharisaic masters who are
presumed to have been Patriarchs, are formulated as stories. But
Neusner (*HMLP* III, p. 195) and Kanter (Conclusions) have also argued
that, while the *ma'aseh* belongs to the patriarchal circle, it is
not unique to that group. The formulation of a large number of
stories about Tarfon, therefore, does not throw this hypothesis
into question. We need not be driven on account of this fact to
accept Alon's theory (*Studies in Jewish History* I [Tel Aviv,
1967[2]] pp. 258-59) that Tarfon served as the Patriarch after the
death of Eleazar b. Azariah. *Ma'asim* are normative stories, and
there is no reason that they may not be told of any authoritative figure.

CHAPTER X

THE LAW

The Issues and the Catalogue

The analysis of the substance of the legal units of traditions, particularly those in M.-Tos.,[1] centers upon two issues: the relationships among these discrete rulings and their relationships to their larger setting within mishnaic law. We ask the first question to determine the coherence of this set of items. A coherent complex of items would cover a clearly delineated thematic agendum and be based upon a limited number of consistently held principles. The coherence of the legal units of tradition would strongly suggest that they have not been assigned randomly to Tarfon. As to the relationship between the legal materials and their larger setting, our problem here is to ascertain Tarfon's role in the mishnaic legal tradition. This question has two aspects. First, we want to know whether or not Tarfon's agendum consists of matters discussed by others and thus lies within the mainstream of mishnaic law. Second, we concern ourselves with the role his rulings and their underlying principles play in the unfolding of that law. In particular, do his views, or those of his opponent, form the conceptual foundation for either a chapter or a tractate, or do they fail to generate significant discussion.

In order to help us answer these questions, we present the legal rulings in M.-Tos. in a chart of three columns. The first column briefly summarizes each ruling. In the second column, by noting the matters mentioned above, we trace Tarfon's role in the law. The third column states the principle, if any, underlying his ruling. The items in the chart are listed under one of the following seven general categories of law: purity, agricultural, Temple, family, Sabbath and festival, liturgical, civil.[2]

Purity

1. M. Kel. 11:7--Wide metal end of a horn--Tarfon declares unclean; sages rule it is clean.

Application of general rules to specific example. Assumes that objects outside of the cult, specifically autonomous objects, are susceptible to uncleanness (M. Kel. 11:2). Many traditions assigned to Yavneans deal with parallel cases.

Horn is an autonomous object.

2. M. Kel. 25:7--Holding place--the anonymous law of M. Kel. 25:7 states that all objects consist of three parts: an inside, an outside, a holding place. Tarfon and Aqiva gloss this ruling by limiting it to a large baking trough and to cups respectively.

Gloss and limitation of a general rule. The anonymous law of M. Kel. 25:1 distinguishes between the insides and the outsides of objects. It does not specify the significance of this differentiation. M. 25:7 divides all objects into three parts. But Tarfon and Aqiva limit this rule. Yose and Meir gloss Aqiva's view. This is the only development of this law.

No discernible principle.

3. Tos. Kel. B.M. 7:1--Earth from a grave area--Tarfon rules that in order to render unclean it must be enough to cover a barleycorn's bulk of bone. The preceding anonymous law states that it must be equal to the size of the upper part of a stopper in a Lachmeite barrel.

Specification of dimensions. The Houses (M. Ohal. 16:4, 18:1), Eliezer (17:2) and the anonymous law of M. 2:3 assume that dirt from a grave area renders unclean. It does so because it contains bone. Tarfon defines the amount of dirt that has this effect. His ruling presumes that a barleycorn's bulk of bone renders unclean by contact and by carrying = M. Ohal. 2:3. A dispute between Eliezer and sages in M. Ohal. 17:5 assumes that dirt from a grave area must be equal to the size of the seal of packing bags. The latter may be identical to sages' stoppers.

A barleycorn's bulk of bone conveys uncleanness.

4. M. Ohal. 13:1--Hole in the door-- Tarfon says it must be a square handbreadth in order to give passage to uncleanness. Aqiva rules it must be the size of a fist. In the parallel version in Sifre Zuṭa the attributions are reversed.

Application of general rules to specific example. This pericope, like the remainder of M. Ohal., assumes that objects other than actual tents either spread uncleanness as a tent or give passage to uncleanness. The underlying presupposition of all views in this pericope, as well as of

Assumes there is not a standard measurement for openings that allow for the passage of uncleanness. M.'s version of Tarfon's saying is based upon the principle that only holes which fulfill functions ordained by man give passage to uncleanness. The version in Sifre

Text	Comment	Principle
the Houses' rulings in 13:1,4, and of the anonymous laws in 13:1,2, namely, that the size of an opening giving passage to uncleanness varies depending upon either the purpose for which it is used or the agent that made it, is not in accord with the fundamental underpinning of the whole tractate. The rest of the tractate assumes that an opening must be a square handbreadth to allow for the passage of uncleanness. According to the anonymous law of 13:1, however, a hole made by nature and not used by man must be the size of a fist. One which is functional, serves man's purposes, must be a square handbreadth. Tarfon's ruling equates the hole in the door with one that is functional.		Zuṭṭa, however, is in accord with the principle that holes which meet the objective criteria of a size of a fist have this effect.
5. Tos. Kel. B.M. 7:2 (M. Kel. 7:12)—Size of the fist—M. Ohal. 13:1 states that a natural hole must be the size of a fist in order to allow for the passage of uncleanness. Tarfon, Aqiva, Yose, and Judah gloss this rule by defining the size of the fist.	Specification of dimensions. Related to the laws discussed in No. 4.	No discernible principle.
6. M. Ohal. 16:1—Moveables bring uncleanness—The anonymous law states that moveables bring uncleanness if they are as thick as an ox-goad = one third of a handbreadth in diameter. Tarfon glosses this ruling by presenting an illustration. Aqiva modifies the rule so that it is in accord with the laws assumed in the remainder of Ohal. Thus according to Aqiva, it conveys uncleanness as a tent only if it is a handbreadth in diameter.	Gloss of a general rule provides an illustration. The meaning of the anonymous law of 16:1 is unclear. The Aqivans interpret it to mean that moveables convey uncleanness as a tent if they are a handbreadth in width. The ruling, interpreted in this manner, does not agree with the assumption underlying the remainder of the tractate that an object must be a handbreadth in width and in length in order to spread uncleanness as a tent.	Variable measurements for conveying uncleanness by overshadowing.

7. Tos. Neg. 8:2—Cedarwood used in the purification rite of a leper—a list of seven rulings: (1) it is made of cypresswood-cedarwood, (2) its head is smooth, (3) its length, (4) its width, (5) one may use same piece of wood more than once, (6) purify both while the Temple is standing and while it is not standing, (7) purify outside the land of Israel.

Specification of dimensions and establishing general rules. None of these matters are discussed in any great detail elsewhere. No. 1 in Scriptural. No. 2 is in agreement with the anonymous law of Sifre Zuṭṭa 19:6 and with Ḥaninah b. Gamaliel, Sifra Mesora Parasha 1:12. The dimensions listed in Nos. 3-4 are also given verbatim at M. Par. 14:6. Tarfon's ruling at No. 5 disagrees with the opinion attributed to Eliezer in Tos. Neg. 8:2. There is nothing parallel to the significant ruling, No. 6. Tos. Neg. 8:1 is in agreement with No. 7.

One may perform the priestly function of purification even after the destruction of the Temple.

8. Tos. Par. 11:5—Paraphernalia set aside for purification rite—Tarfon rules that these objects are not subject to uncleanness caused by carrying. This saying has the tradental attribution, Eleazar says in the name of Tarfon.

Application of general rules to specific example. Tarfon's saying relates to and agrees with the view of sages in M. Par. 11:6. They state, in opposition to Meir, that all unclean individuals do not render unclean by carrying objects set aside for use in the purification rite. This is in contrast to the purification ashes, the purification water mixed with the ashes, and the one who sprinkles the water which are rendered unclean in this manner. The difference between the first and second cases is that the latter concerns items which have already become part of the ceremony, while the former deals with items which have only been set aside for use in the ceremony. The presupposition of both of the rulings is that with regard to the purification rite all unclean persons are comparable to zabs; like zabs they render unclean by carrying. This view is in agreement with Joshua's opinion in M. Par. 10:1. He rules that with regard to the purification rite, objects susceptible to corpse uncleanness are comparable to zabs; they convey uncleanness by carrying.

Present objective criteria and not subjective presumptions about future use determine the status of an object.

9. M. Miq. 10:5--Ring in a chain-- Tarfon glosses the anonymous law that details how much of the handle of a bucket must be immersed. This rule indicates that one has to immerse only that part of the handle that is func- tional. The saying attributed to Tarfon comments upon this law by stating that if only part of a ring falls within the prescribed measure, one immerses the entire ring.

A minor gloss. Presupposes notion of interposition, the theme of M. Miq. chs. 9-10.

Objective and not solely functional criteria determine the law.

10. Tos. Miq. 1:16-19--Immersion pool of Discus of Yavneh measured and found lacking the required amount of water-- Tarfon declared all previous purifica- tions performed in it retroactively fit; Aqiva declared them unfit.

A theoretical question. Assumes that an immersion pool must be of requisite volume in order to purify. Tarfon's ruling is in agreement with the view that we do not need probative evidence to declare clean an unclean person. Aqiva rules that we require such evidence. The Ushans at M. 2:2 refine the discussion of retroactive uncleanness by differentiating between purification on the basis of the location of the pools and on the basis of the type of uncleanness suffered by the person. Simeon concurs with the above principle underlying Tarfon's ruling. Yose's view is in agreement with Aqiva's presupposition.

We act on basis of what we have good reason to assume were the objective facts and not on basis of what we pre- sume may have been the case. In matters of doubt, we may thereby act leniently despite the possibility of transgression.

11. Tos. Nid. 2:8--Male who checks for seminal emissions--his hand should be cut off. Tarfon glosses this anonymous law by stating that it should be cut off upon his belly.

A minor gloss. Anonymous comments and Yose spell out the implications of Tarfon's saying. They disagree about whether or not it should be interpreted literally.

No discernible principle.

12. Tos. Nid. 5:9 (M. Nid. 4:5)-- Duration of protracted labor--Meir: forty or fifty days; Judah in the name of Tarfon: the ninth month; Yose and Simeon: two weeks.

Specification of dimensions. Yavneans, Eliezer and Joshua (M. 4:4) assume that blood associated with hard labor does not render the woman unclean as a zabah. These Yavneans discuss how long a woman may have a respite from pains and still give birth

No discernible principle.

not as a *zabah*. Their dispute assumes that the woman suffers these pains during her eleven clean days. This dispute apparently does not presume that there is a limit to the period of hard labor. The Ushans deal with that matter. Tos. gives illustration for these various rulings.

Definition of intention: a fundamental issue. Both Tarfon and Aqiva assume that the law of "if water be put on" applies only to water which the person put on with approval, which he intended to use. This principle is assigned in M. Maks. 1:3 to Abba Yose. The presupposition of Aqiva's view forms the conceptual foundation for the tractate. Tarfon's opinion is congruent with that of Eliezer (M. Miq. 2:7-9, M. Maks. 6:7) and also with that of Judah (M. Maks. 3:1).

One determines a person's intentions on the basis of his actions. This definition in effect eliminates the opposition between intention and action. We therefore ultimately decide the law on the basis of the objective facts of a situation.

13. M. Maks. 5:4--Water on a rod used to measure a cistern--Tarfon rules that water which comes up from measuring either the depth or the width falls within the category of "if water be put on." Aqiva limits this effect only to the rod used to measure the depth of the cistern.

Specification of dimensions. No other discussion of this issue. The principle behind Aqiva's view, i.e., any amount of land is liable to this rule, apparently underlies other rulings pertaining to land. M. Peah 3:7-8 thus states that, if a woman accepts any amount of land, she forfeits her *ketubah*.

Land of this size is considered a "field"; therefore, it meets the biblical requirement.

Agriculture

14. M. Peah 3:6--Land liable to *pe'ah*-- Dispute between Eliezer, Joshua, Judah b. Bathyra, Tarfon, and Aqiva. Tarfon states that land that is six handbreadths by six handbreadths is liable to *pe'ah*.

A procedural question relating to an unusual case. Assumes that one cannot tithe from already-tithed crops for untithed produce, and that crops in the market place are untithed. Ushans (Tos. Demai 5:21,22) raise the issue of whether or not one may take tithes from one Israelite's crops for those of

Avoids the economic loss of tithing an amount equal to all of the already-tithed crops.

15. Tos. Demai 5:22--Untithed crops mixed with already-tithed crops--Tarfon tells Simeon Shezuri to purchase new crops and tithe the from them in behalf of the untithed crops in the mixture.

another Israelite. Tarfon's advice is in opposition to the laws of M. Hal. 3:8, Tos. Demai 5:12-13, and Tos. Ter. 5:15. In the first two of these pericopae the anonymous law (and in the case of Ter. 5:15) Eleazar b. Azariah rules that, if one does not already have other untithed crops, then he must separate from the mixture enough produce so that the tithe for the untithed crops will be taken from itself.

The appearance of the crop determines its status.

16. M. Kil. 5:8—Hemp—Tarfon rules it is not diverse kinds in a vineyard. Sages rule it is.

Application of general rules to a middle case. Herbs (YRKWT) according to the anonymous law of M. Kil. 5:5 are diverse kinds in a vineyard. Hemp is an herb. But it does not look like an herb. That is, it does not send forth its leaves from its roots as Tos. Kil. 5:15 requires of an herb. It, therefore, is a gray area.

Same as preceding.

17. Tos. Kil. 3:16—Cuscuta in a vineyard—Tarfon rules it is not diverse kinds; sages say it is.

Same as preceding.

18. Tos. Shev. 4:4--Arum and the Sabbatical year--Judah reports that on the authority of Tarfon he ate arum at the conclusion of the Sabbatical year. In M. Shev. Judah 5:5 holds this opinion in a dispute with sages. The latter contend that one may eat arum only after new leaves have formed.

Procedure relating to an unusual case. Assumes that one does not eat crops purposely grown during the Sabbatical year, and that some people do not observe this rule. Arum generates a case of doubt, for it is left in the ground for three years. The arum found at the conclusion of the Sabbatical year, therefore, may be from either the sixth or the seventh year. Several other rulings in M. Shev. Ch. 5 discuss arum.

We act on basis of what we have good reason to presume are the facts. In case of doubt, act leniently despite possible transgressions.

19. Tos. Shev. 5:12--Balsam and the Sabbatical year--Tarfon rules that it is subject to the taboos.	Illustration of the generalization of M. Shev. 7:2: The laws of the Sabbatical year apply to inedible substances which are left growing during the seventh year. The anonymous law of M. Shev. 7:6 is in accord with Tarfon's view.	Laws of Sabbatical year apply to inedible substances.
20. M. Ter. 4:5--Increase heave-offering--Dispute between Eliezer: one-tenth; Ishmael: one-half; Tarfon and Aqiva: almost all.	Specification of dimensions. Houses disagree in M. Ter. 4:3 (Tos. Ter. 5:3) about the minimum measure for heave-offering. The Yavneans discuss the logically secondary issue of the maximum one may give as heave-offering. The opinion attributed to Tarfon and to Aqiva is in accord with the anonymous law of M. Hal. 1:9.	Benefits priests and encourages the performance of the rite. One separates heave-offering *from* his produce (Num 15:21).
21. M. Ter. 9:2--Field mistakenly sown with heave-offering--Anonymous law states that poor Israelites and poor priests glean from it. Tarfon rules that only poor priests may gather.	Procedural question relating to a gray area--The crops of this field are sufficiently like heave-offering such that they are subject to the rules of gleaning, forgotten sheaf, *pe'ah*, and tithes. But at the same time the produce is considered heave-offering. This pre-supposition is in accord with the anonymous law of M. Ter. 9:4--what grows from heave-offering is heave-offering.	Concern for the prerogatives of priests --heave-offering will not be eaten by non-priests, and priest will not have to purchase the heave-offering from them.
22. Tos. Hag. 3:33--Receive heave-offering of wine and of olive oil from anyone all the days of the year--Tarfon states that one may do this. The anonymous law of M. Hag. 3:4 (Tos. Hag. 3:30, 32) rules that the *'amme-ha'areṣ* in Judaea are deemed trustworthy regarding the cleanness of their heave-offering only during the period of the wine presses and of the olive vats.	Fundamental rule. Tarfon asserts that he received this teaching from Yoḥanan b. Zakkai. The anonymous laws of Tos. Demai 2:2,21,22; 3:1,2, as well as that of M. Hag. 3:4 assume, contrary to Tarfon's view, that *'amme-ha'areṣ* do not maintain the cleanness of their heave-offering.	Presumption that everyone, including *'amme-ha'areṣ* are careful to maintain the cleanness of heave-offering. Benefits priests, for they may always receive heave-offering. Encourages the observance of the ritual.

23. M. Yad. 4:3--Tithes given during the Sabbatical year by Israelites in Ammon and Moab--Opinions attributed to Tarfon, Ishmael, Joshua, and Eliezer hold that these people give poorman's tithe. Eleazar b. Azariah contends they give second-tithe.

Procedural question relating to a gray area--The inhabitants of the land of Israel do not separate tithes during the Sabbatical year, for all the crops are treated as ownerless. Ammon and Moab constitute a middle case, for they are sufficiently like the land of Israel such that the produce grown there is subject to agricultural taboos. But they are sufficiently not part of the land of Israel such that they are not subject to the laws of the Sabbatical year. Eliezer asserts that he received a tradition on this matter from Yoḥanan b. Zakkai.

We may act leniently with regard to gray areas; facilitate the observance of agricultural laws.

24. M. Ma. 3:9--Vine in a yard--Tarfon: take the whole grape cluster; Aqiva: pick one grape at a time.

Procedure relating to a gray area--According to M. Ma. 1:6, once crops to be sold in the market have been piled up, one may not eat a temporary meal from them, a meal consisting of one item eaten at a time. If, however, the crops are to be consumed by the grower, he may eat a temporary meal from them until he brings them into his house (M. Ma. 1:6) or into his courtyard (M. Ma. 3:5). But how does one act with regard to crops which grow in a courtyard; how does one pick and eat them such that he does not make them into a pile? According to the anonymous law of M. Ma. 3:8 and M. Ma. 3:9b small items, such as figs, may be picked and eaten one at a time. Tarfon and Aqiva disagree about how one picks a fruit, a cluster of grapes, which consists of more than one part.

Our actions are governed by the present appearance of something and not by what may occur in the future.

25. M. M.S. 2:4--Unclean vetches of second-tithe--Tarfon says they should be distributed among lumps of dough. Sages contend they should be redeemed.

Procedural question relating to an unusual case. According to Deut 14:22-27, one may purchase with second-tithe money only edible substances. Vetches are a middle case, for they may be eaten only when green (M. M.S. 2:4). At other times they serve as animal fodder. The anonymous law of M. M.S. 2:4 does not apply the normal rules for second-tithe to vetches. It allows the person to take them out of Jerusalem. Tarfon agrees in principle with the anonymous law of 2:4, for he also does not subject vetches to the normal rules of second-tithe. One usually redeems unclean second-tithe (M. M.S. 3:9). The Houses also discuss how one treats vetches. They specifically deal with the issue of the cleanness required in their preparation. The concern that the value of second-tithe not decrease runs throughout the entire tractate. This pericope is another illustration of this problem.

Avoid economic loss for the pilgrim; he need not pay the redemption fine of twenty-five percent. A concern that the value of consecrated items not decrease.

26. M. M.S. 2:9--Exchange of second-tithe money in Jerusalem--Disputes of Houses, Aqiva vs. they that made argument: Tarfon and Shammai.

Procedural question. Tarfon agrees in principle with the House of Hillel: exchange "good money" only for "good money." Application of principle that value of second-tithe not decrease.

Concern for value of consecrated produce.

Temple Law

27. Tos. Soṭ. 1:10--Classification of memory-offering of suspected adulteress--Tarfon vs. Aqiva.

This dispute presupposes only Scripture. It is the only discussion of this matter, and is of no legal importance.

Based on interpretation of Num. 5:15, "a meal-offering of memorial, bringing iniquity to remembrance."

28. Tos. Soṭ. 7:16—Lame priest blows the horns in the Temple.	Only discussion of this minor matter. M. Bekh. Ch. 7 deals with the issue of defects which render a priest unfit to serve in the Temple. Many of the rulings are assigned to Yavneans. None deals with the issue of blowing the horns. In later versions of this tradition, Aqivans create a dispute between Tarfon and Aqiva.	No discernible principle.
29. Tos. Bekh. 5:6-7—Priest with extra digits. There are two versions of this story. According to Judah, Tarfon's saying indicates that such a priest is fit. In Yose's opinion, however, Tarfon's comment has nothing to do with priests.	General background is same as in the preceding item. M. Bekh. 7:6 contains a dispute between Judah and sages on this specific matter. Tarfon's opinion serves as a precedent for Judah.	No discernible principle.
30. Tos. Ḥul. 3:7—Animal stripped of its hide—Tarfon declares unfit.	Application of general rule to a specific example. According to M. Ḥul. 3:1, all terminal defects render animals *ṭerefah*. In M. Ḥul. 3:2 (Tos. Ḥul. 3:7) Meir and sages disagree about the status of an animal stripped of its hide. Tarfon's ruling is in accord with that of sages.	An animal of this sort would die on its own; therefore, it is unfit.
31. M. Bekh. 4:4—Cow without a womb— Tarfon fed it to the dogs; it is unfit. Sages permit its consumption.	General background same as in preceding item. The anonymous law of M. Ḥul. 3:2 rules that all animals without wombs are fit. Aqivans use this pericope (M. Bekh. 4:4) in relation to an entirely different matter; the law that an expert who errs need not pay a fine.	Same as preceding.

32. M. Men. 12:5--Free-will offerings of oil--Tarfon rules one may vow such offerings; Aqiva contends one may not do so.

General procedural question. M. Men. 12:3-5 discuss the proper manner for designating various parts of the meal-offering as a free-will offering. The anonymous laws agree with the principle underlying Aqiva's view; one may vow as a free-will offering only those constituent ingredients of the meal-offering that may be offered up by themselves. Simeon raises the subsequent question of whether or not an offering that does not meet this requirement is valid. Tos. Men. 12:10 interprets Tarfon's saying to mean that one may offer up oil as a free-will offering. It glosses his statement by indicating how this is done.

The future use of an item does not determine its present status.

33. M. Bekh. 2:6-8--Uncertainty about birth of firstlings--According to Tarfon the priest takes the better of the two animals. Aqiva rules it belongs to the owner. If one of the animals dies, Tarfon rules that the owner and the priest divide the value of the remaining beast.

Procedure relating to a secondary aspect of a case of doubt. Two sets of disputes between Tarfon and Aqiva have been inserted into a series of anonymous laws. The latter are paralleled by M. Bekh. 1:3-4 (deal with asses) and M. Bekh. 8:3-5 (deal with humans). The anonymous law in M. Bekh. 8:3-5 regarding cases in which one of two children die is in accord with Aqiva's view. Ushans Simeon and Meir raise a tertiary issue: whether or not an animal which may be a firstling is subject to priest's dues. Their rulings presuppose the status of the animal. Yose agrees with Tarfon; it may be a firstling and should be treated as such. Meir holds the opposite view.

Gives the benefit of the doubt to the priest.

34. M. Bekh. 2:9--First animal born Caesarean, second in the normal manner--Tarfon treats both as doubtful firstlings; Aqiva claims that neither is a firstling.

Procedural question relating to a gray area. The problem is generated from the Scriptural verses referring to firstlings. It is not clear whether or not a firstling must be both the first born and be born in the normal manner, by opening the womb. The anonymous law of M. Bekh. 8:3 is in accord with Aqiva's view, for it states that if humans are born in the order described in M. 2:9, neither has to be redeemed. Simeon disagrees and treats the child born in the normal manner as a first-born. He thus goes beyond Tarfon's view.

Concern for consecrated items.

35. Tos. Bekh. 6:14--Tarfon returns the redemption-money.

Story about Tarfon glosses and supports the anonymous law preceding it. That law is the only ruling relating to the procedure for this ceremony.

We act on the basis of the previously certain objective facts.

36. M. Ker. 5:2-3--Procedure for bringing sacrifices for doubtfully committed sacrilege--Sages declare that one is not liable to bring a suspensive guilt-offering in such a case. Aqiva rules one does bring such an offering. Tarfon assumes one brings the suspensive guilt-offering and details the procedure for presenting the various sacrifices. Aqiva holds a different view on this aspect of the matter. The opinions differ in that Tarfon's eliminates the necessity of bringing two guilt-offerings.

Procedure relating to an unusual case. Lev 5:17-19 do not clearly delineate the actions for which one is liable to bring a suspensive guilt-offering. Tarfon and Aqiva agree that one brings a suspensive guilt-offering for a crime for which a person, when certain, brings a guilt-offering. M. Ker. 1:2, however, states that one brings such an offering only for those crimes for which a person, when certain, brings a sin-offering. The whole of the tractate discusses the law of the suspensive guilt-offering only in relation to these latter types of transgressions. The presupposition of Tarfon's ruling thus is contrary to that of the tractate.

Avoid unnecessary economic loss.

37. M. Par. 1:3--Thirteen-month old sheep--Tarfon, Ishmael, and Ben Azzai assign various names to such a lamb. All of these titles refer to useless items.

An insignificant gloss to a law which states that a thirteen-month old lamb is fit neither for sacrifices that require a lamb nor for those that require a ram.

Assumes that such an animal is useless for sacrifices.

Family

38. Tos. Yev. 1:10--Marrying co-wife's daughter--This saying is subject to two interpretations. Accordingly, it may support the views of either of the Houses in M. Yev. 1:4. It may mean that Tarfon would arrange for the girl to marry the priest, in which case it supports the ruling of the House of Hillel. Alternatively, it may mean that Tarfon would marry his daughter's co-wife. According to this interpretation, it supports the view of the House of Shammai.

Fundamental question relating to the laws of levirate marriage: Does a woman forbidden to the levir exempt her co-wives from entering into levirate marriage? House of Hillel rules in M. Yev. 1:4 that she does not. In addition to Tarfon's saying, Tos. contains a statement by Joshua in support of the House of Hillel and a remark by Yoḥanan b. Nuri, which reports that the matter had not yet been resolved.

Since the meaning of Tarfon's comment is unclear, we cannot ascertain its underlying principle.

39. M. Yev. 15:6-7--Cases of insufficient evidence creating doubt--Tarfon rules that the co-wife of a woman who testifies concerning their husband's death may continue to eat heave-offering. Similarly, a man who is not certain about which one of five women he betrothed pays the value of only one *ketubah*. Aqiva holds the co-wife may not continue to eat heave-offering, and that the man leaves a sum equal to the value of five *ketubot*.

Procedural question relating to unusual cases of doubt. The issue between Tarfon and Aqiva may be reduced to the following theoretical question: Do we ignore doubt and act on the basis of previously-known objective facts, or do we take into account the doubt and act accordingly? The given of their dispute, namely, a wife may remarry and claim the value of her *ketubah* on the basis of her own testimony regarding her husband's death in the provinces beyond in the sea is in accord with the ruling of the House of Shammai in M. Yev. 15:2-3. The House of Hillel hold that a wife's testimony is accepted only if it is given in and concerns a matter which occurred in the same province. Furthermore, on the basis of such testimony, according

We act on the basis of the previously certain objective facts.

to the House of Hillel, the woman may only remarry. But she cannot claim her *ketubah*. The ruling that the testimony of the co-wife does not allow the other co-wives to remarry agrees with the anonymous law of M. Yev. 15:4. Aqiva's opinion agrees in principle with the anonymous ruling of M. Yev. 2:6-7. The parallel to this pericope, Tos. Yev. 14:12, contains two different modifications of the disputes in M. 15:6-7. The anonymous comments bring Tarfon over to Aqiva's view. The statement of Simeon b. Eleazar has the opposite effect.

A procedural question relating to a minor aspect of this ceremony. The anonymous description of this ceremony, Tos. Yev. 12:15, states that only the judges recite this verse. Judah disagrees. The story involving Tarfon serves as a precedent for Judah's view.

Interpretation of the words, "and his name shall be called in Israel," Deut 25:10. These words indicate that "all of Israel" present at the ceremony recite the verse.

Minor procedural matter. Story presumes that one witness is sufficient in these matters. It, therefore, is told in accordance with the view attributed to Gamaliel and Aqiva in M. Yev. 15:7. Joshua and Eliezer hold that the testimony of one witness is not sufficient. Story supports the ruling attributed to Tarfon and Aqiva in Tos. 14:10. The opposite view is given anonymously.

One must act with great care in relation to testimony regarding a person's marital status.

40. Tos. Yev. 12:15--*Ḥaliṣah* ceremony--Judah reports that Tarfon directed all those present to recite Deut 25:10.

41. Tos. Yev. 14:10--Cross-examine witnesses who testify in behalf of a woman.

42. M. Ket. 5:2—Food given to a betrothed woman not married within the allotted time—Tarfon: entirely heave-offering; Aqiva: half heave-offering, half common produce.

Procedural question relating to an unusual case. This dispute presumes that a betrothed woman after twelve months acquires the right to be provided for by her husband. If he is a priest, she may eat heave-offering. Aqiva's opinion is in agreement with the anonymous law of Tos. Ket. 5:1. After marriage (*nissu'in*) the woman receives half her provisions as heave-offering and half as common produce. Ushans in Tos. Ket. 5:1 continue the discussion of the anonymous laws of M. Ket. 5:2. None of their comments presupposes the views of Tarfon and Aqiva.

We act on basis of present object facts and not on basis of what we presume will happen in the future. Ruling benefits the priest.

43. Tos. Ket. 5:1H—Tarfon betrothed three hundred women during years of want and fed them heave-offering.

A fundamental question: When does an Israelite woman betrothed to a priest acquire the right to eat heave-offering. Tarfon's action indicates that she may do so immediately after her betrothal. His view is in agreement with Lev 22:11. The anonymous law of M. Ket. 5:2-3 (Tos. Ket. 4:1F) opposes this view, holding that the woman acquires this right only after the performance of *nissu'in*. Rulings attributed to Aqiva and Judah b. Bathyra in Tos. Ket. 5:1 are in agreement with Tarfon.

A woman betrothed to a priest acquires the right to eat heave-offering = Lev 22:11. Acts in behalf of woman.

44. M. Ket. 7:6—Scolding woman does not receive the money prescribed in her *ketubah*.

A minor point. This ruling presumes only that certain women, by virtue of their actions, forfeit the money prescribed in their *ketubot*. Glosses generalization of M. Ket. 7:6 that women who transgress Jewish customs fall into this category.

Certain actions are so unbecoming a married woman that she forfeits her *ketubah*.

45. M. Ket. 9:2-3--Distribution of deceased husband's property--Tarfon says that if a man dies, leaving a wife and creditors, and has either money or items outstanding as col-lateral, or crops uprooted from the ground, these are given to the weakest among the claimants. Aqiva rules the inheritors claim these items.

Procedure relating to a gray area. Inheritors claim all moveable property. If others want to claim these items, they must take an oath. The items mentioned in this pericope do not exactly fall into the category of moveable property. The dis-pute between Tarfon and Aqiva regarding uprooted crops does not presuppose the anonymous law of M. Ket. 8:7. This states that whoever first claims the uprooted crops is entitled to them.

One may act leniently with regard to gray areas; acts in woman's behalf.

46. M. Giṭ. 9:1--Conditional divorce--Eliezer permits a man to divorce his wife on the condition that she not marry a particular individual. Objections to this ruling are attributed to Tarfon, Yose the Galilean, and Aqiva.

Fundamental question regarding husband's rights. M. Giṭ. 9:3 contains an anonymous law which states that one may not give a divorce of this type. Judah offers the exact language which the *get* must contain.

Protects women. A husband has no control over his divorced wife.

47. M. Qid. 3:13--*Mamzerim* can be purified.

A fundamental ruling. The saying is glossed by a dispute between an anonymous law and Eliezer. This anonymous law indicates that the children of *mamzerim* who marry certain classes of people lose that status. The gloss in effect tones down Tarfon's claim. Tarfon's ruling opposes the law of M. Yev. 8:3 which states that *mamzerim* never enter into the congregation of Israel.

The status of *mamzerot* is not permanent.

Sabbath and Festival

48. M. Shab. 2:2--Oil for lamp--Tarfon allows only olive oil. Sages permit all oils.

A minor procedural issue. Yavneans and Ushans discuss this matter.

No discernible principle.

49. Tos. Shab. 5:13b--Tarfon wore a linen covering on the Sabbath to protect himself from the rain.

A secondary question: Must objects look like garments, or may they simply function as garments in order to be worn on the Sabbath? The question of what may be worn on the Sabbath is the theme of M. Shab. Ch. 5 and Tos. Shab. Ch. 5. Tos. Shab. 5:13-14 specifically deal with objects which function like, but do not have the appearance of, garments. Tarfon's actions are in agreement with the anonymous law of this pericope.

The appearance of an item and not a person's intentions determines the law.

50. M. Eruv. 4:4--Tarfon without prior intention entered a town on the Sabbath and acquired the travel-rights of a resident of that town.

A fundamental question discussed throughout M. Eruv. Ch. 4: Is intention necessary in order for a person to acquire the right to travel on the Sabbath? Rulings of Yavneans relate to various cases which illustrate this matter. All of these opinions assume that a person and a city have a Sabbath-limit, and that a resident of a city may travel within the entire city and its Sabbath-limit. According to the rulings attributed to Yoḥanan b. Nuri (M. 4:5), Eleazar b. Azariah (4:1), and Gamaliel (4:1), one does not need intention. Joshua (4:10), Aqiva (4:1), sages (4:5), and Eliezer (4:5) require intention. Judah, who is the tradent for the story about Tarfon, agrees with the first group of masters.

We act on the basis of the objective facts. The person's prior lack of intention is inconsequential.

51. M. Kel. 11:4--Door bolt--Tarfon says one may carry it about a courtyard on the Sabbath; it is like all other utensils.

Application of general rule to specific example. M. Shab. 17:1,5 state that any utensil, any potentially useful object, may be moved on the Sabbath. It is not *muqṣeh*. The fact that an item is useful places it into the category of objects which have been set in readiness. This notion is in accord with the Hillelite opinion in M. Beṣ. 1:9. Tarfon's ruling

The appearance of an item, its classification as a utensil, and not a person's intention, determines its status.

52. M. Zev. 11:7--Cooking in a pot on the festival--Tarfon rules one may use the pot the entire day. Sages hold that one may cook in it only until the time of eating.

apparently presupposes the idea expressed in M. Shab. 17:1, as well as the Hillelite view. It also is in agreement with Eliezer's view in M. Bes. 4:6. The latter states that whatever is in a courtyard falls into the category of items set in readiness.

Application of general rules to specific example. According to Exod 12:16 and M. Bes. 2:1, one may cook on a festival food he intends to eat that day. Furthermore, on a festival one may use only those items, which prior to the beginning of that day, have been set aside for a specific purpose. The dispute between Tarfon and sages comes down to whether or not one's prior intention determines how one may use an item on the festival. This pericope, therefore, deals with the question discussed in the preceding items. Nathan in Tos. Zev. 10:13 treats this saying as a comment upon scouring and rinsing pots used in the Temple.

Present status of an object and not one's prior intention determines the law.

53. M. Suk. 3:4--Broken-off myrtles--Ishmael rules there must be three myrtles; Aqiva says one. According to the gloss of Ishmael's opinion, two of the three myrtles may have broken-off tips and still be fit. Tarfon says all three may have broken-off tips.

Ruling on a minor procedural question. Tarfon's ruling, as well as the gloss of Ishmael's saying, oppose the anonymous law of M. Suk. 3:2. This ruling presupposes Lev 23:40, one takes myrtles on Sukkot, as well as the view that there must be three myrtles.

No discernible principle.

54. Tos. Suk. 2:8--Length of the palm--Anonymous law says it must be four handbreadths. Tarfon says it must measure five handbreadths.

Specification of measurement. Presupposes Lev 23:40.

No discernible principle.

55. M. Ta. 3:9--Fasting for rain--Story relates that Tarfon told the people to call off the fast because rain fell before noonday.

Procedural ruling on a minor point. M. Ta. 3:9 contains a dispute between Eliezer and sages on this matter. Tarfon's ruling is in agreement with Eliezer's view.

The falling of the rain before the expiration of the greater part of the day is grounds for cancelling the fast.

56. Tos. Hag. 2:13--Eulogizing on a festival--According to this story, Tarfon forbade this.

Minor procedural matter. Gloss of Houses' dispute at M. Hag. 2:4, and the anonymous laws of M. Meg. 1:3 and M. M.Q. 3:8 imply that one does not eulogize on the festival. The storyline of the *ma'aseh*, however, suggests that it was normal to do so. It states that all the people from the surrounding villages came to Lydda to mourn Alexsa.

Actions of this sort are not in accord with the spirit of the day.

Liturgical

57. M. Ber. 1:3--Saying the *Shema'*--Tarfon relates that he once turned off the road in order to recite this prayer. Tarfon's saying may also be interpreted to mean that he once reclined in order to recite it.

A minor procedural matter. The Houses and Yavneans discuss various aspects of reciting the *Shema'*. No other ruling in M.-Tos., however, deals with the specific issue noted in Tarfon's saying. A story in M. Ber. 1:2 indirectly relates that Judah once recited the *Shema'* while walking on the way. Tarfon apparently feels that, while traveling, a person cannot have the required attention in order to fulfill the *miṣvah*. His view thus is in accord with Tos. Ber. 4:2 which states that one needs proper attention.

One needs proper attention to fulfill commandment of reciting the *Shema'*. Does not interpret Deut 6:7, "When you walk by the way," literally.

58. M. Ber. 6:8--Blessing over water--It is unclear whether this pericope deals with the blessing said before drinking or whether it relates to the prayer said after drinking. Tarfon prescribes the blessing, "who createst"; sages say, "by whose word."

Specification of prayers. If the anonymous law is treated as a comment about the blessing said before drinking, then it agrees with that of M. Ber. 6:3. One says, "by whose word" over everything which does not grow from the ground.

No discernible principle.

59. M. Pes. 10:6--Prayer of redemption at the Seder--Alternative prayers are attributed to Tarfon and to Aqiva. Tarfon's blessing praises God for past redemption and the present ability to celebrate the festival. The blessing assigned to Aqiva looks forward to the

Specification of prayers. M. Pes. Ch. 10 and Tos. Pisha Ch. 10 deal with the rituals of Passover-evening. Opinions attributed to the Houses and to Yavneans comment upon various aspects of the ceremonies. The Houses disagree in M. Pes. 10:6 about how much of the Hallel one says

No discernible principle.

future, specifically, to the offering
of sacrifices.

60. Tos. Meg. 2:8--Judah relates that
when he was a minor he read the *Megillah*
with Tarfon's approval.

Civil

61. M. B.Q. 2:5--Ox causes damage in the
domain of the injured party--Tarfon declares the owner of the ox liable to pay
a restitution equal to the full amount
of the damage. Sages contend he pays a
half-restitution.

before the meal. The Hillelite view is
that one recites those paragraphs which
speak of redemption. The dispute between
Tarfon and Aqiva, therefore, is set within
the framework of the Hillelite position.

Sages in M. Meg. 2:4 disagree with Judah's
opinion. Judah's ruling apparently con-
tradicts the anonymous law of M. R.H. 3:8.
It states that a minor cannot fulfill the
obligations of others since it is not incumbent upon him to perform the rite.

A fundamental ruling. The Bible does not
discuss the matter of assessing fines on
the basis of the location in which the
accident occurred. The dispute between
Tarfon and sages merely presupposes the
biblical (Exod 21:35-36) distinction between full and half restitutions. The
owner of an ox which is an attested danger
pays the former; the owner of an ox which
is not an attested danger pays only the
half-restitution. Tarfon's ruling is in
accord with the anonymous law of M. B.Q.
1:4. The dispute between Tarfon and sages
has been glossed in accordance with another
portion of M. B.Q. 1:4. Thus the dispute
as it presently is formulated concerns only
damages done by goring, kicking, biting,
pushing, and laying down. Sages agree that
if the damage is that which is classified
as an attested danger, e.g., eating, the
owner pays a full restitution. Simeon in
Tos. B.Q. 1:9 offers four general principles
for the classification of damages. His
ruling regarding damage done in the domain
of the injured party agrees with that attributed to Tarfon. M. B.Q. 5:3 (Tos. B.Q. 5:9-12)

No discernible principle.

The location of the accident determines
the liability of the person whose
property causes the damage.

gives a series of laws which stipulate that an owner of an ox is liable for damages caused by his ox in the domain of the injured party only if the ox was brought there without permission. This view is assigned in Tos. B.Q. 5:12 to Tarfon. Tarfon's view here is consistent with and probably generated from his ruling in M. B.Q. 2:5. A comment attributed to R. Judah the Patriarch (M. B.Q. 5:3) qualifies the rulings of M. 5:2-3 and Tos. 5:9-12. It states that the owner of the ox is liable in all cases unless the owner of the yard agreed to watch the ox. In principle Judah the Patriarch agrees with Tarfon.

62. M. B.M. 2:7--Use of coins received after selling a lost animal which cannot earn its keep--Tarfon says the finder may use the coins; Aqiva rules he may not.

A secondary issue. M. B.M. 2:7-8 discuss the rights of a person to use returnable lost objects. The general rule is that one may use them only for their benefit. Furthermore, one should treat the items in such a way that their value does not decrease. In accordance with these principles, the anonymous law of 2:7 states that one must sell a lost animal which does not earn its keep. Tarfon and Aqiva discuss the secondary issue of the person's right to use the money received after the sale. Aqiva's ruling is in agreement with the general principle that a finder may not use a returnable lost item. Tarfon's opinion opposes this idea.

A person who finds an object may use it for his own benefit.

63. M. B.M. 4:3--Laws of defrauding-- Tarfon rules that an overcharge or an undercharge of one-third constitutes defrauding. The cheated person has the whole day to cancel the sale. The anonymous law defines defrauding as an

Specification of measurements. The opinions in this dispute offer differing definitions of the term "defrauding" found in Lev 25:14. Ushans discuss secondary matters relating to this law, e.g., whether it applies to both the

No discernible principle.

overcharge or an undercharge of one-sixth. But the cheated person has less time to cancel the transaction.

Miscellaneous

64. Tos. Shab. 13:5--Scrolls of sectarians--Tarfon says one burns the divine names contained in them. Yose disagrees. Ishmael rules one blots them out in water.

65. M. Naz. 5:5--Conditional Nazirite vow--House of Shammai rule that a dedication (M. Naz. 5:1) or a vow made in error is binding. House of Hillel rule that if the facts turn out to be what was presupposed at the time the vow was uttered, then it is binding. Tarfon rules that a vow is binding only if the facts are clear when the person pronounced it.

merchant and the consumer or only to the latter.

Procedural question relating to an unusual case. The anonymous law of Tos. 13:5 is in accord with Tarfon's view. It states that on the Sabbath one does not save the divine names.

A fundamental issue. M. Naz. Ch. 5 spells out through various examples the opinions of the Houses. Tarfon's ruling extends the opinion of the House of Hillel.

The sanctity of the divine name depends upon where it appears.

One does not legislate on the basis of what he presumes.

The Agendum of the Legal Issues

Having divided our materials by their larger themes, we are able to identify the broad contours of the agendum. We can see in Figure 1 the range of issues discussed in these items and also the distribution of the materials over the various themes.

Fig. 1. Legal Items Over Themes

Theme	No. Items	Percentage of Whole
Purity	13	20.0
Agriculture	13	20.0
Temple	11	16.9
Family	10	15.4
Sabbath and Festival	9	13.8
Liturgy	4	6.2
Civil	3	4.6
Miscellaneous	2	3.1
TOTAL	65	100.0

The distributions are not even. Two topics (purity and agriculture) each account for 20% of the corpus. Slightly smaller proportions of the traditions deal with Temple, family, and Sabbath law. By contrast, only a few items relate to either civil or liturgical matters. In order to attempt to characterize the orientation of this agendum, let us compare these distributions (in percent) to those available for other authorities.[3] Figure 2 presents this comparison. I give the mean percentage for each category, as well as Tarfon's deviation from it. (Numbers in parentheses present calculations which exclude the data on Gamaliel and Yose. In several instances the statistics for their materials distort the general trends.)

Fig. 2. Distribution of Legal Items over Themes (Percentages)

	Tarfon	Eliezer	Joshua	Eleazar	Ishmael	Houses	Gamaliel	Yose	Mean	Deviation
Purity	20.0	29	33.3	26	25	29.2	14	14	24.4 (28.5)	-4.4 (-8.5)
Agriculture	20.0	18	17.4	21	20	24.5	17	14	18.8 (20.2)	+1.2 (-.2)
Temple	16.9	16	17.4	7	10	6.0	5	26	12.5 (10.2)	+4.4 (+6.7)
Family	15.4	10	10.4	12	4	13.0	14	12	10.8 (9.9)	+4.6 (+5.5)
Sabbath	13.8	15	11.1	19	18	19.3	33	5	17.2 (16.5)	-3.4 (-2.7)
Liturgy	6.2	2	4.2	10	9	6.0	10	5	6.6 (6.2)	-.4 (0)
Civil	4.6	3	1.4	5	7	2.0	8	10	5.2 (3.7)	-.6 (+.9)
Miscellaneous	3.1	6	4.8	0	7	0	6	14		

The order of the themes and their respective percentages in
the Tarfon-corpus are very similar to those for the corpora of the
first five authorities: Eliezer, Joshua, Eleazar, Ishmael, and the
Houses. In these other corpora, purity law and agricultural law
predominate. On the average they together account for 45-50% of
the materials. These same two themes constitute the most frequently discussed issues in the Tarfon-tradition. The percentage
of his items dealing with purity law, however, is slightly low, a
deviation of -8.5%. In the other corpora the above two topics
generally are followed by festival, family, liturgical, and civil
law. Tarfon's agendum differs from this order only in that family
law exceeds festival law by one item. One theme, Temple-law, does
not consistently account for the same percentage of the materials
of the five other masters. Its location in their agenda, therefore, varies. For example, 17.4% of Joshua's units of tradition
deal with cultic concerns, the second most common theme of his
corpus. Only 6% of the Houses' materials, the next to lowest percentage in the corpus, however, relate to this issue. Now the
figure for the Tarfon-tradition is somewhat above the mean, a deviation of +6.7%. But it is almost identical to the corresponding
percentage for the units of tradition of Eliezer and Joshua. Accordingly, Tarfon's agendum in this respect, as well as in all the
other respects noted above, coincides with those of the other five
authorities. We may, therefore, identify Tarfon's agendum as
Pharisaic, for that is the character of these five other corpora.[4]
    What does it mean to say that an agendum is Pharisaic? An
agendum of this type, as can be seen from the above discussion,
primarily focuses upon two topics: purity and agricultural law.
The specific rulings belonging to these two broad themes pertain
to matters of table-fellowship. That is to say, the thrust of
these laws is to insure that the members of the group adhering to
these rulings eat, in a state of cleanness, their properly tithed
produce. The assumption underlying this concern is that everyone
should replicate the cult in his everyday life, consuming his
properly-tithed food in a state of cleanness, as does a priest.
Thus "Pharisaic piety is based upon the Temple and its laws of
uncleanness. The Pharisees simply enlarge the area in which those
laws are to be observed and enforced."[5] This reverence for the
cult, which can be discerned as the underpinning of many of the
Houses' rulings, very likely accounts for the interest of later
Pharisaic authorities, in particular Eliezer, and by extension,

Joshua and Tarfon, in cultic matters. We may surmise that these
masters believed in the efficacy of the cult, and assumed that it
would be restored. They, therefore, ruled on Temple-matters in
the anticipation that in the new Temple their views would be
observed.

In the case of Tarfon an additional factor may explain his
interest in cultic matters. As we shall see, a considerable body
of evidence suggests that Tarfon is a priest. For this reason,
a sizeable portion of his rulings deals with priestly and Temple-
matters. This additional consideration leads us to the conclusion
that Tarfon's general concerns are those of a Pharisee, or perhaps
those of a Pharisaic priest. His agendum, accordingly, coincides
with those of the members of the group whose opinions form the
heart of significant portions of M.-Tos.

Tarfon's Role in the Law

Having discerned the broad contours of Tarfon's corpus, we
turn to his specific rulings and focus our discussion upon their
role in mishnaic law. As noted at the outset of this chapter,
there are two aspects to this issue. First, we want to determine
whether or not Tarfon's agendum is generated from within the mainstream of the law, and if so, what are the types of problems that
his rulings address. Do they articulate general principles, or
relate to the application of general rules to specific cases?
Second, we discuss the relationship between Tarfon's dicta and the
unfolding of mishnaic law.

Our answer to the first of the above questions about Tarfon's
role in the law is that the specific issues he discusses lie within the mainstream of mishnaic law. To begin with, nearly all of
his units of tradition (sixty-one of sixty-five) are on matters
that others also address. His comments and those of the other
authorities relate either to the same general issue (Nos. 3, 6,
11, 21, 33, 36, 39, 40, 41, 45, 52, 53, 54, 57, 58, 59, 62) or
more frequently even to the same aspect of an issue (Nos. 1, 2, 4,
5, 7, 8, 9, 10, 12, 13, 14, 15, 16, 17, 18, 19, 20, 22, 23, 24, 25,
26, 29, 30, 31, 32, 34, 37, 38, 42, 43, 44, 46, 48, 49, 50, 51, 55,
56, 60, 61, 63, 64, 65). Tarfon's unit of tradition concerning the
size of the clump of dirt from the grave area (No. 3) provides an
example of the former. While few pericopae concern themselves with
the size of the clump, many items deal with other aspects of this
dirt. On the other hand, a number of items besides Tarfon's ruling

at No. 15 relate to the specific question of how one tithes on
behalf of crops in a mixture. In this instance, mixtures constitute the general issue, while tithing mixtures is the specific
question. Only the following four items deal with matters with
which the rest of mishnaic law is not concerned: Nos. 27, 28, 35,
and 47. Three of these four units of tradition relate to minor
aspects of Temple-law.

Once we have located Tarfon's units of tradition within the
center of the concerns of Mishnah, we examine the specific role
played by his dicta within that mainstream. Two-thirds (forty-
four of sixty-five) of his sayings, treating all major legal
topics of his agendum, are either rulings on procedural questions
relating to unusual or minute matters (Nos. 10, 15, 18, 21, 25,
26, 28, 33, 34, 35, 36, 39, 40, 41, 42, 45, 48, 49, 53, 55, 56,
57, 60, 64), applications of general rules to specific cases (Nos.
1, 4, 8, 16, 17, 19, 23, 24, 29, 30, 31, 51, 57, 58, 62), or minor
comments upon more general laws (Nos. 2, 6, 9, 11, 44). Seven of
the above items (Nos. 16, 17, 21, 23, 24, 25, 45) treat middle
cases; Tarfon applies established principles to matters that are
problematic, in that they do not squarely fall into either one of
two categories. Another twelve of the above pericopae concern the
more theoretical question of whether objective facts or subjective
presumptions are determinative of which presupposed general rule
applies in a specific instance (Nos. 4, 8, 10, 18, 24, 33, 39, 42,
49, 51, 52, 65). We return to this matter in the following section. Of the remaining 34% of the entire corpus, 17%, again treating all major legal topics, simply specify details. In these dicta
Tarfon gives precise measurements for various items (Nos. 3, 5, 12,
14, 20, 54, 63), classifies sacrificial offerings (Nos. 27 and 37)
or details the text of a prayer (No. 59). Only 17% of all the
dicta, again relating to diverse topics, lay down general rules
(Nos. 7, 13, 22, 32, 38, 43, 46, 47, 50, 61, 65). For example,
No. 7 states that priests may purify lepers even after the destruction of the Temple. According to No. 22, a priest may receive,
from anyone, at any time, heave-offering of olive oil and of wine.
On the whole, the above data indicate that Tarfon's rulings relate
to the fine points of the law. In this respect Tarfon's corpus is
identical to those of other masters.[6]

Although the issues addressed by Tarfon are generated from
within the mainstream of mishnaic law, his rulings do not significantly contribute to its development. Nearly two-thirds of his

opinions (forty-two of sixty-five items: Nos. 1, 3, 6, 7, 8, 9,
14, 16, 17, 19, 20, 21, 23, 24, 25, 26, 27, 28, 29, 30, 31, 34,
35, 37, 38, 40, 41, 44, 45, 46, 47, 49, 50, 51, 54, 55, 56, 58,
59, 60, 63, 64, 65) do not give rise to any further discussion.
No one comments upon Tarfon's ruling or carries forward its underlying conception. Neither does anyone develop the view contrary
to that of Tarfon. In fourteen cases (Nos. 2, 10, 11, 12, 15, 18,
31, 33, 39, 48, 52, 53, 57, 62) later authorities comment and ex-
pand upon the ideas of Tarfon or those of his opponent. But these
secondary developments are limited in scope. In five pericopae
(Nos. 4, 5, 36, 42, 43) Tarfon's view is in accord with a conception contrary to that which underlies a significant portion of M.
In these instances others besides Tarfon, however, also articulate
the rejected position. We, therefore, have no reason to assume
that this rejected point of view originates with Tarfon. In only
four cases (Nos. 13, 22, 32, 61), 6% of the corpus, Tarfon's opinion or that of his opponent generates further important developments in the law. In the first two of these items (Nos. 13 and
22), the views of Tarfon's adversaries form the foundation of a
sizeable portion of M.--a tractate (No. 13) or parts of several
tractates (No. 22). In the latter two examples, only parts of a
chapter have been spun out of Tarfon's ruling (No. 61) or that of
his opponent (No. 32).

The Coherence of the Tradition:
Specific Problems and Concerns

One theoretical problem, the issue of objective facts vs.
subjective presumptions, and a general tendency to rule to the
benefit of priests and to encourage the performance of rituals in
which priests play a central role each unite many of the units of
tradition. Seventeen items (Nos. 4, 8, 9, 10, 13, 16, 17, 18, 24,
32, 39, 42, 49, 50, 51, 52, 65), 26% of the corpus, relate to the
first of these matters. The question of whether we decide how to
act on the basis of objective facts or on that of subjective presumptions is phrased in several different ways. In the case of
M. Ma. 3:9 (No. 24), for example, the issue under dispute amounts
to the following: Is the present appearance of the fruit, an objective consideration, or the person's intention to eat it determinative? Conversely, in M. Eruv. 4:4 (No. 50), if a person is in
fact within the Sabbath-limit of a town, may he enter the town,
even though he lacked this intention prior to the beginning of the

Sabbath? The issue of objective facts vs. subjective presumptions
also arises with regard to the question of the form of an object
vs. its function. Form is comparable to objective facts, while
function is parallel to subjective presumptions. For example (No.
49), may a person wear on the Sabbath any item which functions as
a garment, or must it also look like a garment? Conversely, if an
object (No. 51) has the form of a utensil, is it automatically
considered set in readiness for use on the Sabbath? Several of
the cases that relate to matters of doubt may also be treated
under the question of objective facts vs. subjective presumptions.
For example (No. 39), do we determine the present status of the
co-wife on the basis of previously firmly known facts, her past
status, or on that of what we presume to be her present situation?
The seventeen items relating to the topic under discussion cover
cases falling within all of the major thematic categories of the
agendum. Five rulings (Nos. 4, 8, 9, 10, 13) in purity law; four
(Nos. 16, 17, 18, 24) in agricultural law; one (No. 32) in Temple-
law; two (Nos. 30, 42) in family law; four (Nos. 49-52) in Sabbath
and festival law; one (No. 65) on vows ultimately may be reduced
to the question of objective facts vs. subjective presumptions.

     In sixteen of the seventeen pericopae, Tarfon rules that the
objective facts establish the parameters for action. What people
presume they will do, or what they failed to presume is of no consequence. The person who finds himself within the Sabbath-limit,
for instance, may enter the town. The person may pick the entire
cluster of grapes. We presume that the co-wife's husband still is
alive; therefore, she may continue to eat heave-offering. The one
exception to this pattern in M. Ohal. 13:3 (No. 4). Here Tarfon's
decision takes intention into account. But in the parallel version
of this unit of tradition in Sifre Zuṭṭa, the attributions are reversed; Tarfon thereby holds that objective facts are determinative.
We note in support of the reading in Sifre Zuṭṭa that M. Ohal. 13:3
is only one of two disputes between Tarfon and Aqiva in which the
latter's ruling comes first. In Sifre Zuṭṭa Tarfon's opinion precedes that of Aqiva.

     Several of the above items, as well as others analyzed in
studies of corpora of other Yavneans and in Neusner's work on the
Order of Purities, indicate that the problem of objective facts
vs. subjective presumptions is a fundamental Yavnean concern. In
seven of the items (Nos. 4, 10, 13, 24, 32, 39, 42), Tarfon's ruling is opposed by a view attributed to Aqiva. For the latter,

subjective presumptions are determinative. What people intend to
do, or what they think may have occurred is important. Other rulings attributed to Aqiva, not opposed by Tarfon, agree with this
point of view. For example, throughout the tractate of Kelim,
Aqiva holds that the intention of the user determines whether or
not an object is susceptible to uncleanness. In M. Kel. 12:5,
22:9, 27:5 he thus rules, contrary to the view of sages, that no
act of preparation is needed for an object to serve a new function.
The mere designation by the user that the utensil will now function in a new manner renders it susceptible to uncleanness. Similarly, in M. Miq. 3:3, Aqiva contends that only water which is
drawn intentionally renders an immersion pool unfit. Form alone,
an objective criterion, does not determine the point at which an
oven is susceptible to uncleanness. It must be functional, be
able to serve man's purposes, to fall under these rules (Sifra
Shemini Pereq 10:5-6). For an object to be treated as connected
with another item, formal relationship, its attachment to the
other item is not sufficient. The joined items must be able to
function as a whole.

A number of units of tradition assigned to Joshua (M. Ter.
8:1-3, M. Par. 9:4, Tos. Shab. 15:10, M. Pes. 6:5, Tos. Men. 2:16,
M. Ker. 4:2-3 and M. Miq. 2:7-9) relate to the question of objective facts vs. subjective presumptions or, more specifically, to
the question of deed vs. intention. Joshua consistently holds that
both action and intention are needed in reaching legal decisions.
As Green puts it, "Intention without action is meaningless, and
unconscious action is of no account."[7] For example, Joshua rules
that a person who merely intends to drink sin-offering water does
not render it unfit. He must actually raise the flask containing
it to his lips in order to have this effect.

Several rulings of Eliezer and of Eleazar b. Azariah also
deal with the question at hand. In the case of both of these masters, no consistent position is articulated. Eliezer in several
instances (M. Beş. 4:7, M. Par. 9:4, M. Pes. 6:3, M. Zev. 1:1)
rules that intention alone suffices to establish the law. But in
other cases (M. Ter. 8:1-3, M. Miq. 2:7-9, M. Beş. 4:6), the person's presumptions are irrelevant, and only the fact that an action
was performed determines which rule applies in the situation.
Similarly, Neusner concludes, "What is most striking is that for
Eliezer [in his rulings in Kel.] a consistent stress on either form
or function as a criterion for determining the law seems absent."[8]

Zahavy in his study of Eleazar reaches the same results.   In some
pericopae (M. Ma. 5:1, M. Shev. 3:3, M. M.Q. 1:2, M. Shab. 4:2,
M. Eruv. 4:1), objective criteria form the basis for Eleazar's
ruling.   But in M. Beṣ. 2:8, M. Kel. 3:8, Tos. Kel. 2:6, M. Ket.
5:1, and M. Uqṣ. 1:5, the person's intention is significant.

Our brief review of the corpora of the other masters shows
that these other Yavneans addressed the theoretical question that
unites much of the Tarfon-tradition.   Unlike Tarfon, for all these
other masters subjective presumptions play a role in reaching
decisions.   These other authorities simply differ either about
whether objective criteria or subjective presumptions always are
determinative (Eliezer and Eleazar), or about whether one of the
two considerations alone is sufficient to have this effect (Aqiva,
Joshua, Eliezer).   Tarfon, on the other hand, consistently holds
that presumptions are not significant, and that objective criteria
by themselves dictate the law.

Turning to Tarfon's units of tradition relating to priestly
matters, we find that they cover the various themes of his agendum.
When he rules on matters pertaining to purity law (No. 7), to
agricultural law (Nos. 20-22), to family law (Nos. 39, 42, 43), as
well as to Temple-law, he focuses upon issues concerning priests.
For instance, Tarfon details certain rules governing the priest's
purification of lepers (No. 7).   He comments (No. 42) upon the
right of an Israelite woman betrothed to a priest to eat heave-
offering.   In these items, Tarfon consistently rules in the
priest's behalf and also encourages the performance of those
rituals in which the latter occupies the central role.   In M. Bekh.
2:6-8 (No. 33), he favors the priest over the owner of the lamb,
for he contends that if we are not sure which of two animals is
the firstling, the priest can claim the better one of them.   Similarly, in M. Ket. 7:2 (No. 42), Tarfon asserts that a future husband, who is a priest, may give the woman all her provisions as
heave-offering.   This clearly is to the priest's advantage, for he
either receives heave-offering, or he can purchase it cheaply.   In
M. Ter. 9:2 (No. 21), Tarfon allows only poor priests to glean
from a field mistakenly sown with heave-offering.   The priests,
accordingly, do not have to purchase the crops from the poor
Israelites.   Finally, Tarfon rules in M. Ter. 4:5 that one may
give as heave-offering virtually all of his produce.   This ruling,
in addition to benefitting the priest, also encourages the performance of this ritual.   In light of the disparity between the figures

prescribed by the Houses for the minimum one may give as heave-
offering (2-3%) and the amount allowed by Tarfon, it is safe to
assume that for the latter the setting aside of heave-offering has
a different meaning. Tarfon's ruling in No. 22 (Tos. Hag. 3:33)
is equally as novel. Here he states that a priest may receive
from anyone, at any time during the year, heave-offering of wine
and of olive oil. Tarfon attributes to Yoḥanan b. Zakkai this
view that runs counter to the presupposition of much of mishnaic
law. I have no idea what to make of this claim of authority. The
important thing for us is that, like M. Ter. 4:5, Tos. Ḥag. 3:33
clearly encourages the observance of the ritual. Tarfon's actions
reported in Tos. Bekh. 6:14 have the same effect with regard to
the ritual of redeeming first-born children. This unit of tradition relates that after the completion of the ceremony, Tarfon returned the redemption-coins to the father. People obviously are
more apt to perform a ritual if they know it will not cost them
anything.

     The units of tradition indicate that Tarfon's views foster
the performance of two of the key priestly functions: that of receiving heave-offering and that of the redemption of first-born
children. A third important priestly duty, the purification of
lepers, is mentioned in another of his traditions. In Tos. Neg.
8:2, Tarfon asserts that he has purified lepers, and that it is
permitted to do so even after the destruction of the Temple. In
this item we have a pro-priestly polemic, the assertion that even
after the loss of the cultic center, priests still have a part to
play in the life of the community. Perhaps this is also the hidden agendum underlying Tarfon's other rulings on priestly concerns.

     Three other matters are mentioned in a number of units of
tradition: a concern for the rights of women, an interest in avoiding economic losses, and a concern to protect the sanctity and
value of consecrated items. In five items (Nos. 39, 42, 43, 45,
and 46), Tarfon's ruling benefits the woman. In No. 45 he advo-
cates that we act leniently and allow the weakest claimant, the
woman, to acquire the property. No. 43 relates that Tarfon betrothed women during years of want in order to provide them with
sustenance. In No. 39, he allows the co-wife to continue to eat
heave-offering. Tarfon declares invalid a writ of divorce (No.
46) which prohibits the woman from marrying a particular individual. In all of these rulings, we have a consistent approach to the
question of the rights of women.

Four decisions (Nos. 15, 25, 35, 36) covering various themes demonstrate an interest in avoiding economic losses. In Tos. Demai 5:22 (No. 15), Tarfon advises Simeon Shezuri to purchase crops in the market and separate tithe from them on behalf of his untithed crops in the mixture. By following this course of action, Simeon need not consecrate all of his already tithed produce. In M. Ker. 5:2-3, Tarfon's goal is to save the sinner the unwarranted cost of two guilt-offerings. His action, described in No. 35, indicates that the priest may return the redemption-coins to the father. Finally, the pilgrim who follows Tarfon's view on the matter of unclean vetches of second-tithe does not have to pay the fine of twenty-five percent (No. 25). The above summaries indicate that we again have a consistent position on an issue. The same may be said with regard to four rulings relating to consecrated items (Nos. 21, 25, 26, 34). Underlying Tarfon's decision in all these pericopae is the concern that we protect and maintain the value and the sanctity of consecrated items. No. 21 prescribes that only priests may glean from a field mistakenly sown with heave-offering. Nos. 25-26 both deal with the problem of exchanging second-tithe. In No. 34, Tarfon rules that both animals must be treated as doubtful firstlings.

The above five issues, each discussed in items pertaining to the various themes of the agendum, account for only half of the corpus (thirty-two of sixty-five items). Of the other thirty-three units of tradition, twenty (Nos. 1, 3, 6, 14, 19, 23, 27, 30, 31, 37, 38, 40, 44, 47, 55, 56, 57, 61, 62, 64) are based upon a variety of principles which have nothing in common with each other. In the case of the remaining thirteen items (Nos. 2, 5, 11, 12, 28, 29, 48, 53, 54, 58, 59, 60, 63), I can discern no principle at all. Now although only 50% of the corpus is accounted for by the five recurrent issues, nevertheless the corpus has a considerable degree of coherence when compared with those of other masters, specifically Eleazar and Yose. In the case of Eleazar, Zahavy concludes, "Eleazar's rulings are not based on a single legal principle but on a set of several varied legal considerations."[9] But Eleazar does not even hold a consistent position with regard to some of these principles. As noted above, in some cases he rules on the basis of objective facts, while in others subjective presumptions are determinative. In his study of Yose, Lightstone reaches similar conclusions. No "small set of legal principles operates within the corpus and determines its diverse rulings. One gets the

impression that the tradition is comprised of one unrelated opinion after another."[10] The results of our analysis, on the other
hand, are more in line with those reached by Neusner in his study
of the units of tradition attributed to Eliezer. A number of concerns are evident in a significant portion of his corpus. Eliezer
through logic "attempted to produce an orderly account of what
should be done [in the Temple] in the future." He tried "to sim-
plify what may formerly have been complicated and perhaps internally contradictory rules."[11] At the same time, however, Neusner
notes: "Perhaps Eliezer attempted to legislate according to a coherent philosophy, but we have only a little evidence to suggest
so."[12] Thus there is only a degree of coherence, and even more
important, no inconsistency in the principles operative in the
various pericopae attributed to Eliezer. Our data for Tarfon
point to a similar conclusion. Compared with the legal corpora in
M.-Tos. of other masters, that of Tarfon is coherent.

Legal Units of Tradition First Found
in Later Strata (II-IV)

The analysis of the legal units of tradition that first appear in the later strata of the corpus focuses solely upon the
relationship between these items and those in M.-Tos. We are interested in whether these items discuss themes and articulate
principles not found in the materials in the earliest stratum, or
pertain to the concerns of those materials. We summarize each
item, noting its theme, Tarfon's ruling, and its connection, if
any, to M.-Tos. We also list any textual evidence which suggests
that a tradition bears a questionable attribution. On these
grounds we may exclude from consideration items which may not belong to the Tarfon-corpus.

A. Halakhic Midrashim

    Mekh. Sim.
    1. Mekh. Sim. 12:9 (Mekh. Ish. Pisḥa 6, b. Pes. 74a,
        y. Pes. 7:1)--This is a poorly preserved tradition.
        The various versions have different readings and
        different attributions. Mekh. Ish. knows nothing
        of Tarfon. There is no connection between this
        item which discusses the method for roasting the
        Passover-offering and the materials in M.-Tos.

    Sifra
    1. Sifra 'Emor 16:4 (b. Suk. 31a, y. Suk. 3:1)--Tarfon
        rules that the "palm branches" mentioned in Lev
        23:40 must be in bunches. Aqiva contends that the

verse implies that they need only be branches.
Two items in M.-Tos. (M. Suk. 3:4 and Tos. Suk.
2:8) deal with various aspects of the "four kinds"
mentioned in Lev 23:40.

2. Sifra 'Emor 13:4 (b. Men. 45b)--This exegesis indi-
    cates that one may offer without the bread-offering,
    on Pentecost, the seven lambs. These sacrifices
    are prescribed in Lev 23:18. No tradition in the
    earliest stratum deals with this matter.

Sifre
1. Sifre Num. 148 (b. Men. 68b)--M. Men. 10:6 rules
    that if one brought a meal offering from the new
    grain prior to the bringing of the bread offering,
    it is fit. Tarfon disagrees by claiming it is
    unfit. There is no mention of these matters in
    units of tradition in M.-Tos. But like Sifra
    'Emor 16:4 and Sifra 'Emor 13:4, this item relates
    to one of the commandments found in Leviticus 23
    (vs. 16).

2. Sifre Num. 118a (b. Zev. 57a)--Tarfon deduces (Num
    18:18) that one may consume a firstling for two
    days and one night. This agrees with the anonymous
    law of M. Zev. 5:8.

3. Sifre Num. 118b--One does not redeem dead and unclean
    firstlings; an exegesis of Num 18:15. The rela-
    tionship of this item to those in M.-Tos. is the
    same as the preceding tradition.

The evidence from the halakhic midrashim is mixed. Three
(Sifra 'Emor 16:4, Sifre Num. 118a, and Sifre Num. 118b) items are
closely related to M.-Tos.; three (Mekh. Sim. 12:9, Sifra 'Emor
13:4, and Sifre Num. 148) are not. One (Mekh. Sim. 12:9) of the
latter, however, bears a questionable attribution. As to the
three units of tradition related to M.-Tos., two (Sifre Nos. 2 and
3) deal with firstlings; the third, Sifra 'Emor 16:4, with the
lulav. Both topics are mentioned in at least two pericopae of the
first stratum. These items found in the halakhic midrashim, accordingly, provide evidence for the continuity of the legal portion of the corpus.

Even the units of tradition in this stratum which do not deal
with themes found in materials in M.-Tos. are not random. All
three detail rules for sacrifices. Five of the six items in the
halakhic midrashim thus center upon priestly concerns. Furthermore, the two units of traditions with reliable attributions that
discuss matters not found in the earliest stratum (Sifra 'Emor 13:4
and Sifre Num. 148) are closely related to each other as well as to
Sifra 'Emor 16:4. Each of these three items focuses upon one of
the three agricultural festivals mentioned in Leviticus 23. Sifre

Num. 148 speaks of the 'omer brought on Passover and of the bread-
offering brought on Pentecost. Sifra 'Emor 13:4 deals with a
different aspect of the latter offering. As already noted, Sifra
'Emor 16:4 relates to the lulav. These three items, therefore,
form a commentary upon Leviticus 23.

B. Beraitot

1. b. Shab. 29b--Judah reports that on the Sabbath,
    with Tarfon's approval, he used a perforated egg-
    shell as a lamp. This ma'aseh serves as a prece-
    dent for Judah's opinion in M. Shab. 2:4. This
    item is related in theme and in principle to units
    of tradition in M.-Tos. M. Shab. 2:2 concerns the
    oils one may use on the Sabbath for lighting the
    lamp. The notion that the present appearance of
    an item and not what may happen to it in the future
    determines its legal status underlies many of
    Tarfon's rulings.

2. b. Pes. 118a--Tarfon's saying details the prayers
    one says on Passover evening over the fourth
    (fifth?) cup of wine. M. Pes. 10:6 also relates
    to the liturgy of the Seder.

3. b. R.H. 25b (b. M.Q. 90b)--If the members of a
    Sanhedrin observed a murder, some act as judges
    and some as witnesses. Aqiva contends they all
    serve only as witnesses. No unit of tradition in
    M.-Tos. deals with the matter of testimony and
    court procedures.

4. b. Giṭ. 88b (Tanḥuma Mishpatim 6)--One should not
    make himself dependent upon gentile courts. There
    is no unit of tradition in M.-Tos. relating to
    this matter. She'iltot and Tanḥuma attribute
    this saying to Meir and to Simeon respectively.

5. b. Qid. 24b (b. Giṭ. 42b)--A slave who is set free
    because of an injury inflicted by his master does
    not receive a writ of emancipation. Aqiva con-
    tends he is entitled to this document. There is
    no connection between this unit and M.-Tos.

6. y. Demai 3:4--Simeon says in the name of Tarfon
    that crops deposited with a gentile storehouse-
    owner are demai. In M. Demai 3:4 this saying is
    attributed only to Simeon. Tos. Demai 4:25 assigns
    it to Simeon and to Simeon b. Gamaliel.

7. y. Ḥal. 2:3--This exegetical tradition uses a
    gezerah shavah to prove that dough mixed with oil
    is liable to dough-offering. The attributive
    formula is "Simeon says in the name of Tarfon."
    This item bears no relationship to materials in
    M.-Tos.

8. y. Meg. 1:8 (y. Ket. 3:1)--The attributive formula
    and the exegetical technique found in this unit of
    tradition are identical to those in the preceding
    item, y. Ḥal. 2:3. The exegesis indicates that
    those liable to *karet* are not flogged. No item in
    M.-Tos. deals with this matter.

Six of the eight items first appearing in beraitot are unrelated to materials in M.-Tos. Two of these (b. Giṭ. 88b and y.
Demai 3:4) bear questionable attributions. There is a pattern to
the remaining four units of tradition for three of them (b. R.H.
25b, b. Qid. 24b and y. Meg. 1:8), as well as b. Giṭ. 88b, deal
with diverse aspects of courtroom procedure. Additionally, y.
Meg. 1:8 is closely related to another of the units of tradition
of this sort, y. Ḥal. 2:3. Both are exegeses that employ the
technique *gezerah shavah*, and both have the tradental formula,
"Simeon says in the name of Tarfon."

Like their counterparts in the halakhic midrashim, the two
items closely linked to M. carry forward the concerns and the
principles of the earliest stratum. b. Shab. 29b discusses the
Sabbath-lamp; b. Pes. 118, the liturgy for the *Seder*. In the
former, Tarfon bases his ruling on the principle that objective
facts are determinative.

C. Amoraic Stratum

    1. y. Pes. 10:1--Judah rules that on Passover evening
        one should make women and children happy in ways
        appropriate for each of them. This saying is
        glossed by the statement, "Thus Tarfon used to do."
        A ruling in M. Pes. 10:6 centers upon the procedures
        for Passover evening.

    2. y. Yev. 4:11--This *ma'aseh* relates that Tarfon
        immediately married his sister-in-law after his
        wife's death. I cannot detect any connection be-
        tween this unit of tradition and M.-Tos.

    3. y. Naz. 3:5--Tarfon and Aqiva disagree about whether
        or not a Nazirite who takes his vows in a cemetery
        and subsequently returns there must bring an offer-
        ing for uncleanness. Tarfon rules he must bring
        such an offering; Aqiva contends he need not. A
        unit of tradition found in M. Naz. 6:6 details the
        purification procedures followed by an unclean
        Nazirite. Furthermore, Tarfon's ruling is based
        upon the principle that someone's intrinsic traits,
        and not what may occur to him in the future, is
        legally determinative.

    4. y. Soṭ. 6:2--This pericope deals with a case of
        doubt: Does *one* witness cause a suspected adulter-
        ess to forfeit the money prescribed in her *ketubah*?

             As in M.-Tos., Tarfon rules leniently, claiming
that the woman does not have to give up this money.
This unit of tradition is also thematically related
to items in M.-Tos., for M. Ket. 7:6 and M. Ket.
9:2-3 deal with the collection of the *ketubah*.

5.   b. Bekh. 11a--Tarfon's ruling in this story details
the redemption price for a first-born ass. As already noted, several traditions in M.-Tos. center
upon the matter of firstlings.

The materials that first appear in the fourth stratum of the
corpus are closely related to M., for four (Nos. 1, 3, 4, 5) of
the five items deal with concerns expressed in the earliest stratum. The themes of Nos. 1 and 5 (Passover evening and firstlings),
are mentioned in all levels of the corpus. Nos. 3 and 4 are related in terms of both their issues and their principles to M.-Tos.
The one item in strata IV not related to M.-Tos. (y. Yev. 4:11)
may in fact best be treated as an *aggadah*. Accordingly, all of
the units of tradition in this level of the corpus discuss concerns of its earlier levels.

D.   Summary of Legal Traditions in Strata II-IV and of the
     Entire Legal Corpus

       The materials that first surface in these strata point to the
coherence of the legal portion of the corpus. More than half of
the items with reliable attributions (nine of sixteen) are related
in theme, and in some instances also in principle, to M.-Tos.
These units of tradition focus upon a limited number of issues,
in particular, firstlings and Passover evening. Furthermore, several items deal with the chief philosophical question of the corpus, objective facts vs. subjective presumptions. Of the three
strata, only III, beraitot, contains a large number of traditions
(six) not closely tied to M.-Tos. But even these items, as well
as their counterparts in the halakhic midrashim, are far from random. Of the former, four relate to courtroom procedure, a theme
not found in the materials in the earliest stratum. The latter,
those in halakhic midrashim, center upon the offerings brought on
the various festivals. These items, therefore, are tangentially
related to the dominant interests of the corpus.

       The results of our analysis in this chapter coincide with our
conclusion in Chapter IX. The formal and substantive traits of
the units of tradition indicate that they are situated within the
mainstream of mishnaic law. Except in the area of Temple law,
their concerns also are those of others. For the most part,

Tarfon's role is to apply and refine earlier laws. The few ideas
that apparently are original to his items do not generate significant developments. His decisions reveal a strong coherence in
terms of their underlying principles and concerns. These themes
and interests, covering the major areas of the agendum, unite
large segments of the items in M.-Tos., as well as those first
found in the later layers of the corpus. The legal corpus is a
coherent tradition.

NOTES

CHAPTER X

[1]The results of our analysis of the traditions in M.-Tos.
provide a control for evaluating materials which first appear in
later strata.

[2]We omit the following items: M. Beṣ. 3:5, M. Naz. 6:6, Tos.
Zev. 1:8, M. Ned. 6:6. In the first three, no rulings are assigned to Tarfon. The meaning of the final item is unclear.

[3]Neusner, *Phar.* III, pp. 291ff.; idem, *Eliezer* II, pp. 134ff.,
161ff., 170-224; Zahavy, p. 290; Porton diss., pp. 458-68, 477-78,
Kanter, Conclusions.

[4]The classification of the corpus of the Houses, and by comparison those of the other four masters, as Pharisaic, is based
upon the generally accepted assumption that the former are Pharisees. One fact supports this assumption: namely, the agendum of
the NT Pharisees corresponds to that found in the rabbinic traditions about the Houses.

[5]Neusner, *Eliezer* II, p. 299.

[6]Neusner's analyses in *HMLP* show that rulings of named masters generally pertain to minor details.

[7]Green, *Joshua*, p. 558.

[8]Neusner, *Eliezer* II, pp. 330-31.

[9]Zahavy, p. 296.

[10]Lightstone, p. 340.

[11]Neusner, *Eliezer* II, p. 142.

[12]Ibid., p. 129.

CHAPTER XI

FORMAL EXEGESES

A formally distinct part of the corpus consists of items
containing a comment by Tarfon upon a citation from Scripture.
Our sole concern is to determine whether or not these items form
a coherent set of materials. A positive answer to this question
would indicate that this group of materials constitutes a tradition. By a tradition I mean a body of individual pericopae which
have in common some clearly delineated feature, and whose constituent pericopae, first occurring in later levels of the corpus,
are formulated in line with those in earlier strata of the corpus.
If we should have a tradition, then we may claim that the formulators of these items adhered to the same pattern and included
verses in the units of tradition for the same reason.

The formal exegeses may be coherent in one of the following
ways. First, they may focus upon a particular portion, e.g.,
chapter or book, of Scripture. Second, they may deal with a specific topic. Third, they may employ a limited number of hermeneutical techniques, e.g., the *heqqesh* or the *qal vaḥomer*.[1] Each of
the three patterns suggests that a choice has been made in the
formation of the group of materials, for the items could have
dealt with many parts of Scripture, discussed a broad set of
topics, or used a variety of techniques. Furthermore, commentar-
ies have been organized in these ways;[2] accordingly, we look for
such arrangements in the Tarfon-materials. If we find patterns,
we claim that the items constitute a tradition.

The following chart lists the exegetical units of tradition
according to their occurrence within the strata of the corpus,
thereby illustrating the patterns of their distribution. We
divide the materials into legal and non-legal types. Parallel
versions of a unit of tradition lacking a Scriptural citation are
listed in parentheses.

Fig. 1. Distribution by Strata of the Formally Exegetical Materials

Legal Exegeses

Content	I [M.-Tos.]	II [Halakhic Midrashim]	III [Beraitot]	IV [Amoraic Materials]	V [Later Compilations]
1. Offering of remembrance of the woman suspected of adultery	Tos. Sot. 1:10	Sifre Num. 8	y. Sot. 3:4	--	--
2. Bread-offering	--	Sifra 'Emor 13:4	b. Men. 45b	--	--
3. Palm branches	--	Sifra 'Emor 16:4	b. Suk. 31a,32a; y. Suk. 3:1	--	--
4. Dead firstling	--	Sifre Num. 118	--	--	--
5. Lame priest	(Tos. Sot. 7:16)	Sifre Num. 75	(y. Yoma 1:1); (y. Meg. 1:12); (y. Hor. 3:5)	--	--
6. Free-will offering of oil	(M. Men. 12:5); (Tos. Men. 12:10a); (M. Zev. 10:8)	Sifra Vayiqra 8:7	(b. Zev. 91b)	--	--
7. Dough-offering	--	--	y. Hal. 2:3	--	--
8. *Karet* and stripes	--	--	y. Meg. 1:8; y. Ket. 3:1	--	--
9. Gentile courts	--	--	b. Git. 88b	--	--

Non-Legal Exegeses

Content	I [M.-Tos.]	II [Halakhic Midrashim]	III [Beraitot]	IV [Amoraic Materials]	V [Later Compilations]
1. Merit of the righteous	Tos. Ber. 4:16-18G-M	Mekh. Sim. 14:22G-L; Mekh. Ish. Beshalah 6 A-F	--	--	--
2. Judah and kingship	Tos. Ber. 4:16-18N-OO	Mekh. Sim. 14:22M-GG; Mekh. Ish. Beshalah 6 K-AA	--	--	--

Content	I	II	III	IV	V
3. Praise of Yose	Tos. Miq. 7:11	Sifre Num. 125	- - -	- -	- -
4. *Minim*	Tos. Shab. 13:5	- - -	b. Shab. 116a y. Shab. 16:1	- -	- -
5. God is faithful to redeem	- -	Mekh. Sim. 6:2	- - -	- -	- -
6. God's providence	- -	Mekh. Sim. 16:14 Mekh. Ish. Vayassa 4	- -	- -	- -
7. Priest and heave-offering	- -	Sifre Num. 116 Sifre Zuṭṭa 18:17	b. Pes. 72b	- -	- -
8. Mourn for those doing *miṣvot*	- -	- - -	b. M.Q. 28b	- -	- -
9. Praise of Aqiva	- -	- -	- -	- -	ARN A 6
10. Tarfon's responses to comments	- -	- -	- -	- -	Gen. R. 91:9 ARN B 40
11. Praise of work	- -	- -	- -	- -	ARN A 11
12. Praise God while persecuted	- -	- -	- -	- -	Mid. Ps. 7:13
13. He who does righteousness	- -	- -	- -	- -	Mid. Ps. 106:3 Esther R. 6:1
14. Miracles ordained at creation	- -	- -	- -	- -	PRE 10
15. Nations and Torah	- -	- -	- -	- -	PRE 41

The twenty-four formally-exegetical items (19% of the entire
Tarfon-corpus) are not evenly distributed among its strata. While
only 6% (five of seventy-three)[3] of the units of tradition in
M.-Tos. contain exegeses, 33-50% of the items first appearing in
halakhic midrashim (six of fourteen, 42%), beraitot (four of
twelve, 33%), and later compilations (seven of fourteen, 50%) are
formally-exegetical. These divergent distributions correspond to
the formulary tendencies of the documents of the various strata.
M., and to a lesser extent Tos., do not generally include citations of Scripture and, predictably, the Tarfon-material reflects
this pattern.[4] Halakhic midrashim and many later compilations,
on the other hand, rely on the Bible for their redactional organi-
zation and, as expected, significant proportions of Tarfon's items
here are formally exegetical. In contrast to this uneven distribution, the exegeses are evenly distributed between legal and non-
legal materials. If we exclude from our sample all units of tradition in M.-Tos., nearly equal percentages of legal (six of nineteen, 32%) and non-legal (eleven of thirty-six, 31%) items are
exegetical. We omit M.-Tos., which skews the data, since it contains 80% of all legal pericopae, compared to only 10% of the non-
legal materials and, as I have said, does not usually incorporate
quotations from Scripture.[5]

We turn to the question of the internal coherence of the exegeses, noting in the following chart the verses upon which they
comment.

Fig. 2. Verses Commented Upon in the Exegeses

	Verse	Legal	Non-legal
1.	Gen 37:25		Tos. Ber. 4:16-18G-M
2.	Gen 42:38		Gen. R. 91:9
3.	Exod 4:13		Mekh. Sim. 6:2
4.	Exod 16:14		Mekh. Sim. 16:14
5.	Exod 21:1	b. Giṭ. 88b	
6.	Exod 25:8		ARN A 11
7.	Exod 25:39		Gen. R. 91:9
8.	Lev 2:1	Sifra Vayiqra 8:7	
9.	Lev 10:6		b. M.Q. 28b
10.	Lev 23:18	Sifra 'Emor 13:4	
11.	Lev 23:29	y. Meg. 1:8	
12.	Lev 23:40	Sifra 'Emor 16:4	
13.	Num 5:15	Tos. Soṭ. 1:10	
14.	Num 10:8	Sifre Num. 75	
15.	Num 15:20	y. Ḥal. 2:3	
16.	Num 18:7		Sifre Num. 116
17.	Num 18:17	Sifre Num. 118	
18.	Deut 33:2		PRE 41
19.	Isa 57:8		Tos. Shab. 13:5
20.	Jonah 1:17		PRE 10

	Verse	Legal	Non-legal
21.	Ps 7:1		Mid. Ps. 7:13
22.	Ps 106:3		Mid. Ps. 106:3
23.	Ps 114:2		Tos. Ber. 4:16-18N-OO
24.	Job 28:11		ARN A 6
25.	Dan 8:4-7		Tos. Miq. 7:11

The exegeses do not focus upon a limited section of Scripture.
The cited verses, particularly those in the non-legal materials,
are spread among the books of the Bible.[6] The only interesting
exception is Nos. 10, 11, and 12--three comments upon Leviticus 23.
If a comparable concentration were to characterize a large portion
of the exegeses, we might have evidence of a tradition.

The exegeses must center upon a specific topic, such as the
laws of firstlings, to be considered coherent in content.[7] In the
following chart we note in parentheses the specific topics which
the exegetical items discuss. For the sake of convenience, we
divide the materials according to their more general themes, e.g.,
sacrificial law.

Fig. 3.

Legal

Sacrificial and Temple law
1. Tos. Soṭ. 1:10 (offering of remembrance of the woman suspected of adultery is brought on an unhappy occasion)
2. Sifra Vayiqra 8:7 (free-will offering of oil)
3. Sifra 'Emor 13:4 (one may offer on Pentecost the bread-
   offering without the seven lambs)
4. Sifre Num. 75 (lame priest blows the horns in the Temple)
5. Sifre Num. 118 (one does not redeem dead or unclean
   firstlings)

Civil law
1. y. Meg. 1:8 (those liable to *karet* for violations of Yom
   Kippur are not flogged)
2. b. Giṭ. 88b (do not become dependent upon gentile courts)

Agricultural law
1. y. Ḥal. 2:3 (dough mixed with oil is liable to dough-
   offering)

Festival law
1. Sifra 'Emor 16:4 (the palm branches must be in bunches)

Non-legal

Torah and the rabbi
1. b. M.Q. 28b (mourn for those performing *miṣvot*)
2. PRE 41 (nations reject the Torah)

Praise or criticism of Aqiva
1. Tos. Miq. 7:11 (criticizes Aqiva and praises Yose)
2. ARN A 6 (praises Aqiva)

Messianism
1. Tos. Ber. 4:16-18N-OO (call for activism to bring the
    Messiah)
2. Mekh. Sim. 6:2 (God is faithful to promises of redemption)

Miscellaneous
1. Tos. Shab. 13:5 (*minim*)
2. Tos. Ber. 4:16-18G-M (merit of the righteous)
3. Sifre Num. 116 (priests and heave-offering)
4. Mekh. Sim. 16:14 (God's providence)
5. Gen. R. 91:9 (Tarfon's responses to comments)
6. ARN A 11 (praise of work)
7. PRE 10 (miracles ordained at creation)
8. Mid. Ps. 7:13 (praise God while persecuted)
9. Mid. Ps. 106:3 (identification of he who does righteousness)

The formal exegeses do not deal with a limited set of topics.
The substance of the non-legal items especially is diffuse. At
most only two exegeses relate even to the same theme. The legal
materials, on the other hand, are more focused. Five of the nine
(56%) discuss sacrificial and Temple-law. Still all five units of
tradition deal with different and unrelated topics and, therefore,
do not join together to form a tradition. Similarly, each of the
other four legal items centers upon another topic.

We finally turn to the issue of the hermeneutical techniques
and divide the exegeses according to them.

Fig. 4. Hermeneutical Techniques

I. Grammatical and Syntactical Peculiarities--The following groups
    of exegeses (A-C) build upon either the syntax or grammatical
    features of verses.

    A. Order of Clauses--An explanation based upon the order of
        the clauses of the verse.

        1. Tos. Sot. 1:10 (legal)--By reading the phrases in
            Num 5:15 as appositives, "A meal offering of remem-
            brance, bringing forth iniquity to remembrance,"
            Tarfon deduces that the offering of remembrance of
            the woman suspected of adultery is brought on an
            unhappy occasion.

        2. Sifra 'Emor 13:4 (legal)--The order of the words in
            Lev 23:18, "You shall present with the bread seven
            lambs," shows that the seven lambs are the primary
            sacrifice and may be offered without the bread-
            offering.

        3. Sifre Num. 116 (non-legal)--The order of the words
            in Num 18:7 indicates that the gift received by the
            priest, the heave-offering, is equivalent to their
            performance of Temple-service.

    B. Causal or Sequential Link--An exegesis which claims that
        the clauses of a verse describe causally or sequentially
        related events.

        1. Tos. Ber. 4:16-18N-OO (non-legal)--Tarfon reads Ps
            114:2, "Judah sanctified the name of God; [therefore],
            Israel became his kingdom."

    2. ARN A 11 (non-legal)--Tarfon provides a sequential connection between the clauses in Exod 25:8, "And you shall build Me a sanctuary, and [then] I will dwell in it."

    3. PRE 41 (non-legal)--Tarfon treats the clauses in Deut 33:2 as relating a sequence of events, and then concretizes the verses by supplying referents for the terms.

  C. Verb Tense--The tense of the verb serves as the basis for Tarfon's remark.

    1. PRE 10 (non-legal)--The past tense of the verb "prepare" in Jonah 1:17, "The Lord prepared a great fish to swallow Jonah," allows Tarfon to assert that God ordained miracles at the time of creation.

II. Peculiarity of Words

  A. *Gezerah Shavah*--An analogy based on identical or similar words in two different passages of Scripture.

    1. y. Ḥal. 2:3 (legal)--A *gezerah shavah* upon the word *ḥallah* allows Tarfon to deduce that dough mixed with oil is liable to dough-offering.

    2. y. Meg. 1:8 (legal)--The occurrence of the word *karet* in verses relating to the Sabbath and in those regarding the Day of Atonement is the basis for Tarfon's view that one liable to *karet* for violation of the Day of Atonement may not be flogged.

  B. Inclusion and Exclusion (*ribbui* and *miyy'ut*)--According to this technique, a given word of phrase indicates that the rule in which this word or phrase is found should be limited to the cases mentioned in the verse or should be extended to include additional matters.

    1. Sifre Num. 118 (legal)--"But" ('K) in Num 18:17 indicates that one may not redeem certain firstlings, e.g., dead or unclean ones.

    2. Sifra Vayiqra 8:7 (legal)--Lev 2:1 contains the superfluous word "offering," "And when anyone brings a meal-offering [as an] offering," in order to teach that the constituent elements of a meal-offering, such as the oil, may be brought as such a sacrifice.

    3. b. Giṭ. 88b (legal)--The words "before them" in Exod 21:1, "And these are the ordinances [judgments] that you should place before them," indicate that Israelites should bring their disputes only to Israelite courts.

  C. *Noṭariqon*--Explaining a word by using its letters to form new words.

    1. Mekh. Sim. 16:14 (non-legal)--Tarfon uses this principle to explain the *hapax legomenon* MḤŚPŚ.

  D. Double Meaning--Explanation of an equivocal word.

    1. Sifra 'Emor 16:4 (legal)--Since KPWT (Lev 23:40), "And you shall take KPWT of palms," has two meanings, branches and bunches, Tarfon claims that the palm branches must be in bunches.

E. Metaphor

    1. Tos. Shab. 13:5 (non-legal)--Tarfon treats, "your
memorial" (Isa 57:8), "And they have placed your
memorial behind the doorposts," as a symbol for
Torah. This proves that the *minim* have rejected
God's Torah.

F. Revocalization

    1. Gen. R. 91:9 (non-legal)--Tarfon revocalizes Gen
42:38, "My son (*benî*) shall not go down with you,"
changed to "my understanding" (*bēnî*) to indicate
that he does not agree with someone's view.

    2. Mid. Ps. 7:13 (non-legal)--Tarfon reads "*shiggayon*,"
(Ps 7:1), "A *shiggayon* of David which he sang to the
Lord concerning Cush the Benjaminite," as *siggayon*,
"many," in order to explain this rare biblical word.

III. Logic

A. *Qal Vaḥomer*--An *a fortiori* argument.

    1. Tos. Ber. 4:16-18G-M (non-legal)--Tarfon uses Gen
37:25 to draw the *qal vaḥomer* that God surely has
mercy upon the righteous when he is not angry with
them.

    2. b. M.Q. 28b (non-legal)--Lev 10:6 serves as the
basis for a *qal vaḥomer* which teaches that Israel
should mourn for those who perform many *miṣvot*.

IV. Concretization--Filling in background.

    1. Sifre Num. 75 (legal)--Tarfon specifies the type
of "priests" to which Num 10:8 refers.

    2. Tos. Miq. 7:11 (non-legal)--Tarfon applies Dan
8:4-7 to the disputants, Yose the Galilean and
Aqiva.

    3. Mekh. Sim. 6:2 (non-legal)--Tarfon fills in the
background of Moses' remark in Exod 4:13, "Send
them with whomever you choose."

    4. ARN A 6 (non-legal)--Tarfon identifies Aqiva as
the one who "brings forth to light things hidden
from man" (Job 28:11).

    5. Mid. Ps. 106:3 (non-legal)--Tarfon identifies
"the one who does righteousness at all times"
(Ps 106:3).

Eleven different hermeneutical techniques are used in the
twenty-four items.[8] Except for the concretization of biblical
references, no method occurs in more than three items.[9]

Summary

On the basis of the negative results of our inquiry, we may
claim only that it is impossible to demonstrate that the exegeses
are coherent. We cannot, however, disprove that the items stem
from a single hand, for a commentator may interpret various parts

of Scripture, discuss unrelated topics, and utilize a variety of
hermeneutical techniques.[10] But analyses of the corpora of Yose
and Ishmael, showing that their exegeses follow a pattern, add
weight to the claim that the Tarfon materials are incoherent.[11]

Since the verses appearing in the Tarfon-materials do not
exhibit any patterns, the citation of these verses cannot be explained in terms of a feature common to this complex of items.
The formulators of a given unit of tradition apparently have not
included a verse because other Tarfon-items contain a quotation
from the Bible. They have not deemed it important to assign to
Tarfon a coherent set of formal exegeses. As we have seen, it is
the traits of the documents in which the items appear that explain
why verses are found in them.

The respective roles of exegesis and law in early rabbinism
may account for the contrast between the incoherence of the formal
exegeses and the coherence of the legal materials. If the purpose
of law is to organize correctly and rationally every aspect of
life, then a rabbi ought to be consistent in his legal rulings.
Those responsible for the attribution of materials, as a result,
are concerned about the coherence of an authority's legal rulings.
Establishing the consistency of a master's decisions is in fact
one of the central projects of the amoraim. Interpretation of
Scripture does not serve a goal comparable to that of law. The
various exegeses assigned to a master, therefore, need not be
consistent.

CHAPTER XI

[1]These criteria organize Tarfon's comments in terms of their relationships to Scripture. We do not have sufficient data to look for internal literary patterns.

[2]The commentary to Isaiah at Qumran and halakhic midrashim, for example, use books of the Bible as their organizing principle. Pes. deRav. Kahana, Pes. Rab., and Hebrews, are arranged topically. A uniform approach to Scripture characterizes the Pesharim of Qumran.

[3]We count Tos. Ber. 4:16-18 as two items.

[4]No Tarfon-item in M. contains a citation of Scripture. Similarly, 3% of Joshua's materials in M., 3% of Eleazar's, 5% of Eliezer's, and 9% of Ishmael's are formally-exegetical. Only the units of tradition of Yose diverge from this consistent picture, for 44% of them contain quotations from the Bible.

[5]When M.-Tos. is included, only 10% (nine of eighty-eight) of the legal items in contrast to 36% (fifteen of forty-two) of the non-legal units of tradition are formally-exegetical. In this sample, we count Tos. Shab. 13:5 as a non-legal item, for the section of it containing the exegesis is not legal in content. We also treat Tos. Ber. 4:16-18 as two units of tradition, since it contains that number of interpretations of Scripture.

[6]The exegeses do deal with only a limited part of Scripture. 72% of the items (eighteen of twenty-five) focus upon verses in the Pentateuch; three, 12%, upon Psalms. Moreover, if we exclude from consideration the four exegetical items which are attributed elsewhere to masters other than Tarfon, ARN A 11 (No. 6), PRE 41 (No. 18), PRE 10 (No. 20), and ARN A 6 (No. 24), then sixteen of the twenty-one remaining items (76%) contain verses of the first four biblical books: Genesis, Exodus, Leviticus, and Numbers. Of these sixteen pericopae, five have verses from Leviticus, five from Numbers, four from Exodus, and only two from Genesis. Two-thirds (fourteen of twenty-one) of the remaining exegetical items thus focus upon three biblical books: Exodus, Leviticus and Numbers.

[7]If in the case of a large sample, for example 200 items, 150 deal with the same theme, e.g., sacrificial law, we may claim that they exhibit a pattern. But when the sample of items is small, a comparable shift must be made in the criterion for establishing coherence. The exegeses, therefore, must discuss a specific topic, such as the laws of the firstling.

[8]The various techniques appear in all of the corpus; therefore, no technique characterizes the materials of a particular stratum. In the following chart we note the levels of the corpus in which the exegetical methods are found.

Fig. 5. Distribution by Strata of the Hermeneutical Techniques

Technique	I	II	III	IV	V
Order of clauses	Tos. Sot. 1:10	Sifre 'Emor 13:4 Sifre Num. 116	-- --	-- --	-- --
Causal or sequen- tial connection	Tos. Ber. 4:16-18 N-OO	-- --	-- --	-- --	ARN A 11 PRE 41
Verb tense	-- --	-- --	--	-- --	PRE 10
Gezerah shavah	-- --	-- --	Y. Hal. 2:3 Y. Meg. 1:8	-- --	-- --
Inclusion and exclusion	-- --	Sifre Num. 118 Sifra Vayiqra 8:7	b. Giṭ. 88b	-- --	-- --
Noṭariqon	-- --	Mekh. Sim. 16:14	-- --	-- --	-- --
Double meaning	-- --	Sifra 'Emor 16:4	-- --	-- --	-- --
Metaphor	Tos. Shab. 13:5	-- --	-- --	-- --	-- --
Revocalization	-- --	-- --	-- --	-- --	Gen. R. 91:9 Mid. Ps. 7:13
Qal vaḥomer	Tos. Ber. 4:16-18G-M	-- --	b. M.Q. 28b	-- --	-- --
Concretization	Tos. Miq. 7:11	Sifre Num. 75 Mekh. Sim. 6:2	-- --	-- --	ARN A 6 Mid. Ps. 106:3

[9]Even if on the basis of the two considerations noted below
we exclude nine of the pericopae, ten different methods still are
used in the remaining sixteen items. Five of the excluded items
(Tos. Soṭ. 1:10, Sifre Num. 118, Sifra Vayiqra 8:7, Mekh. Sim.
6:2 and b. M.Q. 28b) apparently belong to larger units of materials in which they now appear, for their formulation and their
hermeneutical techniques are the same as those of the surrounding
pericopae. These items, therefore, may reflect the formulary
choices of the redactor of the document in which they are located. Four other units of tradition (ARN A 6, ARN A 11, PRE 10,
and PRE 41) have questionable attributions, for elsewhere they are
given in the names of authorities other than Tarfon. The following chart illustrates that the remaining sixteen items follow no
patterns.

Fig. 6. Hermeneutical Techniques of the Sixteen Pericopae

Grammatical and syntactical considerations

> *Order of clauses*
> 1. Sifra 'Emor 13:4
> 2. Sifre Num. 116
>
> *Provides causal or sequential connection between clauses*
> 1. Tos. Ber. 4:16-18N-OO

Word choice

> *Gezerah shavah*
> 1. y. Ḥal. 2:3
> 2. y. Meg. 1:8
>
> *Inclusion and exclusion*
> 1. b. Giṭ. 88b
>
> *Noṭariqon*
> 1. Mekh. Sim. 16:14
>
> *Double meaning*
> 1. Sifra 'Emor 16:4
>
> *Metaphor*
> 1. Tos. Shab. 13:5
>
> *Revocalization*
> 1. Gen. R. 91:9
> 2. Mid. Ps. 7:13

Logic

> *Qal vaḥomer*
> 1. Tos. Ber. 4:16-18G-M

Concretization

> 1. Sifre Num. 75
> 2. Tos. Miq. 7:11
> 3. Mid. Ps. 106:3

[10]For example, a preacher each week may deal with a new part
of Scripture, comment upon a new issue, and base his remarks upon
a new technique of interpretation.

[11]Lightstone, p. 342; Portion diss., pp. 429-57.

CHAPTER XII

HOMILETICAL-THEOLOGICAL MATERIALS

The Issues

One-quarter of the corpus (thirty-two of one hundred twenty-eight items) consists of units of tradition which attend to homiletical or theological topics. Two aspects of these materials are of concern to us: first, their coherence, and second, their continuity with the legal portions of the corpus. By dealing with these two issues, we learn about the processes and concerns governing the formulation of these items and their attribution to a single master, Tarfon. For example, if we find that the homiletical-theological items reveal the same formulary preferences, and focus upon a limited, distinct, and conceptually unified agendum of topics, then we may claim that they are not assigned arbitrarily to Tarfon. This in turn indicates that there is a concern to attribute to a master a coherent body of homiletical-theological items. If these items and the legal pericopae discuss the same specific matters, moreover, we may conclude that a similar concern governs the attribution of all items to Tarfon. Failure to find continuities between the legal and non-legal materials, however, does not prove that these two sets of units of tradition do not stem from the same hands, for the two different types of views of a person need not coincide. On the basis of negative findings we may claim only that we cannot demonstrate the unity of the corpus as a whole.

Because of the literary traits of the homiletical-theological materials, we must refine our questions regarding their coherence and continuity. Specifically, we deal with two different types of materials: (1) sayings attributed to Tarfon with homiletical or theological content, and (2) stories in which Tarfon's actions or comments serve as foils for the articulation by others of lessons with this content. Those responsible for the composition of this second type of material, the stories, do not claim that Tarfon holds the views articulated in them. Since Tarfon does not express an opinion, we cannot inquire about the connections between it and the views he enunciates in the sayings assigned to him. We accordingly ask the following question regarding the relationship between these stories and the sayings attributed to Tarfon: Do Tarfon's actions in the stories illustrate lessons which he

413

articulates in other pericopae? Our answer to this question indicates whether or not the formulators of the narratives presuppose
and build upon other homiletical-theological items. Authors of
these stories often implicitly assume that Tarfon has certain
character traits, for instance, that he is a rabbi who asserts the
prerogatives of his office. We therefore look for connections between these traits and the homiletical views assigned to Tarfon.

In the following sections of the chapter, we analyze separately the materials of each stratum. In order to facilitate our
discussion we briefly summarize the items in charts, noting their
formulation, their content, Tarfon's role in them, changes that
occur in parallel versions, and information suggesting a doubtful
attribution. Items with parallels in earlier strata are listed
in square brackets at the end of the charts.

Stratum I, M.-Tos.

1. Tos. Ber. 4:16-18--A dialogue between Tarfon and his
    students consisting of two exegeses by Tarfon on the
    merit of the righteous joined to his teaching about
    drinking water to quench one's thirst (M. Ber. 6:8).
    The first indicates that because of Joseph's merit
    God pitied him. On this basis Tarfon deduces if
    when God is angry He shows kindness toward the righ-
    teous, when He is compassionate He surely does so.
    The second exegesis teaches that Judah merited king-
    ship because he sanctified God's name by jumping into
    the Red Sea. Fulfilling one's duty, confessing sins,
    or atoning for sins do not suffice in order to merit
    political independence.

2. Tos. Shab. 13:5--An independent saying condemning
    minim; they recognize God, yet they deny Him.

3. M. Pes. 10:6--In this dispute Tarfon's prayer for
    redemption focuses upon the exodus from Egypt and the
    ability at present to eat *maṣṣah* and bitter herbs.
    By contrast, the prayer attributed to Aqiva looks
    forward to rebuilding the Temple and to offering
    sacrifices there.

4. M. Mak. 1:10--A saying assigned to Tarfon and to
    Aqiva condemns capital punishment.

5. M. Avot 2:15-16--Tarfon states in his independent
    saying that one receives a reward for whatever amount
    of Torah he studies. But the person must continually
    persist in the effort.

There is no thematic coherence among the five homiletical-
theological items in M.-Tos., for they discuss four unrelated
issues: (1) redemption (Nos. 1 and 3), (2) *minim* (No. 2),

(3) capital punishment (No. 4), (4) the rabbi and the Torah (No. 5). Moreover, the two units of tradition dealing with the theme of redemption pertain to different aspects of this topic.

Only one of the homiletical-theological items (Tos. Shab. 13:5) deals with a matter discussed in a legal unit of tradition assigned to Tarfon, Tos. Shab. 13:5. In this pericope Tarfon first states that before burning books of sectarians one need not cut out the divine names contained in them, and he then condemns *minim* for denying the authority of God.

The five items are formulated as various types of sayings. Three (Nos. 2, 4 and 5) are independent sayings, one (No. 3) an unbalanced dispute, and one (No. 1) a dialogue between Tarfon and his students in which the master is the dominant speaker. None of the dicta forms part of a unit comprised of sayings cast in the same pattern that are assigned to several masters.

Stratum II, Halakhic Midrashim

A. Mekh. Sim.
1. Ex. 6:2--In this exegesis formulated as an independent saying, Tarfon comments that Moses acts improperly, for he shirks his responsibility by asking God to send someone else to lead Israel out of Egypt. God, who has reason not to redeem Israel, faithfully keeps his promises. Furthermore, although, because of their actions, Israel should perish at the hands of Amaleq, God will save them for He has so promised. Tarfon's saying is one of nine exegeses, making the same point, that are attributed to Yavneans and Ushans.

2. Ex. 16:14--Explanation of *hapax legomenon* MḤŚPŚ. Tarfon's interpretation opposes an anonymous exegesis. He claims that this word indicates that the manna fell upon the thresholds of the Israelites' tents. The saying teaches that God performs miracles in a manner advantageous to the beneficiaries of His actions.

[3. Ex. 14:22--Parallels Tos. Ber. 4:16-18: merit of the righteous. This version lacks the *a fortiori* argument about God's compassion upon Israel in the hour of his anger. Tarfon merely comments upon the merit of the righteous = Joseph.]

B. Mekh. Ishmael
1. Baḥodesh 10--The story opens by relating that Tarfon, Joshua, Eleazar, and Aqiva visited Eliezer. The first three masters delivered the same sermon: a rabbi is precious for all of Israel, for he brings them into the world to come. Aqiva's saying, which comes last, focuses upon the preciousness of chastisements. The motif of four sages appears in Tos. Giṭ. 9:1.

[2. Beshalaḥ 6--Parallels Tos. Ber. 4:16-18: merit of the
     righteous. Like Mekh. Sim. 14:22, this version lacks
     the comment about God's compassion in the hour of His
     anger.]

[3. Vayassa 4--Parallels Mekh. Sim. 16:14: explanation of
     MḤŠPŚ.]

C. Sifra
    1. Qodashim 4:9--Tarfon, Eleazar, and Aqiva state in
        identically formulated dicta, that no one of their
        generation knows how to receive or give reproof.
        Yose the Galilean then relates that Aqiva knows how
        to receive reproof.

D. Sifre Num.
    1. 116--Tarfon deduces from Num 18:7 that, after the
        destruction of the Temple, eating heave-offering is
        equivalent to performing Temple-service. There is
        a substitute for the cult after 70. Priests, how-
        ever, still are the cultic officials. This saying
        is set in a narrative framework.

E. Sifre Zuṭṭa
    [1. 18:17--Parallels Sifre 116: eating heave-offering
         is equivalent to Temple-service.]

F. Sifre Deut.
    1. 41--In this dispute Tarfon, Aqiva, and sages disagree
        about whether learning or deeds are of greater impor-
        tance. Tarfon says that actions are more significant;
        Aqiva and sages assert that learning is more important.

    [2. 1--Parallels Sifra Qodashim 4:9: reproof.]

    [3. 32--Parallels Mekh. Ish. Baḥodesh 10: rabbi brings
         Israel into the world to come.]

The six homiletical-theological items first appearing in this
stratum and the one item with a parallel in M.-Tos. (Mekh. Sim.
14:22 [Mekh. Ish. Beshalaḥ 6]), cover five different themes: (1)
redemption (Mekh. Sim. 6:2, Mekh. Sim. 14:22 [Mekh. Ish. Beshalaḥ
6]), (2) God's providence (Mekh. Sim. 16:14 [Mekh. Ish. Vayassa
4]), (3) the rabbi and the Torah (Mekh. Ish. Baḥodesh 10 [Sifre
Deut. 32], Sifre Deut. 41), (4) reproof (Sifra Qodashim 4:9 [Sifre
Deut. 1]), (5) heave-offering and the cult after 70 (Sifra Num.
116 [Sifre Zuṭṭa 18:17]). Self-evidently there are no connections
among these five themes, nor even between the two specific views
assigned to Tarfon on the matter of the rabbi and the Torah (Mekh.
Ish. Baḥodesh 10 [Sifre Deut. 32], Sifre Deut. 41).

There is little continuity between the set of items first
found in halakhic midrashim and that of M.-Tos. Homiletical-
theological units of tradition in the earliest stratum pertain to
only two of the five themes discussed in the halakhic midrashim,

the rabbi and the Torah, and redemption. But again I cannot show
any tight links between these items in the first two levels of the
corpus. As to the connection to Tarfon's legal rulings, there is
a congruence between only one of the homiletical-theological items
(Sifre Num. 116) and a legal unit of tradition. Tarfon's assertion that eating heave-offering after the destruction of the Temple is equivalent to the performance of the Temple-service is
similar in emphasis to his opinions in M. Ter. 4:5 and Tos. Ḥag.
3:33. In both of these pericopae, Tarfon's ruling encourages the
giving of heave-offering. He states in M. Ter. 4:5 that one may
give virtually all his crops as heave-offering. In Tos. Ḥag. 3:33
he asserts that, at any time, a priest may receive, from anyone,
heave-offering of olive oil and of wine. Sifre Num. 116 also
parallels Tos. Neg. 8:2, for in the latter Tarfon reports that,
after the destruction of the Temple, he purified lepers. Both
items give priests a role to play after the destruction of the
Temple.

     Three of the six items (Mekh. Ish. Baḥodesh 10 [Sifre Deut.
32], Mekh. Sim. 6:2, Sifra Qodashim 4:9 [Sifre Deut. 1]) consist
of sayings, cast in the identical formulary pattern, that are
assigned to Tarfon and other masters. In these units of tradition
Tarfon simply provides a name on a list. Two of the three items
(Mekh. Ish. Baḥodesh 10 and Sifra Qodashim 4:9) as well as a
fourth pericope (Sifre Deut. 41) are formulated to highlight
Aqiva's view. Tarfon and the other masters merely serve as foils
for Aqiva. Only two of the units of tradition first found in
halakhic midrashim focus upon Tarfon: Mekh. Sim. Ex. 16:14, a
dispute between Tarfon and an anonymous saying, and Sifre Num. 116,
a dialogue between Tarfon and Gamaliel culminating in the former's
teaching.

Stratum III, Beraitot

1. b. Shab. 25b--A four-party dispute in which Tarfon
    defines wealth as the possession of fields, vine-
    yards, and slaves. Wealth according to Aqiva is
    having a wife pleasant in her ways. Meir and Yose
    also express opinions.

2. b. M.Q. 28b--Another story opening with the storyline
    that four sages visit a fifth master. Tarfon, Yose,
    Eleazar, and Aqiva preach the same message: Ishmael
    should mourn for those who perform *miṣvot*. The tra-
    dition culminates with Aqiva's comment.

3.   b. Qid. 81b--Identically formulated sayings of Meir
     and Tarfon indicate that even sages have sexual urges.
     Tarfon's comment serves as the basis for a story which
     teaches that it is deadly to scoff at a rabbi.

[4. b. Pes. 72b-73a--Parallels Sifre Num. 116: eating
     heave-offering is equivalent to Temple-service.]

[5. b. Qid. 40b--Parallels Sifre Deut. 41: learning vs.
     action.]

[6. b. Sanh. 101a--Parallels Mekh. Ish. Baḥodesh 10:
     rabbi brings Israel into the world to come.]

[7. b. Arak. 16b--Parallels Sifra Qodashim 4:9, Sifre
     Deut. 1: reproof.]

The formal traits of the three items first found in the third
stratum (Nos. 1, 2, 3) are identical to those of the materials of
the earlier levels of the corpus. All three units of tradition
contain sayings assigned to Tarfon. Furthermore, in two of the
three (b. M.Q. 28b and b. Qid. 81b), the dicta of Tarfon and other
masters have the same formulation and make the same point. This
construction is found in half of the units of tradition of the
second stratum.

There is no substantive coherence among the items of this
stratum, nor between these materials and those in earlier levels
of the corpus. Although two of the three items first found in
beraitot (Nos. 2 and 3), and two of the units of tradition with
parallels in the preceding stratum (Nos. 5 and 6) discuss rabbinic
themes, Tarfon's specific views in these four items are unrelated
to each other as well as to other materials in earlier levels of
the corpus. Furthermore, no ideas distinctive to Tarfon found in
the legal portion of the corpus are congruent with comments in the
homiletical-theological beraitot.

Stratum IV, Amoraic Materials

1.   b. Ned. 62a--This story relates that a man releases
     Tarfon after the latter mentions his own name. It
     illustrates the common person's fear of the sage.
     The amoraim use the story to teach that a rabbi
     should not use the crown of the Torah for personal
     benefit.

[2. y. Shev. 4:2--Parallels b. Ned. 62a: fear of sage.
     This version connects Tarfon's action with the
     Shammaite opinion in M. Shev. 4:2, thereby pointing
     out the danger of adhering to their position.]

3. b. Qid. 31b--This narrative reports that, although
   Tarfon greatly honored his mother, sages declare
   that he has not even paid her half of the honor
   demanded by the Torah. In a parallel version in
   y. Peah 1:1, a similar story is told about Ishmael.

[4. y. Peah 1:1--Parallels b. Qid. 31b: honored mother.
   A similar story told about Ishmael follows.]

[5. y. Qid. 1:7--Parallels b. Qid. 31b, y. Peah 1:1:
   honored mother.]

6. b. B.M. 85a--Story of Judah the Patriarch's success
   at reforming Tarfon's daughter's son. A similar
   story in b. B.M. 85a concerns Judah and the son of
   Eleazar b. Simeon.

7. b. Zev. 62b--In this story Tarfon dubs his sister's
   sons ignoramuses for not correctly responding to a
   sage.

8. b. Nid. 24b--Catalogue of sages of successive generations indicating the decline of knowledge.
   Tarfon's name appears between those of Abba Saul
   and Meir.

9. b. Nid. 61a--In this narrative Tarfon advises suspected murderers how to act. Tarfon's action illustrates the maxim, do not believe slander, but
   scrupple about it.

10. y. Demai 1:3--In this story a bad omen keeps Tarfon
    from sin. This pericope also teaches that a sage
    is able to discern the reason for the omen. A
    structurally identical story concerning Ḥaninah b.
    Dosa precedes.

11. y. Yoma 8:4--According to this story, Tarfon advises
    pregnant women to fast on Yom Kippur. The message
    of the story, articulated by Tarfon's students, is
    that religious actions of parents determine the char-
    acter of their children. In similar stories in b.
    Yoma 82b-83a, the women appear before R. Ḥaninah
    and Judah the Patriarch.

All eight items first appearing in this stratum are stories
comprised mostly of narration and little dialogue. By contrast,
stories of the earlier levels consist largely of sayings introduced
by a brief statement detailing the setting in which the dicta were
spoken. The formulation of the majority of the pericopae of the
fourth stratum indicates that their purpose is not to convey the
views of Tarfon, for six of them (Nos. 1 [2], 3 [4,5], 6, 8, 10,
11) are either narratives in which Tarfon serves as a foil, or
allusions to him. Of these six items, four (Nos. 3, 8, 10, 11)
have structurally similar parallels in which a name other than
Tarfon's appears. They, therefore, are standard stories into which
one may insert the name of any master.

Five of the stories (Nos. 1, 6, 8, 10, 11) deal with the
theme, the rabbi and the Torah. But these items share little in
detail. Furthermore, there is no continuity between them and
items in earlier strata. The two stories in which Tarfon proclaims a lesson (b. Zev. 62b and b. Nid. 61a) similarly have no
close ties to other Tarfon-materials.

Stratum V, Later Compilations

1. ARN A 3--Tarfon is a name on a list. The anonymous
   remark proclaims that one should attend upon four
   sages, such as Eliezer, Joshua, Aqiva, and Tarfon.

[2. ARN B 18--Parallels ARN A 3: attend upon four sages.]

3. ARN A 11--In this independent saying Tarfon praises
   work. He deduces from Exod 25:8 that one must work
   in order to merit the *Shekhinah*. ARN B 21 assigns
   the saying to Yose, Mekh. Sim. 20:9 to Eleazar b.
   Azariah.

4. ARN A 41--In this *ma'aseh* Tarfon instructs students
   on how to treat a bride.

5. Lev. R. 34:16--Tarfon gives Aqiva money to buy an
   estate so that they may be supported from it and
   engage in study of Torah. Aqiva invests the money
   in others who study Torah. Point of this long story
   is that Torah is the best investment.

[6. Pes. Rab. 25:2--Parallels Lev. R. 34:16. This version
   teaches that charitable deeds guarantee a person life
   in the world to come. It, however, makes no mention
   of investing money in those studying Torah.]

[7. Kallah Rab. 2:13--Parallels Lev. R. 34:16: Torah and
   charity are the best investments. Adds that one who
   causes someone to give charity is more meritorious
   than the one who gives.]

[8. Kallah 21--Parallels Lev. R. 34:16: Torah the best
   investment. Adds the lesson that one should give
   charity commensurate with his wealth.]

9. Mid. Ps. 7:13--Explanation of the rare biblical word
   shiggayon. Tarfon claims it means "many" and thereby
   interprets Ps 7:1 to mean that one should praise God
   even while persecuted.

10. Mid. Ps. 106:3--Identification of "he who does righ-
    teousness at all times" (Ps 106:3). In the dialogue
    with his students, Tarfon proposes the title belongs
    to the scribe. The students claim it applies to one
    who brings up orphans. A teaching assigned to
    Eleazar of Modin supports their view. In b. Ket.
    50a, Samuel b. Naḥmani gives the answer assigned to
    the students in Mid. Ps.

[11. Esther R. 6:1--Parallels the preceding item.]

12. PRE 10--In this independent saying Tarfon states
     that the verse, "The Lord prepared a great fish to
     swallow Jonah" (Jonah 1:17), indicates that miracles
     are ordained at the time of creation. In Gen. R.
     5:5 a saying with the same message is attributed to
     the amora, Jeremiah b. Eleazar.

13. PRE 41--Long exegetical saying about the rejection
     of the Torah by the nations of the world. Other
     versions of this item are recorded anonymously
     (Sifre Deut. 343), or are assigned to authorities
     other than Tarfon (b. A.Z. 2b to Yoḥanan, Pes. Rab.
     21 to Joshua).

14. Mid. Mishlé 9--Tarfon is a name on a list. Eleazar,
     Ishmael, and Tarfon, on the basis of biblical prece-
     dents, indicate that it is proper for a sage to
     wait upon other masters. The story culminates with
     Gamaliel's assertion that God serves rabbis because
     of their knowledge of Torah. Parallel versions
     (Sifre Deut. 38, Mekh. Sim. 18:12, b. Qid. 32b)
     attribute sayings to Joshua and Ṣadoq, but know
     nothing of Eleazar, Ishmael, and Tarfon.

15. Mid. Sam. 15:2--Tarfon is a name on a list. Simeon
     b. Laqish says that one should study with the sages
     of his own generation and not complain that earlier
     masters, such as Tarfon and Zeira, are no longer
     alive. Mid. Qohelet R. I 4:4 contains a parallel
     saying attributed to Abba b. Kahana in which Aqiva's
     and not Tarfon's name is used.

[16. ARN A 27--Parallels M. Avot 2:15-16: one receives
     reward for whatever amount of Torah he studies.
     This version contains a parable which demonstrates
     that it is irrelevant whether or not the task is
     without end.]

[17. Pes. Rab. 23-24--Parallels b. Qid. 31b: honored
     mother.]

[18. Mid. Ps. 76:2--Parallels Tos. Ber. 4:16-18: Judah
     merited kingship. In this version the students,
     and not Tarfon, give the correct answers.]

     The ten items first found in this stratum (Nos. 1 [2], 3, 4,
5 [6, 7, 8], 9, 10 [11], 12, 13, 14, 15) are cast in four different
literary types. Four units of tradition (ARN A 11, Mid. Ps. 7:13,
PRE 10, and PRE 41) are independent sayings. Mid. Ps. 106:3
(Esther R. 6:1) is a dialogue. Three items (ARN A 41, Lev. R.
34:16 [Pes. Rab. 25:2, Kallah Rab. 2:13, Kallah 21], and Mid.
Mishlé 9) are phrased as stories. ARN A 3 (ARN B 18) and Mid. Sam.
15:2 allude to Tarfon. These items thus exhibit no consistent
literary preferences.

Although the two allusions (ARN A 3 and Mid. Sam. 15:2) and
the one story in which Tarfon's actions allow others to make a
point (Lev. R. 34:16 and parallels) relate to the theme, the rabbi
and the Torah, they have no close ties to each other or to other
homiletical-theological materials in the corpus. The same is true
of the other seven items of the stratum. They discuss four different themes: (1) the rabbi and the Torah (Mid. Mishlé 9, PRE 41),
(2) morality (ARN A 11, ARN A 41, Mid. Ps. 106:3), (3) persecution
(Mid. Ps. 7:13), (4) miracles (PRE 10). More than half, four of
seven (Mid. Mishlé 9, ARN A 11, PRE 10, PRE 41), have parallels in
earlier documents which are either assigned to other masters or do
not include Tarfon's name.

Summary and Conclusions

The homiletical-theological materials exhibit little formal
or substantive coherence and continuity. The formal preferences
that typify the items of the earliest strata do not predominate
in those first found in later levels of the corpus. Specifically,
the units of tradition of the first three strata are formulated as
independent sayings, disputes, and stories consisting of sayings
introduced by a brief statement of the narrative setting. By contrast, thirteen of the eighteen items (72%) first found in amoraic
materials and in later compilations are either stories comprised
mostly of narration, or allusions to Tarfon. Of the five remaining items which are independent sayings, three are assigned in
earlier documents to masters other than Tarfon.

When we examine the substance of the homiletical-theological
materials, we find that they lack coherence and continuity, also
in terms of their content. In the following chart we note the
stratum in which each item first appears. In this way we can
easily see which themes predominate in the earlier levels of the
corpus and which in later strata. We group the units of tradition
under four categories: (1) The Rabbi and the Torah, (2) Redemption, (3) Moral Maxims, (4) Miscellaneous. Allusions to Tarfon
and stories in which his actions or sayings do not teach a lesson
are marked with an asterisk.

Summary of the Content of the Materials

Message	I Item	II Item	III Item	IV Item	V Item
The Rabbi (Sage) and the Torah					
1. Study and reward	*	--	--	--	--
2. Rabbi brings people into world to come	--	*	--	--	--
3. Learning vs. deed	--	*	--	--	--
4. Mourn for those who perform *miṣvot*	--	--	*	--	--
5. Sages have strong sexual urges	--	--	*	--	--
*6. Story illustrating fear of the sage	--	--	--	*	--
*7. Tarfon's grandson and Rabbi Judah the Patriarch re: sage and repentence	--	--	--	*	--
8. Tarfon and his nephews re: proper response to sage	--	--	--	*	--
*9. Decline in knowledge	--	--	--	*	--
*10. Bad omens guard sage from sin	--	--	--	*	--
*11. Parents' observance determines child's nature	--	--	--	*	--
*12. Attend upon four sages, e.g., Tarfon	--	--	--	--	*
*13. Study with sage of generation, Tarfon	--	--	--	--	*
*14. Torah is the best investment	--	--	--	--	*
15. Nations reject the Torah	--	--	--	--	*
16. God waits upon sages	--	--	--	--	*
Redemption					
1. Prayer for redemption	*	--	--	--	--
2. Call for sanctification of God's name	*	--	--	--	--
3. God is faithful to promises of redemption	--	*	--	--	--
Moral Maxims					
*1. Story about Tarfon illustrating honor of parents	--	--	--	*	--
2. Do not believe slander	--	--	--	*	--
3. How to treat a bride	--	--	--	--	*
4. He who does righteousness at all times	--	--	--	--	*
5. Praise of work	--	--	--	--	*
Miscellaneous					
1. Condemnation of *minim*	*	--	--	--	--
2. Capital punishment	*	--	--	--	--
3. Reproof	--	*	--	--	--
4. Heave-offering = Temple-service	--	*	--	--	--
5. God's providence	--	*	--	--	--
6. Wealth = material goods	--	--	*	--	--
7. Miracles ordained at creation	--	--	--	--	*
8. Praise God while persecuted	--	--	--	--	*

The fact that one-quarter of the items are listed under miscellaneous points to the lack of thematic coherence and continuity
of the homiletical-theological materials. Each of these items
discusses an issue mentioned in no other pericope. Six of these
eight units of tradition first appear in the three earliest levels
of the corpus. This means that the interests expressed in these
levels are not developed in materials surfacing in later strata.
Similarly, redemption, a predominate theme of the items in the
earliest levels of the corpus, is not mentioned in any pericopae
that first appear in beraitot, amoraic materials, or later compilations. By contrast, all of the units of tradition in which Tarfon's
sayings or actions teach a moral lesson, and 67% (eleven of sixteen) of those dealing with the theme of the rabbi and the Torah
are first found in strata IV and V. The materials first found in
latest levels of the corpus thus introduce concerns not discussed
in earlier strata.

Turning to various units of tradition on the same theme, e.g.,
the rabbi and the Torah, we see that they pertain to unrelated
topics. The same is true for the allusions to Tarfon and the
stories told about him in which he does not preach a lesson, for
they do not discuss matters mentioned in any of the sayings assigned to him. There is no way of relating the items of the corpus
in terms of their details. Only two of thirty-two homiletical-
theological items (Tos. Shab. 13:5 and Sifre Num. 116) are closely
tied to legal rulings assigned to Tarfon. Both of these items belong to earlier strata of the corpus, have firm attributions, and
focus upon Tarfon. The remaining thirty homiletical-theological
items (94%) are totally unrelated to the legal materials attributed
to Tarfon. The Tarfon corpus consists of two parts that have nothing to do with each other. Both the substance and the literary
traits of these two segments of the materials differ.   Studies of
the corpora of Eliezer and Eleazar reach the same conclusion.[1]

The only factor uniting all of the homiletical-theological
materials is the name Tarfon. But hardly anything mentioned in
these items is distinctive to Tarfon. They are stories that could
be told about, and sayings that could be attributed to, any authoritative figure. Tarfon merely provides a name for such an
individual.

NOTE

CHAPTER XII

[1]See Neusner, *Eliezer* II, p. 225, and Zahavy, p. 338.

CHAPTER XIII

TARFON: THE TRADITION, THE MAN, AND EARLY RABBINISM

The Issues

The one hundred twenty-eight units of tradition attributed to
Tarfon yield two different histories: (1) a history of the formation of a sample body of rabbinic materials, and (2) an account of
the historical Tarfon. These two histories differ in their content and also in their implications. In composing the first of
these accounts, the history of the items attributed to Tarfon, we
trace the various stages in the formation of this group of materials. We find that there is a pattern to some of these items,
while others are unrelated to each other and to the remainder of
the corpus. We discover that certain units of tradition and themes
recur throughout the various strata of the corpus. Others, however, are first introduced during the latest stage in the growth
of this complex of materials. Our most significant finding is
that different factors have governed the formation of the legal
and the non-legal portions of the corpus. These results, which
tell us how and why the name of a master is used in early rabbinism, provide information about the imagination and the values of
the members of that movement.

The study of the configuration of the materials assigned to
Tarfon also forms the indispensable basis for our second history,
our account of the historical Tarfon. We can comment upon the
actual history of this master only after knowing the nature and
the history of the materials that provide the data for his biography. Our findings suggest that we face formidable obstacles in
trying to say anything about the historical Tarfon. First of all,
we have only a few items that report information necessary for a
complete picture of this person. For example, we are not told in
any unit of tradition where and when Tarfon was born, how he was
educated, and where he died. Once we appraise the few bits of
"biographical" information in light of our analyses of the history
of the tradition, we find that these generally appear only in the
latest levels of the corpus, and have been introduced because of
their importance to the authorities who lived long after the death
of Tarfon. If we turn to the items most likely to furnish reliable
information about Tarfon, those which we may date closest to the
time of his life, the items in M.-Tos., we have data that has taken

shape nearly three-quarters of a century after his death. These
items are fairly limited in scope, pertaining almost entirely to
legal matters, and have been formulated not by the immediate disciples of Tarfon but by those responsible for the composition of
the chapters of the earliest documents of rabbinism, M.-Tos. The
units of tradition most likely to disclose anything about the actual Tarfon thus form part of larger complexes of materials, the
chapters of M.-Tos. Moreover, these items have been cast by the
redactors of these documents into highly formalized patterns, in
particular, the dispute and the *ma'aseh*. In his paper, "What's in
a Name?--The Problematic of Rabbinic 'Biography,'"[1] William Green
spells out the problems these types of results raise for the composition of a biography about a rabbinic master. In what follows
we summarize briefly Green's observations.

Green begins his remarks regarding problems raised by the
location of sayings of individual masters within larger documents
by noting the traits of these compositions.

> These documents appear to be no accidental, inchoate
> collections, but carefully and deliberately constructed
> compilations. Each document has its own ideological or
> theological agendum, and it is axiomatic that the agendum
> of any document, though shaped to a degree by inherited
> materials, ultimately is the creation of the authorities,
> most of whom are anonymous, who produced the document
> itself. They have determined the focus, selected the
> materials, and provided the framework that unites the
> discrete pericopae and gives the documents its internal
> consistency and coherence. All of this means that we
> know about early rabbinic figures what the various au-
> thorities behind the documents want us to know, and *we
> know it in the way they want us to know it* [emphasis
> mine]. Consequently, the historical context, the primary
> locus of interpretation for any saying attributed to a
> given master or story about him is the document in which
> the passage appears, not the period in which he is
> alleged to have lived.[2]

At the end of his study, Green states more succinctly the
implications for biographical studies which follow from the location of an individual master's ideas within a document.

> Hopefully the above materials demonstrate that the criti-
> cal study of rabbinic Judaism in every instance depends
> on and must begin with the examination and assessment of
> rabbinic documents themselves. Until we understand the
> motives and techniques of the men responsible for the
> present state of rabbinic literature, it will be difficult
> to apprehend the full meaning of the discrete materials
> it contains. The distinctiveness of any opinion or ruling
> will first emerge in a documentary setting. Before we can
> abstract it from the context, we first need to see it as
> the redactor saw it, then as the tradent manipulated it.

But our understanding of the construction and ideologies
of rabbinic documents is still primitive.[3]

Since in our study we have continually interpreted discrete dicta
without having a full understanding of their redactional context,
the problems Green raises apply to our use of the materials for
drawing conclusions about Tarfon.

Turning to the formalism of rabbinic materials, Green notes
that "forms by nature remove us from a historical figure, because
they 'package' or epitomize his thought, obscure idiosyncracy and
unique modes of expression, and thereby conceal distinctive elements of personality, character, and intellect. The very presence
of forms means at the outset that we cannot claim to have the exact
words spoken by any Yavnean master."[4] Green goes on to observe
that the particular forms used for materials attributed to Yavneans
tend not even to convey accurate representations of *ideas* and
positions held by a given master. He spells out this remark with
regard to the dispute form. He argues that both the superscription, or protasis, and the apodoses of the dispute may obscure the
views of an authority. In all disputes, "it is the referent and
the context provided by superscription (protasis) that makes the
positions of the masters understandable."[5] Thus for example in
the dispute in M. Kel. 11:7,

> The wide metal end of a horn--
> R. Tarfon says, "It is unclean."
> And sages say, "It is clean."

the highly formalized rulings "clean" and "unclean" are meaningful
only because of the superscription. The positions "clean" and
"unclean" could be, and in fact are, applied to any number of
cases within the rules of purity. "By themselves they tell us
little; the significance is wholly a function of the situations to
which they are attached."[6] This means that if the superscription,
which itself is meaningless without its larger context, were
changed, so too would the importance and the meaning of the rulings. It follows that:

> In the dispute-form the language attributed to the master
> himself is secondary for an interpretation of the passage.
> The precision and subtlety of an individual's opinions are
> more likely to be determined by the superscription. But
> the superscriptions themselves are synthetic by definition
> and therefore must admit of a measure of artifice. It is
> clear that the purpose of the dispute-form is to transmit
> in a single context the (usually conflicting) views of
> more than one master. As the example above demonstrates,
> in authentic disputes the superscription must be consensual;

that is, it must be substantively appropriate to at least
two opinions. Since it is unlikely that two individuals
perceive issues, define problems, and express themselves
in identical ways, the dispute-form by nature requires
the alteration and modification of the language and also
perhaps of the precise meaning of the originally independent, individual statements and rulings that almost
certainly stand behind it. This means that we cannot be
certain of the extent to which a master's views on a given
matter have been revised in the tradental and redactional
processes, and we therefore cannot automatically suppose
that the superscriptions in disputes involving him accurately depict his perceptions and definitions of the
issues and problems they represent.[7]

Green's remarks convincingly suggest that we cannot be sure
that a dispute accurately represents even a master's specific per-
ception and definition of issues. But despite this reservation,
it still may be the case that the dispute reports fairly reliable
information regarding the themes upon which a master ruled. That
is to say, although we cannot be sure that a dispute on the question of how one tithes heave-offering that has become mixed with
unclean produce preserves accurate information regarding a given
master's definition of an issue, we may conclude with more certainty that the master at least discussed the theme of heave-
offering. It is much easier to transform a saying on one aspect
of giving heave-offering into a comment on another aspect of this
issue than it is to change a statement on giving heave-offering
into a ruling on how one writes a writ of divorce. We therefore
have some grounds for assuming that the forms in which the materials of a master appear at least do not obscure the themes on
which he ruled. If anything, we may be able to comment upon the
broad themes that interested the historical Tarfon.

Green raises two further objections regarding the use of the
legal sayings of an authority for the construction of his biography. He first questions the reliability of their attributions.
He presents three reasons for doubting attributions, but only the
third (the only one cited below) is relevant to the Tarfon
materials. He states:

Attributions are suspect because of the collective character of rabbinic literature itself and the apparent importance of the disciple-circles in the transmission of
rabbinic materials. It is not unusual for the disciples
of a teacher to perceive in or derive from his teachings
and then to attribute to him positions he did not hold
but which are consonant with their own contemporary concerns. It thus cannot be supposed that all
views assigned to a given master actually originate with
him. Specific opinions may be interpretations or inven-
tions of the followers of a particular sage. The names

> attached to specific sayings consequently may not repre-
> sent an individual at all, but rather a group or circle
> which identified itself with a particular master, or
> others who adhered to his teachings.[8]

In the case of the Tarfon-corpus, the large number of items supporting positions of Judah and introduced by the tradental formula,
"R. Judah says," points to the relevance of Green's remarks.

The final consideration Green advances regarding the use of
the legal sayings of a master for the construction of his intellectual biography concerns our lack of a criterion for determining
that a single mind stands behind all these dicta. We must have
some model which allows us to conclude that these are the views of
a particular individual. Green quotes S. C. Humphreys' remark that
"our understanding of patterns of combination or contrast on the
level of ideas has yet barely progressed beyond pure intuition even
for individual cultures, let alone comparative studies."[9]

All of Green's observations indicate that because of the nature of the materials, we can say very little with any degree of
accuracy about the historical Tarfon. Even if we accept the reliability of the attributions, we can discern only the broad themes
of his agendum. Once we have isolated these general issues, we
still must find criteria for assessing the likelihood that they
give us an accurate account of the matters which Tarfon discussed.
The only two criteria, the appropriateness of these matters to the
period in which Tarfon is supposed to have lived, and the distinctiveness of his agendum, are far from probative. The first consideration proves only that it makes sense for Tarfon to have commented on certain issues. The second consideration is, for the
following reason, somewhat more decisive. Studies of corpora of
other masters show that there are slight differences in the thematic interests of the materials assigned to various authorities.
Each master tends to rule on only certain issues and not to comment
at all upon other matters.[10] While we cannot prove that these distinctions are not accidental, it may be the case that they are
based on the interests of the historical personages themselves.
The entire Tarfon corpus however reveals hardly anything about the
master himself. All we can say with any certainty is that Tarfon
is a Pharisee and a priest who lived at Lydda at the end of the
first and at the beginning of the second centuries A.D. and taught
Judah b. Ilai. The major usefulness of these items lies in the
information they provide about rabbinism.

The History of the Tradition:
The Tarfon of Tradition and Early Rabbinism

The corpus consists of two groups of items: (1) a formally
and substantively coherent complex of materials which are in fact
the legal units of traditions, (2) items which are unrelated to
each other as well as to the remainder of the corpus, virtually
all the non-legal materials. The legal units of tradition comprise the majority of the corpus (70%), for the most part (78%)
appear in its earliest stratum (M.-Tos.) and generally contain
ideas distinctive to Tarfon. By this I mean that the specific
views assigned to Tarfon do not appear elsewhere in the names of
other authorities. The formal coherence of these items is indicated by the casting of the items into a limited number of formulary patterns. In M.-Tos., three-quarters of the units of tradition are either disputes or *ma'asim*. Similar percentages of items
with reliable attributions, first found in later strata, appear in
these patterns. Three factors point to the substantive coherence
of the legal units of tradition in the first stratum and in the
corpus as a whole. First, these items attend to a clearly defined
thematic agendum, a Pharisaic set of concerns. Second, a number
of specific issues is discussed with regard to different areas of
law. Coherence of this sort is fairly unique for materials attributed to named masters. More than one-quarter of all units of
tradition, covering all the broad thematic concerns of the corpus
(e.g., festival law, purity law), relate to the question of whether
one reaches legal decisions on the basis of objective facts or on
that of the agent's subjective presumptions, such as his intention.
Similarly, nearly one-third of the items (32%), again dealing with
the major thematic areas of the agendum, pertain to priestly concerns. That Tarfon rules in a consistent manner on each of these
issues is a third factor indicating the coherence of the legal
items. In Tarfon's view, objective facts are always the determinative criterion in reaching legal decisions. He consistently decides to the advantage of the priest, and also encourages the performance of rituals in which the priest occupies the central role.
In support of our claim for the substantive coherence of the legal
rulings in M.-Tos., we also note that, although there are two formally distinct segments of these items, the disputes and the
ma'asim, both groups of items discuss the recurrent issues noted
above. The substantive coherence of the legal items of the whole
corpus is illustrated by the fact that more than half of the units

of tradition with reliable attributions first appearing in strata II-IV relate to matters found in M.-Tos.

The coherence of the legal portion of the corpus indicates that the name of a master, in this case Tarfon, is not used randomly in the assignment of legal rulings. Tradents and redactors seem to know that a master ruled on only certain topics and in certain ways. In this vein, there is no attempt to reduce all rabbis to the same pattern. A rabbi may hold distinctive legal opinions. Moreover, he should be consistent in his rulings. The function that law plays in rabbinic Judaism may account for the consistency of the legal materials attributed to a master. Law serves to organize all aspects of life in a rational and systematic manner. It accordingly stands to reason that the rulings of a given master should be coherent and consistent. An individual rabbi provides a normative model for how one adhering to the rabbinic point of view should live only if his views conform to these requirements.

By contrast to the legal items, the non-legal units of tradition exhibit entirely different traits. They are an incoherent set of items, do not generally contain ideas distinctive to Tarfon, and first appear largely in the later levels of the corpus. In discussing the traits of the non-legal materials, we must distinguish between those that attend to homiletical-theological issues and those that are biographical in nature. Items whose primary purpose is to convey biographical information about Tarfon (and other masters) first appear in later levels of the corpus. The claims made about Tarfon in these items are unrelated to the incidental biographical data found in materials of the earliest stratum. They also are generally identical to those made about other masters, e.g., he is wealthy, he studies in the *Bet Midrash*. On the other hand, the three bits of biographical information contained in units of tradition in M.-Tos., each of which is fairly distinctive,[11] are ignored or changed in later strata. Specifically, a number of pericopae in M.-Tos. relate either that (1) Tarfon is a priest, (2) that he is the advisor and teacher of Judah b. Ilai, or (3) that he lived at Lydda and served as a leader of that community. The fact that Tarfon is a priest however is mentioned in only two of the twelve units of tradition in halakhic midrashim and not at all in the forty-three items in strata III-V. Similarly, in strata II-V, only one item in a halakhic midrash depicts Tarfon as Judah's advisor. The most striking change occurs with regard to the assertion that Tarfon lived in Lydda. In the second level of the corpus,

Tarfon is placed at Yavneh. The change in Tarfon's location is
reflected in items first found in this stratum, as well as in units
of tradition having parallels in M.-Tos. which either mention no
location or place Tarfon at Lydda. This switch suggests that there
is an attempt to homogenize Tarfon with other Yavnean masters. He
is just another authority of that period and, accordingly, he belongs at Yavneh. Additionally, Tarfon is not allowed to have a
distinctive personality for, as Green suggests, an individual with
particular traits "might threaten or serve as a focus of resis-
tance against the rabbinic collective itself."[12] The idiosyncratic
traits and personal history of an individual could serve as the
basis for claims regarding the normative quality of his rulings.
By eliminating or ignoring these traits and thereby reducing all
rabbis to the same model, it is made clear that the authoritative
quality of the rulings of all masters derives from the single fact
that they are the views of rabbis. It is the rabbinization of
Tarfon which characterizes the materials of the later levels of
the corpus.

Turning to the homiletical-theological items, we find a group
of materials with traits similar to those of the units of tradition
containing biographical claims. They are an incoherent complex of
items, for they cover a wide range of unrelated themes. Matters
mentioned in earlier strata, such as redemption, do not appear in
later levels of the corpus. Conversely, some issues, e.g., moral
questions, are discussed only in the latest strata. These probably are issues of concern to the rabbis who lived during the period to which we may date these items found in the later levels of
the corpus. But without firm data on the nature of rabbinism from
the fourth until approximately the tenth century, I cannot be certain. The homiletical-theological items generally do not differentiate Tarfon from other masters. He and other authorities are
assigned the same opinion, or he appears in a story which has a
parallel containing the name of another master. The lack of coherence of these items and their failure to ascribe to Tarfon distinctive views indicates that a master simply provides an authoritative name to which non-legal opinions are assigned. Moreover,
by using the name of an early rabbi, tradents give a sense of
"pastness," traditionally, to particular views. There is no concern about the consistency of a given master's non-legal opinions,
for items of this sort do not have the same function as does law.
They do not organize all aspects of life in a logically consistent

manner. Thus the function served by law and non-legal views in
rabbinic Judaism accounts for the divergent tendencies in the
attribution of items to Tarfon.

The composition of the Tarfon-corpus as a whole is identical
to those of other Yavnean authorities. The legal materials assigned to virtually all Yavnean masters (Yose the Galilean is the
one exception) reveal a fair degree of formal and substantive coherence. By contrast, the non-legal items attributed to each of
these masters have little to do with each other, as well as with
their legal units of tradition.[13] The factors that determine the
formation of the Tarfon-corpus are the same as those governing the
construction of these other corpora. In one respect the Tarfon-
corpus differs from those of Yavnean authorities who are major
figures for rabbinism, viz., many stories first found in amoraic
materials and in later compilations fill in details of the "biog-
raphies" of masters such as Eliezer and Yoḥanan b. Zakkai. For
example, we have pericopae pertaining to the deaths of both of
these authorities. Items of later strata also comment upon the
roles Yoḥanan and Eliezer play in early rabbinism. Thus we have
many versions of the story describing Yoḥanan's escape from Jerusalem, and his establishment of the center at Yavneh. A number of
items center upon Eliezer's excommunication. Why no one constructed materials of this sort about Tarfon cannot be determined.
From the fact that items in later strata seem purposely to ignore
Tarfon's personal history and tend to treat him as a minor figure,
we cannot conclude that he was in fact an unimportant personality
in the early history of rabbinism. What we can say about the historical Tarfon may be set forth only after we have discussed in
detail the materials most likely to contain the relevant information, the legal units in M.-Tos.

Characterization of the Earliest Stratum, M.-Tos.:
The Historical Tarfon and Judaism
in the First and Second Centuries A.D.

The formal and substantive traits of the legal items in M.-Tos.
indicate that they lie within the mainstream of the mishnaic tradition. In the case of virtually all these units of tradition, we
can discern only one stage of formulation, viz., the point at which
they were placed in their present redactional contexts. This means
that those who composed the chapters of M. cast the items into
their current highly formalized patterns and obliterated any prior
stages of formulation. Since the construction of these units of

tradition is the product of the penultimate redactors of M., they
are not put together by circles primarily interested in Tarfon.

   The editors of M. cast the majority of the items assigned to
Tarfon in the same patterns used for most traditions attributed to
other named masters. Thirty-one of the forty-one units of tradition in M. are disputes. An additional four items consist of juxtaposed independent sayings in the semblance of a dispute. 86% of
the legal materials in M., therefore, are either disputes or ap-
proximations of that form. The Tarfon-materials conform to the
formal traits of M. in one further way. Not one of these units of
tradition contains a citation from Scripture.[14]

   A high proportion of well-formulated disputes and a corre-
spondingly low percentage of independent sayings comprise the corpora of masters who deal with the central concerns of M. Thus
most of the opinions in M.-Tos. attributed to Eliezer, Joshua,
Houses, Aqiva, and Tarfon are in the dispute-form and, as we shall
see, pertain to issues discussed in their larger redactional settings. By contrast, in the case of Ishmael, Eleazar, and Yose,
whose rulings often are not germane to their contexts, we can
still detect a stage when their dicta were phrased as independent
sayings.[15] These sayings have been juxtaposed with dicta of other
masters, generally Aqiva, only at a secondary redactional level.
In virtually all instances it is the intersection with Aqiva circles that accounts for the preservation of these masters' lemma.
The same holds true for Tarfon's rulings, for Aqiva occurs in more
than two-thirds of his disputes. Two facts conclusively indicate
that the disputes between Tarfon and Aqiva are the products of
pro-Aqivan circles. First, in a number of cases, the formulation
favors Aqiva. For example, in debates appended to three of the
disputes, Tarfon is not an equal partner; he is assigned arguments
that set up Aqiva's explanations. Three disputes are worded so as
clearly to give Aqiva the final say. Second, and more important,
the traits of the disputes between Tarfon and Aqiva correspond to
those of disputes between Aqiva and masters other than Tarfon.
Nearly 60% of the disputes between Aqiva and Joshua, Aqiva and
Eleazar, Aqiva and Ishmael, and Aqiva and Yose, contain balanced
dicta. In 90% of all these items, Aqiva's name comes last. Disputes between masters other than Aqiva exhibit neither of these
types of consistencies.[16] Where we find these traits, we may assume that the items are the products of Aqivan circles.

A second distinct, non-Aqivan, segment of the Tarfon-materials
of the earliest stratum, found mostly in Tos., consists of *ma'asim*.
These are highly formalized narratives whose purpose is to report
the authoritative actions of a master. A properly constructed
ma'aseh contains the opinion of only one authority. We, as expected, find no mention of Aqiva in the *ma'asim* about Tarfon.
These items are not products of Aqivan circles, but of groups interested in Tarfon. In the case of half of the *ma'asim*, we can
assume that this circle consists of disciples of Judah b. Ilai,
for these items are preceded by the attributive chain, "Said R.
Judah." Furthermore, Tarfon's actions described in them serve as
precedents for opinions assigned to Judah. All seven of these
ma'asim have been formulated to conform to their redactional contexts. Like the disputes, these items have taken shape within the
mainstream of the mishnaic redactional process.[17]

The two patterns used for the formulation of most of the
items in M.-Tos., the disputes and the *ma'asim*, highlight different aspects of Tarfon. The disputes focus upon Tarfon's words,
while the *ma'asim* stress his deeds. Taking these two views together, we see that in early rabbinism a master teaches law both
by what he does and by what he says. By contrast, the non-legal
materials of the first three strata are sayings. Only in the
later levels of the corpus are stories with non-legal content told
about Tarfon.

Turning to the content of the rulings in M.-Tos., we learn
that 95% of these items pertain to matters discussed by other
Yavnean authorities. This indicates that the topics of the Tarfon-
materials fall within the concerns of M.-Tos. One-quarter of all
items deal with general issues, e.g., the separation of tithes,
commented upon by other masters. Two-thirds of Tarfon's decisions
focus upon more specific, commonly raised questions, such as how
to separate already-tithed produce from a mixture containing untithed crops.

A further factor indicating that the traits of the Tarfon-
materials correspond to those of M. as a whole is that, like rulings of other masters, they generally pertain to minor details of
law. Moreover, only two of all the rulings assigned to Tarfon
form the logical foundation for a chapter or a tractate of M. In
this respect Tarfon's materials in M.-Tos. serve a function similar to that of other assigned items. Now although we have determined the function which the Tarfon-units of tradition play in

M.-Tos., we still know nothing about why the redactors of these
documents have chosen to use named sayings for this purpose, and
how they selected materials to fulfill this goal. To put matters
differently, assigned materials usually discuss the fine points of
the law, often glossing anonymous rulings. But in other instances
anonymous statements add these minor details. We cannot at present determine why the redactors of M., who formulated most of the
materials in that document, chose in certain cases to preserve
assigned sayings. I suspect that even after the completion of the
form, literary, and redactional criticism of all of M.-Tos., we
still will not be able to determine how and why the redactors
selected materials for these documents, for without knowing what
was excluded, it is impossible for us to ascertain the reasons for
the inclusion of other materials.

Let us now summarize the picture M. gives us of Tarfon in
order to comment upon the historical Tarfon and the times in which
he lived. The Tarfon of the earliest stratum is a Yavnean. He
has little contact with Yavnean authorities other than Aqiva. The
latter, who disagrees with Tarfon regarding many different questions, is wiser than Tarfon, for he always wins the debates between them. In fact, compared to Aqiva, Tarfon often looks like a
fool. Tarfon is a Pharisee and a priest. He is particularly
interested in two issues: (1) the question of whether objective
facts or subjective presumptions are the determinative factors in
making legal decisions, and (2) the rights and the functions of
priests. With regard to each of these matters, he consistently
articulates the same position. He always rules that objective
facts are determinative; he decides to the advantage of priests.
Tarfon's non-legal concerns are very limited, pertaining only to
the issues of redemption, *minim*, capital punishment, and the importance of Torah-study. Finally, the Tarfon of M. lives at Lydda
and is the teacher of Judah b. Ilai.

Assessing the above account in terms of the criteria detailed
at the outset of this chapter for using rabbinic data to construct
the biography of a master, we find that much of this description
has a high degree of plausibility. To restate these criteria: we
argued that if we assume the reliability of the attributions, then
materials which can be dated close to the time of a master preserve
an accurate record of the themes discussed by him. If these themes
are pertinent to the period in which the master lived, their likelihood to contain reliable information about him is further

strengthened. Finally, the distinctiveness of the range of issues
attributed to a master, or the biographical statements made about
him, adds further weight to their claim of reliability. Turning to
the first bit of biographical information stated above, the assertion that Tarfon is a Yavnean, we cannot evaluate it in terms of
the just-mentioned criteria. But in support of this claim, we
note that (1) Tarfon in all but one case disagrees only with Yavneans, and (2) where we can correlate the substance of his rulings
with those of other named masters, we find that his views presuppose opinions of earlier authorities, and logically precede
those of Ushans and later rabbis. The chronological and substantive data are congruent.[18] It, therefore, is highly probable
that masters actually lived during the periods in which we normally assume they flourished. We conclude that Tarfon is a Yavnean. The Tarfon-materials, however, do not preserve reliable information regarding his contacts with other masters. Our examina-
tions indicate that the construction of the items attributed to
Tarfon is the result of complex literary processes. We have no
way of knowing whether the historical situation reflected in these
items corresponds to actual historical circumstances or merely is
the creation of the formulators of these materials. For example,
we cannot ascertain that Tarfon even met Aqiva, and that the latter is smarter than him, or by contrast, that Tarfon only on rare
occasions came into contact with masters other than Aqiva. We,
however, do know the history of the formation of the Tarfon-
materials. As noted, many of these items are the products of
Aqivan formulators who often use Tarfon's name in a schematic
manner.

    When evaluated in terms of our criteria for reliability, the
claim that Tarfon is a Pharisee and a priest is very plausible,
because his agendum agrees with that which has been identified as
Pharisaic and conforms to what we assume a priest would discuss.
The fact that it is understandable for an early Yavnean to have
Pharisaic leanings supports the claim that Tarfon is a member of
that group. The distinctiveness of the assertion that Tarfon is a
priest, and the congruence between the biographical data suggesting
that he has this status and the substance of his rulings add
weight to the notion that he is a priest.

    We have determined that Tarfon is concerned with the question
of objective facts vs. subjective presumptions and with priestly
rights and functions from the details of his opinions and not just

from the themes which he discusses. Since the claim that Tarfon
deals with these two matters is based on the facticity of the details of the items assigned to him, it does not have a high degree
of reliability. But three other considerations further the plausibility of the notion that Tarfon is concerned with these questions. First, as we shall see below, both of these issues are
important concerns to Jews of the late first and early second centuries. It is highly appropriate for Tarfon to have discussed
these questions. Second, the specific views attributed to Tarfon
regarding these two matters are fairly distinctive. Third, each
of these topics is dealt with in nearly one-third of the Tarfon
corpus, covering all the major themes of the agendum.

We may briefly discuss the other three aspects of the picture
of Tarfon in M. With regard to his non-legal views, we note that
it is very unlikely that Tarfon only rarely commented on such matters. The traits of M.-Tos. account for the fact that we have so
few statements on non-legal issues. Of the four themes mentioned
in the five non-legal units of tradition, two, redemption and
minim (or "Who is Israel?"), are appropriate concerns for a late
first and early second century authority. The limited nature of
our data, however, precludes us from making any statements about
Tarfon's non-legal views. That assertion that Tarfon lived at
Lydda is difficult to judge. I cannot, however, think of any
reason for questioning this bit of biographical data. Similarly,
the depiction of Tarfon as the teacher of Judah b. Ilai probably
corresponds to actual historical facts. The claim is distinctive
and is supported by the substantive congruence of the rulings of
these two masters on the question of objective facts vs. subjective
presumptions.

The few assertions we may safely make about Tarfon (that he is
a Pharisee and a priest who lived at Lydda at the end of the first
and the beginning of the second centuries, and is the teacher of
Judah b. Ilai) tell us little about him and the times in which he
lived. If, however, we add to this account the fairly reliable
claim that Tarfon dealt with the issues of objective facts vs.
subjective presumptions and of priestly rights and functions, and
also include his specific views on these two topics, then on the
basis of the earliest stratum of the Tarfon-corpus, we may make
some detailed comments about Judaism at the end of the first and
at the beginning of the second centuries. The question of whether
objective facts or subjective presumptions are the determinative

factors in evaluating action, or as it is more frequently put,
whether intention or deed is the key consideration, is an important concern of various Jews of the first century. On this matter
Tarfon consistently rules that objective criteria set the parameters for action. The human mind can neither create realities
not grounded in objective facts nor simply impose its will upon
such facts. Reality rather is defined by external factors, and
man must conform to them. For instance, one judges the status of
items in terms of formal characteristics and not in terms of how
one decides to use the items. If a rod used for measuring the
width of a cistern becomes wet, the water renders foodstuffs susceptible to uncleanness even though it does not serve the intended
purpose of the person. Similarly, it does matter that a person
prior to the performance of an action did not intend to do it.
For example, as long as one is within the Sabbath-limit of a town
prior to the beginning of the Sabbath, he acquires the rights of
travel of a resident of that town despite his prior lack of intention to have these rights. In a similar vein, the fact that an
item is already being used in a certain way overrides restrictions
regarding its use arising from previous intentions to treat it in
a different manner.

In his study of the history of the mishnaic laws of Purities,
Jacob Neusner determines that the issue of intention first becomes
a major concern during the Yavnean period. The various rabbis who
introduce the question of intention in their comments upon the
rules of uncleanness ultimately are saying that man can subject
the processes of nature to the human mind. As Neusner states, "In
the system of uncleanness, it is man who inaugurates the processes
by which food and utensils become subject to uncleanness. The
mysterious, supernatural force of contamination therefore is sub-
jected to human manipulation, specifically, to human will."[19]
Aqiva is the authority who most clearly and consistently holds
this view which serves as the basis for much further discussion in
M.-Tos. In Aqiva's opinion, what man thinks and wants establishes
parameters for action. For example, the water which comes up on
the rod when measuring the width of a cistern does not render
foodstuffs susceptible to uncleanness, for it is irrelevant to the
person's immediate intent. In his study of Aqiva's contribution
to the law of the order of Seeds, Charles Primus similarly finds
that the question of intention is a recurring concern of Aqiva.[20]
In Aqiva's rulings in this order of M., the will of man defines

reality. For example, "Aqiva frequently proposes to set boundaries or define domains by reference to the intentions expressed by the actions of the individual man."[21]

While Aqiva and Tarfon disagree about the extent to which the human mind may define reality, they concur that man's thoughts are important because they provide a context for human action. In the opinion of both of these masters, man should use his mind for the purpose of constructing a rationally ordered life. Thoughts alone are not sufficient. They must give rise to proper conduct encompassing the smallest details of life. In their stress on the connection between thought and action, Tarfon and Aqiva stand in opposition to other Jews of the first century who emphasize the exercise of the mind to the exclusion of human conduct. For example, Philo reports, "There are some, who regarding the laws in their literal sense in the light of symbols of matters belonging to the intellect, are over punctilious about the latter, while treating the former with easy-going neglect."[22] These individuals are concerned with the message for which the laws of the Bible serve as symbols and not with the laws themselves. Philo's comments suggest that in the opinion of these people what one thinks ultimately is important. Philo offers a rationale for observing the laws while still stressing their inner meaning.

> Why, we shall be ignoring the sanctity of the Temple and
> a thousand other things if we are going to pay heed to
> nothing except what is shown us by the inner meaning of
> things. Nay, we should look on all these outward ob-
> servances as resembling the body, and their inner mean-
> ings as resembling the soul. It follows that, exactly
> as we have to take thought for the body, because it is
> the abode of the soul, so we must pay heed to the letter
> of the laws. If we keep and observe these, we shall
> gain a clearer conception of those things of which
> these are the symbols.[23]

Those whom Philo denounces apparently are concerned only that people should think correct thoughts. A similar view, but expressed in negative terms, is attributed to Jesus in the Sermon on the Mount (Matthew 5). Here, for example, Jesus states that one who merely looks upon a woman lustfully has already committed adultery in his heart. One who is angry with his brothers is liable to judgment. One thus need not perform an overt action to be liable to judgment. Thinking is equivalent to action. By contrast, Aqiva and Tarfon hold that thought and action must be joined together.

The views assigned to Tarfon and to other rabbis presuppose
that man has the ability to control his nature and his fate by
either imposing his will on external forces, or at least by bringing his thoughts into conformity with those objective factors. In
the conclusion to his study, Primus contrasts this point of view
with that of other Jews of the first century. He cites the opinion of the author of 4 Ezra (7:72-74; 8:35) who claims that man
inevitably sins. The mind merely makes man conscious of transgression. Similar views are contained in the Synoptic Gospels
(Matt 18:8-9 [Mark 9:43-47]), and in Paul (Rom 7:15), "I do not
understand my own actions. For I do not do what I want, but I do
the very thing I hate."

In his comments on the rulings of Yavneans on the issue of
intention, Neusner raises the question about the connection between these views and the situation of the Jews after the destruction of the Second Temple.[24] He contends that the inner logic of
mishnaic law accounts for the interest of the Yavneans in the
question of intention. But despite the lack of a causal connection between the events of A.D. 70 and the rabbis' concern with
the issue at hand, it is a fact that the latter is congruent with
the effects of the Temple's destruction. By stressing the power
of the human mind, the rabbis indicate that man is responsible for
his actions and his fate. They are not helpless; their deeds and
thoughts are very important. The rulings of Tarfon and Aqiva testify to this fact. These two however, as noted, differ about the
exact role the human mind plays. For Tarfon, by using his mind
man deduces rules allowing him to live within the reality established by objective facts. Aqiva allows man to create partially
the reality in which he lives.

Tarfon's numerous rulings on matters relating to priests also
constitute a system of thought congruent with the situation of the
Jews after A.D. 70. We can interpret these decisions as a priestly
response to the destruction of the Temple. The loss of the Temple
caused a crisis in Judaism, for the locus of holiness was eliminated. The point of contact between man and the divine disappeared.
The destruction also raised the question, who shall rule Israel.
In particular, since priests could no longer perform their sacred
task of offering sacrifices, they now lost their basis of authority.[25] Tarfon's rulings respond to these problems by indicating
that priests still have sacred duties to perform. The purification
of lepers continues after the destruction of the Temple. Priests

may receive heave-offering and firstlings. Tarfon's rulings encourage the performance of these rites. He states that a priest
may receive heave-offering of wine and of oil from anyone, at any
time during the year. People may give virtually all their produce
as heave-offering. Sifre Num. 116 contains the logical outcome of
this line of reasoning, for here Tarfon states that eating heave-
offering after the destruction of the Temple is equivalent to the
offering of sacrifices. While in Tarfon's opinion priests still
have a central role to play in the religious life of the Jews,
other rulings assigned to him indicate that the non-priest also
has rites to perform. Like other Yavneans, Tarfon comments upon
the *lulav*, the Passover-liturgy, and kindling lights on the Sabbath. Just because the Temple has been destroyed, Jewish religious life need not cease.

    The distinctiveness of Tarfon's view stressing the centrality
of the priest for Judaism becomes evident when compared with those
of other Jews of this period who reflected on the role of the
Temple, the cult, and the priesthood. In his essay, "Judaism in a
Time of Crisis, Four Responses to the Destruction of the Second
Temple,"[26] Jacob Neusner sketches the opinions of the authors of
4 Ezra and 2 Baruch, the members of the Qumran sect, some Chris-
tians, and certain rabbis on these issues. We briefly summarize
Neusner's comments and supplement them with remarks on Philo,
Josephus, Sibylline Oracles, and rabbis he does not mention.

    A number of individuals living prior to A.D. 70 in essence
had already faced the loss of the Temple. They had either rejected the Temple in Jerusalem because of its impurity and that of its
priests (Qumran-sect), become indifferent to it (Christians), or
were at such a distance from it that it could not play an active
role in their religious life (Philo and other Diasporan Jews).
The adherents of each of these positions had found substitutes for
the Temple and its cult. Philo[27] spiritualizes and moralizes the
cult so that the essence of sacrifice is living in harmony with
the cosmos, being virtuous, and following the dictates of philosophy. It is the inwardness of the sacrificiant that is important
to God. Philo allegorizes the biblical laws relating to the
priesthood to convey this message. Now it is true that he is hor-
rified by Calligula's defilement of the Temple (*Legatio*), and that
he even went and offered sacrifices there (*Prov.* 2.64), but his
justifications for the need for a Temple are not very strong and
do not seem to be terribly important to him. Temples ultimately

are concessions to men who must serve God with bodily actions
(*On Drunkenness* 87), means for testing piety, and a device to
bring about the brotherhood of people.

> There is also the temple made by hands; for it was right
> that no check should be given to the forwardness of those
> who pay their tribute to piety and desire by means of
> sacrifices either to give thanks for the blessings that
> befall them, or to ask for pardon and forgiveness for
> their sins. But he provided that there should not be
> temples built either in many places or many in the same
> place, for he judged that since God is one, there should
> be also only one temple. Further, he does not consent
> to those who wish to perform the rites in their houses,
> but bids them rise up from the ends of the earth and come
> to this temple. In this way he also applies the severest
> test to their dispositions. For one who is not going to
> sacrifice in a religious spirit, would never bring him-
> self to leave his country and friends and kinsfolk and
> sojourn in a strange land, but clearly it must be the
> stronger attraction of piety which leads him to endure
> separation from his most familiar and dearest friends
> who form as it were a single whole with himself. And
> we have the surest proof of this in what actually hap-
> pens. Countless multitudes from countless cities come,
> some over land, others over sea, from east and west and
> north and south at every feast. They take the temple
> for their port as a general haven and safe refuge from
> the bustle and great turmoil of life, and there they
> seek to find calm weather, and, released from the cares
> whose yoke has been heavy upon them from their earliest
> years, to enjoy a brief breathing-space in scenes of
> genial cheerfulness. Thus filled with comfortable hopes
> they devote the leisure, as is their bounden duty, to
> holiness and the honouring of God. Friendships are
> formed between those who hitherto know not each other,
> and the sacrifices and libations are the occasion of
> reciprocity of feeling and constitute the surest pledge
> that all are of one mind.[28]

As Lloyd Gaston puts it, "The temple at Jerusalem, something like
the Queen in the British Commonwealth, was the symbol of the unity
of the people of the one true God, and as such it was honored
throughout the Diaspora."[29] Given the above views on cult, priesthood, and the Temple, the actual loss of this building would not
have greatly affected Philo.

In distinction to Philo, the members of the Qumran sect took
very seriously the need for a temple and a cult.[30] For them the
problem was that "the old Temple was, as it were, destroyed in the
times of the Maccabees. Its cult was defiled by the rise of a
high priest family other than theirs."[31] Their solution to this
crisis was:

To create a new Temple until God would come and, through
the Messiah in the line of Aaron, would establish the
Temple once again. As Bertil Gärtner points out, "Once
the focus of holiness in Israel had ceased to be the
Temple, it was necessary to provide a new focus. This
focus was the community, which called itself 'the Holy
place' and 'the holy of holies.'"[32] Thus the Qumran
community believed that the presence of God had left
Jerusalem and had come to the Dead Sea. The community
now constituted the new Temple, just as some elements in
early Christianity saw the new Temple in the body of
Christ, in the Church, the Christian community. In some
measure, this represents a spiritualization of the old
Temple, for the Temple, as Gärtner points out, was the
community and the Temple worship was affected through
the community's study and fulfillment of the Torah.
The response of the Dead Sea sect, therefore, was to
reconstruct the Temple and to reinterpret the nature
and substance of sacrifice. The community constituted
the reconstructed Temple. The life of Torah and obedi-
ence to its commandments formed the new sacrifice.[33]

While the Qumranians saw the whole community as a Temple and as a
priesthood, priests still occupied a special position in the community. They performed their tasks of blessing and cursing, deciding legal cases, and controlling the property of the group.
All Israelites ultimately are not priests. Given the chance to
return to Jerusalem and assume the leadership in the Temple, the
Qumranians would have done so and reconstructed Israel with the
Temple at its center. In the interim, however, the elect, the
True Israel, must remove from the rest of mankind and live the
holy life in preparation for the final battle. By contrast, Tarfon rules that a priest may receive heave-offering from any one at
any time.

Christian thoughts on the issues of Temple, priesthood, and
cult are varied and complex.[34] One first of all is faced with the
problem of separating, if possible, the views of Jesus from those
of his followers. One must carefully distinguish between attitudes towards cult and those toward the Temple. When various
Christians use the imagery of the new Temple, some have in mind
the body of Christ, others, the Church. Both Christ and the
Church are the Temple either in the sense that they are the locus
for the presence of God, or that they offer atoning sacrifices to
God. A final difficulty in discussing Christian views is that for
some Christians, the Temple foreshadowed the true mode of sacrifice and has been surpassed or annulled by it. Others, such as
Stephen (Acts 7), however, think that the Temple and its cult was
from the beginning a product of human invention and part of the
Jewish rebellion against God. Neusner's statement on the Christian

attitude toward the Temple takes into account these complexities
and presents what seems to be the point of view of most Christians.

> Because of this faith in the crucified and risen Christ,
> Christians experienced the end of the old cult and the
> old Temple before it actually took place, much like the
> Qumran sectarians.... Like the Qumranians, the Chris-
> tian Jews criticized the Jerusalem Temple and its cult.
> Both groups in common believed that the last days had
> begun. Both believed that God had come to dwell with
> them as he had once dwelled in the Temple. The sacri-
> fices of the Temple were replaced, therefore, by the
> sacrifice of a blameless life and by other spiritual
> deeds. But the Christians differ on one important point.
> To them, the final sacrifice had already taken place;
> the perfect priest had offered up the perfect holocaust,
> his own body.[35]

The position taken by most Christians has roots in what Lloyd
Gaston convincingly argues is Jesus' own views on these issues.
"Jesus was fundamentally indifferent to the cult, and for him, the
functions of the old Temple were to be fulfilled in the new Temple
which Jesus had come to found. From the beginning the Church was
uninvolved in the cult of the Temple."[36] For the Christians long
before 70, the Temple had ceased to exist as a holy place.

Each of the three groups we have rapidly reviewed found re-
placements for the Temple considerably before its actual destruction. After the loss of the Temple in 70 A.D.,[37] a number of other
programs emerged to deal with this crisis. Some Jews, like the
author of the fourth Sibylline Oracle (we assume he is a Jew and
lived after 70 A.D.)[38] sees the destruction of the Temple as a
blessing and not as a crisis. In his prophecy (lns. 115-16, 125-
26), he describes the loss of Jerusalem.

> To Solyma too the evil blast of war shall come from Italy,
> and shall lay in ruins God's great Temple.... And a
> Roman leader shall come to Syria, who shall burn down
> Solyma's Temple with fire and therewith slay many men,
> and shall waste the great land of the Jews with its broad
> way.[39]

That this loss is a blessing can be inferred from the Sibyll's
comments in lines 8-12 and 27-30 regarding temples and sacrifices.

> For He has not as His habitation a stone set up in a
> temple, dumb and helpless, a bugbear of many woes to
> mortals. But He is one whom none can see from earth,
> nor measure with mortal eyes, seeing He was not fashioned
> by mortal hand. With all-embracing view He beholds all,
> yet Himself is seen by none.... Who, when they see
> them, shall disown all temples and altars, vain erec-
> tions of senseless stones, befouled with constant blood
> of living things and sacrifices of four-footed beasts.[40]

The response of the authors of 4 Ezra and 2 Baruch to the events of 70 is "essentially negative. All they had to say is that God is just and Israel has sinned, but in the end of time there will be redemption. What to do in the meantime? Merely wait."[41] Josephus' views on the destruction of the Temple to some extent parallel the above opinion. He agrees that the Temple was destroyed because of Israel's sin. Those responsible for this sin are the Zealots who on many occasions defiled the Temple by using its sacred objects for the purposes of war, and by shedding human blood within its precincts.[42] The destruction of the Temple was willed by God in order to purge it and the city.[43] The *Shekhinah* had departed from the Temple long before its destruction.[44] But the people of Israel should not desert their God, for, "Yet might there be hopes for an amelioration of thy lot, if even thou wouldst propitiate that God who devastated thee."[45] Exactly what Josephus thought the nature of a restored Israel would be, and even what were his views on Jewish life for the interim are diffi cult to determine. But from his remarks in *Antiquities* and in his apologies, *Against Apion* and the *Life*, it is clear that he was not in any way opposed to sacrifices and the priesthood. The best type of a religion and a government is one which is organized around a priesthood.[46] Jewish worship in the Temple is service in behalf of all mankind.[47] Even in the year 100, for Josephus, it is still a source of pride to be a priest.[48] In light of the lack of serious criticisms of sacrifices and priests, it seems safe to assume that, for Josephus, these factors would play a part in his Judaism of the future.

Within rabbinism we can distinguish between two different responses to the destruction of the Temple. On the one hand Eliezer believed in the efficacy of the cult, apparently approved of the actions in the former Temple, and "presumed that the Temple would soon be restored, and that life would go on pretty much as it had in the past. His solution to the problem of the cessation of the cult was not to replace the old piety with a new one, but rather to preserve and refine the rules governing the old in cer-tain expectation of its restoration in a better form than ever. His concern for the Temple marks him once again as a Pharisee, for as stated, Pharisaic piety was based upon the Temple and its law of uncleanness; the Pharisees simply enlarged the area in which these laws were to be observed."[49] By contrast to Eliezer's lack of a new program for the period after the loss of the Temple,

Yohanan b. Zakkai developed a system that takes account of this
event and that creates a new basis for authority. The enactments
attributed to Yohanan provide the best and most reliable evidence
for this program. Neusner summarizes the implications of these
enactments as follows.

> Yohanan, first, assumed the liturgical authority formerly
> vested *de facto* in the Temple priests to determine the
> proper calendar. Second, he exercised judicial and legal
> authority earlier held by the Sanhedrin in Jerusalem.
> Third, he performed certain rites formerly reserved for
> the Temple.... He thereby announced immediately that the
> commandments which had depended on the Temple would con-
> tinue to be observed even though the Temple was in ruins....
> Yohanan attempted to endow his court with prerogatives
> hitherto reserved to the sanctuary to preserve the memory
> and the sanctity of the Temple, while providing for its
> temporary inaccessibility.[50]

Yohanan's actions indicate that he took the priest's claims seriously. His solution was to place the priests under the authority
of the sages. Priests no longer are the leaders of Israel, and
there are rituals to replace their former duties. Yohanan in this
respect stands in opposition to Tarfon who still seems to place
the priests at the center of Jewish life. In the history of Judaism, Yohanan's point of view prevailed for, "as the rabbis gained
control within the Jewish community, they gradually effected their
program of attempting to make all Jews into priests, which to them
meant into rabbis."[51]

Let us speculate upon what Judaism would have been like if
Tarfon's view had become normative. Judaism would have been similar to Jewish religious life prior to the destruction of the Temple, with the exception that Temple-rituals could not be performed.
In point of fact, nothing would have changed with the loss of the
Temple. Priests could and should continue to perform their non-
sacrificial rituals. They still purify lepers and receive agricultural offering from non-priests. The non-priestly Jew for his
part should continue to give his tithes and firstlings to priests.
Non-priests also are able to observe the other laws prescribed in
the Torah. For example, if they cannot eat the Passover-offering
on the first night of the holiday, they can consume *maṣṣah* and
bitter herbs. Tarfon's post-destruction Judaism thus is very
similar to that of Eliezer. We look in vain in the most reliable
sayings and stories of both masters for anything pertaining to the
Torah-myth of rabbinic Judaism. Nothing in these items suggests
that study of Torah constitutes the central rite. We do not know

for sure that if Tarfon's program had prevailed, there would have
been no rabbinic Judaism.[52]   But nothing in his sayings suggests
the basic motifs thereof.

NOTES

CHAPTER XIII

[1]This paper appears in *Approaches to Ancient Judaism: Theory and Practice* (ed. W. S. Green).

[2]Ibid., p. 80.

[3]Ibid., pp. 86-87.

[4]Ibid., p. 81.

[5]Ibid., p. 82.

[6]Ibid.

[7]Ibid.

[8]Ibid., p. 84.

[9]S. C. Humphreys, "'Transcendence' and Intellectual Roles," *Daedalus* 106/2 (1975) p. 91.

[10]See Neusner, *Eliezer* II, pp. 134-42, 160-69; Green, *Joshua*, pp. 555-58; Porton diss., p. 477; Zahavy, p. 290; Kanter, Conclusions; and Lightstone, p. 335.

[11]No other Yavnean master with a sizeable corpus of traditions is depicted in M.-Tos. as a priest. Eliezer is the only other Yavnean who is placed at Lydda in a significant number of traditions in M.-Tos. (Tos. Suk. 2:1, Tos. Ta. 2:5, Tos. M.S. 5:16, M. Yad. 4:3). In the case of other masters, only one or two items locate them at Lydda (Aqiva: M. R.H. 1:6, Tos. Ah. 4:2; Gamaliel: Tos. Pisḥa 10:12; Eleazar b. Sadoq: Tos. Pisḥa 10:10; Judah b. Ilai: Tos. Eruv. 9:2, Tos. Shab. 2:5; Judah the Patriarch: Tos. Nid. 6:3, Tos. Ah. 18:18). Although Judah b. Ilai is the tradent for traditions assigned to virtually all Yavneans, no one besides Tarfon is portrayed in M.-Tos. as his advisor and teacher.

[12]Green, "Name," p. 84.

[13]Neusner, *Eliezer* II, pp. 287-421; idem, *Development*, pp. 265-301; Zahavy, pp. 309-32.

[14]Examining the disputes in more detail, we find that most are tightly constructed. Thirty-seven of the thirty-eight disputes in M.-Tos. are true disputes, that is to say, the opinions respond to the same problem and to each other. Thirty-one of the items in this form contain only two opposing opinions. Only two disputes consist of conflicting opinions assigned to Tarfon and to an Ushan, e.g., Meir or Yose. In the other thirty-six items, Tarfon disagrees either with Yavneans, sages, or an anonymous law. Finally, three-quarters of the disputes are mnemonically formulated.

[15]See above, p. 350.

[16]Disputes of the Houses and of Joshua have similar traits. We have argued above (p. 332) that the same circles of formulators are responsible for the composition of these materials as well as for those of Aqiva.

[17]Like the Tarfon-corpus, that of Eliezer is the product of two different circles, the Aqivans and the circle of Judah b. Ilai (see above, p. 333). In this respect the materials assigned to Tarfon are similar to those of a master belonging to the main-stream of the mishnaic tradition.

[18]Neusner reaches a similar result in his analysis of the Order of Purities; see *HMLP* XXII, p. 4.

[19]Ibid., p. 186.

[20]Primus, pp. 194-97.

[21]Ibid., p. 194.

[22]Philo, *The Migration of Abraham* 89 (trans. F. H. Colson), p. 183.

[23]Ibid., 92-93 (p. 185).

[24]Neusner, *HMLP* XXII, pp. 186-89.

[25]On the role of the Temple in Judaism and various reactions to its destruction, see the following: Jacob Neusner, *A Life of Rabban Yoḥanan ben Zakkai, Ca. 1-80 C.E.* (Leiden, 1970[2]); idem, *HMLP* XXII, pp. 182-99; Sheldon Isenberg, "Power Through Temple and Torah," pp. 24-52 in *Christianity, Judaism and other Greco-Roman Cults* II (ed. J. Neusner; Leiden, 1975); H. J. Schoeps, "Die Tempelzerstörung des Jahres 70 in der jüdischen Religions-geschichte," pp. 144-83 in *Aus frühchristlicher Zeit* (Tübingen, 1950); Hans Wenschkewitz, *Die Spiritualisierung der Kultusbegriffe: Tempel, Priester, und Opfer im Neuen Testament* (Leipzig, 1932); R. Patai, *Man and Temple in Ancient Jewish Myth* (London, 1947); Jonathan Z. Smith, "Earth and Gods," *Journal of Religion* 49 (1969) pp. 103-27.

[26]This essay appears in *Judaism* 21/3 (1972) pp. 313-27.

[27]Philo's views on the cult and the Temple are dealt with in the following works: Valentin Nikiprowetzky, "Spiritualisation et Culte Sacrificiel chez Philon d'Alexandrie," *Semitica* 17 (1967) pp. 97-116; J. Daniélou, "La Symbolique du Temple de Jerusalem chez Philon et Josephe," pp. 83-90 in *Le Symbolism Cosmique des Monuments Religieux. Serie Orientale Roma* 14 (Rome, 1957); E. J. Goodenough, *By Light, Light* (New Haven, 1935), esp. pp. 95-120; H. A. Wolfson, *Philo* (Cambridge, 1968), esp. pp. 240-48.

[28]*Special Laws* 1.67-71 (trans. F. H. Colson), pp. 139-41.

[29]Gaston, p. 131.

[30]The following works discuss the attitudes of the Qumranians to Temple and priesthood: Bertil Gärtner, *The Temple and the Community in Qumran and the New Testament* (Cambridge, 1965); Valentin Nikiprowetzky, "Temple et Communauté," *REJ* 126 (1967) pp. 7-25; Hans Kosmala, *Hebräer, Essener, Christen* (Leiden, 1959); Georg Klinzing, *Die Umdeutung des Kultus in der Qumrangemeinde und in Neuen Testament* (Göttingen, 1971).

[31]Neusner, "Judaism," p. 318.

[32]Gärtner, p. 15.

[33]Neusner, "Judaism," pp. 318-19.

[34]In addition to Gaston, the following works discuss Christian views on the Temple, the cult, and the priesthood: Oscar Cullmann, "L'opposition contre le temple de Jérusalem, motif commun de la théologie johannique et du monde ambiant," *NTS* 5 (1959) pp. 157-73; A. E. Harvey, "New Wine in Old Skins II: Priest," *ET* 84 (1973) pp. 200-203; W. M. Horbung, "New Wine in Old Skins IX: The Temple," *ET* 86 (1975) pp. 36-42; C. F. D. Moule, "Sanctuary and Sacrifice in the Church of the NT," *JTS* 1 (1950) pp. 29-41; Frances M. Young, "Temple, Cult, and Law in Early Christianity," *NTS* 19 (1973) pp. 325-38; M. Fraeyman, "La Spiritualisation de l'idée du temple dans les épitres pauliniennes," *Ephem. Theol. Louvan.* 33 (1947) pp. 378-412; A. F. J. Klijn, "Stephen's Speech--Acts 7:2-53," *NTS* 4 (1958) pp. 25-31; W. F. Brownlee, "The Priestly Character of the Church in the Apocalypse," *NTS* 5 (1959) pp. 224-25; R. J. McKelvey, *The New Temple, The Church in the NT* (London, 1969); Valentin Niki-prowetzky, "Le Nouveau Temple," *REJ* 130 (1971) pp. 5-30; Marcel Simon, *Verus Israel* (Paris, 1948), esp. pp. 19-125; idem, "St. Stephen and the Jerusalem Temple," *JEH* 2 (1951) pp. 127-42; idem, "Retour du Christ et reconstruction de la Temple dans la pensée chrétienne primitive," pp. 247-58 in *Aux Sources de la Tradition Chrétienne* (Neuchâtel, 1950); Paul Minear, *Images of the Church in the NT* (Philadelphia, 1960); K. Baltzer, "The Meaning of the Temple in Lukan Writing," *HTR* 58 (1965) pp. 263-77; A. Cole, *The New Temple* (London, 1951); John Hall Elliott, *The Elect and the Holy* (Leiden, 1966); Yves Congar, *The Mystery of the Temple* (London, 1962).

[35]Neusner, "Judaism," p. 319.

[36]Gaston, p. 131.

[37]We assume that the cult did not continue after the destruction of the Temple. For a more detailed discussion of this issue, see Emil Schürer (*The History of the Jewish People in the Age of Jesus Christ* I [rev. ed., edited by Vermes and Millar (Edinburgh, 1973)], pp. 521-23); E. Mary Smallwood (*Jews Under Roman Rule* [Leiden, 1976], pp. 443-45); Alexander Guttmann ("The End of the Jewish Sacrificial Cult," *HUCA* 38 [1967] pp. 137-48); K. W. Clark ("Worship in the Jerusalem Temple after A.D. 70," *NTS* 6 [1960] pp. 269-80).

[38]For current views on the Sibylline Oracles, see James H. Charlesworth (*The Pseudepigrapha in Modern Research* [Missoula, 1976], pp. 184-89) and J. J. Collins (*The Sibylline Oracles of Egyptian Judaism* [Missoula, 1975]).

[39]Translated by H. C. O. Lanchester in R. H. Charles, *The Apocrypha and Pseudepigrapha of the O.T.* II (Oxford, 1913), p. 395.

[40]Ibid., pp. 393-94.

[41]Neusner, "Judaism," p. 317.

[42]See *War* 2.121-22; 4.151-54, 202; 5.15, 19, 36, 562-69; 6.95-102, 165.

[43]*War* 2.539; 4.323; 5.412; 6.249-50.

[44] *War* 6.300.

[45] *War* 5.19 (trans. H. Thackeray), p. 207.

[46] *Against Apion* 2.83, 184-98.

[47] *War* 4.324; 5.18-19, 212-14.

[48] He opens his *Life* with remarks about his priestly lineage.

[49] Neusner, *Eliezer* II, pp. 298-300.

[50] Idem, *First*, pp. 183, 190-91.

[51] Idem, "Judaism," p. 324.

[52] This argument seems to ignore two facts: (1) Tarfon is called a rabbi, and (2) he seems to have studied Torah and commented upon its laws. The first consideration is not probative, for we should not anachronize by viewing those mishnaic authorities with the title rabbi in the model of later rabbinic masters. What is meant exactly by the title rabbi in M. is an issue needing further study. A comparison of the agenda of post-70 masters lacking the honorific title rabbi with those of masters with this title may provide data for answering this question. With regard to the second consideration noted above, the fact that Tarfon seems to have offered legal rulings relating to the Bible does not make him a rabbinic Jew. The study of Scripture does not make a person a rabbi, for priests, Essenes, and other Jews of Late Antiquity read and interpreted the Bible.

INDEXES

BIBLE